RACE REBELS

RACE REBELS

*Culture, Politics, and the
Black Working Class*

ROBIN D. G. KELLEY

THE FREE PRESS
A Division of Macmillan, Inc.
NEW YORK

Maxwell Macmillan Canada
TORONTO

Maxwell Macmillan International
NEW YORK   OXFORD   SINGAPORE   SYDNEY

The Free Press
A Division of Macmillan, Inc.
866 Third Avenue, New York, N.Y. 10022

Maxwell Macmillan Canada, Inc.
1200 Eglinton Avenue East
Suite 200
Don Mills, Ontario M3C 3N1

Macmillan, Inc. is part of the Maxwell Communication Group of Companies.

Printed in the United States of America

printing number

1 2 3 4 5 6 7 8 9 10

Library of Congress Cataloging-in-Publication Data

Kelley, Robin D. G.
     Race rebels : culture, politics, and the Black working class /
Robin D. G. Kelley.
         p. cm.
     ISBN 0-02-916706-X
     1. Afro-Americans—History—1877–1964. 2. Afro-Americans—
History—1964– 3. Afro-Americans—Politics and government.
4. Working class—United States—History—20th century.
5. Radicalism—United States—History—20th century. I. Title.
E185.61.K356   1994
973'.0496073—dc20   94-27097
                                                              CIP

Permission Credits

The Free Press and the author gratefully acknowledge permission to reprint excerpts from the following poems, song lyrics, or book chapters.

To my two best friends,

DIEDRA AND ELLEZA,

who taught me more about resistance

than I ever cared to know.

Contents

PART III. REBELS WITHOUT A CAUSE?

Foreword

It is getting hotter all the time on the streets of America's cities. Two years after the most destructive civil insurrection in U.S. history, many things have changed and few things have improved. Homeless men, women, and children congregate on downtown streets or seek shelter in abandoned warehouses and factories. The seeming permanence of a low-wage, low-employment economy undermines morale in the present and curtails hope for the future. Racial antagonisms spark outbursts of hate, hurt, and fear in high schools, in shopping centers, and on the streets themselves. An entire generation of young people can see that they are society's lowest priority: that they have been allocated the very worst in education, health care, transportation, and social services; that they are unwanted as workers, as students, as citizens, or sometimes, even as consumers.

At the same time, there is a powerful and almost desperate desire for change. In schools and on street corners, in medical clinics and community centers, in places of work and places of worship, the verdict is in on the disaster created in this country by twenty years of neoconservative economics. Most people have suffered terribly from the systematic dismantling of the human and social capital of the United States that took place in the 1970s and 1980s, at the same time that taxpayer dollars went to subsidize the spending sprees and speculative schemes of a wealthy few. In organized protest, but more in embryonic cultural coalitions calling attention to the contradictions of our time, the contours of a new kind of social movement are starting to emerge.

Things are moving very fast, but in opposite directions—oscillating between the renewed racism and class stratification of the 1970s and 1980s, and the emergence of egalitarian, multi-issue, pan-ethnic antiracist coalitions. The present and the future are up for grabs in a way that happens rarely in history. Our problem is that we don't know enough—enough about how egalitarian social change takes place, about how social movements start and how they succeed, about how people find the will to struggle and the way to win when they are facing forces far more powerful than themselves.

Race Rebels arms us with what we need to know. It provides us with knowledge, with descriptions and analyses of what struggles for social change actually entail. Robin D. G. Kelley presents us with a picture of masses in motion, of people as they actually are rather than as others wish them to be. He shows that political activism can never be a perfect, pure, or noncontradictory endeavor, that it is messy and cannot be held in place by simple slogans suggested from the outside. Instead, Kelley looks to history to learn how we can make sense out of what is happening before our very eyes, how we can participate in a movement that speaks from people rather than for them, and that allows people to openly acknowledge the things that divide them even as they rally together for common goals.

In his discussion of black working-class opposition to racism and exploitation, of fights over public space on Birmingham's public buses, of the relationship between the civil rights movement and the black poor, of the currents of black nationalism nurtured within the Communist Party (USA), and his positively brilliant and inspiring readings of rap music and the zoot suit as icons of opposition among aggrieved peoples, Kelley reads back to us the political truth of the lives we live. He shows how hard people have to fight to speak for themselves, to find spaces for action, and to defend the gains they've won. Furthermore, Kelley frames these lively, insightful, and subtle studies within a broader analysis that delineates the bankruptcy of prevailing social science theories about culture while pointing the way toward new ones. *Race Rebels* is a book for our time, a book that is on time, and a book that understands it is past time to face up to our responsibilities and to make the most of our opportunities.

—GEORGE LIPSITZ
Department of Ethnic Studies
University of California at San Diego

Introduction

Writing Black Working-Class History from Way, Way Below

> Against this monster, people all over the world, and particularly ordinary working people in factories, mines, fields, and offices, are rebelling every day in ways of their own invention. Sometimes their struggles are on a small personal scale. . . . Always the aim is to regain control over their own conditions of life and their relations with one another. Their strivings have few chroniclers. They themselves are constantly attempting various forms of organization, uncertain of where the struggle is going to end.
>
> —C.L.R. James, Grace C. Lee, and Pierre Chaulieu, *Facing Reality*[1]

"McDonald's is a Happy Place!"

I really believed that slogan when I began working there in 1978. For many of us employed at the central Pasadena franchise, Mickey D's actually meant food, folks, and fun, though our main objective was *funds*. Don't get me wrong; the work was tiring and the polyester uniforms unbearable. The swing managers, who made slightly more than the rank-and-file, were constantly on our ass to move fast and smile more frequently. The customers treated us as if we were stupid, probably because 90 percent of the employees at our franchise were African Americans or Chicanos from poor families. But we found inventive ways to compensate. Like virtually all of my fellow workers, I liberated McDonaldland cookies by the boxful, volunteered to clean "lots and lobbies" in order to talk to my friends, and accidentally cooked too many Quarter Pounders and apple pies near closing time, knowing fully well that we could take home whatever was left over. Sometimes we (mis)used the available technology to our advantage. Back in our day, the shakes did not come ready mixed. We had to

1

pour the frozen shake mix from the shake machine into a paper cup, add flavored syrup, and place it on an electric blender for a couple of minutes. If it was not attached correctly, the mixer blade would cut the sides of the cup and cause a disaster. While these mishaps slowed us down and created a mess to clean up, anyone with an extra cup handy got a little shake out of it. Because we were underpaid and overworked, we accepted consumption as just compensation—though in hindsight eating Big Macs and fries to make up for low wages and mistreatment was probably closer to self-flagellation.

That we were part of the "working class" engaged in workplace struggles never crossed our minds, in part because the battles that were dear to most of us and the strategies we adopted fell outside the parameters of what most people think of as traditional "labor disputes." I've never known anyone at our McDonald's to argue about wages; rather, some of us occasionally asked our friends to punch our time cards before we arrived, especially if we were running late. And no one to my knowledge demanded that management extend our break; we simply operated on "CP" (colored people's) time, turning fifteen minutes into twenty-five. What we fought over were more important things like what radio station to play. The owner and some of the managers felt bound to easy listening; we turned to stations like K-DAY on AM or KJLH and K-ACE on the FM dial so we could rock to the funky sounds of Rick James, Parliament, Heatwave, The Ohio Players, and—yes—Michael Jackson. Hair was perhaps the most contested battle ground. Those of us without closely cropped cuts were expected to wear hairnets, and we were simply not having it. Of course, the kids who identified with the black and Chicano gangs of the late seventies had no problem with this rule since they wore hairnets all the time. But to net one's gheri curl, a lingering Afro, a freshly permed doo was outrageous. We fought those battles with amazing tenacity—and won most of the time. We even attempted to alter our ugly uniforms by opening buttons, wearing our hats tilted to the side, rolling up our sleeves a certain way, or adding a variety of different accessories.

Nothing was sacred, not even the labor process. We undoubtedly had our share of slowdowns and deliberate acts of carelessness, but what I remember most was the way many of us stylized our work. We ignored the films and manuals and turned work into performance.

Women on the cash register maneuvered effortlessly with long, carefully manicured nails and four finger rings. Tossing trash became an opportunity to try out our best Dr. J moves. The brothers who worked the grill (it was only *brothers* from what I recall) were far more concerned with looking cool than ensuring an equal distribution of reconstituted onions on each all-beef patty. Just imagine a young black male "gangsta limpin'" between the toaster and the grill, brandishing a spatula like a walking stick or a microphone. And while all of this was going on, folks were signifying on one another, talking loudly about each other's mommas, daddys, boyfriends, girlfriends, automobiles (or lack thereof), breath, skin color, uniforms; on occasion describing in hilarious detail the peculiarities of customers standing on the other side of the counter. Such chatter often drew in the customers, who found themselves entertained or offended—or both—by our verbal circus and collective dialogues.[2]

The employees at the central Pasadena McDonald's were constantly inventing new ways to rebel, ways rooted in our own peculiar circumstances. And we never knew where the struggle would end; indeed, I doubt any of us thought we were part of a movement that even had an end other than punching out a time card (though I do think the "Taylorizing" of McDonald's, the introduction of new technology to make service simpler and more efficient, has a lot to do with management's struggle to minimize these acts of resistance and recreation).[3] But *what* we fought for *is* a crucial part of the overall story; the terrain was often cultural, centering on identity, dignity, and fun. We tried to turn work into pleasure, to turn our bodies into instruments of pleasure. Generational and cultural specificity had a good deal to do with our unique forms of resistance, but a lot of our actions were linked directly to the labor process, gender conventions, and our class status.

Like most working people throughout the world, my fellow employees at Mickey D's were neither total victims of routinization, exploitation, sexism, and racism, nor were they "rational" economic beings driven by the most base utilitarian concerns. Their lives and struggles were so much more complicated. If we are to make meaning of these kinds of actions rather than dismiss them as manifestations of immaturity, false consciousness, or primitive rebellion, we must begin to dig beneath the surface of trade union pronouncements, political institutions, and organized social movements, deep into the daily lives, cultures, and communities which make the working classes so much more than people who work. We have to step into the complicated maze of experience that renders "ordinary" folks so extraordinarily multifaceted, diverse, and complicated. Most importantly, we need to break away from traditional notions of politics. We must not only redefine what is "political" but question a lot of common ideas about what are "authentic" movements and strategies of resistance. By "authentic" I mean the assumption that only certain organizations and ideologies can truly represent particular group interests (e.g., workers' struggles must be located within labor organizations, or African American concerns are most clearly articulated in so-called "mainstream" civil rights organizations such as the NAACP or the Urban League). Such an approach not only disregards diversity and conflict within groups, but it presumes that the only struggles that count take place through institutions.

If we are going to write a history of black working-class resistance, where do we place the vast majority of people who did not belong to either "working-class" organizations or black political movements? A lot of black working people struggled and survived without direct links to the kinds of organizations that dominate historical accounts of African American or U.S. working-class resistance. The so-called margins of struggle, whether it is the unorganized, often spontaneous battles with authority or social movements thought to be inauthentic or unrepresentative of the "community's interests," are really a fundamental part of the larger story waiting to be told.

Race Rebels begins to recover and explore aspects of black working-class life and politics that have been relegated to the margins. By focusing on the daily lives of African American working people, strategies of resistance and survival, expressive cultures, and their involvement in radical political movements, this book attempts to chronicle the inventive and diverse struggles waged by black workers during the twentieth century and to understand what they mean for rethinking the way we construct the political, social, and cultural history of the United States. I chose the title *Race Rebels* because this book looks at forms of resistance—organized and unorganized—that have remained outside of (and even critical of) what we've come to understand as the key figures and institutions in African American politics. The historical actors I write about are literally *race rebels* and thus have been largely ignored by chroniclers of black politics and labor activism. Secondly, the title points to the centrality of race in the minds and experiences of African Americans. Race, particularly a sense of "blackness," not only figures prominently in the collective identities of black working people but substantially shapes the entire nation's conceptions of class and gender. Part of what *Race Rebels* explores is the extent to which black working people struggled to maintain and define a sense of racial identity and solidarity.

Some of the questions *Race Rebels* takes up have their roots in works by an older generation of radical scholars who chose to study slavery and its demise when fascism was on the rise in Europe and the future of colonialism was uncertain. The two most influential books in this respect were written nearly three decades before E. P. Thompson's *The Making of the English Working Class*—namely, W.E.B. DuBois's *Black Reconstruction* (1935) and C.L.R. James's study of the Haitian Revolution titled *Black Jacobins* (1938). These majestic histories of revolution, resistance, and the making of new working classes out of the destruction of slavery anticipated the "new" social historians' efforts to write "history from below." They also contributed enormously to revising the history of Western revolutions by placing race, culture, and the agency of African people—the slaves and ex-slaves—at the center of the story. Neither author viewed the newly created black proletariat as merely passive products of economic exploitation and dislocation. In DuBois's account freedpeople are on the move, undermining slavery at every halting step. The men and women who fought to reconstruct the South were more than servants and cotton pickers; they were Negroes with a capital *N*, they belonged to families and churches, and they brought with them a powerful millenarian vision of fairness and equality. And the white poor who supported efforts to stop them, the folks whose most valuable possession was probably their skin, put the noose around their own neck in exchange for membership in the white race. *Black Reconstruction* may still be the most powerful reminder of how fundamental race is for understanding American culture and politics. For C.L.R. James the slaves' memories of Africa, the world they created in the quarters bordering the cane fields, the social meaning ascribed to skin color, the cultural and religious conflicts *within* African-descended communities, were as critical to creating and shaping the Revolution as were backbreaking labor and the lash.[4]

The "new labor" or "new social historians," who set out to write "history from below" in the early to mid-1960s, traveled even further down the road opened up by their predecessors. Unlike DuBois and James, whose work on black "labor" entered the scholarly world either quietly or amid vehement opposition, this new generation of historians caused a revolution. The story of its origins is so familiar that it may one day be added to the New Testament. The late E. P. Thompson was the Moses of it all, along with his British ex-Communist comrades and fellow travelers like Eric Hobsbawm and Africanists like Terrence Ranger; across the Channel were prophets like George Rudé, and across the Atlantic were disciples like Herbert Gutman, David Montgomery, Eugene Genovese, and so on.[5] They differed in time, place, and subject matter, but they all shared the radical belief that one could, indeed, write history "from below." Of course, there were those critics who felt the new genre failed to take on the state or ignored political economy. And for all of its radical moorings, "history from below" started out very manly and very white (or at least Euro-ethnic), though that changed somewhat with the emergence of women's and ethnic studies.

Yet, as old as the "new" labor history is, "history from below" in its heyday had a very small impact on the study of African Americans.[6] Certainly, there are those who might argue that all black history is "from below," so to speak, since African Americans are primarily a working-class population. This view has its problems, however. Aside from the fact that every racial or ethnic group in the United States was primarily working class, it denies or minimizes diversity and conflict within African American communities. Unable to see a world that left few written records, many scholars concerned with studying "race relations" folded the black working class into a very limited and at times monolithic definition of the "black community." By overlooking or playing down class and gender differences, mainstream middle-class male leaders have too often been regarded as, in historian Nell Painter's words, "representative colored men."[7]

The chapters in part I not only question whether a handful of "representative Negroes" can speak for the mass of working-class African Americans, but also suggest that some of the most dynamic struggles take place outside—indeed, sometimes in spite of—established organizations and institutions. All four chapters explore the political significance of everyday forms of resistance at work and in public space, the pleasures and politics of culture, and community institutions that are usually not defined as "working-class" organizations. In other words, I sought to dig a little deeper, beneath "below," to those workers whose record of resistance and survival is far more elusive. I'm referring here to evasive, day-to-day strategies: from footdragging to sabotage, theft at the workplace to absenteeism, cursing to graffiti.

These chapters also explore the double-edged sword of race in the South, which is why I called part I "We Wear the Mask" from Paul Laurence Dunbar's poem of the same title. The mask of "grins and lies" enhanced black working people's invisibility and enabled them to wage a kind of underground "guerrilla" battle with their employers, the police, and other representatives of the status quo. Although the South certainly had its share of militant African American and interracial movements, and the status quo was sufficiently afraid of rebellion to expend a tremendous amount of resources on keeping the peace and surveilling black communities, the mask worked precisely because most Southern whites accepted their own racial mythology; they believed that "darkies" were happy and content, and that any open, collective acts of defiance were probably inspired from the outside. On the other hand, the "mask" exacted a price from black folks as well. The inner pain generated by having to choke back one's feelings in the face of racism could create tensions. Writer Gloria Wade-Gayles, who grew up in a Memphis housing project and came of age on the eve of the civil rights movement, beautifully captured this dilemma: "As teenagers, many of us were caught between our anger at white people and our respect for our black elders; between a need to vent our rage in the light of day and a desire to remain alive; and between two images of our people: one for downtown and the other for ourselves."[8] As I suggest in my discussion of black resistance during World War II and during the civil rights movement, the "mask" was no longer viable; evasive strategies continued, to be sure, but often with a militant face.

No matter what we might think about the "grins and lies," the evasive tactics, the tiny acts of rebellion and survival, the reality is that most black working-class resistance has remained unorganized, clandestine, and evasive. The driving questions that run through this book include: how do African American working people struggle and survive outside of established organizations or organized social movements? What impact do these daily conflicts and hidden concerns have on movements that purport to speak for the dispossessed? Can we call this politics?

"History from below" clearly pushed me to explore the politics of the everyday. The approach I take is deeply influenced by scholars who work on South Asia, especially political anthropologist James C. Scott. Scott maintains that, despite appearances of consent, oppressed groups challenge those in power by constructing a "hidden transcript," a dissident political culture that manifests itself in daily conversations, folklore, jokes, songs, and other cultural practices. One also finds the hidden transcript emerging "onstage" in spaces controlled by the powerful, though almost always in disguised forms. The veiled social and cultural worlds of oppressed people frequently surface in everyday forms of resistance—theft, footdragging, the destruction of property—or, more rarely, in open attacks on individuals, institutions, or symbols of domination. Together, the "hidden transcripts" created in aggrieved communities and expressed through culture, and the daily acts of resistance and survival, constitute what Scott calls "infrapolitics." As he puts it, "the circumspect struggle waged daily by subordinate groups is, like infrared rays, beyond the visible end of the spectrum. That it should be invisible . . . is in large part by design—a tactical choice born of a prudent awareness of the balance of power."[9]

Like Scott, I use the concept of infrapolitics to describe the daily confrontations, evasive actions, and stifled thoughts that often inform organized political movements. I am not suggesting that the realm of infrapolitics is any more or less important or effective than what we traditionally understand to be politics. Instead, I want to suggest that the political history of oppressed people cannot be understood *without* reference to infrapolitics, for these daily acts have a cumulative effect on power relations. While the meaning and effectiveness of various acts differ according to the particular circumstances, they do make a difference, whether intended or not.

One measure of the power and historical importance of the informal infrapolitics of the oppressed is the response of those who dominate traditional politics. Daily acts of resistance and survival have had consequences for existing power relations, and the powerful have deployed immense resources in order to avoid those consequences or to punish transgressors. Knowing how those in power interpret, redefine, and respond to the thoughts and actions of the oppressed is just as important as identifying and analyzing resistance. The policies, strategies, or symbolic representations of those in power—what Scott calls the "official" or "public" transcript—cannot be understood without examining the infrapolitics of oppressed groups. The approach I am proposing will help illuminate how power operates, and how seemingly innocuous, individualistic acts of survival and resistance shape politics, workplace struggles, and the social order generally. I take the lead from ethnographer Lila Abu-Lughod who argues that everyday forms of resistance ought to be "diagnostic" of power. Instead of seeing these practices merely as examples of the "dignity and heroism of resisters," she argues that they could "teach us about the complex interworkings of historically changing structures of power."[10]

Writing "history from below" that emphasizes the infrapolitics of the black working class requires that we substantially redefine politics. Too often politics is defined by *how* people participate rather than *why*; by traditional definition the question of what is political hinges on whether or not groups are involved in elections, political parties, or grass-roots social movements. Yet the how seems far less important than the why, since many of the so-called real political institutions have not always proved effective for, or even accessible to, oppressed people. By shifting our focus to what motivated disenfranchised black working people to struggle and what strategies they developed, we may discover that their participation in "mainstream" politics—including their battle for the franchise—grew out of the very circumstances, experiences, and memories that impelled many to steal from their employer, join a mutual benefit association, or spit in a bus driver's face. In other words, I am rejecting the tendency to dichotomize people's lives, to assume that clear-cut "political" motivations exist separately from issues of economic well-being, safety, pleasure, cultural expression, sexuality, freedom of mobility, and other facets of daily life. Politics is not separate from lived experience or the imaginary world of what is possible; to the contrary, politics is about these things. Politics comprises the many battles to roll back constraints and exercise some power over, or create some space within, the institutions and social relationships that dominate our lives.[11]

When people decide that they want to devote their life or part of their life to rolling back those constraints, then many choose to support movements or institutions that speak to their concerns. But given the multiplicity of constraints and the wide range of issues black working people have dealt with (as African Americans, wage laborers, women, men, consumers, neighbors, creative persons, victims of police brutality, etc.), what kinds of organizations were they drawn to and why? How have they reshaped those movements to incorporate more of their concerns and how have they been changed in the process? Although I cannot promise to answer these questions in any broad and comprehensive way, and I doubt that they can be answered in any single volume, they are the main themes in part II: "To Be Red and Black." I chose to explore African American involvement in the Communist Party because it challenges any easy assertions about what political movements are "authentic" or marginal to black working-class experience. I am not suggesting that the Communist Party is a better representative of black working-class politics than a more familiar organization like the NAACP. But during the interwar period, thousands of African Americans were drawn to Communist circles, and they entered not as malleable vessels ready to be molded by Party ideology. They put their own stamp on the Party, especially locally, and turned it into an important site of black working-class politics.

The questions this section takes up grow out of my first book, *Hammer and Hoe: Alabama Communists during the Great Depression*, which locates a distinctive black radical tradition within the larger scope of working-class politics. But by looking at black working-class radicalism within the context of an international movement, I soon realized that whatever "traditions," beliefs, or ideologies these largely illiterate industrial, agricultural, and service workers brought with them, they ultimately changed. The Communist Party was not simply a neutral vehicle for the darker proletariat to realize some predetermined agenda. Nor did the black rank-and-file Communists check their racial politics at the door. For example, the first chapter in part II ("'Afric's Sons With Banner Red'") argues that a lot of the poetry and songs written by African American rank-and-file Communists bore a closer resemblance to Garveyism than to proletarian literature—a rather odd development given the CP's vigilant battle against all forms of "petty bourgeois racial chauvinism." In the chapter on the experiences of African American volunteers in the Spanish Civil War, I suggest that what motivated almost ninety predominantly working-class black men and one black woman to risk life and limb to fight fascism abroad was a kind of race-conscious, Pan-Africanist internationalism. Awakened by Italy's invasion of Ethiopia, these Black Communists and sympathizers fought Franco as a backhanded response to Mussolini. But their unexpected experiences in the Spanish Republic and as members of a radical International Brigade changed them forever. In both cases, these black radicals created a kind of hybrid movement that combined Garveyism, Pan-Africanism, African American vernacular cultures and traditions, and Euro-American Marxist thought. Their actions and the ways in which they constructed their identities should lead us to question categories that we too frequently regard as mutually exclusive in African American communities: nationalism and communism, religion and communism, Pan-Africanism and internationalism.

The kind of redefinition of politics I am calling for has been one of the main projects of cultural studies scholars, whose insights have deeply influenced my recent work, especially in part III: "Rebels Without a Cause?" These last two chapters examine black working-class male youth culture in two periods: the 1940s and the 1980s and 1990s. Through an examination of Malcolm X's teenage years, chapter 7 tries to unravel the cultural politics of the zoot suit, bebop, and the hipster ethic. Chapter 8 explores the aesthetics and politics of gangsta rap, from its irreverent and misogynist roots in early vernacular traditions to its dark rendering of black life in the postindustrial ghetto.

By including a section on black youth culture, I wanted to make a case for placing young people's experiences squarely within the context of working-class history. Of course, there are issues unique to studying youth that we must consider: unlike more mature adults, young people are in the process of discovering the world as they negotiate it. They are creating new cultures, strategies of resistance, identities, sexualities, and in the process generating a wider range of problems for authorities whose job it is to keep them in check. Never-

theless, because the young black men who strolled down Harlem's
125th Street in the 1940s, or "gangsta limped" along L.A.'s Crenshaw Boulevard in the 1990s, were partly products of dramatic economic transformations, they are central to telling the story of the
black working class. Thus I try to place Malcolm X's teenage years, his
politics, style, and the significance of the hipster culture, within the
context of race, class, and gender relations and the changing political
economy during World War II. Similarly, the transformation of South
Central Los Angeles as a result of deindustrialization and recent de-
velopments in policing is important for understanding the prevalence
of gangsta rap in L.A. That chapter looks at what the transformation
of L.A. has meant *to*—not just *for*—African American youth.

This last section of *Race Rebels* brings us closer to the present but
further away from the world we traditionally think of as the "working
class." We travel to the darkest recesses of "history from below," to
the cultural world beneath the bottom. Both chapters engage aspects
of culture regarded by some on the Left (and all on the Right) as nihilistic, apolitical, or simply worthless. These are people—in this
case, young urban black males—whose behavior has been regarded
by many critics within African American communities as well outside
the mainstream. They are race rebels very much like Richard Wright's
"Bigger Thomas," products of capitalist transformation, urban decay,
persistent racism, male pathos, and nihilistic imaginations, struggling
to create a collective identity that reflects their race, gender, class, and
location in the city.

Increasingly, I have come to see that the global restructuring of the
economy during the last three decades or so has marked a significant
moment in the history of the black working class. In fact, in the public and scholarly discourse on the contemporary urban crisis, the
term "working class" has somehow disappeared. In its place is a fairly
new and amorphous category called the "underclass." Of course, we
hear of the successful black middle class, and, on occasion, the
phrase "stable black working class" appears in the texts of some left-
leaning scholars—but the latter is generally used as a moral category
to distinguish the people we like from the people we don't like, the
good Negroes from the bad apples, the Amos's from the Andy's. As
my friend and brilliant historian of Atlantic labor history Peter
Linebaugh has said on many occasions, the working class occupies

many different locations: sometimes they're at work, sometimes they're at home, sometimes they're in jail, and sometimes they're drunk lying in a gutter. They are neither devils nor angels, selfish individuals nor socialists. They don't share a common worldview or even a single culture (especially when you compare across time, space, race, and gender). They are simply people whose very survival depends on work or some form of income (i.e., public assistance, charity, unemployment insurance, crime). This is what the African American working class looks like from way, way below, and it is not always a pretty sight.

Race Rebels is less concerned with giving readers heroic role models or romantic stories of triumph than with chronicling and rethinking black working-class politics, culture, and resistance. More than anything, these chapters try to make sense of people where they are rather than where we would like them to be. This book is just a small and very incomplete step toward suggesting ways to connect everyday struggles to formal politics; to break down the iron triangle by refusing to privilege race, class, or gender; to reject formulaic interpretations in favor of the complexity of lived experience; to erase the boundaries between social, cultural, and political history; to pay attention to cultural hybridity; and reject the kind of subtle essentialism that treats African American culture in the singular. If we want to make sense of those McDonald's workers, or the rebellions written about by C.L.R. James, Grace Lee, and Pierre Chaulieu almost four decades ago, those of us committed to writing working-class history must look way, way, way below, to the places where the noble and heroic tradition of labor militancy is not as evident.

PART I

"WE WEAR THE MASK"

Hidden Histories of Resistance

We wear the mask that grins and lies,
It hides our cheeks and shades our eyes—
This debt we pay to human guile;
With torn and bleeding hearts we smile,
And mouth with myriad subtleties.

Why should the world be overwise,
In counting all our tears and sighs?
Nay, let them only see us, while
  We wear the mask.

We smile, but, O great Christ, our cries
To Thee from tortured souls arise.
We sing, but oh, the clay is vile
Beneath our feet, and long the mile;
But let the world dream otherwise,
  We wear the mask.

—Paul Laurence Dunbar, "We Wear the Mask"[1]

Chapter 1

Shiftless of the World Unite!

If "conspicuous consumption" was the badge of a rising middle class, "conspicuous loafing" is the hostile gesture of a tired working class.

—DANIEL BELL, *Work and Its Discontents*[1]

All observers spoke of the fact that the slaves were slow and churlish; that they wasted material and malingered at their work. Of course they did. This was not racial but economic. It was the answer of any group of laborers forced down to the last ditch. They might be made to work continuously but no power could make them work well.

—W.E.B. DuBois, *Black Reconstruction in America*[2]

Nearly a quarter century ago, a historian named George Rawick published an obscure article in a small left political journal that warned against treating the history of the working class as merely the history of trade unions or other formal labor organizations. If we are to locate working-class resistance, Rawick insisted, we need to know "how many man hours were lost to production because of strikes, the amount of equipment and material destroyed by industrial sabotage and deliberate negligence, the amount of time lost by absenteeism, the hours gained by workers through the slowdown, the limiting of the speed-up of the productive apparatus through the working class's own initiative."[3] Unfortunately, few historians have followed Rawick's advice. Still missing from most examinations of workers are the ways in which unorganized working people resisted the conditions of work, tried to control the pace and amount of work, and carved out a modicum of dignity at the workplace.

Not surprisingly, studies that seriously consider the sloppy, undetermined, everyday nature of workplace resistance have focused on

workers who face considerable barriers to traditional trade union organization. Black domestic workers devised a whole array of creative
strategies, including slowdowns, theft or "pan-toting" (bringing home
leftovers and other foodstuffs), leaving work early, or quitting, in order to control the pace of work, increase wages, compensate for un-
derpayment, reduce hours, and seize more personal autonomy. These
individual acts often had a collective basis that remained hidden from
their employers.

Black women household workers in the urban South generally
abided by a "code of ethics" or established a sort of blacklist to collectively avoid working for employers who proved unscrupulous, abusive, or unfair. Quitting or threatening to quit just prior to an
important social affair to be hosted by one's employer—commonly
called an "incipient strike"—was another strategy whose success often depended on a collective refusal on the part of other household
workers to fill in.[4] Likewise, in the factories strategies such as feigning
illness to get a day off, slowdowns, sometimes even sabotage, often
required the collective support of co-workers.

Studies of black North Carolina tobacco workers reveal a wide
range of clandestine, yet collective, strategies to control the pace of
work or strike out against employers. When black female stemmers
had trouble keeping up with the pace, black men responsible for sup-
plying tobacco to the stemmers would pack the baskets more loosely
than usual. When a worker was ill, particularly black women who operated stemmer machines, other women would take up the slack
rather than call attention to her condition, which could result in lost
wages or dismissal. On the factory floor, where stemmers were generally not allowed to sit or talk to one another, it was not uncommon
for women to break out in song. Singing in unison not only reinforced a sense of collective identity but the songs themselves—religious hymns, for the most part—ranged from veiled protests against
the daily indignities of the factory to utopian visions of a life free of
difficult wage work.[5]

Theft at the workplace was among the more common forms of
working-class resistance, and yet the relationship between pilfering—
whether of commodities or time—and working-class opposition has
escaped the attention of most historians of the African American

working class.[6] Any attempt to understand the relationship between theft and working-class opposition must begin by interrogating the dominant view of "theft" as deviant, criminal behavior. First of all, what theft is must be placed in historical context. As E. P. Thompson and Peter Linebaugh point out in their studies of English workers, changes in the law in response to workers' actions often turned accepted traditions—what Thompson calls "the moral economy"—into crime. At the center of class conflict in the eighteenth century were dock workers in London who suddenly lost the right to dip into tobacco cargoes for their personal use; farmers who were denied access to "common" lands for grazing and gathering wood; shipwrights, caulkers, and other laborers in the shipbuilding industry who discovered that they could be jailed for continuing the very old practice of taking "chips" of excess wood home with them. For years afterward, workers continued to take things from work, but now they were stealing. For some the consequences were unemployment, jail, deportation to the "New World," or the gallows.[7]

The idea of the moral economy certainly operated in the Jim Crow South, as is evident in the actions of domestic workers. While "pantoting" was regarded as theft by many employers, household workers believed they had a right to take home leftovers, excess food, and redundant or broken utensils for their home use. Not only was it the moral thing to do, given the excesses and wastefulness of wealthy families and the needs of the less privileged, but pan-toting also grew out of earlier negotiations over the rights and obligations of waged household labor. Insisting that pan-toting was not theft, one Southern domestic worker declared, "We don't steal; we just 'take' things— they are a part of the oral contract, exprest [sic] or implied. We understand it, and most of the white folks understand it." The "white folks" who tolerated pan-toting viewed it as either further proof of black women's immorality or justification for low wages. In other words, because pan-toting entailed the loss of food and clothing, low wages were intended to compensate for the *employer's* loss. Others simply treated pan-toting as a form of charity. As one employer put it, "When I give out my meals I bear these little blackberry pickaninnies in mind, and I never wound the feelings of any cook by asking her 'what that is she has under her apron.'" Aside from the more familiar instances of pan-toting, washerwomen throughout the South occasionally kept their patrons' clothes when they were not paid in a timely and adequate fashion.[8]

From the vantage point of workers, as several criminologists have pointed out, theft at the workplace is also strategy to recover unpaid wages and/or compensate for low wages and mistreatment.[9] In the tobacco factories of North Carolina, black workers not only stole cigarettes and chewing tobacco (which they usually sold or bartered at the farmer's market) but, in Durham at least, workers figured out a way to rig the clock in order to steal time. And in the coal mines of Birmingham and Appalachia, miners pilfered large chunks of coke and coal for their home ovens. Black workers sometimes turned to theft as a means of contesting the power public utilities had over their lives. During the Great Depression, for example, jobless and underemployed working people whose essential utilities had been turned off for nonpayment literally stole fuel, water, and electricity: people appropriated coal, drew free electricity by tapping power lines with copper wires, illegally turned on water mains, and destroyed vacant homes for firewood.[10]

Unfortunately, we know very little about black workplace theft in the twentieth-century South and even less about its relationship to working-class resistance. Historians might begin to explore, for example, what philosopher and literary critic Michel de Certeau calls "wigging," a complicated form of workplace resistance in which employees use company time and materials for themselves (e.g., repairing or making a toy for one's child, writing love letters). By using part of the workday in this manner, workers not only take back precious hours from their employers but resist being totally subordinated to the needs of capital. The worker takes some of that labor power and spends it on herself or her family. One might imagine a domestic who seizes time from work to read books from her employer's library. A less creative though more likely scenario is washerwomen who wash and iron their own family's clothes along with their employers' laundry.[11]

Judging from the existing histories, it seems that domestic workers adopted sabotage techniques more frequently than industrial workers. There is ample evidence of household workers scorching or spitting in food, damaging kitchen utensils, and breaking household appliances, but these acts were generally dismissed by employers and white contemporaries as proof of black moral and intellectual inferiority. Testifying on the "servant problem" in the South, a frustrated employer remarked:

> the washerwomen . . . badly damaged clothes they work on, iron-rusting them, tearing them, breaking off buttons, and burning them brown; and as for starch!—Colored cooks, too, generally abuse stoves, suffering them to get clogged with soot, and to "burn out" in half the time they ought to last.[12]

Although most of the literature is silent on industrial sabotage in the South, especially acts committed by black workers, there is no question that it existed. In his work on tobacco workers in Winston-Salem, Robert Korstad introduces us to black labor organizer Robert Black, who admitted to using sabotage as a strategy against speedups:

> These machines were more delicate, and all I had to do was feed them a little faster and over load it and the belts would break. When it split you had to run the tobacco in reverse to get it out, clean the whole machine out and then the mechanics would have to come and take all the broken links out of the belt. The machine would be down for two or three hours and I would end up running less tobacco than the old machines. We had to use all kind of techniques to protect ourselves and the other workers.[13]

It is surprising to note how little has been written about workplace theft and sabotage in the urban South. Given what we know of the pervasiveness of these strategies in other parts of the world, and the fact that sabotage and theft were common practices among slaves as well as rural African Americans in the postbellum period, the almost universal absence of these sorts of clandestine activities among black industrial workers in historical accounts is surprising.[14] Part of the reason, I think, lies in Southern labor historians' noble quest to redeem the black working class from racist stereotypes. The company personnel records, police reports, mainstream white newspaper accounts, and correspondence have left us with a somewhat serene portrait of folks who, only occasionally, deviate from what I like to call the "Cult of True Sambohood." Southern racist ideology defined pilfering, slowdowns, absenteeism, tool-breaking, and other such acts as ineptitude, laziness, shiftlessness, and immorality.[15] But rather than escape these categories altogether, sympathetic labor historians are often too quick to invert them, remaking the black proletariat into the hardest-working, thriftiest, most efficient labor force around. Part of the problem, I suspect, lies in the tendency of historians to either assume that all black workers lived by the Protestant work ethic or shared the same values usually associated with middle-class and prominent working-class blacks. But if we regard most work as alienating, especially work performed in a context of racist and sexist oppression, then we should expect black working people to minimize labor with as little economic loss as possible.

When we do so, we gain fresh insights into traditional, often very racist documents. Materials that describe "unreliable," "shiftless," or "ignorant" black workers should be read as more than vicious, racist commentary; in many instances these descriptions are the result of employers, foremen, and managers misconstruing the meaning of working-class activity which they were never supposed to understand. Fortunately, many Southern black workers understood the "Cult of True Sambohood" all too well, and at times used the contradictions embedded in racist ideology to their advantage. In certain circumstances, their inefficiency and penchant for not following directions created havoc and chaos for industrial production or the smooth running of a household. And all the while the appropriate grins, shuffles, and "yassums" mitigated potential punishment.[16]

The effectiveness and acceptability of this sort of "masking" is partly shaped by gender. Although both men and women were known to adopt these kinds of evasive tactics to protect themselves, they often countered racially defined notions of appropriate masculine and feminine behavior. Because black women—especially household workers—were often regarded as less violent than men, and were thought, by many employers at least, to be more closely integrated into the familial networks of the homes in which they worked, they might have had slightly more space to speak their minds to the people they worked for. But we have to be careful not to overstate the case: grievances and complaints by household workers had to be expressed in such a way as to minimize what might be interpreted as insubordination. Despite claims that domestics were "part of the family," household worker Dorothy Bolden remembers having "to walk a chalk line.

And if you talked back in those days, you was an uppity nigger, you was sassy, and you was fired and put out."[17]

On the other hand, while there might have been fewer opportunities for black men to jettison the mask of deference since public insubordination sometimes led to violence, they also had to contend with gender conventions that regarded deference and retreat from conflict as less-than-manly behavior. The racial politics of manhood has not only centered on publicly "standing up" to racism and other indignities, but the failure or inability to do so has been frequently described in terms of "feminizing" black men. When combined with a U.S. labor movement characterized by a long history of using masculine language and imagery to describe workers' struggles, the race-gender matrix can make for interesting expressions of labor politics. A powerful example is the Memphis sanitation workers' strike of 1968, in which hundreds of black picketers marched silently with placards bearing the slogan, "I Am a Man."[18]

As David Roediger has demonstrated in a penetrating essay on Covington Hall, a radical labor journalist and supporter of the interracial Brotherhood of Timber Workers in Louisiana (an affiliate of the Industrial Workers of the World or IWW), race and gender operated simultaneously in the rhetoric defending interracial working-class resistance. First, the BTW sought to use appeals to "manhood" as the foundation for building biracial unity. Hall, and before him BTW leader Ed Lehmann, insisted that there be no "Niggers," or "white trash" (i.e., scabs)—only MEN—(i.e., militant union activists). Second, because these timber workers were united by a universalizing notion of manhood, Hall made sure that strategies of resistance were sufficiently manly; in short, militant and directly confrontational. Yet, because sabotage was a popular tactic of the BTW's, it had to be recast not as clandestine but as openly rebellious. Roediger writes, "it is hard to believe the zeal with which [sabotage] was propagandized was not intensified by the tremendous emphasis on manhood, in part as a way to disarm race, in BTW thinking. And, of course, the fear of emasculation and the need to assert manhood applied with special force among white male workers because to be 'cringing' and 'servile' meant not only being unsexed, but less than white as well." Thus to be manly meant not only to be confrontational but to be as far away from servile (read: "Negro") labor as possible. Hall even symbolized sabotage by invoking the image of a rattlesnake rather than the quieter image of the black cat, which was more common elsewhere. Roediger astutely observed, "A greater appreciation of African American patterns of resistance might have argued for using Brer Rabbit as the symbol for sustained, creative, gritty struggle. Instead, the BTW not only sought confrontation but, like the rattlesnake, made noise about doing so."[19]

Employers and probably most white workers viewed what black male workers were doing as less than manly; proof of their inferiority at the workplace and evidence that they should be denied upward mobility and higher wages. For some black male industrial workers, efficiency and the work ethic were sometimes more effective as signifiers of manliness than sabotage and footdragging. As Joe Trotter's powerful book on African Americans in southern West Virginia reminds us, theft, sabotage, and slowdowns were two-edged swords that, more often than not, reinforced the subordinate position of black coal miners in a racially determined occupational hierarchy. As he explains, "Job performance emerged as one of the black miners' most telling survival mechanisms. To secure their jobs, they resolved to provide cooperative, efficient, and productive labor." More than a few black workers apparently believed that a solid work record would eventually topple the racial ceiling on occupational mobility. Furthermore, black men and women workers were taught the virtues of hard, efficient work in church. The National Baptist Convention, for example, issued pamphlets and reports criticizing workers for laziness and idleness, suggesting that hard work—irrespective of wages of the nature of the work itself—would lead to success and respectability for the race as a whole.[20]

Yet, efficiency did not always lead to improved work conditions, nor did sabotage and footdragging always go unnoticed or unpunished. Therefore, what we need to know is why certain occupations seemed more conducive to particular strategies. Was efficiency more prevalent in industries where active, interracial trade unions at least occasionally challenged racially determined occupational ceilings (i.e., coal mining)? Was the extent of workplace surveillance a deterrent to acts of sabotage and theft? Were black workers less inclined toward sabotage when disruptions made working conditions more difficult or dangerous for fellow employees? Were evasive strategies more common in service occupations, particularly those that employed women? These questions need to be explored in greater detail. They suggest that to really understand strategies of resistance we need to explore with greater specificity the character of subordination at the workplace.[21]

But it is even more complicated than this. Where we find a relative absence of resistance at the "point of production," it does not necessarily follow that workers acquiesced or accommodated to the conditions of work. On the contrary, the most pervasive form of black protest was simply to leave. Central to black working-class infrapolitics was mobility, for it afforded workers some freedom to escape oppressive living and working conditions, and power to negotiate better working conditions. Of course, one could argue that in the competitive context of industrial capitalism—North and South—companies did not necessarily suffer from this sort of migration since wages for blacks remained comparatively low no matter where black workers ended up. And employers depended on legal and extralegal measures to limit black mobility, including vagrancy laws, debt peonage, blacklisting of union activists, intimidation of Northern labor recruiters, and outright terror. Thus the very magnitude of working-class mobility challenges the idea that Southern black working people accommodated. Besides, there is plenty of evidence to suggest that a significant portion of black migrants, especially black emigrants to Africa and the Caribbean, were motivated by a desire to vote, provide a better education for their children, and/or live in a setting in which Africans or African Americans exercise power. One's ability to move represented a crucial step toward empowerment and self-determination; employers and landlords understood this, which explains why so much energy was expended limiting labor mobility and redefining migration as "shiftlessness," "indolence," or a childlike penchant to wander.[22]

Location plays a critical role in shaping workplace resistance, identity, and—broadly speaking—infrapolitics. By location I mean the social spaces of work and community, as well as black workers' position vis-à-vis existing racial and class hierarchies. Southern labor historians and race relations scholars have established in no uncertain terms the degree to which occupations and, in some cases, work spaces were segregated by race.[23] But only recently has scholarship begun to move beyond staid discussions of labor market segmentation and racial (and more recently, gender) inequality to an analysis of what these distinctions at work *and* home mean for black working-class politics and for collective action.[24]

Earl Lewis offers a poignant example. During World War I, the all-black Transport Workers Association of Norfolk began organizing African American waterfront workers irrespective of skill. Soon there-after, its leaders turned their attention to the ambitious task of orga-nizing all black workers, most notably cigar stemmers, oyster shuckers, and domestics. The TWA resembled what might have hap-pened if Garveyites took control of an IWW local: their ultimate goal seemed to be One Big Negro Union. What is important about the Norfolk story is the startling success of the TWA's efforts, particularly among workers who had been dismissed as unorganizable. Lewis is not satisfied with simplistic explanations like the power of charismat-ic leadership or the primacy of race over class to account for the mass support for the TWA; rather, he makes it quite clear that the labor process, work spaces, intraclass power relations, communities and neighborhoods—indeed, class struggle itself—are all racialized. The result, therefore, is a "racialized" class consciousness shaped by the social locations of work and home. Lewis writes,

> In the world in which these workers lived nearly everyone was black, ex-cept for a supervisor or employer. Even white workers who may have shared a similar class position enjoyed a superior social position because of their race. Thus, although it appears that some black workers manifest-ed a semblance of worker consciousness, that consciousness was so imbedded in the perspective of race that neither blacks nor whites saw themselves as equal partners in the same labor movement.[25]

A racialized class consciousness shaped black workers' relations with interracial trade unions as well. Contrary to popular belief, black workers did not always resist segregated union locals. Indeed, in some instances African American workers preferred segregated lo-cals—as long as they maintained control over their own finances and played a leading role in the larger decision-making process. To cite one example, black members of the Brotherhood of Timber Workers in Louisiana found the idea of separate locals quite acceptable. How-ever, at its 1912 convention black delegates complained that they could not "suppress a feeling of taxation without representation" since their dues were in the control of whites, and demanded a "coloured executive board, elected by black union members and designed to work 'in harmony with its white counterpart.'"[26]

Gender also undoubtedly shaped the work spaces and collective consciousness of Southern black workers. Recent work on black female tobacco workers, in particular, has opened up important lines of inquiry. Not only were the dirty and difficult tasks of sorting, stemming, and rehandling tobacco relegated to black women, but the spaces in which they worked were unbearably hot, dry, dark, and poorly ventilated. The coughing and wheezing, the tragically common cases of workers succumbing to tuberculosis, the endless speculation as to the cause of miscarriages among co-workers, were constant reminders that these black women spent more than a third of the day toiling in a health hazard. If some thought the physical space in which they worked was a prison or a dungeon, then they could not help but notice that all of the "inmates" were black women like themselves. And if that were not enough, foremen referred to them only by their first names, or changed their names to "girl" or something more profane, regarding their bodies as perpetual motion machines as well as sexual objects. Thus, in addition to race, gender bonds were reinforced by the common experience of sexual harassment.

Women, unlike their black male co-workers had to devise a whole range of strategies to resist or mitigate the daily physical and verbal abuse of their bodies, ranging from putting forth a sort of "asexual" persona, to posturing as a "crazy" person, to simply quitting. Although these acts might seem individual and isolated, they were not. In the tobacco factories, these confrontations usually took place in a collective setting, the advances of lecherous foremen were discussed among the women, and strategies to deal with sexual assault were observed, passed down, or learned in other workplaces. (Some women who had previously worked as domestics, for example, had experience staving off the sexual advances of male employers.)[27]

Yet, in the eyes of most male union leaders, these sorts of battles were private affairs that had no place among "important" collective bargaining issues. Unfortunately, most labor historians have accepted this view, unable to see resistance to sexual harassment as a primary struggle to transform everyday conditions at the workplace.[28] Out of

the common social space and experience of racism and sexual exploitation, black female tobacco workers constructed "networks of
solidarity." They referred to each other as "sisters," shared the same
neighborhoods and institutions, attended the same churches, and
displayed a deep sense of community by collecting money for co-
workers during sickness and death and by celebrating each other's
birthdays. These "networks of solidarity" were indispensable for organizing tobacco plants in Winston-Salem and elsewhere.[29]

In rethinking workplace struggles, black women's work culture,
and the politics of location, we must be careful not to overemphasize
the distinct character of home and work. Recent studies of paid
homework remind us that working women's homes were often extensions of the factory. For African American women, in particular, as
some scholars have shown, the decision to do piece work or take in
laundry grew out of a struggle for greater control over the labor
process, a conscious effort to avoid workplace environments in which
black women have historically confronted sexual harassment, and
"the patriarchal desires of men to care for their women even when
they barely could meet economic needs of their families or from
women's own desires to care for their children under circumstances
that demanded that they contribute to the family economy."[30]

The study of homework opens up numerous possibilities for rethinking black working-class opposition in the twentieth century.
How do homeworkers resist unsatisfactory working conditions? How
do they organize? Do community and neighborhood-based organizations protect their interests as laborers? How does the extension of
capital-labor relations into the home affect the use and meaning of
household space, labor patterns, and the physical and psychological
well-being of the worker and her family? How does the presumably
isolated character of work shape their consciousness? How critical is
female homework as a survival strategy for households in which male
wage earners are involved in strikes or other industrial conflicts?

For many African American women, homework was indeed a way
to avoid the indignities of household service, for as the experience of
black tobacco workers suggests, much workplace resistance centered
around issues of dignity, respect, and autonomy. Sexual harassment
was part of the job. "It was always attempts made on black women
from white men," one domestic worker remembers. "Sometimes he

had a knack for patting you on the back, not on your back but on your behind, and telling you that you was a nice-looking black gal and this type of thing. And I resented that."[31]

Less dramatic but of immense importance was the practice of requiring black domestics to don uniforms, which had the effect of reducing their identities to that of "employee" and ultimately signified ownership—black workers became the property of whoever owned the uniform. Household workers in Washington, D.C., for example, resisted wearing uniforms because they were symbols of live-in service. Their insistence on wearing their own clothes was linked to a broader struggle to change the terms of employment from a "servant" (i.e., a live-in maid) to a day worker. "As servants in uniform," historian Elizabeth Clark-Lewis writes, "the women felt, they took on the identity of the job—and the uniform seemed to assume a life of its own, separate from the person wearing it, beyond her control. As day workers, wearing their own clothes symbolized their new view of life as a series of personal choices rather than predetermined imperatives."[32]

But struggles for dignity and autonomy often took on an *intra*class character. Black workers endured some of the most obnoxious verbal and physical insults from white workers, their supposed "natural allies." We are well aware of dramatic moments of white working-class violence—the armed attacks on Georgia's black railroad firemen in 1909, the lynching of a black strikebreaker in Fort Worth, Texas, in 1921, the racial pogroms in Mobile's shipyards during the Second World War[33]—but these were merely explosive, large-scale manifestations of the verbal and physical violence black workers experienced on a daily basis. Without compunction, racist whites in many of the South's mines, mills, factories, and docks referred to their darker co-workers as "boy," "girl," "uncle," "aunt," and more commonly, just plain "nigger." Memphis UAW organizer Clarence Coe recalls, "I have seen the time when a young white boy came in and maybe I had been working at the plant longer than he had been living, but if he was white I had to tell him 'yes sir' or 'no sir.' That was degrading as hell [but] I had to live with it." Occasionally white workers kicked and slapped black workers just for fun or out of frustration. Black workers took whatever opportunity available to them to contest white insults and reaffirm their dignity, which, more often than we might imagine, exploded into fisticuffs after work or at the workplace. Black tobacco worker Charlie Decoda recalled working "with a cracker and they loved to put their foot in your tail and laugh. I told him once, 'You put your foot in my tail again *ever* and I'll break your leg.' " Even sabotage, a strategy usually employed against capital, was occasionally used in the most gruesome and reactionary intraclass conflicts. In Michael Honey's work on the Memphis working class, he tells us about a black UAW leader named George Holloway whose attempts to desegregate his local and make it more responsive to black workers' needs prompted racist white union members to tamper with his punch press. According to Honey, this unfortunate act of sabotage "would have killed or maimed him had he turned it on." But as Honey also points out, personal indignities and individual acts of racist violence prompted black workers to take collective action, sometimes with the support of antiracist white workers. Black auto workers in Memphis, for example, waged a wildcat strike after a plant guard punched a black woman in the mouth.[34]

This sort of intraclass conflict was not merely a manifestation of "false consciousness" or a case of companies' fostering an unwritten policy of "divide and rule." Rather, white working-class consciousness was also racialized. The construction of a white working-class racial identity was a dynamic process emerging from the peculiar nature of class conflict in a society where wage labor and chattel slavery existed side by side. Studies by Roediger, Eric Lott, and others are especially important for explaining how European workers came to see themselves as white and as part of a white working-class racial identity.[35] While racism was not always in the interests of Southern white workers, it was nonetheless very "real."

Racist attacks by white workers did not need instigation from wily employers. Because they ultimately defined their own class interests in racial terms, white workers employed racist terror and intimidation to help secure both a comparatively privileged job and what W.E.B. DuBois and David Roediger call a "psychological wage." A sense of superiority and security was gained by being white and *not* being black. And in some cases white workers obtained very real material benefits by institutionalizing their strength through white-controlled unions which used their power to enforce ceilings on black mobility and wages. Black workers had to perform "nigger work." Without the existence of "nigger work" and "nigger labor," to white workers whiteness would be meaningless.[36]

Determining the social and political character of "nigger work" remains essential for an understanding of black working-class infrapolitics. First, by racializing the division of labor, it has the effect of turning dirty, physically difficult, and potentially dangerous work into *humiliating* work. To illustrate this point, we might examine how the meaning of tasks once relegated to black workers changed when industrial settings became predominantly, if not exclusively, white. For example, as sociologist Michael Yarrow points out in his study of coal miners in Appalachia, where not only are there fewer black workers but racial ceilings have been largely (though not entirely) removed, difficult and dangerous tasks that used to be humiliating "nigger work" are now engendered with masculinist meaning. The miners believed that "being able to do hard work, to endure discomfort, and to brave danger" is an achievement of "manliness." While undeniably an important component of the miner's work culture, it has the ultimate effect of "obscuring its reality as class exploitation." On the other hand, the black miners in Trotter's study were far more judicious, choosing to leave a job rather than place themselves in undue danger. This is not at all to suggest that black miners did not take pride in their work. On the contrary, they often challenged dominant categories of skill and performed what had been designated as menial labor with the pride of a skilled craftsman. But once derogatory social meaning is inscribed upon the work itself (let alone the black bodies that perform the work), it has the effect of undermining its potential dignity and worth—which frequently means rendering "nigger work" less manly. In order to retain the socially constructed categories in which work designated as masculine is valorized, the racialization of the same work can, in effect, change the gendered meaning of certain jobs. Ethnographer Paul Willis found this to have been the case in his own study of British working-class youth. Racism, as Willis observed,

> marks the bottom limit of the scope of masculinity and delivers it not as a vulgar assertion of everything physical and menial, but as a more carefully judged cultural category. But elsewhere, where immigrant racial groups are still likely to take the worst and roughest jobs, they are not considered

"harder" and "more masculine." It is untenable that such social groups should take the mantle of masculine assertiveness, so such jobs are reclassified to fall off the cultural scale of masculinity into the "dirty," "messy," and "unsocial" category.[37]

Because black men and women toiled in work spaces in which both bosses and white workers demanded deference, freely hurled insults and epithets at them, and occasionally brutalized their bodies, it becomes even clearer why issues of dignity informed much of black infrapolitics in the urban South. Interracial conflicts between workers were not simply diversions from some idealized definition of class struggle; white working-class racism was sometimes as much a barrier to African American's struggle for dignity and autonomy at the workplace as the corporate-defined racial division of labor.[38] Thus episodes of interracial solidarity among working people, and the fairly consistent opposition by most black labor leaders to Jim Crow locals, are all the more remarkable.[39] More importantly, for our purposes at least, the normative character of interracial conflict opens up another way to think about the function of public and hidden transcripts for *white* workers. For Southern white workers to openly express solidarity with African Americans was a direct challenge to the public transcript of racial difference and domination. Indeed, throughout this period Southern biracial union leaders, with the exception of certain left-wing organizers, tended to apologize for their actions, insisting that the union was driven by economic necessity and/or assuring the public of their opposition to "social equality" or "intermixing." Thus, even the hint of intimate, close relations between workers across the color line had consequences that cut both ways. Except for radicals and other bold individuals willing to accept ostracism, ridicule, and even violence, expressions of friendship and respect for African Americans had to remain part of the "hidden transcript" of white workers. This is an important observation, for it means that acts and gestures of *antiracism* on the part of white workers had to be disguised and choked back; when white workers were exposed as "nigger lovers" or when they took public stands on behalf of African Americans, the consequences could be fatal.[40]

This chapter, and some of the work on which it draws, just begins to explore the realm of workplace infrapolitics. It aims to recover daily acts of resistance by African Americans who, until recently, have been presumed to be silent or inarticulate. Given the incredibly violent and repressive forms of domination in the South, workers' dependence on wages, the benefits white workers derived from Jim Crow, the limited influence black working people exercised over white dominated trade unions, and the complex and contradictory nature of human agency, clandestine forms of resistance should be expected.

Whether or not battles were won or lost, the mere threat of resistance elicited responses from the powerful which, in turn, shaped the nature of struggle. Repression and resistance are inextricably linked and African American resistance did make a difference. We know, for example, that Southern rulers during this era devoted an enormous amount of financial and ideological resources to maintaining order; police departments, vagrancy laws, extralegal terrorist organizations (e.g., the Ku Klux Klan and the White Legion), and the spectacle of mutilated black bodies were part of the landscape of domination surrounding African Americans. Widely publicized accounts of police homicides, beatings, and lynchings, as well as black protest against acts of racist violence, abound in the literature on the Jim Crow South.[41] Yet, while dramatic acts of racial violence and resistance are usually well documented and make good stories, they represent only the tip of a gigantic iceberg.

We need to recognize that infrapolitics and organized resistance are not two distinct realms of opposition to be studied separately and then compared; they are two sides of the same coin that make up the history of working-class resistance. As I have tried to illustrate, the historical relationships between the hidden transcript and organized political movements during the Age of Jim Crow suggest that trade unions and political organizations able to mobilize segments of the black working class were successful because they at least partially articulated the grievances, aspirations, and dreams that remained hidden from public view. On the other hand, we must be careful not to assume that organized movements are merely articulating a full-blown hidden agenda that had been percolating until the proper moment. Such a view underestimates the impact that social movements themselves have on working-class consciousness. Involvement in a movement often radicalizes workers who might have otherwise expressed their grievances silently.[42] Hence, efforts on the part of grass-roots

unions to mobilize Southern black workers, from the Knights of Labor and the Brotherhood of Sleeping Car Porters to the Communist
Party and the Congress of Industrial Organizations (CIO), clearly
played a role in shaping or even transforming the hidden transcript.
Successful struggles that depended on mutual support among working people and a clear knowledge of the "enemy," not only strengthen
bonds of solidarity but also reveal to workers the vulnerability of the
powerful and the potential strength of the weak. Furthermore, at the
workplace as in public space, the daily humiliations of racism, sexism, and waged work, combined with the presence of a labor movement, embolden workers to take risks when opportunities arise. And
their failures are as important as their victories, for they drive home
the point that even the smallest act of resistance has its price. The
very power relations that force them to resist covertly also make clear
the terrible consequences of failed struggles.

African American workers' actions, thoughts, conversations, and
reflections were not always, or even primarily, concerned with work,
nor did they fit well with formal working-class institutions, no matter
how well these institutions might have articulated *aspects* of the "hidden transcript." In other words, we cannot presume that trade unions
and similar labor institutions were the "real" harbingers of black
working-class politics; rather, even for organized black workers they
were probably a small part of an ensemble of formal and informal avenues through which people struggled to improve or transform daily
life. For a worker to accept reformist trade union strategies while stealing from work, to fight streetcar conductors while voting down strike
action in one's local, to leave work early in order to participate in religious revival meetings or rendezvous with one's lover, or to choose to
attend a dance rather than a CIO mass meeting is not necessarily a
sign of an "immature" class consciousness, but reflects the multiple
ways working people live, experience, and interpret the world around
them. It is to this larger world, the places where the African American
working class spend at least one-third of their day, that we now turn.

Chapter 2

"We Are Not What We Seem"

The Politics and Pleasures of Community

Each day when you see us black folk upon the dusty land of the farms or upon the hard pavement of the city streets, you usually take us for granted and think you know us, but our history is far stranger than you suspect, and we are not what we seem.

—RICHARD WRIGHT, *Twelve Million Black Voices*[1]

[T]he Negro, in spite of his open-faced laughter, his seeming acquiescence, is particularly evasive. You see we are a polite people and we do not say to our questioner, "Get out of here!" We smile and tell him or her something that satisfies the white person because, knowing so little about us, he doesn't know what he is missing.

—ZORA NEALE HURSTON, *Mules and Men*[2]

"In the dark, we vented our rage. But in the bright of day and out in the open, we were often well-behaved and cooperative." The darkness to which Gloria Wade-Gayles is referring was a segregated movie theater in Memphis, Tennessee. The "rage" she and her friends vented took the form of popcorn raining from the "Negroes Only" balcony, on to the unexpectant heads of "white people who sat beneath us in cushioned chairs, secure, they thought, in their power."[3]

This passage is more than a revealing anecdote about resistance; it is a metaphor for the pleasures and politics of black communities under segregation. Like the passages from Richard Wright and Zora

Neale Hurston, the crucial lesson she offers us is that in order to "know" the history of black working people we must slip into the darkness. We must strip away the various masks African Americans wear in their daily struggles to negotiate relationships or contest power in public spaces, and search for ways to gain entry into the private world hidden beyond the public gaze. For it is here, in the homes, social institutions, cultures, thoughts, actions, and language that one finds an essential component of Southern black working-class consciousness and politics in the Age of Jim Crow.

Building Community in the Bright of Day

Several Southern labor and urban historians have already begun to unveil the hidden social and cultural world of black working people and assess its political significance. A number of recent studies have established that during the era of Jim Crow, black working people carved out social space free from the watchful eye of white authority or, in a few cases, the moralizing of the black middle class. These social spaces constituted a partial refuge from the humiliations and indignities of racism, class pretensions, and wage work, and in many cases they housed an alternative culture that placed more emphasis on collectivist values, mutuality, and fellowship.[4]

This is not to say that there were no vicious, exploitative relationships within Southern black communities, or that black institutions were immune from the tentacles of Jim Crow. Black working-class *families*, for example, were sites for internal conflicts as well as key institutions for sustaining a sense of community and solidarity.[5] If patriarchal families are, at the very least, a system by which exploited male wage earners control and exploit the labor of women and children, then one would presumably find a material basis for a good deal of intrafamily conflict, and perhaps an array of resistance strategies, all framed within an ideology that justifies the subordinate status of women and children.[6] We might ask, therefore, how do conflicts and the exploitation of labor power within the locus of the family and household shape larger working-class politics?

Surprisingly, very few U.S. labor and African American historians have asked this question. Indeed, the role of families in the formation of class consciousness and in developing strategies of resistance has not been sufficiently explored, in part because most scholarship continues to privilege the workplace and production over the household and reproduction. Critiquing E. P. Thompson's oft-cited formulation of class formation, feminist labor historians Carolyn Steedman and Elizabeth Faue remind us that class identities and ideologies are not simply made at work or in collective struggles against capital. Steedman, for example, points out that because radical histories of working people are so invested in a materialist, workplace-centered understanding of class, it leaves very little space "to discuss the *development* of class consciousness (as opposed to its expression), nor for an understanding of it as a learned position, *learned* in childhood, and often through the exigencies of difficult and lonely lives." Likewise, Elizabeth Faue asks us to look more carefully at the formation of class, race, and gender identities long before young people enter the wage labor force. She adds that "focusing on reproduction would give meaning to the relationship between working class family organization and behavior and working class collective action and labor organization."[7]

Such a reexamination of black working-class families should provide richer insights into how the hidden transcript informs public, collective action. We might return, for example, to the common claim that black mothers and grandmothers in the Age of Jim Crow raised their boys to show deference to white people. Were black working-class parents "emasculating" potential militants, as was argued by several black male writers in the 1960s, or were they arming their boys with a much more sophisticated understanding of the political and cultural terrain of struggle?[8] And what about the recollections of black women who remember their mothers teaching them values and strategies that helped them survive and resist race, class, and gender oppression?[9] Once we begin to look at the family as a central (if not *the* central) institution where political ideologies are formed and reproduced, we may discover that the households themselves hold the key to explaining particular episodes of black working-class resistance. A brilliant example is Elsa Barkley Brown's essay on African American families and political activism during Reconstruction. She not only demonstrates the central role of black women (and even children) in Republican Party politics despite the lack of female suffrage, but persuasively argues that newly emancipated African Americans constructed a notion of citizenship in which the franchise was the collective property of the whole family. Men who did not vote according to the family's wishes were severely disciplined or ostracized from community institutions.[10]

While the politics of family life remains elusive, the role that community organizations played in shaping black working-class politics, culture, and ideology is much clearer. Grass-roots institutions such as mutual benefit associations, fraternal organizations, and religious groups not only helped families with basic survival needs, but created and sustained bonds of fellowship, mutual support networks, and a collectivist ethos that ultimately informed black working-class political struggle. Fraternal and mutual benefit societies, in particular, provided funds and other resources to members in need and to the poor generally, including death benefits (mainly to cover burial costs) and assistance for families whose members became seriously ill or lost their job.

The social links created through organizations such as the Knights of Pythias, the Odd Fellows, the Masons, the Elks, and the Independent Order of St. Luke occasionally translated into community and labor struggles. In Atlanta, for example, benevolent and secret societies among black women constituted the organizational structures through which washerwomen waged a citywide strike in 1881. Organized under the auspices of the "Washing Society," a secret protective association that operated much like a mutual benefit society, the strikers not only demonstrated incredible solidarity (in some cases prompting other domestic workers in the city to demand higher wages) but raised money to pay fines and post bail when strikers were arrested. In addition to relying on their own treasury, they received donations from churches and fraternal orders with which many of the strikers were also affiliated. In West Virginia, where black membership in fraternal orders reached nearly 33,000 in 1922, the black rank and file entered the United Mine Workers with considerable organizational experience. The bonds of fellowship developed in these fraternal orders played an important role in consolidating black union support, even if some of the orders' middle-class leadership opposed unionization.[11]

Although the balance of power within these organizations was not always equal, at times leaning toward male dominance and the middle class exercising more influence than their numbers, benevolent societies were structured in a democratic manner that allowed all voices to play some kind of role in constructing a vision of the community.[12] Black workers, therefore, entered the workplace or the labor movement with their own political culture. Anchored in a prophetic religious ideology, these collectivist institutions and practices took root and flourished in a profoundly undemocratic society.

Yet, while black institutions were built and maintained on fairly democratic principles, we need to acknowledge that cross-class alliances, fellowship, and mutuality were constructed in the context of intraracial class and gender tensions. There was a hidden transcript of mutual disdain, disappointment, and even fear which occasionally found its way into the public transcript. For some middle-class blacks, for example, the black poor were regarded as lazy, self-destructive, and prone to criminal behavior. Geraldine Moore, a black middle-class resident of Birmingham and author of *Behind the Ebony Mask*, wrote that many poor African Americans in her city "know nothing but waiting for a handout of some kind, drinking, cursing, fighting and prostitution."[13] From the other side, in his study of a small Mississippi town during the late 1930s, sociologist Allison Davis found that "lower-class" blacks often "accused upper-class persons (the 'big shots,' the 'Big Negroes') of snobbishness, color preference, extreme selfishness, disloyalty in caste leadership, ('sellin' out to white folks'), and economic exploitation of their patients and customers."[14]

To understand the significance of internal conflict among African Americans, we need to examine how communities are constructed and sustained rather than begin with the presumption that a tight-knit, harmonious black community has always existed (until recently) across time and space. This sort of romantic view of a "golden age" of black community—an age when any elder could beat a misbehaving child, when the black middle class mingled with the poor and offered themselves as "role models," when black professionals cared more about their downtrodden race than their bank accounts—is not only disingenuous but has stood in the place of serious historical research on class relations within African American communities. As a dominant trope in the popular social science literature on the so-called "underclass," it has hindered explanations of the contemporary crisis in urban America by presuming a direct causal relationship between the disappearance of middle-class role models as a result of desegregation and the so-called moral degeneration of the black jobless and underemployed working class left behind in the cities.[15]

The concept of "role models" overstates the extent to which notions of respectability, morality, and community responsibility are passed down by individual example. It not only presumes that these values originate solely with the black middle class, but it obscures the role that community institutions play in determining and instilling modes of behavior, beliefs, expectations, and moral vision. When we begin to look at, say, black churches as places where cultural values were enacted, taught, and policed, we discover that the so-called "lower class" was not always on the receiving end.[16] Occasionally it was the wealthier black folk who violated Christian principles—especially those who did not help the less fortunate or whose tithe was insufficient. Working-class women demonstrated as much vigilance as their middle-class counterparts in enforcing the general principle that cleanliness is next to Godliness. Baptist women of all classes distributed small pamphlets published by the National Baptist Convention bearing titles such as "How to Dress," "Anti-Hanging Out Committee," and "Take a Bath First."[17]

More importantly, working people built and sustained black churches with their own hard earned wages. In West Virginia, black coal miners raised thousands of dollars to construct and maintain churches, and when money was tight during the Depression, they held rallies and fundraisers to pay debts and retain ministers. Black religious leaders understood the crucial importance of their working-class congregations, especially the women. In 1915, a report from the Women's Convention of the National Baptist Convention acknowledged that it was "the poor washer-woman, cook and toiler [who] has built up nine-tenths of all our institutions and churches."[18]

Black church members also helped build Southern labor unions, especially during the era of industrial unionism in the 1930s and 1940s, when the Congress of Industrial Organizations sought to organize industries that employed large numbers of African Americans. Unions such as the Food, Tobacco, Agricultural, and Allied Workers (FTA), the Steel Workers Organizing Committee (SWOC), and the International Union of Mine, Mill and Smelter Workers, often held meetings in black churches and actively recruited sympathetic black ministers to their cause.[19] And when black working people entered the house of labor, they brought the spirit, culture, and rituals of the house of God with them. Southern CIO organizer Lucy Randolph Mason had vivid memories of how black workers turned union gatherings into revival meetings: "Those meetings were deeply religious. A colored member would pray and lead in singing and dismiss the gathering with a blessing. In one group there was an elderly Negro who 'lined out' the Lord's prayer verse by verse while others repeated the words after him. They were praying for more of the Kingdom of God on earth."[20] At a meeting of the Mine, Mill and Smelter Workers' union in Bessemer, Alabama, journalist George Stoney witnessed a similar scenario:

> It was an "open meeting," and Brother Harris (formerly minister) was there to preach a sermon on the goodness of unions and why people ought to join them. His was the shouting, epigrammatic style of the evangelist. If you substitute "God" for "union," "devil" for "employer" and "hell" for "unorganized" you would have had a rousing sermon. The illustrations, minus their profanity, might well have been used to show the power and goodness of God instead of the union. And his "why not join" was so much in the church tone, I was afraid he was going to have us sing the hymn of invitation.[21]

During the late 1930s in Birmingham, black gospel quartets turned out to be crucial for the expansion and legitimation of unionism. The Steel Workers' Organizing Committee even had its own vocal group known as the Bessemer Big Four Quartet. Made up of former members of the West Highland Jubilee Singers, a popular quartet active in the 1920s, the Bessemer Big Four Quartet performed at union meetings and were heard occasionally on local radio broadcasts. Like most other quartets, the Bessemer Big Four did not simply use the gospel form to create secular union songs. Rather, they performed deeply religious compositions that sanctioned, or rather sanctified, unionism. Here are some lines from a song they recorded entitled "Satisfied":

> Well you read in the Bible,
> You read it well.
> Listen to the story,

That I'm bound to tell.
Christ's last Passover,
He had his Communion.
He told his disciples,
Stay in the union.
Together you stand,
Divided you fall.
Stay in the union,
I'll save you all.
Ever since that wonderful day my soul's been
    satisfied.

The religious groundings of the Southern labor movement not only provided a cultural and moral basis for working-class solidarity, but gave its members a reason for interracial unity beyond basic utilitarianism, or what the Industrial Workers of the World called "stomach equality." Black and white workers were all "children of God together in a collective struggle."[22]

Even if religious ideology, spiritual values, and gospel music united Southern working people and offered a moral justification to fight the bosses, Southern black church leaders were, more often than not, hostile or indifferent to organized labor. Part of their reluctance to support trade unions had to do with organized labor's rather mixed record on racial equality (which is why the CIO's explicit attempt to attract black workers gained the support of some ministers who had been hostile to unions in the past). A few ministers opposed unions because they either benefited from white patronage, or were simply intimidated by local authorities and corporate interests.[23]

No matter where individual clergy stood in relation to unionism, the faith of most black congregations seemed unshakable. The church was more than an institution. In addition to providing fellowship, laying the foundation for a sense of community, and offering help to those in need, churches were first and foremost places of reflection and *spiritual empowerment*. By spiritual empowerment, I do not simply mean a potential site for political organizing. Rather, the sacred, the spirit world, was often understood and invoked by some African Americans as veritable weapons to protect themselves or to attack others. How do we interpret divine intervention, especially when one's prayers are *answered*? How does the belief that God is by one's side affect one's willingness to fight with police, leave an abusive relationship, stand up to a foreman, participate in a strike, steal, or break tools? How do historians make sense of, say, conjure or "hoodoo" (magic) as a strategy of resistance, retaliation, or defense in the daily lives of some working-class African Americans? Can a sign from above, a conversation with a ghost, a spell cast by an enemy, or talking in tongues unveil the hidden transcript? If some worker turns to a root doctor or prayer rather than a labor union to make an employer less evil, is this a case of "false consciousness"? These are not idle questions. Most of the oral narratives and memoirs of Southern black workers speak of these events or moments as having enormous material consequences.[24]

Of course, the divine and netherworlds of conjure were rarely, if ever, the only resistance or defense strategies used by black working people, but in their minds, bodies, and social relationships this was real power—power of which neither the CIO, the Populists, nor the NAACP could boast. With the exception of Vincent Harding, no historian that I know of since W.E.B. DuBois has been bold enough to assert a connection between the spirit and spiritual world of African Americans and political struggle.[25] Anticipating his critics, DuBois's *Black Reconstruction* boldly considered freedpeople's understanding of divine intervention in their narratives of emancipation and, in doing so, gave future historians insight into an aspect of African American life that cannot be reduced to just "culture":

> Foolish talk, all of this, you say, of course; and that is because no American now believes in his religion. Its facts are mere symbolism; its revelation vague generalities; its ethics a matter of carefully balanced gain. But to most of the four million black folk emancipated by civil war, God was real. They knew Him. They had met Him personally in many a wild orgy of religious frenzy, or in the black stillness of the night.[26]

Building Community in the Dark

Not every nighttime "frenzy" was sacred. Many African American working people pierced the stillness of the night with the sounds of blues and jazz, laughter and handclapping, moans and cries. These were times when they had hoped God looked the other way.

These secular nights are key to understanding the hidden transcript, the private worlds of black working people where thoughts, dreams, and actions that were otherwise choked back in public could find expression. These secular spaces of leisure and pleasure are no less important than churches or mutual benefit societies. But what can we know about this side of community? After all, the places of rest, relaxation, recreation, and restoration rarely maintained archives or recorded the everyday conversations and noises that filled bars, dance halls, blues clubs, barber shops, beauty salons, and street corners of the black community. However, folklorists, anthropologists, oral historians, musicians, and writers fascinated by "Negro life" preserved a relatively large body of cultural texts which have allowed scholars access to the hidden transcript. A handful of pioneering scholars and critics, including Amiri Baraka, Lawrence Levine, and Sterling Stuckey, demonstrate that African American working people created a rich, dynamic culture that served as both a window into a hidden consciousness and a "weapon of the weak." These authors not only insisted that black culture represents at least a partial rejection of the dominant ideology, but that it was forged within the context of struggle against class and racial domination. As archaeologists of African American rural and urban working-class culture whose site/sight extends widely, they have exhumed and interpreted an array of materials. A few scholars in literature, folklore, even political science, have re-examined much of this material to reinterpret historically the politics of race, gender, and class. The challenge for Southern labor historians is to determine precisely how this rich expressive culture—which was frequently in conflict with formal working-class institutions—shaped and reflected black working-class infrapolitics.[27]

Of course, not all blues or gospel lyrics spoke to oppression, nor could one assign political meaning to the entire body of folklore, jokes, and various other oral texts. Black working-class culture was created more for pleasure, not merely to challenge or explain domination. But people thought before they acted, and what they thought shaped, and was shaped by, cultural production and consumption. Besides, for a working class whose days consisted of backbreaking wage work, low income, long hours, and pervasive racism, these social sites were more than relatively free spaces in which the grievances and dreams of an exploited class could be openly articulated. They enabled African Americans to take back their bodies for their own pleasure rather than another's profit.

Studies conducted during the 1920s and 1930s of public recreation in Southern cities reveal that opportunities for *whites* were meager, which meant that facilities for African Americans were woefully inadequate. Movie theaters, parks, recreational centers, swimming pools, and beaches were either segregated, available to African Americans on designated days, or completely off limits. Few Southern cities had outdoor amusement parks, but they, too, were either completely segregated or for whites only.[28] Although African Americans were less than pleased with third-rate segregated facilities, they nevertheless made the most of Jim Crow's parks, theaters, and nickelodeons. In the shadow of "Whites Only" signs and police officers aggressively monitoring the color line, they found pleasure and fellowship, fun and games, in these segregated spaces. Historian Earl Lewis put it best: Southern black folk turned segregation into "congregation." Congregation, Lewis writes, "symbolized an act of free will, whereas segregation represented the imposition of another's will. . . . [African Americans] discovered, however, that congregation in a Jim Crow environment produced more space than power. They used this space to gather their cultural bearings, to mold the urban setting."[29]

But these secular forms of congregation frequently drew the wrath of black sacred congregations. The church's strict moral codes and rules for public behavior often came into conflict with aspects of black working-class culture, particularly their engagement with commericalized leisure. Baptists and Methodists disciplined members for patronizing gin joints, for wild dancing, and for gambling. Through newspaper colums and leaflets, male and female activists in the church railed against a range of improprieties, such as "gum chewing, loud talking, gaudy colors, the nickelodeon, jazz," to name but a few. A leader of the Baptist church warned that "The sure way to ruin is by way of the public dance hall."[30]

Indeed, the moral panic over commercialized leisure among black middle-class spokespersons had reached crisis proportions by the eve of World War I. In 1914, W.E.B. DuBois and Augustus Dill surveyed several hundred leading African Americans about the state of "manners and morals" among young people, and many pointed to popular culture as the root cause of moral degeneracy. "Movies, I believe," replied one informant, "have an unwholesome effect upon the young people. Roller skating, ragtime music, cabaret songs, and ugly suggestions of the big city are all pernicious. The dancing clubs in the big cities are also vicious." Another respondent feared that young people "assemble in dives and hang around the corners in great numbers, especially the boys. Many of them are becoming gamblers and idlers."[31]

Women were scrutinized much more closely than men. They were told how to dress and warned not to even venture into "unwholesome" amusements. Both men and women of the church insisted that the home sphere is where the female belongs—unless, of course, she is performing the worthy labors of organizing for the church, helping the community, or earning money to put food on the table. As Evelyn Brooks Higginbotham points out,

> the competing images of the church and the street symbolized cultural divisions within the mass of the black working poor. . . . [T]he church and the street constituted opposing sites of assembly, with gender-laden and class-laden meanings. The street signified male turf, a public space of worldly dangers and forbidden pleasures. . . . Women who strolled the streets or attended dance halls and cheap theaters promiscuously blurred the boundaries of gender.[32]

But resistance from ministers, middle-class leaders, upright working-class congregants—not to mention white employers—did not stop African American working people from "hanging out"; nor did it stop them from showing up in church on Sunday morning. "Every Friday and Saturday night," recalls Atlanta blues musician Roy Dunn, "somebody in a different place had what you call an open house. They'd give some kind of party, a barbecue or something, in order to give people somewhere to go. Cause there wasn't nowhere until Sunday, and that was church." Aside from house parties, some of the most popular sites of Friday and Saturday night congregation were dance halls, blues clubs, and "jook joints."[33] In darkened rooms ranging in size from huge halls to tiny dens, black working people of both sexes shook and twisted their overworked bodies, drank, talked, engaged in sexual play, and—in spite of occasional fights—reinforced their sense of community. Whether it was the call and response of a blues singer's lyrics or the sight of dozens of sweaty brown bodies in motion, doing the "slop," the "snake hips," or any of the familiar dances of the day, the form and content of such leisure activities were unmistakably collective.[34]

I am not suggesting that parties, dances, and other leisure pursuits were merely guises for political events, or that these cultural practices were clear acts of resistance. Instead, much if not most of African American popular culture can be characterized as, to use Raymond Williams's terminology, "alternative" rather than oppositional.[35] Most people attended those events to escape from the world of assembly lines, relief lines, and color lines, and to leave momentarily the individual and collective battles against racism, sexism, and material deprivation. But this is still only part of the story, for seeking the sonic, visceral pleasures of music and fellowship, the sensual pleasures of food, drink, and dancing, was not just about escaping the vicissitudes of Southern life. Black patrons went with people who had a shared knowledge of these cultural forms, people with whom they felt kinship, people to whom they told stories about the day or the latest joke, people who shared a common vernacular filled with a grammar and vocabulary that struggled to articulate the beauty and burden of their racial, class, and gender experiences in the South. They were often spaces which allowed for freer sexual expression, particularly for women whose sexuality was often circumscribed by employers, family members, the law, and the fear of sexual assault in a society with few protections for black women. One scholar of black dance wrote, "In the atmosphere of increasing urban anonymity and the pleasures of a good time, dance in the honky-tonk became more directly associated with sensation and sexual coupling." Coot Grant, a performer who grew up in Birmingham watching dancers through a "peephole in the wall" at her father's honky-tonk, remembers that the popular dances of the turn of the century bore provocative titles like "the Fanny Bump, Buzzard Lope, Fish Tail, Eagle Rock, Itch, Shimmy, Squat . . . and a million others."[36]

Knowing what happens in these spaces of pleasure can help us understand the solidarity black people have shown at political mass meetings, illuminate the bonds of fellowship one finds in churches and voluntary associations, and unveil the *conflicts* across class and gender lines that shape and constrain these collective struggles. Furthermore, when we consider the needs of employers and the power of the Protestant work ethic in American culture, these events undermined labor discipline while, in many cases, reinforcing black working-class ties to consumer culture. Black working people who spent time and their precious little money at the dance halls, blues clubs, and house parties, cultural critic Paul Gilroy astutely observes, essentially

> see waged work as itself a form of servitude. At best, it is viewed as a necessary evil and is sharply counterposed to the more authentic freedoms that can only be enjoyed in nonwork time. The black body is here celebrated as an instrument of pleasure rather than an instrument of labor. The nighttime becomes the right time, and the space allocated for recovery and recuperation is assertively and provocatively occupied by the pursuit of leisure and pleasure.[37]

Yet, we must keep in mind that places of leisure were also places of work for some segments of the black working class, particularly women for whom there existed few opportunities outside of domestic service. Local singers and dancers, for instance, frequently held day jobs, turning to performance as both a means of artistic self-expression as well as an additional source of income. Besides waitresses, barmaids, coat checks, and assorted service workers whose tips derived largely from the wages of black working-class male consumers, we must also consider the work experiences of a wide range of "sex workers" and escorts. Some dance halls employed young women to dance with unescorted men for a small "per-dance" fee of a nickel or dime. Sexual liaisons and companionship could be purchased by men, and the men and women involved in the trafficking of female bodies made their living selling women's sexuality. To look at the urban pleasure/sex industry in the South by exploring labor relations and the labor process would yield some interesting results, no doubt.

Given the coercive and illicit nature of this part of the underground economy, the hazards involved, the particular gender and racial dimensions, a labor history approach alone has obvious limitations. For instance, while prostitution offered women a means of income to supplement wage labor or enable them to escape domestic service, we must consider the extent to which anonymous sex or dancing was a source of pleasure, especially compared to cleaning and cooking. So much so that women who traveled unescorted at night in public were frequently assumed to be prostitutes, especially if they were anywhere near the places of amusement. In Atlanta, for example, the police had what was called "a sundown law with women." Often it did not matter if the woman was a known prostitute or not; if she was by herself in a restaurant or club, she was likely to be arrested.[38] Furthermore, in light of the ways in which black women's sexual expression or participation in popular amusements (especially in heterosocial public places) has been constrained, not only by Jim Crow but by Victorian mores, black women's involvement in the pleasure industry might be seen as both typical and transgressive. Typical in that black women's bodies have historically been exploited as sites of male pleasure; transgressive in that women were able to break the straightjacket of what Evelyn Brooks Higginbotham calls the "politics of respectability" in exchange for the possibility of female pleasure. It is also potentially empowering since it turn labors not associated with wage work—dancing, sexual play, intercourse—into income.[39]

While Friday and Saturday nights in Southern cities were moments set aside for the "pursuit of leisure and pleasure," some of the most intense skirmishes between black working people and authority erupted after weekend gatherings. During World War II in Birmingham, for example, racial conflicts on public transportation on Friday and Saturday nights were commonplace; many of the incidents involved black youth returning from dances and parties. This should not be surprising since these young men and women who rode public transportation in groups were emboldened by a sense of social solidarity rooted in a shared culture, common friends, generational identity, not to mention a level of naiveté as to the possible consequences of "acting up" in white-dominated public space. Leaving social sites which ultimately reinforced a sense of collectivity through shared culture, combined possibly with the effect of alcohol and reefer, emboldened many young black passengers. On the South Bessemer line, which passed some of the popular black dance halls, white passengers and operators dreaded the "unbearable" presence of large numbers of African Americans who "pushed and shoved" white riders at will. As one conductor noted, "negroes are rough and boisterous when leaving downtown dances at this time of night."[40]

The nighttime also afforded black working people the opportunity to become something other than workers. In a world where clothes constituted signifiers of identity and status, "dressing up" was a way of shedding the degradation of work and collapsing status distinctions between themselves and their oppressors. As one Atlanta domestic worker remembers, the black business district of Auburn Avenue was "where we dressed up, because we couldn't dress up during the day. . . . We'd dress up and put on our good clothes and go to the show on Auburn Avenue. And you were going places. It was like white folks' Peachtree."[41]

Seeing oneself and others "dressed up" was enormously important in terms of constructing a collective identity based on something other than wage work, presenting a public challenge to the dominant stereotypes of the black body, and reinforcing a sense of dignity that was perpetually being assaulted. Many poor black parents dressed their children in a manner that camouflaged class differences. "Only by our address," Gloria Wade-Gayles recalls, "could our teachers identify many of us as residents of the project. We wore starched hand-me-downs or inexpensive clothes bought on time and in basement sales at stores on Main Street. Shinola polish kept our shoes white or shiny, and shoe repairmen on the corner kept them soled." Ironically, "better class Negroes," who often criticized working-class African Americans for their slovenly appearance, sometimes found their efforts to dress stylishly annoying and unproductive. In his book, *The Georgia Negro: A History* (1937), Asa Gordon admonished the state's black working-class population for spending more on clothes "than circumstances demanded and income suggested." African Americans "insist on wearing clothes, that, for them, represent extravagant luxury. Negroes with small incomes insist on wearing the best clothes 'money can buy.'"[42]

These efforts to re-present the body through dress were a double-edged sword since the styles African Americans adopted all too frequently reinforced rather than challenged bourgeois notions of respectability. Indeed, by ridiculing black efforts to appear "respectable," white elites secured their own status as the measure of taste and respectability. Minstrelsy and popular film commonly lampooned African Americans who dressed stylishly for public outings, recasting this black version of the bourgeois promenade as another example of Rastus aping "better-class" white citizens.[43]

Nevertheless, the political implications of dress as an assertion of dignity and resistance should not be dismissed as peripheral to the "real" struggles of Southern black working people. Clothes have their own social meanings, depending on the context in which they are worn. Understandably, clothing could serve as a badge of oppression or a sign of transgression.[44] The obvious and most extreme cases involved returning black veterans who were beaten and lynched for wearing their military uniforms in public. In Georgia alone, where twenty-two African Americans were lynched in 1919, it was clear that black soldiers were singled out. One veteran was beaten to death by a mob in Blakely, Georgia, "for wearing his uniform too long." There are several cases during the Second World War in which black uniformed soldiers—most of them stationed in the South—were beaten or shot by white civilians or police officers. As military personnel representing a higher authority, the uniforms emboldened some African Americans to challenge segregation (see chapter 3). More often than not, however, the uniforms turned black soldiers into moving targets. To ensure their safety, many African American soldiers chose to wear only their civilian clothes when out on furlough "on account of intimidation."[45]

Protecting the Veil

Culture and community are essential for understanding black working-class infrapolitics. Hidden in homes, dance halls, and churches, embedded in expressive cultures, is where much of what is choked back at work or in white-dominated public space can find expression. "Congregation" enables black communities to construct and enact a sense of solidarity; to fight with each other; to maintain and struggle over a collective memory of oppression and pleasure, degradation and dignity; to debate what it means to be "black," "Negro," "colored," and so forth.

Congregation can also be a dangerous thing. While Jim Crow ordinances ensured that churches, bars, social clubs, barber shops, beauty salons, even alleys, would remain "black" space, segregation gave African Americans a place to hide, a place to plan. When white ruling groups had reason to suspect dissident activities among African Americans, authorities tried to monitor and sometimes shut down black social spaces—usually swiftly and violently. Mere rumors of black uprisings made any black gathering place fair game for illegal, often brutal, invasions.[46]

To penetrate the other side of the veil, employers and police officials actively cultivated black "stool pigeons" or informers to maintain tabs on the black community. According to Hosea Hudson, a black labor organizer and Communist Party member in Alabama during the 1930s and 1940s, police and welfare agencies often relied on "stool pigeons" to inform on their neighbors. "Many times when these welfare officials came into a community, first thing they do, was going to a [stool pigeon's] home before they go round to see anybody else on this block." The agent would then proceed "from house to house, and could near about tell you if you had done anything to earn any money from last week until this time, because that's what these stooges in the community would do."[47] The success of stool pigeons often depended on the same strategies black working people used to resist exploitation. Black informers had to maintain a low profile and don a mask in front of other black folk since they were less effective as spies without entry into the community of workers.

That stool pigeons can exist in black communities, and that their reasons for turning informant might be motivated by the same circumstances that led many of Hosea Hudson's comrades into the Communist Party (i.e., joblessness and poverty), reinforce the idea that neither mutual oppression nor common skin color alone explain black working-class solidarity. The bases and forms of resistance were not only a product of their experiences with racism, wage labor, and sexism, but were also rooted in African American communities' conversations, cultural practices, and collective efforts to make their lives better. When we search for the locus of working-class opposition, we ought to look not only at antiracist activities or workplace conflicts but at the dynamic processes by which social and cultural institutions were constructed and time and space for leisure appropriated.

The culture of African American working people shaped and was shaped by black community institutions, constantly recreated and reinforced a sense of collective identity, and was itself passionately contested. Individual and collective experiences, grievances, and dreams were talked about and reflected upon in the hidden social spaces that tend to fall between the cracks of political history—spaces as diverse

as barber shops, bars, and benevolent societies. By ignoring or belit-
tling these shared practices and privileging the public utterances of
black middle-class leadership, several race relations scholars, like
Lester Lamon in his study of Tennessee, decided that black working
people "remained silent, either taking the line of least resistance or
implicitly adopting the American faith in hard work and individual effort."[48] If they had looked deeper beyond the veil, beyond the public
transcript of accommodation and traditional protest, they would have
found more clamor than silence.

Chapter 3

Congested Terrain

Resistance on Public Transportation

A young soldier, in uniform, was seated in the front of a Birmingham bus, in the days when the white folks of that city had not yet gotten straightened out about civil rights. At the next stop a white man boarded the vehicle, paid his fare, and approached the ebony soldier. "I'll take that seat," he said imperiously. "You move to the back where you belong." The soldier didn't budge. "I have a question for you," he said, his voice low and even. "If we were on the battlefield, would you still want me to move to the back while *you* stayed up front?"

—POPULAR AFRICAN AMERICAN JOKE DURING WORLD WAR II[1]

Moving Theaters

In an address before the Bessemer Kiwanis Club in 1942, Alabama white supremacist leader Horace Wilkinson relayed a conversation he had had in which a Birmingham bus driver pointed to a group of black passengers in the back of the bus and declared, "Right there, mister, is where our next war will break out, and it may start before this one is over."[2] That public spaces were frequently the most embattled sites of black working-class opposition during World War II is not surprising. Social, economic, and political upheaval caused by the war was largely responsible for heightened conflict on public conveyances. Wartime rhetoric unintentionally undermined the legitimacy of white supremacy. Black Americans were expected to support a war against Hitler—whose plan for Aryan supremacy was treated as a

55

threat to Western democracy—while white supremacy and segregation continued to be a way of life in the Deep South. African Americans, especially the youth, believed racism could no longer be
justified on home soil, and those who were unwilling to tolerate it
any longer exhibited greater militancy in public spaces such as
busses, streetcars, or on city streets.[3]

These daily battles on public transportation have enormous implications for the study of African American working-class opposition.
Contrary to the experiences of white workers, for whom public space
eventually became a kind of "democratic space" where people of different class backgrounds shared city theaters, public conveyances,
streets, and parks,[4] for black people white-dominated public space
was vigilantly undemocratic and potentially dangerous. Jim Crow
signs, filthy and inoperable public toilets, white police officers, racial
epithets, dark bodies standing in the aisles of half-empty busses, were
daily visual and aural reminders of the semicolonial status black people occupied in the Jim Crow South. Of course, throughout most of
the twentieth century individual African Americans have fought back
in an effort to at least ameliorate public accommodations, but their
struggles have largely been ignored by historians. While the primary
project of civil rights scholarship has been to examine desegregation,
the study of black resistance to segregated public space remains one
of the least developed areas of inquiry. There are countless studies of
well-organized movements with defined goals, spokespersons, and
formal organizations behind them, but historians as a whole have not
examined in any detail the everyday posing, discursive conflicts, and
physical battles that created the conditions for the success of organized, collective movements.[5] This has been an unfortunate oversight
since most black working-class resistance, as I emphasized in the previous chapters, has remained unorganized, clandestine, and evasive.
Moreover, examples of black working-class resistance in public spaces
offer some of the richest insights into how race, gender, class, space,
time, and collective memory shape both domination and resistance.
The purpose of this chapter, therefore, is to "remap" black working-
class opposition by shifting focus away from the workplace and community to public space, namely Birmingham's streetcars and busses
during the Second World War.

As the wartime economy generated more employment opportunities and rural residents migrated to the city to fill these jobs, the sheer number of people moving to and from work overtaxed an already limited fleet of streetcars and busses. Because public transportation provided limited space that had to be shared—even if racially divided—between blacks and whites, battles over space, as well as the manner in which space was allocated, resulted in intense racial conflict. Even police commissioner Eugene "Bull" Connor, who was more inclined to blame outside agitators for any action resembling black militancy, placed much of the blame on the wartime economy: "The war has brought unprecedented conditions. Stations, depots, carriers, busses, streetcars . . . are crowded to capacity; sidewalks . . . are congested; stores and elevators are filled with people."[6]

In some ways, the design and function of busses and streetcars rendered them unique sites of contestation. An especially apt metaphor for understanding the character of domination and resistance on public transportation might be to view the interior spaces as "moving theaters." Theater can have two meanings: as a site of performance and as a site of military conflict. First, dramas of conflict, repression, and resistance are performed in which passengers witness, or participate in, a wide variety of "skirmishes" that shape their collective memory, illustrate the limitations as well as possibilities of resistance to domination, and draw more passengers into the "performance." The design of streetcars and busses themselves—enclosed spaces with seats facing forward or toward the center aisle—lent a dramaturgical quality to everyday discursive and physical confrontations.[7]

Theater as a military metaphor is particularly appropriate in light of the fact that all bus drivers and streetcar conductors in Birmingham carried guns and blackjacks, and used them pretty regularly to maintain order. As one Birmingham resident recalls, during the 1940s streetcar conductors "were just like policemans [sic]. They carried guns too."[8] African American and some white liberal riders found streetcar conductors and bus drivers to be particularly racist. One leading white progressive noted that "the Klan has picked up a good many members from the street-car and bus operators."[9] And they policed the aisles with a vengeance. Even the mildest act of resistance, from talking too loud to arguing over change, could lead to ejection without a fare refund or, in some cases, arrest. Profanity or physical contest could result in a six-month jail sentence or, in most cases, a substantial fine and court costs.[10]

A transgressive act frequently led to violence, which was surprisingly commonplace on Birmingham's city transit system. In August 1943, for example, when a black woman riding the South East Lake–Ensley line complained to the conductor that he had passed her stop, he followed her out of the streetcar and, in the words of the official report, "knocked her down with handle of gun. No further trouble."[11] Two months later on a North Bessemer streetcar, a black man loaded down with luggage was beaten severely for not moving fast enough for the conductor and for cursing. In the words of the official report, "Operator hit him with his fist and knocked him out of car." Angry but apparently undaunted, the man boarded the car again "and kept talking so operator hit him with [a] black jack."[12] The task of policing public transportation was also taken up by white male *passengers*, many of whom were working-class. There were dozens of incidents in which white men threw African American men and women off the vehicle, slapped black women, or drew guns on black passengers. Rarely were they prosecuted or even charged. One of the most dramatic incidents—among the few to receive some publicity—involved Steven Edwards, a black passenger who was shot several times during an altercation with a bus driver on the Avenue F line. Incensed that several black passengers were forced to move further back to make room for white passengers, Edwards demanded his fare be refunded. When the driver would not return the correct fare, the indignant Edwards began cursing and a fight ensued. The driver shot him twice and an armed, unidentified white passenger who had just boarded the bus shot him two more times. Neither the driver nor the armed passenger were blamed; Edwards was found guilty of disorderly conduct and fined $50.[13]

Despite the repressive, police-like atmosphere on public transportation, black passengers still resisted. Over the course of twelve months beginning September 1941, there were at least eighty-eight cases of blacks occupying "white" space on public transportation, fifty-five of which were open acts of defiance in which African American passengers either refused to give up their seats or sat in the white section. But this is only part of the story, since the total number of reported incidents and complaints of racial conflict reached 176: including at least 18 interracial fights among passengers, 22 fights between black passengers and operators, and 13 incidents in which black passengers engaged in verbal or physical confrontations over being shortchanged.[14]

What is more striking than the sheer number of incidents is the fact that, in most cases, the racial compartmentalization of existing space was not the primary point of contention. For many black working-class riders, simply getting on the bus was a struggle in and of itself. It was not uncommon, for instance, for half-empty busses or streetcars to pass up African Americans on the pretext that space needed to be reserved in anticipation of additional white riders. According to a 1944 report, the largest number of reported "racial" incidents involved black passengers who had been passed up, or those who fought drivers/operators who attempted to stop them from boarding.[15] Aside from the obvious problems of not being able to get to one's destination on time, or being stranded at a bus stop as five or six busses pass by, riders' transfers expired if they had to wait too long, which meant paying a full fare all over again. Another company policy (the Birmingham Electric Company or BECO owned and operated the public transit system) that had a similar effect was the practice of forcing blacks to pay at the front door and enter through the center doors. On numerous occasions, black passengers paid their fare at the front door but before they had a chance to board the bus drove off.[16] The rule itself was not only obnoxious but ambiguous: drivers were instructed to "collect fares at the front entrance and direct negroes to board at the center entrance of all vehicles *when they are crowded*" (emphasis added). What was meant by crowded was always subject to interpretation, leading to immense confusion and, at times, intense disagreement.[17] Besides, company policies were thought to be less authoritative, and therefore more vulnerable to challenges, than municipal ordinances. One black passenger on the Pratt–Ensley streetcar who was arrested for repeatedly boarding on the white side, insisted that "it was not a law to board on [the] colored section, just a company rule."[18]

Public transportation, unlike most forms of public space (e.g., a waiting room or a water fountain) was an extension of the market-place. Passengers paid for transportation, which if used on a daily basis could add up to a significant portion of the working poor's income. And transportation companies depend on fares for profit (although operators and conductors did not always operate on the basis of economic rationality). This explains why divisions between black and white space had to be relatively fluid and flexible. When a bus or streetcar traveled through black neighborhoods, one could expect more black riders; indeed, a bus completely full with black passengers was not an uncommon sight, especially on Birmingham's West Side. With no fixed dividing line, black and white riders were continually contesting adjustments to what was a fluid boundary. In short, the lack of a fixed color line rendered public transportation far more vulnerable to everyday acts of resistance.

The ambiguity of the color line and the variety of ways individual drivers and conductors interpreted Jim Crow laws meant that the resistance dramas played out in Birmingham's moving theaters were not always predictable. In February of 1944, for example, a large crowd of black passengers on the College Hills line—which had a reputation for having the most brutal, racist bus drivers—sat in awe as one driver asked three white women to move to the side seats in order to make room for black passengers![19] An even more dramatic scene took place two months later on the the South East Lake–Ensley line. Around mid-afternoon a police officer boarded the car and noticed two white men sitting behind the color boards on one side and African Americans sitting across from them. The officer demanded that the color boards be moved further back, but the conductor argued that to do so would mean making some black passengers stand unnecessarily; the two white men had planned to transfer to another bus in a few stops. When the officer realized that he could not convince him to move the color boards, he angrily took the conductor's badge number and filed a complaint.[20]

One particularly startling exchange took place during the peak morning hours in April 1944, on the Mountain Terrace bus. The official report is worth quoting in its entirety:

> White woman boarded bus and started a tirade against negroes, which was her usual custom. At 29th Street she said she was going to see that

the color boards were not moved this morning to give the negroes more room, and moved as far back in bus as she could in the white section. Later she came to Operator and asked him to make the negroes stop laughing at her. He told her he could not stop them from laughing, she then went into a tirade. A negro girl made some remark, she rushed back and a fight started. Operator separated them and had no further trouble. *This woman causes some trouble every morning.*[21]

The story is remarkable, for here we have a group of African American passengers freely ridiculing a white women, who—given the racial and gender politics of chivalry—is supposed to be protected by the operator. In this narrative it is the *white* woman who is the "trouble-maker." More significantly, the operator implicitly sides with the black passengers and shifts the balance of power, thus acknowledging and thereby unveiling what could have been a hidden transcript: the laughter (and ridicule) among black passengers.

Incidents such as these were important, for they illumined to black riders that small victories were indeed possible within the framework of "separate but equal," not to mention instilling a sense of fear or frustration in those white riders who witnessed successful acts of black resistance or white operators who defended black space at the expense of whites.

As with the rest of the marketplace, African Americans experienced public transportation as a form of economic exploitation. One source of frustration was the all-too-common cases of black passengers who had been cheated out of their fare or shortchanged. Some unscrupulous drivers and conductors made extra money by returning the wrong change, presuming that black working people could not count. One tactic was to give back only coins for large bills. One woman on the East Lake–West End line paid the ten cents fare with a $5 bill and the operator returned her change in dimes, despite her insistence on receiving "greenbacks." When she finally counted the handful of dimes it only amounted to $1.40.[22]

Unlike in the workplace, where workers entered as disempowered producers dependent on wages for survival and beholden, ostensibly at least, to their superiors, working people entered public transportation as consumers—and with a sense of consumer entitlement. Arguments and fights over being shortchanged were fairly common during the war, and acts of resistance sometimes took on more material than symbolic forms. There were numerous cases in which black passengers in fact refused to pay their fare or attempted to pay only a portion to protest their second-class status.[23]

Small War Zones

The commoditized nature of public transportation, the growing number of black and white working-class passengers, and the highly charged political atmosphere caused by the war turned busses and streetcars into theaters in the sense of small war zones as well. They provided microcosms of race, class, and gender conflict that raged in other social spaces throughout the city (i.e., sidewalks, parks, and streets) but otherwise rarely found a place in the public record. Some of these battles reflected the frustrations of an embittered black working class which still experienced racist employment practices despite the booming economy. Although a rather large percentage of jobless black males found employment, either in the armed services or in the lower echelons of industry, and thousands left Alabama to take advantage of Northern employment opportunities, racism nevertheless limited the options available to African American working people. The majority of blacks were denied access to employment training programs, and white-controlled industrial unions actively limited black occupational mobility. The Fair Employment Practices Committee, which held hearings in Birmingham in 1943, was apparently powerless to bring about changes. In fact, during the war the percentage of blacks employed in the steel industry actually declined from 41 percent in 1940 to 38 percent in 1945, and black steel workers on average earned 80 percent of what their white co-workers earned. Conditions for black women were certainly no better; many tried desperately to escape domestic work and take advantage of industrial jobs, but in Birmingham virtually all "female positions" were reserved for white women. Those who successfully moved out of domestic work merely filled other kinds of service jobs—such as dishwashers, cooks, bus girls, mechanical laundry workers—jobs white women had vacated.[24]

White working-class bus and streetcar passengers were also embittered, though for different reasons. Many were unskilled workers (or

their children) who had been drawn into the orbit of industrial production and feared blacks were taking "their" jobs. A race riot erupted in Mobile and wartime hate strikes took place in several locations.
These tensions fueled intense battles over space on the Boyles–Tarrant City line, which serviced Tarrant City, an industrial suburb of
Birmingham that was home to a large white working-class community. More fights between black and white passengers broke out on this
line than on any other bus or streetcar line in the city. Numerous cases were reported of white men spitting on black women, white working-class youth assaulting black passengers through streetcar
windows after exiting, and fistfights and verbal exchanges breaking
out on a regular basis. Between December 1941 and May 1942, at
least eight reported incidents took place of black and white passengers brawling on the bus. In one reported incident, occurring at
around 2:40 AM, a group of "White boys refused to let negro man
ride, and ejected him."[25]

At the forefront of black resistance were young people who had
been radicalized by the war and whose backgrounds ranged from servicemen to zoot suiters, militant female high school students to
young household workers. According to an internal report by the
Transportation Department of the Birmingham Electric Company, the
majority of "racial disturbances" on public transportation were "pro-
voked, to a large extent, by younger negroes." It was indeed true that
resistance to racist practices on public transportation took place at an
especially early age. The evidence suggests that black male children
and teenagers not only engaged in verbal and physical confrontations
with white authorities, but they tended to direct their attacks on
physical property. Groups of black youth spent some summer
evenings disengaging trolley cables and escaping into dark Birmingham alley ways, the South Bessemer line being a prime target. One
black youth was arrested for throwing rocks at a South East Lake–Ensley streetcar; another was jailed for setting off a "stink bomb" on a
Boyles streetcar. Moreover, it wasn't uncommon for black schoolchildren returning home from school to place their hands "in [the]
center doors causing [the] signal bell to ring." Some of these forms of
behavior could be regarded as playful pranks, but given the repressive, racist atmosphere on the bus and the black youth's sense of
alienation and frustration, it is hard to imagine these acts as anything

but oppositional, much like the original motivation behind subway graffiti, which was initially called "bombing."[26]

As previous scholarship has already demonstrated, black servicemen gained a reputation as militant opponents of Jim Crow.[27] Numerous reports came from Birmingham of black soldiers attempting to move the color boards, sitting or standing in the white section, and fighting with operators as well as white passengers over any act of injustice. In March of 1943, on the Avenue F bus, a black soldier (whom the official report claimed was from New York) refused to move out of the white section, clashed with a knife-wielding white passenger, and was seriously injured. The white passenger was arrested but found not guilty; the black serviceman was taken away by military authorities.[28] A few days later, a black soldier and a female companion boarded the South 15th Street bus late one evening and occupied seats in the white section. When asked to move they complained and then asked for their transfers back. As soon as they stepped off, they began cursing the driver, who then alighted and pulled a gun on them. The soldier, who was carrying a "long blade knife," was arrested.[29]

In a world where clothes carried a great deal of social meaning and were often signifiers of power (or the lack thereof), black men in uniform saw themselves as representing a higher authority and, therefore, felt empowered to act on principle. More importantly, their uniforms signified a clear, active opposition to fascism and Aryan supremacy, which is precisely what African Americans experienced in the South as far as black soldiers were concerned. Occasionally black servicemen tried to turn individual acts of resistance into collective battles, by either drawing other passengers or military personnel into the fray. On the East Lake–West End Line, for example, two black soldiers boarded and promptly sat in the white section. When the conductor asked them to move back, one started to get up but "the other pulled him back in his seat and talked him into remaining in white section." They were eventually ejected.[30] In another incident, a lone black soldier boarded a North Birmingham bus and stood in the white section. When told to move to the back, he responded with "objectionable language." At the next stop, the soldier blocked the aisle in a vain effort to compel several black passengers who had just boarded the bus to join his one-man protest. When the driver tried to eject him, the soldier fought back, knocked him down, and fled the scene before the police arrived.[31]

Despite the tendency on the part of historians to write the history of individual resistance on Jim Crow busses as a good versus evil, justice versus injustice narrative, not all of the incidents involving black servicemen could easily translate into demands for collective equity, fairness, and justice. Often the battles were more personal. Issues of personal autonomy, masculinity, dignity, and freedom to transgress the boundaries of accepted behavior—a negation of an assigned "place" as a black "boy" in the Jim Crow South—were the bases for dozens of physical conflicts.

In almost every case, transgressive acts were met by violence. When the driver of an Acipco bus closed the door on a black soldier's hand as he was tossing a cigarette butt while boarding, the soldier perceived it as a vicious, deliberate act of racism. Words were exchanged between the two, which quickly escalated into a fistfight: "Soldier drew back to hit operator, who struck soldier on head with gun. He reached in his pocket and operator told him to take his hand out or he would kill him. He withdrew his hand and left bus."[32] Another violent incident occurred after two black servicemen boarded a Wylam–Bush Hills streetcar reportedly cursing. The operator attempted to throw them off the car, but one of the servicemen drew a knife and held him at bay. The two men were finally subdued by another conductor from a nearby streetcar and one of his white passengers, who just happened to have a gun.[33]

We must not exaggerate the extent to which resistance on busses was initiated by black servicemen. Most of the young men who contested the power of operators to confine blacks to inadequate spaces, who challenged racist remarks and gestures, or who engaged in outrageous acts of rebellion as a means of "testing the limits" of Jim Crow had more in common with the zoot suiters of Los Angeles or Detroit than the upright soldiers who tended to be more acceptable role models. There are clear differences between the two. The soldiers' clothes and style signified an antifascist, pro-democratic message. By contrast, the language and culture of the "hipster" represented a privileging of ethnic identity and masculinity, and a rejection of subservience. Young black males created a fast-paced, improvisational language which sharply contrasted with the passive stereotype of the stuttering, tongue-tied Sambo. In a world where whites commonly addressed them as "boy," zoot suiters made a fetish of calling each other "man." The zoot suiters constructed an identity in which their gendered and racial meanings were inseparable; opposition to racist oppression was mediated through masculinity. They also cultivated reputations for being "tough"—very few traveled without weapons. As Howard Odum recorded during the war, the mere image of these draped-shape-clad hipsters struck fear in the hearts of white Southerners.[34] As the official reports seem to suggest, black youth who were products of this dissident subculture were particularly unruly on Friday and Saturday nights, as discussed earlier in this chapter.

To many of the passengers familiar with traditions of black folklore, a lot of these young men must have seemed like modern-day "Stagolees," "baaad niggers" who put on public displays of resistance that left witnesses in awe, though their transgressive acts did not lead directly to improvements in conditions, nor were they intended to. Some boldly sat down next to white female passengers and, often with knife in hand, challenged operators to move them. Others refused to pay their fare, or simply picked fights with bus drivers or white passengers. In the middle of the day on the Fourth of July, a black man riding the South Bessemer line pulled a knife on an operator after he was asked to move to the back of the bus. In another incident, a black passenger on the Ensley–Fairfield line boarded, moved the color dividers forward to increase space allotted to black passengers, and sat down next to a white man. The operator expelled him, but he reboarded on the return trip and this time "sat between two white men and began to laugh and make a joke about it." He was then moved bodily to the black section, but a few stops later approached the driver with an open knife. Before the police arrived, he jumped out of the window and escaped. When the bus returned later in the evening, he had the audacity to board again.[35]

The South East Lake–Ensley Line attracted some of the roughest black men in the city, in part because its route serviced areas where a number of dance halls and blues clubs were located. One such incident took place in November of 1943, after a black man not only refused to move to the back of the vehicle in order to make more seats available to white passengers, but audaciously "leaned back and stuck his feet out in the aisle. Conductor struck him with his gun and negro made a break for doors and said, 'I'll see you as you come back.' " Before he had a chance to make good on his threat, he was arrested.[36] Another case involved a black man who, after being forced to move out of the white section, demanded that his fare be returned. When the conductor refused, the man began arguing with the white passengers and "invited them to come over if they wanted a fight." He was subsequently arrested.[37] One of the most violent incidents occurred during the peak evening hours. A fight started when the conductor tried to make an allegedly intoxicated black passenger stop cursing. The official report, despite its cryptic language, describes the scene in detail:

> [The] negro made lunge at conductor who shoved him back. Fight started and negro kicked conductor back in seat. Motorman came to his assistance and negro took out knife. Conductor took out gun and hit negro on head and knocked him down. Another negro offered to take him off car and they alighted. Car made down town loop and stopped at 2nd Ave. and 17th St. where this negro boarded with open knife in upraised hand. Fight started again and negro was shot by conductor.[38]

Nevertheless, like the folk hero, the Stagolee-type rebel was not always regarded as a hero to other working-class black passengers. Some were embarrassed by his actions; the more sympathetic feared for his life. On the Pratt–Ensley streetcar, for instance, a near altercation took place between the conductor and a black man who had complained loudly of having to board on the "colored side." He was already familiar to the conductor since he had had previous arguments about the color boards. After threatening words were exchanged, the passenger "put hand in pocket and cursed conductor. When he did conductor grabbed his [gun] but did not pull it out of holster, but told the negro if he pulled a knife he was going to kill him." The black passengers, however, told him "to hush before he got killed." A few stops later he decided to disembark.[39]

The large number of incidents involving black women also challenge the myth that most opposition to Birmingham's segregated transit system was waged by black male soldiers. In fact, although the available records are incomplete, it seems that black women outnumbered black men in the number of incidents of resistance on busses and streetcars. Between 1941 and 1942, nearly twice as many black women were arrested as black men, most of them charged with either sitting in the white section or cursing. This should not be surprising given the fact that black women had a long tradition of militant opposition to Jim Crow public transportation, a tradition that includes such celebrated figures as Sojourner Truth, Ida B. Wells-Barnett, and, of course, Rosa Parks.[40] More significantly, however, black working women in Birmingham generally rode public transportation more often than men. Male industrial workers tended to live in industrial suburbs within walking distance of their place of employment, while the vast majority of black working women were domestics who had to travel to wealthy or middle-class white neighborhoods on the other side of town.

Unlike the popular image of Rosa Parks's quiet resistance, most black women's opposition tended to be profane and militant. In Birmingham, there were dozens of episodes of black women sitting in the white section, arguing with drivers or conductors, and fighting with white passengers, and in most cases the final scene of the "drama" ended with the woman either being ejected, receiving a refund for her fare and leaving of her own accord, moving to the back of the vehicle, or going to jail. Throughout the war, dozens of black women were arrested for merely cursing at the operator or a white passenger. In October of 1943, for example, a teenager named Pauline Carth attempted to board the College Hills line around 8:00 PM. When she was informed that there was no more room for "colored" passengers, she forced her way into the bus anyway, threw her money at the driver, and cursed and spit on him. The driver responded by knocking her out of the bus, throwing her to the ground, and holding her down until police arrived.[41]

Fights between black women and white passengers were also fairly common. In March of 1943, a black woman and a white man boarding the East Lake–West End line apparently got into a shoving match, which angered the black woman to the point where she "cursed him all the way to Woodlawn." When they reached Woodlawn she was arrested, sentenced to thirty days in jail, and forced to pay a $50 fine.[42] On several occasions the violence was worse than simple shoving. One black woman boarded a Lakeview bus and promptly took the closest available seat—next to a white man. The man responded by striking her; blows were exchanged, hers with an umbrella, his including a closed fist upon her jaw. Only the woman was arrested, however.[43] On a North Birmingham bus a fight ensued when a black woman allegedly pushed a white woman out of the way while she was boarding through the front door during a rainstorm. Soaking wet, these two women "went down the aisle . . . fighting with their umbrellas." But the battle did not end there. A white man standing in the aisle who had witnessed the fight walked up to the black woman (who by then had found a seat) and hit her with his own umbrella. She, in turn, "grabbed [his] umbrella and [the] handle came off, and she struck back at man with the part she had. Operator separated them and there was no further trouble." Surprisingly, no one was arrested.[44]

Although black women's actions were no less violent or profane than men's, gender differences did shape black women's resistance. Household workers were in a unique position to contest racist practices on public transportation without significantly transgressing Jim Crow laws or social etiquette. First, company rules permitted domestics traveling with their white employers' children to sit in the section designated for whites. The idea, of course, was to spare white children from having to endure the Negro section. While this was the official policy of the Birmingham Electric Company (owner of the city transit system at the time), drivers and conductors did not always obey it, and a number of employers filed complaints.[45] Nonetheless, the mere existence of the rule enabled black women to challenge the indignity of being forced to move or stand when seats were available.

Second, when employers were willing to intervene on behalf of their domestics, it had the effect of redirecting black protest into legitimate, "acceptable" avenues. Soon after a white employer complained that the Mountain Terrace bus regularly passed "colored maids and cooks" and therefore made them late for work, the company took action. According to the report, "Operators on this line [were] cautioned."[46] Although a few of the reported grievances reflect a genuine concern on the part of white employers for the way domestic workers were treated on the busses and streetcars,[47] most protests were motivated by more utilitarian concerns. Employers complained frequently of vehicles passing their workers, which made them late for work. And when busses continually passed black women late into the night, a few employers grudgingly chose to drive their maids home.[48]

Yet the historian must beware—it is very possible that black women exaggerated the number of incidents in which public transportation was responsible for tardiness. The unreliability of public transportation provides a plausible excuse for absenteeism, for stealing a few extra hours of sleep, for attending to problems or running errands—all of which were standard resistance strategies, or purely strategies for making ends meet, waged by household workers.[49]

Because most black domestics had to travel alone at night, the fear of being passed or forced to wait for the next vehicle was very real among black women. Standing at a poorly lit, relatively isolated bus stop late at night left them prey to sexual and physical assault by white and black men. As sociologist Carol Brooks Gardner reminds us, in many neighborhoods the streets, particularly at night, are perceived as belonging to men, and women without escorts—no matter how well they could defend themselves—were often treated as available or vulnerable. In the South, this applied largely (though not exclusively) to black women, since the ideology of chivalry presumably compelled most white men to come to the defense of most white women—though this was not always the case for working-class white women. Although one might make the argument that open resistance on the buses contradicts the idea that these same women might be afraid in the streets, it misses the crucial point that busses and streetcars, though sites of vicious repression, were occupied, lighted spaces where potential allies and witnesses might be found.[50]

Making Noise

Open black resistance on Birmingham's public transit system conveyed a sense of dramatic opposition to Jim Crow, before an audience, in a powerful way. But discursive strategies, an apparently more evasive form of resistance, carried dramatic appeal as well. No matter how well drivers, conductors, and signs kept bodies separated, black voices could always flow easily into the section designated for whites, serving as a constant reminder that racially divided public space was contested terrain. Black passengers were routinely ejected, and occasionally arrested, for making too much noise, which in many cases turned out to be harsh words directed at a conductor or passenger, or a monologue about racism in general. For example, a black soldier boarded the East Lake–West End line late one evening in May 1944, and immediately began "loud-talking" so everyone on the bus could hear him. First, he asked what the car fare was, and then he commented on how cheap it was, adding "but this is Alabama." When the operator returned his change he defiantly threw it away and swaggered slowly down the aisle. He then "started talking in a loud voice to negroes about white people, but did not curse." His actions and words were enough to render him a suspicious character, so the streetcar motorman had a police vehicle follow the car. A few stops later the soldier began arguing with a white passenger, so the police arrested him.[51]

Verbal attacks on racism made for excellent theater. Unlike pedestrians passing a street corner preacher, passengers were trapped until they reached their destination. The official reports reveal a hypersensitivity to black voices from the back of the bus. Indeed, any verbal protest or complaint registered by black passengers was frequently described as "loud"—an adjective almost never used to describe the way white passengers articulated their grievances. One morning in August 1943, during the peak hours, a black man boarded an Acipco bus and immediately began "complaining about discrimination against negroes in a very loud voice." After a failed attempt to have the color boards moved forward, the man "became so loud that operator asked him to leave bus which he did."[52]

Although one could argue that "making noise" was not always a clear-cut act of resistance or protest, even the act of cursing took place in a specific sociohistorical context in which repressive structures and institutions circumscribed black mobility and access to public space. The voices themselves, especially the loud and profane, literally penetrated and occupied white spaces. Moreover, the act of cursing, for which only black passengers were arrested, elicited police intervention, not because the state maintained strict moral standards and would not tolerate profanity but rather because it represented a serious transgression of the racial boundaries. While modern scholars might belittle the power of resistive, profane noise as opposition, Birmingham's entire policing structure did not. Cursing was among the most common crimes for which black passengers were arrested. On the South Bessemer line in 1942, for example, one black man was sentenced to six months in jail for cursing. In most instances, however, cursing was punishable by a $10 fine and court costs, and jail sentences averaged about thirty days.[53]

Another forgotten or overlooked discursive strategy is humor. Making jokes about racist, oppressive conditions before an operator or other passengers was probably more pervasive than the documents suggest, particularly since humor could disguise protests so much as to keep them out of the reports. Only when black ridicule of Jim Crow public transportation and its operators led to violence or arrests was it recorded. On the Acipco bus a black passenger alighted, walked around to the driver's window, and said—addressing him by his driver's badge number—"1686 I'm going to see why more colored passengers don't ride on this bus." The passenger then walked over to the curb and stood there, staring at the driver and the bus. The driver, angry and humiliated, walked over to him and "said he was going to give him something to report and hit him with his gun." Evidently, this passenger had a history of verbally attacking drivers for their racism, for he "rode bus every morning and fussed and abused the operator all the way to town."[54]

Unity at the Back of the Bus

Some might argue that these hundreds of everyday acts of resistance—from the most evasive to the blatantly confrontational—amounted to very little since they were primarily individual, isolated events which almost always ended in defeat. But such an argument misses the uniquely dramaturgical quality of social intercourse within the interior spaces of public conveyances. Whenever passengers were present, no act of defiance was isolated, nor were acts of defiance isolating experiences. On the contrary, because African American passengers shared a collective memory of how they were treated on a daily basis, both within and without the "moving theaters," an act of resistance or repression sometimes drew other passengers into the fray, thus escalating into collective action, and always impressed itself on other passengers' memories. A very interesting report from an Avenue F line bus driver illustrates just such a moment of collective resistance: "Operator went to adjust the color boards, and negro woman sat down quickly just in front of board that operator was putting in place. She objected to moving and was not exactly disorderly but all the negroes took it up and none of [the] whites would sit in seat because they were afraid to, and negroes would not sit in vacant seats in rear of bus." In some instances, black riders invented collective ways to protest which protected their anonymity. On the College Hills line in August 1943, black riders grew impatient with a particularly racist bus driver who, in the course of a few minutes, twice drew his gun on black passengers, intentionally passed one black woman's stop, and ejected a man who complained on the woman's behalf. According to the report, "the negroes then started ringing bell for the entire block and no one would alight when he stopped."[55]

Resistance to material domination could also take on a collective character, as black passengers attempted to compensate for the daily indignities, losses due to incorrect change, inconveniences caused by passing vehicles, or the many times passengers never reached their destination. When the Airport bus met a large crowd of black and white passengers on their way to work, everything proceeded as normal until someone discovered a way to open the center door, allowing an entire crowd of African-Americans to invade the bus without paying their fare. The back of the bus became so crowded that the startled driver could not get on, "so he asked someone to collect transfers for him. When they refused he made them all alight so that he could collect transfers as they boarded. They refused to board bus the second time." Their collective refusal to reboard the bus was a remarkable show of solidarity, particularly since some of the passengers presumably risked being late for work.[56]

But all oppositional and transgressive acts took place in a context of extreme repression. The occupants sitting in the rear who witnessed or were part of the daily guerrilla skirmishes learned that punishment was inevitable. The arrests, beatings, and ejections were intended as much for the individual transgressor as for all other black passengers on board. The fear of an incident escalating into collective opposition often meant that individuals who intervened in other conflicts received the harshest punishment. On the South Bessemer line early one evening in 1943, a young black man was arrested and fined $25 for coming to the defense of a black woman who was told to move in back of the color dividers. His crime was that he "complained and talked back to the officer."[57] Likewise, the fear of arrest or ejection could persuade individuals who initially joined collective acts of resistance to retreat. Even when a single, dramatic act captured the imaginations of other black passengers and spurred them to take action, there was no guarantee that it would lead to sustained, collective opposition. To take one example, a black woman and man boarded the South East Lake–Ensley line one evening in 1943 and removed the color dividers, prompting all of the black passengers on board and boarding to occupy the white section. When the conductor demanded that they move to their assigned area, all grudgingly complied except the couple who had initiated the rebellion. They were subsequently arrested.[58]

Occasionally specific protests continued long after the incidents that incited them. Sometimes the passengers themselves approached formal civil rights organizations to intercede on their behalf or lead a campaign against the BECO. Following the arrest of Pauline Carth in 1943, a group of witnesses brought the case to the attention of the Birmingham branch of the NAACP, but aside from a perfunctory investigation and an article in the Birmingham *World*, no action was taken. The Southern Negro Youth Congress (SNYC), a left-wing youth organization based in Birmingham, actually attempted a small-scale direct-action campaign on the Fairfield bus line after receiving numerous complaints from black youth about conditions on public transportation. Mildred McAdory and three other SNYC activists attempted to move the color boards on a Fairfield bus in 1942, for which she was beaten and arrested by Fairfield police. As a result of the incident, the SNYC formed a short-lived organization called the Citizens Committee for Equal Accommodations on Common Carriers. However, the treatment of African Americans on public transportation was not a high-priority issue for Birmingham's black protest organizations during the war, partly because black middle-class leaders, particularly left-leaning radicals, were more concerned with supporting the war effort, and partly because very few middle-class blacks rode public transportation. Thus working people whose livelihood depended on city transit generally had to fend for themselves.[59]

Lessons to Be Learned

There are at least three lessons to be learned from examining black working-class resistance on Birmingham's busses and streetcars. First, unorganized, seemingly powerless black passengers made governing public transit more difficult by their acts of transgression. And they brought to the forefront the most hotly contested aspects of Southern regulation of public space. Second, *what* they resisted and the sorts of oppositional practices they adopted serve as a window into the elusive and complex consciousness of African American working people. Sitting with whites, for most black riders, was never a critical issue; rather, African Americans wanted more space for themselves, they wanted to receive equitable treatment, they wanted to be personally treated with respect and dignity, they wanted to be heard and possibly understood, they wanted to get to work on time, and above all, they wanted to exercise power over institutions that controlled them or on which they were dependent.

Finally, the bitter struggles waged by black working people on public transportation, though obviously exacerbated by wartime social, political, and economic transformations, should force us to rethink the meaning of public space as a terrain of class, race, and gender conflict. Although the workplace and struggles to improve working conditions are certainly important, for Southern black workers the most embattled sites of conflict were frequently public spaces. Part of the reason has to do with the fact that policing proved far more difficult in public spaces than in places of work. Not only were employees constantly under the watchful eye of foremen, managers, and employers, but workers could be dismissed, suspended, or have their pay docked on a whim. In the public spaces of the city, the anonymity and sheer numbers of the crowd, whose movement was not directed by the discipline of work (and was therefore unpredictable), required more vigilance and violence to maintain order. Although arrests and beatings were always a possibility, so was escape. Thus, for black workers, public spaces both embodied the most repressive, violent aspects of race and gender oppression and, ironically, afforded more opportunities than the workplace itself to engage in acts of resistance.

Chapter 4

Birmingham's Untouchables

The Black Poor in the Age of Civil Rights

So long as we confine our conception of *the political* to activity that is openly declared we are driven to conclude that subordinate groups essentially lack a political life or that what political life they do have is restricted to those exceptional moments of popular explosion. To do so is to miss the immense political terrain that lies between quiescence and revolt and that, for better or worse, is the political environment of subject classes. It is to focus on the visible coastline of politics and miss the continent that lies beyond.

—JAMES SCOTT, *Domination and the Arts of Resistance*[1]

The underclass itself is, as always, relatively quiescent politically.

—NICHOLAS LEMANN, *The Promised Land*[2]

One way to think about the emergence of the modern civil rights movement is as a public declaration of the hidden transcript; a direct challenge to Jim Crowism by people who had heretofore resisted quietly. Of course, such a characterization is not entirely accurate. At the same time ordinary black working people were finding creative ways to resist and survive in the South, organized movements—from the Populists and organized labor to the NAACP and the Communist Party—were also fighting the status quo. And, as we have seen, spontaneous, unorganized conflicts became more pervasive and intense as time went on, especially during the Second World War. Yet, the movements of the 1950s and 1960s were fundamentally different, since they mobilized many more people and ultimately toppled Jim Crow.

While it is tempting to argue that the hidden transcripts of the Jim Crow era emerged into the overt politics of the civil rights movement, the story is far more complicated. As the example of Birmingham continues to show, established black leaders did not always address the issues most directly affecting working people, especially the most impoverished section of the working class. Many working poor and jobless residents waged battles that remained hidden or appeared as spontaneous rebellions. Thus poor people not only challenged the civil rights leaders, but their daily acts of resistance and survival substantially shaped the movement, efforts to police the movement, and subsequent race relations in the city of Birmingham.

As World War II came to a close, African Americans in Birmingham and other Southern cities found that the war at home was far from over. The streetcars and busses might have been a little quieter, but that had to do with more vigilant policing on public transportation. After the wartime crackdown on black resistance, a substantial segment of the black poor, youth in particular, grew increasingly militant as well as optimistic that an Allied victory overseas would make Birmingham a little less racist and more democratic. Yet, history soon proved that the poor did not have a whole lot to be optimistic about. Not only did police-civilian conflict and incidents of police brutality increase in black communities, but the material conditions of the working class went from bad to worse. In Birmingham, signs of postindustrial decline began to appear as early as the 1950s, and in the racial and class hierarchy that characterized the urban South, these signs spelled disaster for African American working people.

That the modern civil rights movement was born at the very moment when segments of Birmingham's black industrial working class faced displacement, expanding poverty, and increased dependency on public assistance is a critical fact that few scholars have paid attention to. Very few official civil rights leaders recognized or responded to deindustrialization in the 1950s and early 1960s, nor were they necessarily knowledgeable about or sensitive to the specific problems, needs, and desires of the poor. And, with few exceptions, mainstream civil rights spokespersons did not encourage poor blacks to participate in decision-making or leadership capacities within their organizations.

Examining interactions between the civil rights movement and Birmingham's black poor provides an excellent case study for exploring how everyday forms of resistance shape, and come in conflict with, formal political movements. The poor, I argue, developed their own strategies of survival and resistance which, in some cases, placed as much emphasis on issues of personal dignity and/or state-sanctioned violence as on material needs. Indeed, political protest and survival strategies, ranging from the reappropriation of property to the violent uprisings in 1963, often came in conflict with the political agenda of the civil rights movement. And yet the very presence of mass demonstrations, increased police repression, and organizational militancy served to partly "unveil" the hidden transcript. Resistance strategies were less evasive and more confrontational, especially after 1963.

Civil Rights in the Age of Deindustrialization

Much like Detroit and other rustbelt cities, Birmingham experienced industrial decline and an expansion of black poverty and unemployment after the war. During the 1950s, seven out of every ten black miners in Birmingham lost their jobs, in part because Birmingham steel companies began importing higher grade ore from South America and the coal industry introduced a machine called the "continuous miner" which replaced scores of black underground workers. Furthermore, the transition to "strip mining" led to greater mechanization overall, thus reducing the need for unskilled (i.e., black) labor. However, there are significant differences between Detroit and Birmingham that underscore the specificity of race and region in the urban South. First, whereas the auto industry in Detroit experienced growth in the 1950s and 1960s, Birmingham's steel industry did not significantly increase production and its mining industry actually declined once the Tennessee Coal, Iron, and Railroad Company (TCI), the largest corporate entity in the Birmingham region, began importing iron ore. The corporate leaders of TCI, which remained linked to its parent company, U.S. Steel, contributed to Birmingham's no-growth economy by blocking nearly all efforts to diversify. In 1945, for example, TCI executives successfully opposed efforts by Ford and General Motors to open plants in Birmingham.[3]

Second, whereas trade union activity in Detroit was of little consequence in altering racist practices in hiring and promotion, the United Auto Workers there at least made some motions on behalf of black workers, especially during the late 1960s. In Birmingham, however, the white-dominated locals of the United Steel Workers of America (USWA) put pressure on companies *not* to promote blacks to skilled positions. The union, therefore, became a tool to maintain white supremacy, which had the effect of undermining any vestiges of hope for job security for black steel workers. The only major industrial union which consistently fought against discrimination—the International Union of Mine, Mill, and Smelter Workers of America—not only operated in Birmingham's fastest declining industry but had been weakened considerably by racist and anti-Communist attacks from the state CIO council and USWA locals.[4] Thus industrial opportunities for black workers began to diminish much earlier and more rapidly in Birmingham than in other cities: the percentage of blacks employed in heavy industry declined from 54 percent in 1930, to 41 percent in 1950, to 33 percent in 1960.[5]

Third, unlike most Northern and Midwestern cities where industries expanded and moved out of the central city to the suburbs, most of Birmingham's heavy industry, as well as a large number of black working-class residences, was already located in suburban areas. Some workers who lost their jobs were forced out of company housing, and many returning black veterans unable to secure work in the mines and mills had to turn to public housing concentrated in the inner city or multifamily housing located near the already overcrowded black business district. Black communities in the industrial suburbs had already become crowded, and racist zoning practices made expansion impossible. Moreover, at least 88 percent of the city's black dwellings were deemed substandard by the Birmingham Housing Authority, and the Jefferson County Board of Health found a direct correlation between poverty, housing conditions, and the high rates of infant mortality and tuberculosis in black communities.

Although the city instituted a massive slum clearance program which left thousands of African Americans homeless, its public housing projects fell far short of fulfilling the housing needs of poor blacks. By 1959, Birmingham's seven housing projects, consisting of 4,862 units, designated only 1,492 for black residents.[6] The city also severely restricted potential housing sites by limiting the number of areas zoned for black residence. In 1948 Birmingham had only one residential area in the city zoned for blacks; most black dwellings were located in areas zoned for industrial or commercial use. Homeowners in areas zoned industrial/commercial were not eligible for Federal Housing Administration (FHA) loans. In the eyes of most African Americans, the poor as well as the middle and working class, racist whites conspired to limit black housing opportunities. Federally supported and private lending institutions regularly turned down black home loan applicants; Birmingham Water Works refused to extend piping to potential black subdivisions; and several blacks who purchased homes in or near white neighborhoods during the late 1940s were victims of bombings.[7]

Thus, during the 1950s Birmingham's displaced jobless or underemployed black workers were forced to reside in the housing projects, two-family shotgun houses, and dilapidated apartments, most of which were concentrated within a two-mile radius extending out from the center of the city. By 1960 the census tracts located in this area had both the highest percentage of African Americans as well as the highest percentage of families below the poverty line. What occurred in Birmingham, therefore, was not a case of corporations fleeing the central city for the suburbs, leaving the unemployed behind. Rather, Birmingham's coal and steel industry discarded a large segment of its black labor force, while racist zoning laws, an uneven and overcrowded housing market, and public housing policies propelled some ex-industrial workers and other poor people deeper into the inner city and left pockets of unemployed black workers in the industrial suburbs.

If significant northern migration of Alabama blacks had not taken place after World War II, the material conditions of the poor might have been a lot worse. Although the mechanization of agriculture in the countryside drove thousands of rural African Americans into the city during and after the war, Birmingham did not receive the mass influx of black migrants that most Northern industrial cities had to absorb. Instead, Birmingham experienced a net loss of over 21,000 black and white residents between 1950 and 1960. When we compare changes in black population in Birmingham with other urban centers, especially after World War II, we find that the percentage of

African Americans in Birmingham remained virtually the same throughout the twentieth century, hovering between 39 percent and 43 percent. But during the Jim Crow era, at least, while white income rose, conditions for poor black families had hardly changed because of the combination of racist hiring practices and Birmingham's slow growth industrial economy. By 1955, 42.1 percent of black families earned less than $2,000 compared to 8.4 percent of white families. Public assistance remained woefully inadequate; the city could barely afford to maintain its welfare program, which mainly consisted of distributing surplus food. Altogether, some 35,000 residents took advantage of the program, many of whom stood in lines that stretched at least four blocks.[8]

When war contracts reinvigorated Birmingham's economy, it seemed as though both mainstream black political leaders and white liberals were taking a greater interest in the plight of the black poor. As early as 1943, traditional black leaders and a handful of white liberals attempted to establish a chapter of the National Urban League in Birmingham, but the project was eventually aborted in the face of virulent white opposition. The idea of an interracial organization with national, specifically Northern, links was not very popular among Southern white liberal or conservative politicians. Despite the fact that the short-lived chapter counted a few major Birmingham corporate executives among its executive board, it did not have sufficient support and was abandoned in 1950.[9]

After the war, the Jefferson County Coordinating Council on Social Forces, founded in 1939, took on most of the responsibility for assisting the city's poor. In 1951, an interracial organization was created within the Council consisting primarily of business people, social workers, liberal politicians, educators, and ministers. The Interracial Committee (IC) was created to administer to the needs of black residents, serving as an acceptable substitute for the Urban League.[10]

Not surprisingly, committee members never talked directly to, or requested input from, the poor. Indeed, its policies ostensibly on behalf of the poor reflect the class interests and ideologies of its black leadership. In the area of recreation, for instance, black IC leadership placed at the top of its agenda the construction of a nine-hole Negro golf course. Also placed under the rubric of recreation was the "distressing number of young unmarried parents." Mrs. H. C. Bryant, longtime black club woman and YWCA leader, believed that the growing number of unwed mothers in poor black communities stemmed from a lack of guidance and recreational facilities for young black women. Perhaps most revealing was the black IC leaders' emphasis on the "development of a real estate subdivision for high class Negro homes" rather than low-income rental units.[11]

Although poor working women were in dire need of daycare facilities, the IC never made it a top priority issue. There had not been any public service daycare facilities since the war, and the three daycare centers run by the Community Chest were exclusively for mothers too sick to care for their children. Moreover, the primary daycare center for black children in Birmingham was composed mainly of children whose parents were "not disadvantaged." When the Committee, with the support of the Community Chest, finally succeeded in establishing an extra daycare facility, the cost to parents was set at $6.50 per week, a relatively high figure in relation to the earnings of single working mothers, or even two-parent working-class families who had to survive on as little as $20 to $30 per week.[12]

Likewise, IC's subcommittee on employment was not always cognizant of the specific needs of the black poor, as well as of the disastrous effects that technological change and racist hiring practices were having on black industrial labor. First, committee members did not attempt to use their influence to improve wages and working conditions for existing black industrial workers, in part because its members clearly sided with employers. Second, the committee put more emphasis on hiring college-educated blacks in civil service and public relations positions.[13]

By the time the Interracial Committee was disbanded in 1956, it had accomplished very little for the poor. Yet racist white residents and politicians viewed the committee as a radical threat to the status quo. White members of the committee decided to disband because "of the violent attacks upon it by proponents of the White Citizens Councils." The decision was made unilaterally, without input from black members. Moreover, the Jefferson County Coordinating Council on Social Forces decided that, while continuing to work toward improving social services for black residents, it "would not engage, directly or indirectly, in any activity toward desegregation."[14]

Birmingham civil rights organizations that were devoted to desegregation, however, were only slightly more sensitive to the needs and problems of the black poor in the 1950s and early 1960s, in part because most leading civil rights activists were middle-class African Americans who tended to misunderstand or overlook the plight of the poor. The Alabama Christian Movement for Human Rights (ACMHR), under the leadership of the Reverend Fred Shuttlesworth, had the largest working poor membership of any of the city's civil rights organizations. Yet, in 1959 only one-third of its membership earned less than $2,000, 55 percent of its members were homeowners, and 40 percent earned more than $4,000 annually (in the city as a whole, only 20 percent of black residents earned that much or more). What is most significant is that practically all of its members were employed.[15]

Although Shuttlesworth was far more sympathetic to working people than Birmingham's traditional black bourgeoisie had been, the strategies and long-term goals of the ACMHR were not directed at the material impoverishment of the poor or the horrible conditions in the black slums. Of course, issues such as school and bus desegregation and the hiring of black police officers affected, and even drew support from, the black poor, but ACMHR leadership defined racial equality in employment in terms of civil service and professional jobs for qualified blacks and viewed conditions in the slums as essentially a moral dilemma rather than a product of unequal opportunity. Meanwhile, according to a report produced by the Jefferson County Coordinating Council, in 1960 at least 70,000 people of Jefferson County were malnourished, most of whom were black Birmingham residents. In this same year, when the city experienced a recession in steel and related industries, the median income for black wage earners was a paltry $1,287 compared to $3,456 for whites; of black adults, 28.6 percent earned less than $1,000 annually.[16]

In addition to poverty, police repression became a major issue for African Americans during and after the war, particularly for slum residents. Beginning in 1941, a wave of police homicides and beatings re-ignited resistance to police brutality. Nearly all of these incidents were sparked by an act of insubordination—in most cases, a young black man arguing with a white person. The best-known incidents resulted in the deaths of O'Dee Henderson and John Jackson, both of whom were killed by police in Fairfield—an industrial suburb of

Birmingham. Henderson, who was arrested and jailed for merely arguing with a white man, was found the next morning in his jail cell handcuffed and fatally shot. A few weeks later, John Jackson, a black metal worker in his early twenties, was shot to death as he lay in the backseat of a police car. Jackson made the fatal mistake of arguing with the arresting officers in front of a crowd of blacks lined up outside a movie theater.[17]

These and other incidents attracted the attention of civil rights organizations because they were dramatic, clear-cut cases of injustice resulting in injury or death. By contrast, poor people's attitudes toward the police were informed by an accumulation of daily indignities, whether or not they were experienced or witnessed. What must be understood is the semipublic discourse between the police and the black poor that rarely appears in the evidence historians must rely on. The case of Bessie Ammons, a fifty-year-old janitor employed by Smithfield Court Housing Project, is instructive in this respect. On January 20, 1951, at about 5:45 AM, Mrs. Ammons was on her way to work when two police officers pulled up and one asked "Gal, where are you going? Come here!" She not only refused to walk over to the car, but would not get in the car when ordered to do so, despite the fact that one of the officers had drawn his gun. Taken aback by her open defiance of the law, the two officers continued to harass her. "I ought to put your black a—— in jail for vagrancy," one of the officers declared. "Whenever any policeman tells you to get in the car, you had better do it. I mean what I say. I'm the law. Get on down the street." These incidents took place in public spaces on a daily basis, witnessed by many, although there is very little public record of such exchanges.[18]

Of course, not all African Americans arrested or harassed by police were consciously engaged in acts of public insubordination. The fact remains that more African Americans, especially poor black male youth, were arrested and prosecuted than any other group in relation to the proportion of the total population. Many criminological studies suggest that the high arrest rate of marginalized black male youth can be attributed to at least three factors. First, of course, poverty and relative deprivation, exacerbated by a lack of employment opportunities due to race, leads to greater incidents of criminality. Because African Americans made up the majority of Birmingham's poor, it is not surprising that blacks would commit a higher percentage of crimes than whites. A report submitted by a Birmingham police official in charge of the vice squad concluded that most juvenile arrestees came from families dependent on welfare or some form of charity, or whose parents earned extremely low wages.[19] Second, gender differences help explain the higher incidence of male criminality, a pattern that is consistent across regional and national boundaries. Although the matter is far too complicated to discuss in detail here, several scholars attribute these patterns to higher rates of male unemployment, greater freedom from the restraints of the household compared to females (i.e., more opportunities to engage in criminal activity), and a patriarchal culture that socializes men to be more aggressive and makes earning power a measure of manhood.[20]

The third reason for the higher black arrest rates—the fact that the criminal justice system tends to cast all marginalized black male youth as criminals—ironically mitigates the importance of the first two factors. In addition to reflecting the relative poverty of African Americans, the disproportionate rate of black arrests is also indicative of the racist assumptions and practices of police officers, judges, and juries that African Americans are criminal by nature.[21] During the war, for example, although the number of black juvenile delinquency cases in Birmingham actually decreased, crime among black youth was viewed by government officials, social workers, police officers, and mainstream black leaders as a growing and alarming problem. In 1943, a Committee for the Prevention of Delinquency was created, and the Jefferson County Youth Protective Association decided to invite black leaders to a special "Negro meeting." Out of this meeting emerged a Birmingham Negro Youth Council in 1945 whose stated agenda was to offer religious guidance, provide recreational and educational opportunities, and improve employment and health conditions for poor black youth. City Commissioner Cooper Green even invited FBI director J. Edgar Hoover to Birmingham to speak on the subject. "In this large industrial area," Green reported to Hoover, "of which 38 percent of the residents are Negro, we have an immediate and growing problem."[22]

Many middle-class blacks unwittingly reinforced stereotypes by accepting the image of poor blacks, especially young people, as lazy, self-destructive, and prone to criminal behavior. Geraldine Moore, a black middle-class resident of Birmingham and author of *Behind the Ebony Mask*, wrote the following description of the Magic City's "truly disadvantaged":

> For some Negroes in Birmingham, life is a care-free existence of wallowing in the filth and squalor typical of the slums with just enough money to eke out a living. Some of these know nothing but waiting for a handout of some kind, drinking, cursing, fighting and prostitution. But many who live in this manner seem to be happy and satisfied. They apparently know and desire nothing better.[23]

The demand for black police officers in Birmingham made by a score of mainstream black political organizations during the 1940s and 1950s was motivated as much by their desire to reduce black crime as by their interest in ending police brutality. Birmingham *World* editor Emory O. Jackson waged a campaign during and after the war to clean up black crime. In 1946 he called on Birmingham police to step up their work in the predominantly black 4th Avenue district and get rid of the "profaners, number racketeers, bootleggers, and foulmouthers" once and for all.[24] In Jackson's view, he was merely fighting a situation he found embarrassing for fellow African Americans. Although most residents probably shared Jackson's concern for cleaning up the district, it is doubtful that all shared his sentiments. Aside from the fact that some local residents depended on illicit activities as a source of income, many of Birmingham's poor understood that a greater concentration of police in the area without reforms in law enforcement practices opened the doors for greater police repression.

1963 and Beyond: A Turning Point

The contradictions between the goals of the civil rights movement to desegregate public space and the daily struggles of the black poor—most notably declining employment opportunities, inadequate housing, and police repression—came to a head during the Southern Christian Leadership Conference's (SCLC's) nonviolent mass demonstrations in May of 1963. One need only examine film footage of the Birmingham confrontation to know that the hundreds of schoolchildren who crowded into Sixteenth Street Baptist Church, recruits of the direct-action campaign who marched peacefully into the hands of Eu-

gene "Bull" Connor's waiting police officers, were *not* products of
Birmingham's worst slums. Rather, the vast majority of neat, well-
dressed, and orderly children were the sons and daughters of activists
or movement supporters. The slum dwellers, teenagers and young
adults alike, did show up at Ingram Park to participate *on their own
terms* in the May demonstrations. Historians and activists have labeled them "onlookers," "spectators," or "bystanders" merely because they were not directed by any civil rights organization. But
when Bull Connor ordered the use of police dogs and clubs on the
demonstrators, the crowd of so-called "onlookers" taunted police, retaliated with fists, profanity, rocks, and bottles, and if possible escaped into their own neighborhoods. On the very next day, a group
of "spectators were seen brandishing knives and pistols along the
fringes of the demonstrations." Shocked by the show of armed force,
SCLC leadership decided to call off the demonstration that day.
While these "fringe dwellers" had no intention of filling the jails, they
were clearly demonstrating their utter contempt for the police, in particular, and racist oppression, in general.[25]

A more dramatic example of collective opposition on the part of
the poor occurred late Saturday night, May 11, after the home of the
Reverend A. D. King and A. G. Gaston's motel were bombed by
racists. An angry crowd gathered in front of the Gaston Motel and began throwing bottles and bricks at police officers on the scene. The
fighting escalated into a full-scale riot, as hundreds of black residents
destroyed glass storefront windows, overturned cars, set buildings on
fire, and seized all the commodities they could get their hands on. Police officers themselves were prime targets. One patrolman chased a
group of rioters down a dark alley and emerged with three stab
wounds in his back. A police inspector was found soaked in blood,
having been "brained by a rock." Armed with megaphones, SCLC
leaders A. D. King and Wyatt T. Walker implored the rioters to stop
the violence and go home, but their efforts were to no avail. Walker
himself was struck in the leg by a brick tossed by a rioter. The uprising finally came to an end after state troopers intervened with unbridled violence.[26]

Civil rights leaders treated the uprising as an impediment to the
progress of the "real" movement and variously described the rioters
as "wineheads" or "riffraff." While the epithets were uncalled for, this

was not an unreasonable posture for mainstream black leaders to assume. On the eve of the uprising, white liberals, the Chamber of Commerce, along with the silent support of moderate black political figures, barely won a battle to scrap Birmingham's city commission system for a mayor-city council structure. Whereas the old system concentrated municipal power in the hands of three men and enabled segregationists like Bull Connor to entrench themselves in office, the new system would expand representation to districts and, presumably, entice the outlying suburbs to join the Birmingham municipality. Most important, however, was the presumption that the more democratic mayor-council structure could incorporate the demands of moderate blacks and facilitate the transition to a more equitable system of segregation without disrupting business. By the time the crisis occurred, white liberal David Vann, who had been elected mayor just days before the Birmingham confrontation, was locked in battle against segregationists for control over city government, as the old city commission under Bull Connor initially refused to disband. Black leaders who supported SCLC's civil disobedience campaign feared that the rioters would jeopardize both the movement's gains as well as the new administration's stability.

But the rioters felt their own lives had been in jeopardy far too long. Despite the protestations of black leaders, the people of Birmingham's slums and segregated pool halls resisted injustice and oppression on their own terms, which included attacking police officers and taking advantage of the crisis to appropriate much needed or desired commodities. The irony is that the very movement which sought to control or channel the aggressive, violent behavior of the poor was the catalyst for their participation.[27]

In spite of the movement's failure to deal with the specific problems of the poor, the 1963 peaceful demonstration was a powerful declaration of aspects of the usually veiled dissident political culture.[28] However, from the perspective of the poor, the accumulation of indignities and level of anger were so great that they precluded, for younger people in particular, the possibility of nonviolent resistance. Their unmitigated rage directed at the police reflected years of brutalities, illegal searches and seizures, and incidents of everyday harassment. As James Scott surmises about subordinate groups in general, "if the politics they engender is tumultuous, frenetic, delirious, and occasionally violent, that is perhaps because the powerless are so rarely on the public stage and have so much to say and do when they finally arrive." The black poor, I would argue, had more to be angry about and much more to say about their plight; grievances over which even their "leaders" were unaware. So when the opportunity came in the series of crises of 1963, they seized it.[29]

The change in the public posturings of black poor youth and young adults caught much of white Birmingham off-guard. Throughout the mid-1960s, complaints by white residents of the growing impudence and discourteousness of Birmingham blacks flooded the police department and Mayor's office. In 1964, a white woman whose residence bordered a black community observed to her utter horror "Negro boys . . . step out in front of the car driven by a white woman—wanting to ride. Hitch-hiking." In her view, the attitudes and actions of black passengers after desegregation rendered public transportation unbearable: "Can't get on the bus and ride to town because the colored have taken the buses."[30] But the same circumstances that unleashed such fervent opposition to the powerful and emboldened the powerless to assert a public oppositional presence also unleashed a more sustained effort on the part of the state to put things back in order. The public posturings on the part of African Americans actually led to an increase in confrontations with the police, whose reputation for racial tolerance left much to be desired. Police repression reached an all-time high between 1963 and the early 1970s, and, of course, black male youth from poor communities accounted for the majority of incidents.

During the tumultuous year of 1963, a large proportion of confrontations between black youth and police were more explicitly political than the run-of-the mill criminal cases.[31] For example, although the number of black juvenile delinquency cases increased 40 percent between 1962 and 1963, 550 of those cases, or 23.4 percent of all cases brought to juvenile court in 1963 (irrespective of race or sex), were placed under a new category called "Demonstrating." Property offenses, which usually account for the majority of juvenile cases, comprised only 34.1 percent of the total cases. Altogether, although African Americans comprised about 39 percent of Birmingham's total population, in 1963 black males made up 1,012, and black females 626, of the total cases, whereas white males and females constituted

556 and 255 of the total cases, respectively.[32] Moreover, police frequently used excessive force in politically volatile situations. On September 15, 1963, hours after the bombing of Sixteenth Street Baptist Church killed four black girls, sixteen-year-old Johnny Robinson was fatally wounded by police after he and an unidentified black youth were seen throwing rocks at a passing car full of white teenagers. "Negroes Go Back to Africa" was scrawled on one side of the car in shoe polish, and a Confederate flag draped the other side. The white youth, who were apparently celebrating the murder of the four black children, yelled racial epithets at the two black teenagers. As soon as police in the vicinity observed Robinson and his companion throwing rocks at the passing car, they gave chase. According to the police version, they told Robinson several times to halt, but he kept running away. When the smoke cleared from a volley of police gunfire, Robinson lay dead.[33]

Two years after the mass demonstrations of 1963, arrests of black youths were still disproportionately higher than arrests of white youths, though the absolute numbers were now much closer; and blacks fared worse at the hands of police. By 1966 the number of white juveniles convicted of crimes nearly equaled that of blacks; white males and white females accounted for 662 and 282 of total cases, respectively, whereas black males and females accounted for 712 and 263 cases, respectively. In the fourteen months between January 1966 and March 1967, ten black men, the majority teenagers or young adults, were killed by Birmingham police. During this same period there were no white victims or black female victims of police killings.[34]

Besides black youth, other segments of the poor fell victim to police brutality. An arrest or beating prompted by a mistaken identity or a particularly racist patrolman could prove to be a substantial setback for poor working residents whose families depended on meager wages to stay afloat. A case in point is the arrest of North Birmingham resident Catherine McGann, a single mother of seven children who worked for a living as a domestic. On the night of September 4, 1964, she and two black men whom she did not know were standing in front of a store in her neighborhood when several police officers drove up and forcibly shoved the two men into a police car. When she tried to walk away, two of the officers "rushed up and grabbed me and were hollering, 'Get in this car nigger.'" She struggled desperately to break free, but they hit her several times, dragged her into the vehicle, and slammed the door on her ankle. McGann was subsequently taken to jail and refused medical attention, though she was not charged with anything until her son appeared to post bail. The court found her guilty of resisting arrest and loitering after a warning, for which she was fined $125. The beating and arrest turned out to be much more than "a very terrible and humiliating experience." It nearly devastated Catherine McGann financially. "All my children are in school and I do not have the money to get books for them or to pay their fees. I don't earn much and then to have what little I earn to be taken away from me for no reason at all is very hard."[35]

By 1967, local civil rights organizations, spearheaded by the ACMHR, placed the rising tide of police brutality at the top of their agenda. This marked a significant change since the late 1940s and early 1950s, when black middle-class spokespersons were more concerned about reducing black crime than police use of excessive force. Although the movement's tactics had not changed (the ACMHR organized a sixty-day boycott of downtown stores to protest recent police killings), its rhetoric revealed a heightened level of militancy. Shuttlesworth not only threatened to build alliances with black militant organizations, but his group distributed a flyer proclaiming in no uncertain terms that "Negroes are TIRED of Police Brutality and Killing Our People. Negroes are tired of 'One Man Ruling' of 'Justifiable Homicide' every time a NEGRO IS KILLED!" More significantly, the ACMHR was less willing to negotiate; instead, Shuttlesworth attempted to file suit against the city in order to obtain police department and coroners' records so they might investigate past cases of police homicides.[36]

The ACMHR's efforts failed to bring about any major improvements in police practices. Both Mayor Boutwell and his successor, Mayor George Seibels, refused to form civilian review boards. Indeed, no significant progress was made on the issue of police brutality until the fatal shooting of Bonita Carter by Birmingham police in 1979. During the early 1970s, a number of poor and working-class African Americans joined grass-roots organizations that investigated and fought police misconduct, such as the Committee Against Police Brutality and the Alabama Economic Action Committee (which investigated at least twenty-seven separate incidents in 1972), but these movements received very little support from the black elite. The utter refusal of "old guard" leadership to deal with the problem of police brutality led Richard Arrington, Jr., Birmingham's first black mayor, to the following conclusion:

> The failure of the so-called black leaders in this community to speak out about police brutality simply confirms my belief that there is really no such thing as black leaders in this community—they are people who are used by the white power structure in this community who take an ego trip because they are called upon by some powerful white citizens to fit black folk into an agenda that has been set up by the white community, particularly the business structure here.[37]

Meanwhile, long-term structural changes were forcing more and more African Americans into an increasingly marginalized existence. Deindustrialization, which began, as we noted, in the 1950s, picked up steam, dealing a devastating blow to young black workers entering the workforce and to existing black industrial laborers. Although antidiscrimination laws and successful litigation on the part of the NAACP removed racially based ceilings to occupational mobility, by the late 1960s and throughout the 1970s it no longer mattered. TCI, for example, laid off thousands of workers in the 1970s and by 1982 ceased operating altogether. The Sloss-Sheffield furnace shut down in 1971, and Pullman-Standard closed shop in the early 1980s. The shift from industrial to service-sector jobs, combined with discrimination, meant that the ratio of black male income to white male income actually decreased slightly after World War II. In 1949, black men in Birmingham earned an average of 53 percent of what white men earned; the ratio dropped to 48.8 percent in 1959, recovering only to 51.5 percent in 1969.[38]

Demographic shifts continued and accelerated as well, contributing to the concentration of poverty in core city and North Birmingham census tracts. While Northern cities generally grew in the sixties, Birmingham's population declined by 11.7 percent between 1960 and 1970. During this decade, urban renewal—particularly slum clearance programs and the expansion of the University of Alabama Medical Center—played a more significant role in this shift and its accompanying concentration of poverty. The Medical Center, which is located in the heart of the inner city, displaced 1,000 black families. As a result, the percentage of African Americans in census tract 44 decreased from 76 percent in 1950, to 48 percent in 1960, to 28 percent in 1970, whereas tract 15 increased its percentage of black residents from 17 percent in 1950, to 30 percent in 1960, to 94 percent in 1970. Tract 44's substantial decrease in black residents is especially significant since it had the fifth-largest percentage of poor families in 1960 out of ninety-two tracts, suggesting that the poor were disproportionately affected by urban renewal programs.[39] Moreover, although it was one of the nine inner-city tracts, the percentage of African Americans and families below the poverty line still increased significantly between 1960 and 1970, which suggests that the remaining eight tracts underwent an even greater concentration of poor black families.[40] Even more dramatic shifts in the racial composition of Birmingham's inner city occurred in the mid- to late 1970s, as a result of white flight to the suburbs. This, plus the city's successful annexation of low- and middle-income black communities on the fringe of the city limits, meant that African Americans became the majority in Birmingham in 1980.[41]

It was in the midst of massive deindustrialization and demographic shifts that President Lyndon Johnson's Great Society was established in Birmingham. From the outset, Mayor Albert Boutwell welcomed the adoption of the Economic Opportunity Act (EOA), which he regarded as a much-needed infusion of federal aid into Birmingham's economy. Following a somewhat rocky start,[42] the Jefferson County Committee for Economic Opportunity (JCCEO) was established in June of 1965 to administer a total of twenty-four different service programs in the ten years after its founding. Broadly speaking, the black poor, who constituted about 95 percent of the participants in JCCEO agencies, took advantage of these programs; through employment opportunities in human services, through job training programs, through early childhood education, through free legal services, and through emergency food and medical aid. The Committee also hired some middle-class and working-class African Americans to work in administrative posts in social welfare agencies.

But overall, neither the city nor the state contributed the necessary financial support to render JCCEO agencies effective tools to fight poverty. Largely because the state legislature refused to appropriate sufficient funds to match available federal funds, all recipients of benefits received payments below the poverty level throughout the 1960s, and Aid to Dependent Children, whose caseload in 1965 consisted of 80 percent black children, allocated only 35 percent of the minimum survival budget to each family. Furthermore, by 1970 the state still had no basic assistance program and the food stamp program reached only 10 percent of eligible families because of an especially complicated application process and a lack of information available to the poor. Thus, in the period between 1957 and 1967, the city actually *decreased* its total expenditures on welfare from $31,000 to a paltry $12,000. By 1970 over one-third of all black families in Birmingham fell under the poverty line (compared to 14.7 percent of white families).[43]

While the War on Poverty might have failed to reverse the deteriorating conditions for the black poor, it ultimately played an important role in mobilizing an already politicized segment of them, as well as in strengthening ties between white liberals and mainstream black leadership, and in providing poor residents a greater voice in the affairs of certain social agencies—especially Head Start. As a result of pressure from both the federal government and the black poor themselves, the JCCEO evolved after two years from a twenty-one member board of directors, consisting entirely of mayoral appointments, to a forty-eight member board composed of sixteen public officials or representatives of public agencies, sixteen representatives from private community groups, and sixteen representatives from poor "target" communities, each elected by their respective neighborhood advisory councils. The new structure, established in 1967, not only allowed the black poor direct representation for the first time in the history of Birmingham's welfare agencies, it also substantially reduced the power of the mayor within the Committee. In the end, however, the neighborhood councils exercised very little power to shape the long-term agenda of the JCCEO. The committee not only allocated insufficient funds for projects initiated by the neighborhood councils, but the bureaucratic independence of various agencies made long-term planning virtually impossible. Moreover, the employment of African Americans in responsible positions within JCCEO agencies initially prompted a backlash from white social workers who argued that these newly appointed men and women "lacked qualifications."[44]

Even if the neighborhood councils turned out to be relatively ineffective in terms of determining the long-range agenda of the JCCEO, they managed to provide a new forum for a new generation of "race rebels." Their constituents exhibited a militant sense of entitlement reminiscent of the Communist-led movements of the 1930s, the public transportation battles of the 1940s, and the uprisings surrounding the SCLC's direct-action campaigns. In nearly all of the conflicts between the black poor and JCCEO, protesters found themselves fighting black as well as white bureaucrats. One particularly memorable confrontation occurred in 1969 when a predominantly black women's organization, called the Poor People's Action Committee (PPAC), protested what it felt were discriminatory practices within the JCCEO's Concentrated Employment Program. The program, which coordinated the work of several public and private agencies into a comprehensive training program for the poor, had placed the majority of black women who had completed the program in a chicken packing plant rather than in human relations positions as promised. The PPAC also complained of being threatened and intimidated by two staff members—the director, who was white, and the black assistant director—for participating in the protest. Ironically, with the assistance of another agency under the JCCEO's jurisdiction, the Legal Services Program, the PPAC won their case, exposed the deficiencies in the Concentrated Employment Program, and ultimately forced the director to resign and the JCCEO to take disciplinary action against the assistant director. A second major struggle erupted in 1971, when the United Neighborhood Improvement Association (UNIA) picketed JCCEO headquarters to protest the dismissal of two black employees. Despite several stormy meetings, the JCCEO board of directors did not accede to the UNIA's demands, which included the removal of two black project directors and the white executive director. The UNIA came away from the battle quite bitter, accusing the JCCEO of not doing an effective job assisting the poor since "these hard-core people are not being reached."[45]

The rise of militant opposition to the JCCEO, combined with deteriorating conditions of the poor caused by deindustrialization, urban renewal, concentrated poverty, police repression, the limitations of the civil rights agenda, and a general mistrust of traditional black leadership, compelled some poor African Americans to turn to more radical alternatives. In 1970 several community-based interracial organizations were created specifically to concentrate on poor people's needs, including the Jefferson County Welfare Rights Organization—a local chapter of the National Welfare Rights Organization—the Southside Action Committee, the Alabama Economic Action Committee, the Committee for Equal Job Opportunity, and the Southern Organizing Committee for Economic Justice (formerly the Southern Conference Educational Fund).[46] The black poor also turned to black nationalist organizations influenced by Malcolm X, the Black Power philosophies of the late 1960s, and/or the Nation of Islam. These movements—much like the Communist Party three decades earlier—showed more sensitivity to the specific problems of poor residents and sought change through alternative means of opposition.

They were ultimately crushed by police repression, which served as a powerful deterrent to the participation of the vast majority of poor people. The most important example is the Alabama Black Liberation Front (ABLF), a short-lived organization that attracted considerable attention from both the black poor and city officials. Like the Black Panther Party, the ABLF went beyond demonstrating against police brutality to advocating armed self-defense groups. Its primary agenda, however, was to help the poor resist evictions, obtain relief, and establish collective self-help programs to provide food, clothes, and other necessities to community folks. Its long-term goal was to educate black residents and prepare the groundwork for revolution.[47]

Most of its leaders were poor young residents who had at one time or another been arrested or engaged in petty crimes. One of its founding members in 1970 was twenty-three-year-old Ronald Williams: "I guess I used to be what you'd call an illegitimate capitalist. I acted for myself alone—whatever I could take, I took it. I did time. I'm not ashamed of all that. I learned to survive the way people had to survive in this society. Until I got hip—and I learned how we have to organize and help each other and change the system." Another founding member, forty-three-year-old Wayland Bryant, was radicalized by his utter disappointment with the "so-called civil rights movements" in which he had participated for over twenty years. He came to realize that integration was not the panacea he believed it would be since it did not attack the fundamental problems of poor people under capitalism.

From the outset, the police and FBI made it virtually impossible for the ABLF to operate in Birmingham. Literally within weeks of their founding, its members were rounded up *en masse* and arrested in a preemptive strike by police to stop a "planned ABLF ambush." The incident centered around Bernice Turner, a fifty-five-year-old domestic who was being forced out of her home by land developers. Before the ABLF had an opportunity to investigate the case, Turner was served an eviction notice on September 14, 1970. Five Liberation Front activists, including Bryant, Williams, Harold Robertson, and another man and a woman—both unidentified—decided to stay with Mrs. Turner that night and leaflet the community the next morning. The next day, after Mrs. Turner had left for work, nearly two dozen police officers surrounded her home to arrest the ABLF activists. "A Malcolm X record was playing," recalled Wayland Bryant, "when I heard the door crash open—I never heard any knock." The officers tossed tear gas through the doors and windows, shot Ronald Williams, and beat the remaining members occupying the house. Five ABLF members were jailed and Bryant and Williams charged with assaulting a police officer with a deadly weapon and intent to murder. Over the next few weeks, practically the whole membership of the ABLF was arrested for distributing literature and other assorted charges, breaking the backbone of the organization before it had an opportunity to mobilize mass support.[48]

The rapidity with which the Birmingham police crushed the ABLF served as an important reminder that, no matter how many reforms the civil rights movement secured in terms of extending participatory democracy to African Americans, the poor still remained powerless to alter conditions and relationships that affected them the most. Although some segments of the black poor did not totally abandon organized politics, especially since newly formed community-based organizations were more concerned with issues of poverty, joblessness, survival, and police brutality than earlier civil rights organizations, they were reminded of the consequences of militant action. Some, like Mrs. Turner, viewed the collapse of the ABLF with anger and remorse. As she expressed soon after the arrests, "those men are in jail and it's just not right. . . . All they wanted to do was help."[49]

The failed efforts of the 1970s were not a complete loss. The political stirrings of poor and working-class residents prompted city government to form the Citizen Participation Program (CPP) in 1974, a well-structured "grassroots bureaucracy" of neighborhood associations with a limited voice in issues affecting their communities (e.g., city services, zoning, development). As Steven Haeberle's recent study of the CPP argues, residents from low-income black neighborhoods had the highest participation rate in the program throughout the 1970s and 1980s. When these government-sponsored institutions were not responsive enough, black poor and working-class residents often formed their own voluntary associations to tackle specific problems. More significantly, the dramatic shift in the city's racial makeup during the 1970s contributed to black political empowerment.

Richard Arrington's successful bid for mayor in 1979 heightened the entire black community's sense of power. Although class distinctions and tensions within the African American community by no means disappeared, the black poor generally believed that a black administration was a marked improvement over the past century of white, largely racist city governments. (In many cases they were right: incidents of police brutality, for example, decreased dramatically after Arrington implemented reforms in police operations.) Coming out of a decade in which Black Power slogans shaped much of African American political discourse, Birmingham's black poor showed greater interest in mainstream politics and were much more willing in the 1980s to support municipal government and to participate in political institutions intended to improve the quality of life, including those originating in city hall. Yet, despite their new sense of enfranchisement, their protests continued, suggesting a failure on the part of Arrington's administration to provide essential city services for the poorest neighborhoods. This dual sense of empowerment and dissatisfaction is revealed in Philip Coulter's recent study of residents who take advantage of the Mayor's Office of Citizens Assistance (MOCA), established soon after Arrington's election. Coulter demonstrated that in 1983 African Americans with incomes of less than $5,000 (along with the wealthiest whites) were most likely to file complaints with MOCA. Because the majority of complaints center on city services, the persistent protest of the poorest communities suggest that the administration has been unable to solve most of their problems. Not only do these studies challenge William Wilson's hypothesis that the "underclass" is socially isolated from and indifferent toward political institutions, but, as I have suggested throughout this chapter, their high participation rate also reflects a tradition of activism. The only difference is that they now have greater access to legitimate political avenues.[50]

The two decades after 1963 turned out to be a mixed bag of victories and defeats. During the 1960s, the black poor exhibited greater militancy and political participation, on the one hand, but faced an intensification of police repression, poverty, and joblessness, on the other. Although the civil rights movement succeeded in desegregating public space, winning the franchise, securing federal job antidiscrimination legislation, and eventually paving the way for black empowerment, neither the vote nor legislative initiatives were effective weapons against poverty, joblessness, and plant shutdowns. Today, as more Birmingham steel and iron mills are turned into museums and fewer high-wage industrial jobs are made available, increasing numbers of unskilled African Americans are forced to turn to public assistance, low-wage service sector positions, or in some cases crime.

Although the black poor continue to resist and survive the best way they know how, the complex set of issues they must face and the contradictory, hidden world of the poor make predicting what future struggles might look like a difficult task indeed. To understand the politics of poor and displaced working people, as I have argued throughout this chapter and the three preceding chapters, requires both a redefinition of politics and a long-term historical perspective.

But we cannot end there. We also have to look beyond the hidden transcripts, beyond the quotidian world of sabotage and rock throwing, to the organizations and cultural forms that gave voice to working-class African Americans who might not otherwise have found it in the black middle class's struggle for racial uplift and respectability. To do this we must begin where people are rather than where we expect them to be, which means broadening our scope to include black participation in the class-oriented, interracial movements of the American Left. In part II we shall go back to the 1930s, when another group of "race rebels" tried to develop a distinctive strand of class-conscious racial politics within the American Communist movement. Even when they failed, their struggles within the Party to define communism and internationalism on their own terms changed the movement, and themselves, in some surprising ways.

PART II

TO BE RED AND BLACK

Revolt! Arise!
   The Black
   And Red World
   Now Are One!
The past is done!
   The Red Flag
   Flies against the
   Sun!
—Langston Hughes, "A New Song"[1]

Chapter 5

"Afric's Sons With Banner Red"

African American Communists and the Politics of Culture, 1919–1934

Rise, Afric's sons with banner
   red.
Freedom's path we too must tread.
We've fought for it and bled.
   Black men, United!

Long we've borne the nation's
   shame.
Long we've bow'd both meek and
   tame.
'Tis right that now our anger
   flames.
In its might.

Face the lynchers, the Southern
   Cossacks.
Face the demons. Strike them
   back.
Face them dying but striking back.
   For our right.

—J. THOMPSON, "Exhortation"[1]

I first discovered Thompson's poem a few years ago buried in a barely readable microfilm edition of the *Liberator*, the official newspaper of the Communist-led League of Struggle for Negro Rights. Though the

103

poem had no direct bearing on my research (I was working on a dissertation about Communists in Alabama), I was fascinated by it because it struck me as so peculiar and out of place. Published in 1933, it appeared during a time when the CP was waging war against "petty bourgeois Negro nationalism" and "racial chauvinism." Yet, "Exhortation" is in many ways a black nationalist manifesto. Thompson does not paint the portrait one might expect of black and white workers together fighting the bosses; rather, he introduces us to a different sort of Manichean world in which white lynchers and black men are poised to battle one another. The implication that dignity is embodied in the masculine act of resistance places "Exhortation" in the tradition of Claude McKay's celebrated poem, "If We Must Die," which also inspired many of Thompson's contemporaries who published in the Garveyite *Negro World*. Like McKay, his appeal for the united resistance of black men centers not on the fruits of possible victory, but on the very act of fighting. Indeed, except for keywords like "banner red" and "Southern Cossacks," there is nothing in Thompson's "Exhortation" that would indicate he is a Communist writing for a Communist paper.

As I continued perusing Communist publications for obscure information about the South, these kinds of creative expressions of black nationalism became less anomalous and more pervasive, particularly in Communist publications geared toward the African American community. It seemed to fly in the face of everything I thought to be "proletarian internationalism," and the very presence of this work—irrespective of its aesthetic worth—seemed to undermine the common assertion that the Communists imposed integrationist values on black artists.[2] Of course, studies of the politics of culture during the Popular Front and the recent string of biographies of black radical artists—namely Langston Hughes, Claude McKay, Richard Wright, and Paul Robeson—have already challenged the notion that Party discipline transformed these artists into Moscow automatons.[3] But most of this work still assumes that the Communists had a clear-cut "line" on cultural production that was naturally in conflict with the work of black artists. What scholars have yet to explain is how, especially during the more radical "Third Period" (the period from 1928 to 1933 when the Communist Party of the United States [CPUSA] shifted from a more gradualist approach to a belief that revolution was just around the corner), Party theoreticians simultaneously thwarted "racial chauvinism" and "petit bourgeois nationalism" in all manifestations of political action, while race-conscious themes and nationalist sentiment appeared in so much black expressive and literary culture inside and on the margins of the Communist Party.

The following, then, is a preliminary effort to unravel this paradox by exploring the relationship between Communist debates about aesthetics and some of the cultural work produced by African American radicals from the mid-1920s to the mid-1930s. It is my contention that some of the answers could be found partly in the changing make-up of the Party during the Third Period which enabled African American working people—many of whom left Garveyite movements in various stages of decline—to insinuate themselves into the Party's culture. I also want to suggest that the Communists' position on the "Negro Question" (implicitly, at least) and its own interpretation of "proletarian realism" unintentionally created an opening for African Americans to articulate nationalist ideologies in spite of the Party's formal opposition to "Negro nationalism." In other words, by the late 1920s and early 1930s, black nationalism(s)—especially as expressed in culture—had much more in common with American communism than most scholars have admitted. Thus, like American Jewish and Finnish Communists, whose cultural and national identities constituted a central element of their radical politics, ethnic nationalism and internationalism were not mutually exclusive.

Black Radicalism Meets the Class Struggle

African Americans who joined the Party in the 1920s and 1930s were as much the creation of American communism as of black nationalism; as much the product of African American vernacular cultures and radical traditions as of Euro-American radical thought. Many were products of Garveyism and/or the emerging postwar black Left that had been deeply touched by the Bolshevik Revolution as well as by workers' uprisings and racial violence in American cities during and after World War I. While these events did not propel large numbers of African American radicals into the American Communist Party, it did reinforce their belief that socialist revolution was possible within the context of a complicated matrix of "race politics" and working-class unity. A. Philip Randolph and Chandler Owen attempted to build African American support for the Socialist Party of America (SPA) by emphasizing class as well as race-specific goals, but the Socialists' official position regarded racist oppression secondary to the class struggle and held steadfastly to the idea that socialism was the only way to solve the problems of blacks.[4]

Perhaps the most enigmatic group among the postwar black Left was the African Blood Brotherhood (ABB), a secret, underground organization of radical black nationalists led largely by West Indian immigrants. Founded in 1918 by Cyril Briggs, the ABB advocated armed defense against lynching, the right to vote in the South, the right to organize, equal rights for blacks, and the abolition of Jim Crow laws. According to Briggs, the ABB was the first organization to demand self-determination for black Americans in the Southern United States. Although it is doubtful that the ABB's leadership worked out a theory based on the idea of an oppressed nation, Briggs consistently demanded self-determination, in some form or another. As early as 1917, while editor of the *Amsterdam News*, Briggs advocated the creation of a "colored autonomous state." In the pages of the *Crusader*, he attacked Woodrow Wilson for not applying the concept of self-determination to Africa, and during the "Red Summer" of 1919 when race riots broke out in several major cities, Briggs demanded "government of the Negro, by the Negro and for the Negro." A unique experiment in black Marxist organization, the ABB was short-lived, killed off by its own internal logic; by the early 1920s its Marxist leadership decided that an interracial proletarian party would be a more effective form of organization and therefore opted to join the CPUSA.[5]

Like the Socialists before them, American Communists initially regarded black radicalism as a subset of the class struggle. The Party's 1921 program asserted that "the interests of the Negro worker are identical with those of the white." Two years later, Communist leadership recognized that black people in the United States constituted an "oppressed race," but considered black nationalism "a weapon of reaction for the defeat and further enslavement of both [blacks] and their white brother workers." However, pressure from the Communist International, primarily V. I. Lenin and Indian Communist M. N. Roy, and popular support for black nationalist movements within African

American working-class communities, compelled the CPUSA to seriously reconsider its approach to the "Negro Question."[6]

The Fourth World Congress of the Comintern in 1922 adopted a set of theses describing blacks as a nationality oppressed by worldwide imperialist exploitation.[7] Because black workers' struggles were now considered inherently anti-imperialist, American Communists were obliged to view Garveyism and other notable nationalist movements anew. During the 1924 UNIA Convention, the *Daily Worker* thoroughly covered the proceedings and praised the organization for its militancy. And at the Fourth National Conference of the Communist Party in 1925, it recognized that the Garvey movement was "an almost universal phenomenon among American Negro workers."[8]

While Party leadership praised the UNIA for its mass base and anticolonial position, it was critical of its strategy and rhetoric. The Party opposed the UNIA's mass-based nationalism and emphasis on race pride; its 1925 platform equated Garveyism with "reactionary" Jewish Zionism. On the other hand, the same platform expressed faith in the ability of Communists to work within the UNIA and transform it into "an organization fighting for the class interests of the Negro workers in the United States."[9] The CPUSA's new-found respect for Garvey's appeal came a bit too late, however, since the UNIA was already on the verge of collapse. The Party responded by forming the American Negro Labor Congress (ANLC) in 1925, an organization led chiefly by former ABB leaders whose primary purpose was to build interracial unity in the labor movement. Chapters were to be established throughout the United States, particularly in the South, but because of poor leadership and ill-conceived planning, the ANLC never gained popular support.[10] In the end, although the Communists utterly failed to redirect Garveyism, they did attract a handful of ex-Garveyites into their ranks.

The Communists' failure to mobilize significant black support in the early and mid-1920s can be partially attributed to the Comintern's vision of internationalism which extended beyond Pan-Africanism and/or racial solidarity. While Comintern officials recognized differences between anticolonial and European working-class movements, peasants and proletarians, they still insisted that these struggles be united under the same banner. Even their conferences emphasized an international unity that few Americans, black or white, could ever imagine. In 1927, for example, African American delegates were invited to attend a conference in Brussels held under the auspices of the League Against Colonial Oppression. Organized in 1926 by the German Communist Party (KPD) to combat pro-colonial sentiments emerging in Germany, the League was an important step toward coordinating various struggles for national liberation in the colonies and "semicolonies," and it served as an intermediary between the Communist International and the anticolonial movement. It was at this conference that former ABB leader Richard B. Moore witnessed Europeans, Asians, and Africans pass a general resolution that proclaimed: "Africa for the Africans, and their full freedom and equality with other races and the right to govern Africa." It was indeed a remarkable sight for anyone who believed the struggle for African freedom was *only* an African struggle.[11]

The Communist movement's internationalism not only appropriated the familiar idioms of Pan-Africanism, but in many respects it cleared the way for a vision of black anti-imperialism that could transcend without negating a completely racialized worldview. Moreover, internationalism became a vehicle for African American radicals to cross cultural boundaries, to escape and challenge essentialist presumptions common among some segments of the CP about what the "authentic" Negro proletariat looked and talked like. Lovett Fort-Whiteman, an early recruit who rose quickly within the Chicago CP's ranks, was emblematic of this sort of cultural internationalism. Soon after his return from the Soviet Union, the Texas-born Communist became a popular spectacle on the Southside of Chicago for strolling the streets draped in a Russian *rubaschka* (blouse). Yet this same internationalist vision sometimes hindered the Party's work in the African American community. For example, black delegates from the Workers (Communist) Party and the ABB attending the first All-Race Conference in 1924 were treated with suspicion when they attached to their proposal for armed self-defense and working-class organization a statement endorsing the "Internationale" as the "anthem of Negro Freedom." Similarly, at the ANLC's first mass meeting in Chicago, organized by Lovett Fort-Whiteman, hundreds of black workers in attendance became disenchanted with the Congress as soon as the entertainment appeared: a Russian ballet and a one-act play written by Pushkin—performed entirely in Russian![12]

A major turning point for the Party's racial politics occurred in 1928. That year, the Sixth World Congress of the Comintern passed a resolution asserting that African Americans in the black belt counties of the American South constituted an oppressed nation and therefore possessed an inherent right to self-determination. Not surprisingly, the resolution met fierce opposition from white, and some black, Party leaders, but for many black Communists, particularly those in the urban North, the resolution on black self-determination indirectly confirmed what they had long believed: African Americans had their own unique revolutionary tradition. As historian Mark Naison observed, "By defining blacks as an oppressed nation . . . the Comintern had, within the Leninist lexicon of values, endowed the black struggle with unprecedented dignity and importance." Black Communists published dozens of articles in the Party press supporting the idea that African Americans have their own identifiable, autonomous traditions of radicalism. "Aside from the purely Marxian analysis," wrote one black CP organizer, "the Negro's history is replete with many actual instances of uprising against his exploiters and oppressors."[13] In short, history and culture—whether it was to celebrate traditions of black resistance or recuperate the "folk" art of the black working class—became the vehicles through which black Communists could both "express" and justify their collective right to self-determination.

Race Men in Red Face

The Comintern's new position on the "Negro Question" compelled black Communists to call upon African American writers, artists, and historians to focus their work on the age-old tradition of black rebellion. As early as 1928, William L. Patterson, a prominent black Harlem lawyer who had joined the Party in the mid-1920s, criticized virtually all contemporary black poets in an article entitled "Awake Negro Poets." Although Patterson was pleased that they "have persistently called themselves black men, have proclaimed their songs Negro songs, have triumphantly hailed the emergence of a *Negro* culture," he hoped more young writers would write revolutionary verse that described the conditions of the black masses and captured the tradition of resistance instead of catering to patrons.[14]

Writers of the genre Patterson hoped for were drawn to left-wing circles during the 1930s because of the Party's new focus on African American issues. Even more than the self-determination slogan, the Party's defense of the Scottsboro Nine (young black men who had been falsely accused of raping two white women near Paint Rock, Alabama, in 1931), its vigorous denunciation of racism, and its unrelenting fight for the concrete economic needs of poor blacks attracted a significant section of America's submerged black intelligentsia, many of whom were former Garveyites or Pan-Africanist ideologues. Many were drawn to the League of Struggle for Negro Rights (LSNR), a CP-sponsored auxiliary created in 1930 intended to replace the defunct American Negro Labor Congress. Its somewhat radical nationalist program supported black self-determination in the South, advocated militant resistance on the part of African Americans, and called for a resolute campaign against lynchings and white terrorist organizations.[15] The LSNR newspaper, the *Liberator*, the source in which I discovered J. Thompson's "Exhortation," was established under the able editorship of former ABB founder Cyril Briggs, and conceived of as the "agitator and organizer of the Negro Liberation Movement."[16]

Yet, while the Central Committee of the CPUSA agreed to the formation of the LSNR and the publication of the *Liberator*, it did not agree with Briggs's assessment that the movement and its paper should be in the vanguard of the "Negro Liberation Movement." Indeed, white Communist leaders exhibited ambivalence toward the LSNR as early as the League's first national convention in St. Louis in 1931. The Central Committee resolved that the LSNR should not become "a substitute for the Party, which at all times must retain its leading role in the struggle for full equality, and in the South, for the right of self-determination." Furthermore, the Central Committee insisted that the League not become a "Negro organization" and that the *Liberator* not be characterized as a "Negro" paper.[17] These kinds of political pressures from national CP leadership ultimately led to the demise of the *Liberator*. After first suspending publication in January of 1932, it resumed again a year later but was limited primarily to Harlem. By 1934, the League had been reduced to little more than a skeleton of its former self.[18]

During the five years the *Liberator* remained in existence, however, its readership understood it to be a "Negro paper" irrespective of Central Committee concerns. As veteran Alabama Communist Hosea Hudson remembered, the *Liberator* "carried news items on the whole question of the oppressed people, like Africa. . . . It always was carrying something about the liberation of black people, something about Africa, something about the South. . . . We would read this paper and this would give us great courage."[19] The *Liberator* incubated a renascent black nationalist literary movement, publishing not only the verse of writers such as Langston Hughes but also more obscure works like Thompson's "Exhortation." And like Thompson's poem, much of the verse which appeared in the *Liberator* combined class consciousness, prevailing Pan-African ideas, and an emphasis on struggle as a form of masculine redemption.

A provocative example is Ruby Weems's "The Murder of Ralph Gray," a narrative poem about the Communist-led Share Croppers' Union's (SCU) first martyr. One of the founders of the all-black union, Gray was murdered in a shoot-out with law enforcement officials near Camp Hill, Alabama. Like Thompson, Weems transcends the simple class basis of antilabor repression and goes directly for the racial jugular vein. Her opening stanza reads:

> O white masters of the mulatto South,
> Thin lips emitting froth,
> Pale eyes shining like the upturned belly
> Of a decaying snake carcass,
> You killed Ralph Gray . . .

It is hard not to notice her linking of Caucasian physical features and the white ruling class's profligate character. Not only does Gray's willingness to die for the cause of freedom epitomize a kind of symbolic manhood, but his individual death cannot stop the millions of black people who allegorically stood behind Gray and the SCU. As if a massive ghost were rising from Gray's grave, Weems warned the "landowners and slave-drivers" of the consequences of their actions:

But white masters,
Why do you hurry through the cornfields late at night?
Are you running away from Ralph Gray?
Too late, too late!

His muscles swelling into a mighty challenge
Mount into a vision of a million clenched fists.
He wears his death like a joyous banner of solidarity,
A specter of militant Negro manhood.
He lies still and silent—but under his unmoving form
Rise hosts of dark, strong men,
The vast army of rebellion![20]

Much of this poetry could have easily appeared in the *Negro World*'s column, "Poetry for the People." Although the themes were far more varied and eclectic than those which appeared in the *Liberator*, Garveyite poems shared the gendered language which defined the act of resistance as a masculine rite of passage. Garveyites published poems such as "A Call to Race Manhood" and "Ku Klux Klan Beware" which emphasized the redeeming quality of male violence against their oppressors. Witness, for instance, Robert Poston's poem, "When You Meet a Member of the Ku Klux Klan" (1921):

When you meet a member of the Ku Klux Klan,
Walk right up and hit him like a natural man;
Take no thought of babies he may have at home,
Sympathy's defamed when used upon his dome.[21]

Thus, whereas racial themes might have been in conflict with the Communists' version of proletarian realism, these black artists—including most male writers outside of the Party—found common ground on the terrain of gender. Proletarian realism consciously evinced masculine images and defined class *struggle* as a male preserve. Communist cultural theoretician Michael Gold did not mince words in 1926 when he wrote: "Send a strong poet, a man of the street . . . send a man." As Paula Rabinowitz insightfully points out, "By linking the proletariat, and its culture, with masculinity, the metaphors of gender permeated the aesthetic debates of male literary radicals throughout the 1930's."[22] In fact, dozens of poems written

Working people fought constantly to control the pace of work and increase leisure time. Here a group of stevedores in Houston, Texas, seize a free moment to rest. (*Photo by Russell Lee. Courtesy Library of Congress*)

Washing clothes was hard work, but it gave African American household workers more autonomy and allowed them to escape the watchful eye of employers. In this photo, taken about November 1941, two women in Greensboro, Georgia, lug bags of soiled laundry home to be washed. (*Courtesy Schomburg Center for Research in Black Culture, New York Public Library*)

Two black men outside a store near Reserve, Louisiana, take time out for a few hands of cards. Although this is a rural town scene, cards, dominoes, and other games of chance were played on front porches and sidewalks in black communities throughout the urban South. *(Courtesy Schomburg Collection for Research in Black Culture, New York Public Library)*

For many black workers, the "nighttime was the right time." One photographer captured a jovial scene of African American men hanging out in a popular bar in Atlanta during the 1940s. *(Courtesy J. Neal Montgomery Collection, Atlanta Public Library)*

Working people, like these pictured here in Woodville, Georgia, built and sustained churches with their wages. Women were the backbone of the congregation. Black churches not only provided fellowship, a sense of community, and help to those in need, but were first and foremost places of reflection and spiritual empowerment. (*Courtesy Schomburg Center for Research in Black Culture, New York Public Library*)

Although black household workers in the urban South usually depended on public transportation to get to and from work, they did not always accept the terms of Jim Crow. They were at the center of many day-to-day battles against segregation, harassment by drivers and passengers, and a variety of other indignities. In this picture, two domestic workers wait for a streetcar in downtown Atlanta, circa 1939. (*Photo by Marion Post Wolcott. Courtesy Library of Congress*)

NEGROES

ARE CALLING A 60-DAY PERIOD OF—

MOURNING FOR THE DEAD!

Ten (10) Negroes Have Been Killed

By Law Enforcement Officers in 14 Months—NO White Person Has Been Killed
BY POLICE DURING THIS TIME!

THIS MOURNING PERIOD MEANS:

NO SHOPPING Downtown—or in the SHOPPING CENTERS WHILE WE ALL MOURN.
Human life is sacred; and Negroes are TIRED of Police Brutality and Killing Our People.
Negroes are tired of "One Man Ruling" of "Justifiable Homicide" every time a
NEGRO IS KILLED!

Wear OLD Clothes to express old, old, grief—Wear Old Clothes to PREVENT NEW
KILLINGS! Remember, it may be YOU, your CHILD, or Your Relative Next Time!

LET'S NOT BE FOOLED ANYMORE!

Six Organizations—Alabama Christian Movement For Human Rights, B'ham Baptist Ministers Conference, Birmingham
NAACP, Interdenominational Ministerial Alliance, Jefferson County Housewives League, Alabama Council On Human
Relations have PROTESTED THESE KILLINGS! County and City Officials quickly MADE PROMISES to have Police
Officers enforce laws fairly; to stop cursing and using abusive language; and to use NO unnecessary force in making
arrests. . . BUT they REFUSE NOW to BACK THIS UP by agreeing to an AUTOMATIC GRAND JURY INVESTI-
GATION OF ANY HOMICIDE BY POLICEMEN.

NEGROES ARE TIRED OF EMPTY PROMISES—

We want FULL JUSTICE NOW! Let us get TOGETHER—AND STAY TOGETHER!

1. Stay out of Downtown and the Shopping Centers—Pass this message on to all your friends.
2. ATTEND MASS MEETINGS EACH NIGHT—AND BRING ALL YOUR FRIENDS!
3. JOIN IN THE MARCHES FOR FREEDOM . . . The PICKETING OF STORES that love your money, but not you!
4. GET IN THE FIGHT FOR FREEDOM—WE STILL HAVE A LONG WAY TO GO!
5. CALL THE MOVEMENT OFFICE: 251-8734 FOR INFORMATION.

(Distributed by Alabama Christian Movement For Human Rights, and Supporting Groups and Friends.)

Above: Photographer Charles Moore powerfully
captures what might be described as a "public
declaration of the hidden transcript." Here
young people confront police during the Birmingham demonstrations in May 1963, presumably expressing feelings and frustrations they
would normally keep to themselves. One cannot help but notice the expressions of anger and
joy, fear and fearlessness on their faces. It is a far
cry from the more common image of black
youth on their knees praying before Eugene
"Bull" Connor. (©1963 Charles Moore/Black Star)

Left: By the mid- to late 1960s, the civil rights
movement had become increasingly militant, as
reflected in this uncompromising flyer protest-
ing police brutality in Birmingham. (Courtesy
Albert Boatwell Papers, Department of Archives
and Manuscripts, Birmingham Public Library)

Above: More than eighty African Americans traveled to Spain in 1936–37 to defend the Spanish Republic from a fascist takeover. This incredible act of heroism and deep commitment to antifascism caught the attention of several leading writers, including Langston Hughes. In this photo, Hughes spends a free moment with Abraham Lincoln Brigade volunteer Crawford Morgan. (*Courtesy Abraham Lincoln Brigade Archives, Brandeis University*)

Left: Among the African Americans who served in the Lincoln Brigade was one woman, Salaria Kee. She initially tried to volunteer through the Red Cross, but was told they did not accept "Negro" nurses. (*Courtesy Abraham Lincoln Brigade Archives, Brandeis University*)

Many black Lincoln Brigade volunteers were drawn to Spain through their work in the "Hands Off Ethiopia" campaign. Spain became an alternative battlefield for African Americans to get back at Mussolini for his invasion of Africa's last truly sovereign state in 1935. In this photo, Harlem residents protest Italy's aggression against Ethiopia by boycotting a local Italian merchant. (AP/Wide World Photos)

During the 1930s and 1940s, the Savoy Ballroom was one of Harlem's hottest dance spots. It was a favorite of young Malcolm Little whenever he was in New York. (Courtesy Schomburg Center for Research in Black Culture, New York Public Library)

Here is a rare image of Malcolm Little, conked and zooted down, posing with his half sister Ella in Boston. Malcolm remembered: "I couldn't wait for eight o'clock to get home to eat out of those soul-food pots of Ella's, then get dressed in my zoot and head for some of my friends' places in town, to lindy-hop and get high, or something, for relief from those Hill clowns." (*Courtesy Schomburg Center for Research in Black Culture, New York Public Library*)

From Malcolm Little to Malcolm X—dignified, bespectacled, upright, conservatively attired. (*Courtesy Schomburg Center for Research in Black Culture, New York Public Library*)

South Central Los Angeles after the 1992 uprising. Photographer James W. Jeffrey brilliantly captures the devastation and the way in which that event was "framed." This photo also offers a powerful visual metaphor for what many L.A. gangsta rappers set out to do: turn the cameras on everyday realities. And yet, like the coverage of the L.A. Rebellion itself, their "reality" is also a product of televised fictions and active imaginations. (©Jeffrey, "Eye on L.A.," *from* Life in a Day of Black L.A.: The Way We See It, *published by UCLA CAAS Publications*)

by white Communists dealing directly with race made their pleas for interracialism in a wholly masculinist discourse. As Sadie Van Veen wrote in her poem "Scottsboro," published in the *Liberator*, "Scottsboro long will you be remembered/ By men and the children of men./ For all that you stand for."[23] Kenneth Patchen's "Southern Organizer" invokes an image of state-sanctioned vigilante violence, of which men are its victims, and "true" men, black and white, are those who stand against it:

> Badges gleam; they dump the sack
>   into the water, turn and go.
> It is peaceful in the Southland; tomorrow
> They will hang and shoot some more
> Of ours: but tonight, as all true men
>   with southern blood will tell you.
> The possum is abroad, the bloodhounds sleep,
> And it is beautiful. Comrades.
>   "Let us do this thing together.
> Black man, comrade, we must together.
> And he is dead. There is work for living
> Men to do. We salute him.
> We have no tears for him."[24]

Similarly, V. J. Jerome's poem, "To a Black Man," written as a companion to Langston Hughes's "An Open Letter to the White Men of the South," counters what he perceives to be black racial separatism with a sustained appeal for unity against capital, but his appeal is to men about men. And like all of these authors, retaliatory violence is as much a matter of male redemption as it is class struggle. The final stanza reads:

> Call back your sons, brother
> and tell them
> the cause is not in the skin
> It's war over wheat-fields and coal pits
> over clothing and houses milk and bread.
> We against them.
> Slaves against masters.
> Fuse the fires

you from the black breast
I from the white
It's war for the earth!
Workmen fieldmen
Every hammer a gun
Every scythe a sword
War for the earth![25]

The language of masculinity, in fact, dominated representations of grass-roots organizing and Party propaganda, especially during the 1930s. Elizabeth Faue makes this point in her excellent study of working-class struggles in Minneapolis. Speaking of the labor movement's iconography as a whole, Faue writes: "They forged a web of symbols which romanticized violence, rooted solidarity in metaphors of struggle, and constructed work and the worker as male."[26] It stands to reason, then, that African American radical writers' and artists' persistent theme of manhood and violent resistance struck an enticing chord that probably reverberated louder than allusions to racial pride. This tendency was even evident among Communist music critics: in the pages of the *New Masses*, writer Richard Frank proclaimed that black music was deserving of high status within proletarian culture because it "possesses such virility."[27]

Besides, the Party's position on black liberation after 1928—their insistence on self-determination for African Americans—not only took precedence over women's struggles, but it essentially precluded a serious theoretical framework that might combine the "Negro" and "Woman" questions. Furthermore, the Party's advocacy of black self-determination conjured up masculine historical figures such as Toussaint L'Ouverture, Denmark Vesey, and Nat Turner. Writers such as Eugene Gordon and V. J. Jerome portrayed the movement as a struggle for "manhood," which is partly why armed resistance was such a powerful trope. When the central black character in Grace Lumpkin's novel *A Sign for Cain*, a young Southern-born Communist, observed "shot guns stacked in the corner of the cabin," he assured his comrades, "we ain't dealing with cowards, but men."[28]

But this is only part of the story. Those who entered radical circles toting the baggage of cultural nationalism found support in Communist theory. Ironically, Stalin's mechanical definition of a nation, which embraced a "community of culture" as a central concept, simply reinforced the modern nationalist idea that the basis of nationhood was a single, identifiable culture. Stalin certainly did not invent this idea. Indeed, African, African American, and West Indian nationalists who identified with the "Negritude movement" were also searching for that essential "Negro" or African culture that could lay the basis for Pan-African identity. Stalin's notion of a "community of culture" merely provided a Marxist justification for black Communists to join the search for the roots of a national Negro culture. As William L. Patterson wrote in 1933, the African American nation was bound by a common culture: "The 'spirituals,' the jazz, their religious practices, a growing literature, descriptive of their environment, all of these are forms of cultural expression. . . . Are these not the prerequisites for nationhood?"[29] Black Party leader Harry Haywood traced the roots of a "national Negro culture" in "ancient African civilization [and] Negro art and literature reflecting the environment of oppression of the Negroes in the United States."[30]

The self-determination slogan might have inspired a few black intellectuals already in the CP, but it did not do much to build black working-class support. Instead, the horrendous conditions brought on by the Great Depression, the Party's stand on racial justice, and its fight for the concrete economic needs of the poor were much more important for attracting African Americans. The presence of black working-class activists, especially from the South, infused Party circles with what might best be described as radical "folk" traditions. Like other visible ethnic groups before them (i.e., Jews, Finnish Americans, Chicanos, Asian Americans), working-class African Americans brought their grass-roots, race-conscious cultural traditions to the Party.[31]

Although the songs, rituals, religious practices, and styles of ordinary black working people were in conflict with Communist ideology and practice (many African Americans not only showed irreverence for the Party's interracialism but refused to even consider questioning their religion), this level of black cultural production rarely faced the critical scrutiny of CP cultural critics. In his critique of the Harlem Renaissance poets, William L. Patterson, for example, vacillated between demanding a culture that would focus on and celebrate the black masses, and rejecting the very idea that working-class African

Americans in the South—those whom he designated as "pure-black"—ever made any cultural contributions. He not only attacked the Harlem writers for voicing "the aspirations of a rising petty bourgeoisie," but he challenged them for refusing to "echo the lamentations of the downtrodden masses." While he rejected racialist claims that the emergence of a Negro literati can be explained by intermixture, his attack on that argument implicitly accepted that "racially pure" blacks do not or cannot make the same sort of cultural contribution: "Obviously, it is easy to say that the fact that the new Negro culture is the creation of a white-black group proves that the white blood is dominant. Not at all. The scientific explanation is simply that the pure-blacks, living in the South, are so oppressed, so debased by white exploiters, that any cultural expression is impossible for them."[32]

Patterson's views were in the minority, however, and even he developed a greater appreciation for the culture of the Southern black masses. Yet, while his fellow Communist cultural critics often exhalted Southern black culture as resistive, they nonetheless held on to an essentialist, race-bound definition of culture. Furthermore, like most American interpreters of culture, they tended to place virtually everything black people did under the rubric of "folk." Paradoxically, this limited vision of African American culture ultimately had the effect of insulating even the most nationalist expressions from censure. As Paul Buhle explains, "folk" expressions within Communist cultural criticism were sheltered from the current debates which raged over the meaning of "proletarian realism": "Few guidelines already existed on the left or elsewhere for popular art. That very absence provided breathing space for the cultural innovator. . . . No one could say what the significance might be, for instance, between Marxism and Black field hollers . . . "[33] In other words, folk artists were not subject to the same criticism and scrutiny that "legitimate" intellectuals faced. With the possible exception of Langston Hughes, most of the contributors whose work appeared in the *Liberator*, and in other Party-related publications, were usually treated as folk or popular culture.[34]

Most Communist theoreticians assumed (even during the Third Period) that "genuine" black folk culture was at least implicitly, if not explicitly, revolutionary. This is precisely why a Communist critic as antireligious as Mike Gold could describe the spiritual expressiveness of black vernacular culture in such celebratory terms. Writing about the black cadre on the Southside of Chicago, Gold writes: "At mass meetings their religious past becomes transmuted into a Communist present. They follow every word of the speaker with real emotion; they encourage him, as at a prayer meeting with cries of 'Yes, yes, comrade' and often there is an involuntary and heartfelt 'Amen!'"[35] Likewise, for white Communists such as Harold Preece, "the throbbing note of protest . . . is even in the spirituals. The Negroes were denied the most elementary civil rights. But they could sing and those songs were living prophesies of deliverance."[36]

Of course, not all CP cultural critics agreed. A handful of left-wing musicologists of the Third Period found revolutionary content in black secular song, but displayed greater ambivalence with respect to spirituals and gospel music. Critical of Hollywood's attempted cooptation of African American religious music, Philip Schatz remarked: "music which was once so soothing a balm for their oppression has misled most of America's cultural world into a belief that these songs are the only genuine artistic expressions of the Negro." Instead, he argued that "workaday songs" were the only "pure" musical expression of the black working class. On the other hand, Lawrence Gellert, probably the Party's most enthusiastic champion of black music, dismissed the content of black religious music from the institutional church as essentially reactionary but thought the *form* of the spiritual provided a foundation for revolutionary music. He pointed to secular songs with anticlerical undertones as a reaction to the black preacher, "a pompous, fat-headed, blow-hard parasite, prating meaningless platitudes about 'de Lawd and his By an' By Kingdom.'"[37] Nevertheless, all of these writers agreed that there was a common, identifiable, "pure Negro culture," and it was the most genuine expression of the black working class.

While the Party's essentializing of black culture created more space for cultural expressions which otherwise would be in conflict with Communist ideology, it also obscured the degree to which "folk" culture was actually bricolage, a cutting, pasting, and incorporating of various cultural forms which then become categorized in a racially/ethnically coded aesthetic hierarchy. Consider, for instance, the way in which black Party members transformed old spirituals into Communist anthems or secular protest songs. African American

Communists gave classics like "We Shall Not Be Moved" and "Give Me That Old Time Religion" new lyrics and completely new messages. In the latter, the verse was changed to "Give Me That Old Communist Spirit," and Party members closed out each stanza with "It was good enough for Lenin, and its good enough for me."[38] The lyrics were also rewritten as "The Scottsboro Song" after the nine young defendants were spuriously found guilty of raping two white women:

> The Scottsboro verdict,
> The Scottsboro verdict,
> The Scottsboro verdict,
> Is not good enuf for me.
>
> Its good for big fat bosses,
> For workers double-crossers,
> For low down slaves and hosses.
> But it ain't good enuf for me . . . [39]

In some respects, these kinds of alterations were very much in the tradition of improvisation, and the insertion of secular lyrics into spiritual song forms was certainly not unique to black Communist culture. But by employing a Marxist-Leninist discourse with its attendant language, idioms, and metaphors, the way in which African American Communists transformed "traditional" music subverted both the Party's own racialized cultural categories as well as the black musical forms upon which they inscribed new lyrics. What they produced was hardly "folk" music; it was a bricolage drawn from the Party's ideology, black cultural traditions and collective memories, and a constellation of lived experiences.

Black radical artists, in particular, self-conscious of this sort of pastiche of proletarian internationalism and "pure Negro" folk culture, were frequently prone to more parodic or satirical expressions. Black Chicago Communists, for instance, came up with a hilarious, tongue-in-cheek rendition of "Lift Every Voice and Sing" (what is acknowledged as the black national anthem) by James Weldon Johnson and J. Rosemond Johnson. It provides an implicit critique of mainstream black leadership for failing to adopt a radical internationalist vision, and yet acknowledges what is possible when black and red traditions of resistance come together:

> Sing a song full of the strife that the dark past
>   has taught us.
> Sing a song full of the hope Communism has
>   brought us.
> Facing a Red! Red! Sun of a new day begun
>   Let us fight on till victory is won.[40]

Similarly, a contributor to the *Liberator* borrowed an old nineteenth-century slave song to create a humorous parody entitled, "No Mo', No Mo.'" While the tune embodies practically all of the elements found in the Communist literary tradition, including anticlericalism and a prophetic vision of an insurmountable revolutionary movement, it contains a whole host of "cotton patch" stereotypes. And like the poetry of Weems and Thompson, the creator of this song makes no reference to black and white marching together:

> No mo' pickin cotton fo' ten
>   cents a day,
> No mo' raisin' taters without
>   gittn' pay.
> Yo gits no bread in church fo'
>   pray:
> No mo' God, no mo' bosses, we
>   folkses say.
>
> [chorus]
> Negroes ain' black—but RED!
> Teacher Lenin done said
> Brothers all oppressed an' po.'
> Ain't it so? Sho!
> ....
> No mo' KU-KLUX KLAN with
>   their burnin' crosses.

No mo' chain-gangs, we's no
    dogs no' ho'ses.
The NAACP, God no' Moses
    can stop us blackies fightin'
    the bosses.[41]

The chorus leaves one with an image of an army of militant, atheist "darkies" poised for a battle against racism *and* the black middle class, guided by the teachings of Lenin. Once again, both the popular conception of the "Negro folk" and the Communists' own image of the proletariat are subverted.[42]

Because we still do not know how the Party's intelligentsia collectively fashioned a notion of "folk" culture that differed from, say, high culture, modernism, or socialist realism, several questions remain: to what extent does the presence of a singular "Negro Question" constrain or structure efforts to interpret African American culture? Does the very idea of a "Negro Question" assume the existence of a single black community, and thus a single, "authentic" culture to be reckoned with? By what criteria do Communist critics categorize black cultural forms as "folk?" These and other questions will have to await further research and reflection.

"The Black and Red World Are Now One"

The cultural world of African American Communists and sympathizers was a mosaic of racial imagery interpenetrated by class and gender. During the 1930s the Party attracted thousands of African Americans who toted their cultural and ideological baggage to the movement, shaped the cultural landscape of American communism, and occasionally found spaces within Communist circles to create an expressive culture which, in some respects, contradicted the movement's goal of interracial solidarity.

As I have tried to demonstrate, this dichotomy between official Communist politics and Communist literary culture reflects a political concession to its new constituency. The Party desperately wanted to present itself as the legitimate heir of Garveyism, particularly in communities like Harlem and Chicago. Moreover, a number of factors converged within Party politics and culture that opened up space for creative expressions of black nationalism and race pride. For one, despite all the antagonism and invective separating Communists from Garveyites and other black nationalists during this period, their writers and artists had one thing in common: they agreed that struggle was a *man's* job. The languages of class struggle and "race" struggle employed a highly masculinist imagery that relied on metaphors from war and emphasized violence as a form of male redemption. Thus, on the terrain of gender, Communists and black nationalists found common ground—a ground which rendered women invisible or ancillary.

Further, the Comintern's thesis on self-determination in the black belt—frequently pointed to as evidence *par excellence* of the CPUSA's subservience to Moscow—contributed to blacks' greater cultural freedom within the Party. It might not have directly *encouraged* the development of an artistic expression of black self-determination, but it certainly did not hurt the production of the kind of rebellious, nationalist sentiment implicit in the notion of self-determination. Besides, white Party critics and theoreticians tended to accept without question anything they believed was "folk" culture, for this was presumably the genuine expression of the laboring and farming masses. Since much of black expressive culture was categorized as "folk," some surprisingly race-conscious, nationalist-inspired art survived in Party circles without censure.

Although the Party rejected racial politics in favor of interracial action, it did not (and could not) stifle the creative contributions of black radicals. On the contrary, during this period African American culture created a home for itself in Communist circles because of the growing presence of black working people. And, as we shall see in the next chapter, they found a way to embrace both the Communists' internationalism and their own vision of Pan-Africanism simultaneously. The place where it all came together was Spain.

Chapter 6

"This Ain't Ethiopia, But It'll Do"

African Americans and the Spanish Civil War

All you colored peoples
Be a man at last
Say to Mussolini
No! You shall not pass
—LANGSTON HUGHES, "The Ballad of Ethiopia" [1]

The Making of Black Internationalists

Some of you might recognize the famous Loyalist slogan, "No Pasaran, You shall not Pass" in Langston Hughes's poem. But when Hughes wrote these words the Republican defense of Spain was still a year away. Entitled "The Ballad of Ethiopia," the poet was referring to an earlier international confrontation with fascism that rocked the Pan-African world: Mussolini's invasion of Ethiopia in 1935. Indeed, the first stanza reads: "All you colored peoples/ No matter where you be/ Take for your slogan/ Africa be free." Nonetheless, Hughes's verse could easily have been retitled "The Ballad of Spain," for its call to action is precisely what prompted over eighty black men and one black woman to risk life and limb to defend the Spanish Republic from a fascist takeover. When the Communist International asked for volunteers to come to Spain in the fall of 1936, African Americans who

123

joined the Abraham Lincoln Brigade regarded the Civil War as an extension of the Italo-Ethiopian conflict.

Black Lincoln Oscar Hunter captured this race-conscious evaluation of the war in a short story titled "700 Calendar Days." One of the characters, a wounded black soldier, explained why he volunteered: "I wanted to go to Ethiopia and fight Mussolini. . . . This ain't Ethiopia, but it'll do." At the same time, black volunteers linked the struggles of the Iberian peninsula to racism and poverty in America; for them Spain had become the battlefield to revenge the attack on Ethiopia and part of a larger fight for justice and equality that would inevitably take place on U.S. soil.

It is no accident that the majority of African Americans who joined the Lincoln Brigade comprised part of a small but significant black Communist Left which came of age sometime between the First World War and the economic crisis of the 1930s (see chapter 5). Their unique background and experiences suggest that their decision to go to Spain was motivated largely by a political outlook that combined black nationalism and Pan-Africanism with a commitment to the Communists' vision of internationalism. Like the American Jewish brigadists whose cultural and national identities constituted a central element of their radical politics, ethnic nationalism and internationalism were not mutually exclusive. Although African American brigadists were a diverse bunch that included Northerners and Southerners, the college-trained and semiliterate, unemployed workers and self-styled intellectuals, most were Party members or supporters who interpreted communism through the lenses of their own cultural world and the international movement of which they were a part. They joined the movement out of their concern for *black people*, and thus had much in common with the black nationalists and mainstream black political figures whose leadership they challenged.

On the other hand, they were part of an organization that encouraged black-white unity without completely compromising black nationalist politics and introduced them to an entirely different interpretation of the way the world worked. The Party, in short, offered African Americans a framework for understanding the roots of poverty and racism, linked local struggles to world politics, and created an atmosphere in which ordinary people could analyze, discuss, and criticize the society in which they lived. Thus, as one black volunteer noticed when he arrived in Spain, "the ideas of all the Negroes from the United States were practically the same though these men did not know one another."[2]

These words were spoken by Mack Coad, an illiterate steel worker originally from Charleston, South Carolina, who had joined the Party in Birmingham in 1930. Although Coad was never singled out for his heroics in Spain, he had known war in the South. In March 1931, he was sent to Tallapoosa County, Alabama, to organize the Communist-led Share Croppers' Union.[3] Unfortunately, because Tallapoosa landlords would not tolerate a surreptitious organization of black tenant farmers and agricultural workers, Coad and other union recruits were caught in a shoot-out with police within weeks of the SCU's founding. When it was all over, SCU leader Ralph Gray lay dead and Coad was forced to flee the state. The following year Coad was sent to the Lenin School in the Soviet Union where his sense of the world and knowledge of international politics had expanded immensely, though he could still neither read nor write when he left. After he returned to the South in 1934, he resumed Party work in Raleigh, North Carolina, Birmingham, and rural Alabama, before heading to Spain in 1937.[4]

There were other Southern-born blacks who went to Spain, but most of them left the South at rather young ages and became acquainted with left-wing causes in Northern cities. Abe Lewis, born and raised in Alabama, joined the Communist Party in Cleveland. A struggling laundry worker, Lewis always remained firmly grounded in black community institutions, having been active in the Future Outlook League, the local NAACP, as well as the black church. He was a prime mover behind the Cleveland Scottsboro Defense Campaign and a consistent contributor to the local black press. Vaughn Love, a native of Tennessee who began working in the coal mines at fourteen, made his way to New York in 1929 and became acquainted with the Communist Party through the League of Struggle for Negro Rights.[5] James Yates, whom we know more about, was born in 1906 in Quitman, Mississippi. He was nourished on stories of how African Americans enjoyed democracy during Reconstruction; was taught by a schoolteacher who insisted that one day America would have a black president; was touched by the vision of his Garveyite uncle, who eventually moved to the all-black town of Boley, Oklahoma; and was

told over and over again about his other uncle who had armed himself to defend his family from the Klan, and of the Irish immigrant
neighbor who assisted him by providing ammunition. It was here, in
the small town of Quitman, Mississippi, that young Yates witnessed
not only countless episodes of racism and violence, but stark examples of internationalism, black nationalism, Pan-Africanism, and interracial solidarity. Quitman was apparently an appropriate place to raise
a black antifascist.[6]

Yates arrived in Chicago in 1923, during the height of the Garvey
movement. Even his boss at the stockyards was a member of the
UNIA. Although Yates himself never joined, he was clearly impressed
by Garvey's overall message and the idea of black self-organization.
By the time the depression hit home, he discovered in the streets
and parks of Southside Chicago an even more impressive bunch of
men and women, some of whom would eventually join him in
Spain. They were activists in the Communist Party and/or the unemployed councils. It's not clear whether Yates joined the Party or not,
but he was unmistakably a part of the unemployed movement and
even began organizing dining car waiters in Chicago and New York.
During his first mass demonstration—a march to Springfield, Illinois, that had been organized by the Party—he came to realize the
international significance of the Communist Party's struggle for jobs,
relief, and equality:

> I was a part of their hopes, their dreams, and they were a part of mine.
> And we were a part of an even larger world of marching poor people. By
> now I understood that the Depression was world-wide and that the un-
> employed and the poor were demonstrating and agitating for jobs and
> food all over the globe. We were millions. We couldn't lose.[7]

One of the leaders of the Springfield demonstration was Oliver
Law, a native of Texas who is undoubtedly the most celebrated
African American to have served in Spain. After spending six long
years in the U.S. Army and never surpassing the rank of corporal, Law
left the service and became a building trades worker. By the time the
Great Depression hit Chicago and left most construction workers jobless, he was sufficiently disillusioned with American capitalism to join
the Communist Party. Like Mack Coad, he not only rose through the
Party's ranks quite rapidly, becoming chairman of the Southside

chapter of the International Labor Defense and a principal leader in the "Hands off Ethiopia" campaign, but he, too, found himself engaged in a war at home. He was hospitalized in 1930 after being severely beaten by police for his role in leading a demonstration of the unemployed.[8]

Despite white Communists' intentions, race relations within the Chicago CP were not always smooth. Oscar Hunter, a black Party member who served in Spain, was constantly criticized by the local Party leadership for his views on race. "I was *always* in trouble," he recalled, "I didn't have the correct line, I didn't have the correct approach," and to make matters worse, his white comrades thought they knew "more about blacks and the history of blacks [than] I did." He remembered vividly one meeting on the Southside at which he made the mistake of referring to black folk as "my people" while appealing to the Party to work on the issue of the high rate of illiteracy among black Chicagoans. For uttering those words he was attacked by the leading cadre who, according to Hunter, "[gave another black Communist] the job of putting me in my place . . . so he comes right out and says what's this shit MY PEOPLE. . . . There's no such a god damn thing."[9]

Hunter's problem with the white CP leadership probably had more to do with his background and education than his unreconstructed black nationalist politics. Born to a working-class family in Orange, New Jersey, in 1908, Hunter and his brothers and sisters had to practically raise themselves after their father left and their mother died. He dropped out of school at age fourteen and moved to Cleveland in search of work. Soon after he arrived, a friend offered to send him to Hampton Institute, where he became actively involved in student politics and met a radical religion teacher who introduced him to Marxist literature. He went on to West Virginia State and then, upon the suggestion of another professor, continued his education at Brookwood Labor College in Katonah, New York. Impressed by some of the Communists he met at Brookwood, Hunter eventually moved to Chicago and joined the CP. As an independent black intellectual whose training in Marxism predated his membership in the Party, Hunter's vocal presence threatened a number of leading cadres in the Chicago area, black and white. Nevertheless, he continued to pursue his intellectual interests at Northwestern University's School of Journalism and at the lively meetings of the local John Reed Club, where he hung out with the likes of Richard Wright and Nelson Algren. Yet, despite his intellectual training, Hunter never took the movement as seriously as his leaders. "I joined the party, and I don't think I was the best communist in the world, I know I wasn't. I think that I had certain corruptions, I liked women. I liked to drink now and then, I liked to have fun."[10]

Oscar Hunter was not the only African American volunteer whose left-wing roots predated his membership in the Communist Party. Admiral Kilpatrick, whose background was as unique as his name, was born in Colorado in 1898 and raised in a Socialist family. His mother had been born a slave in Kentucky and his father, an American Indian from Oklahoma, had been a member of the Socialist Party since the turn of the century. Having grown up around radicals, Kilpatrick was about nineteen when he joined the Industrial Workers of the World. Like many of his comrades, he was influenced by the Russian Revolution and the Sacco and Vanzetti case, and was a victim of antiradical repression in 1919 under the direction of Attorney General A. Mitchell Palmer. He eventually joined the Communist Party in 1927 and went to the Soviet Union in 1931 to study at the Lenin School.[11]

By the mid-1930s, a combination of events had radicalized a segment of the Africans American community. Black men and women had witnessed the incarceration of nine young men falsely accused of raping two white women near Scottsboro, Alabama; the lynching of Claude Neal in Florida; New Deal legislation leave millions of blacks jobless and landless; a callous economic system keep over half the black population in some cities unemployed; and groups like the Klan, the American Nazi Party, the White Legion, and the Black Shirts beat, rape, and humiliate their people without compunction. So when Mussolini invaded the only independent black African nation in 1935, their simmering anger turned to outrage.

The defense of Ethiopia did more than any other event in the 1930s to internationalize the struggles of black people in the United States. Also known as Abyssinia, this particular section of the Horn of Africa held considerable historical, religious, and cultural significance for black communities throughout the world. Not only had the Ethiopians under Emperor Menelik II managed to maintain their independence while the rest of Africa was being carved up by Europeans, but their land had developed a reputation as the cradle of civilization, having been among the first countries in the world to adopt Christianity. In the black Christian world, Ethiopia has remained one of its principal icons and, in some ways, might be called an "African Jerusalem." As historian William Scott explained, many African Americans, particularly the followers of "Ethiopianism," believed that "Ethiopia had been predestined by biblical prophecy to redeem the black race from white rule." Their point of reference, of course, was the biblical passage "Ethiopia shall stretch forth her hands unto God" (Psalm 68:31). The best-known institutional manifestation of Ethiopianism in the United States was perhaps Harlem's own Abyssinian Baptist Church, founded in 1809. During the 1930s, Abyssinian's pastor, Adam Clayton Powell, Sr., developed a reputation for his radical race-conscious sermons and strident support for Ethiopian resistance to Italy.[12]

The Garvey movement, whose official anthem was entitled "Ethiopia, Thou Land of Our Fathers," made constant reference to this African nation in its songs, rituals, and symbols. Likewise, the Star Order of Ethiopia, founded by Grover Cleveland Redding, went so far as to advocate emigration there. The movement was deemed subversive by authorities in Chicago when one of its leaders "burned an American flag to symbolize the surrender of allegiance to the United States and the assumption of allegiance to Ethiopia." While Redding's organization was unable to persuade African Americans to move to the mother country, the Ethiopian ambassador to the United States was slightly more successful. By 1933 the African American community in Ethiopia numbered between 100 and 150.[13]

The African American response to the Italian invasion in some ways prefigured the Left's response to Franco's rebellion in Spain. Almost overnight an array of support organizations were formed, mainly in New York, Chicago, and Los Angeles, to raise money for relief and medical aid; and men from across the nation volunteered to fight. Individuals, such as Walter J. Davis of Fort Worth, Texas, and organizations, such as the Pan-African Reconstruction Association (PARA) headed by Samuel Daniels, initiated efforts to recruit men for Emperor Haile Selassie's army. According to Daniels, his organization had already mobilized an estimated 1,000 volunteers in New York, 1,500 in Philadelphia, 8,000 in Chicago, 5,000 in Detroit, and 2,000 in

Kansas City. While these figures are undoubtedly exaggerated, the overwhelming response from black men suggests a potential volunteer army equal to, and perhaps greater than, the number of Americans who joined the Lincoln Brigade.[14]

Initially Selassie was willing to accept African American combatants, but pressure from the U.S. government compelled Ethiopia to cease all recruitment efforts. Furthermore, potential volunteers were warned that they would be in violation of a federal statute of 1818 governing the enlistment of U.S. citizens in a foreign army. If convicted they could have faced a maximum three-year prison sentence, a $2,000 fine, and loss of citizenship. Despite the law, the Garveyite Black Legion allegedly established a training camp in upstate New York for some 3,000 volunteers, while another group made plans to purchase a freighter to carry black men to the Horn of Africa. Because of Selassie's fear of upsetting relations with the United States, none of these efforts came to fruition. According to most accounts, only two African Americans ever reached Ethiopia—airmen John C. Robinson of Chicago's Southside, and Harlem's Hubert F. Julian.[15]

Most mainstream black political figures opposed sending a brigade of black troops to Ethiopia and counseled young men against breaking the law, but the League of Nations' refusal to protect Ethiopia left many rank-and-file African Americans disillusioned. Black nationalists generally believed that indifference on the part of Western nations (most of which had their own African colonies to contend with) was nothing short of an act of racism. The invasion of Ethiopia was merely the first skirmish in what they viewed as a worldwide race war. Robert Ephraim, founder and president of the Negro World Alliance, stated in the summer of 1935: "the refusal of the United States to throw its influence against Mussolini . . . can only be taken as an indication that the white races are lining up definitely against the black."[16]

Such a racial interpretation of the invasion created a dilemma for the Communist Party and other left-wing movements, since most of the leading black nationalists refused to work with whites. Black Communists in Harlem, with the help of a few friendly Garveyites, created the Provisional Committee for the Defense of Ethiopia (PCDE) which worked tirelessly to redirect antiwhite and anti-Italian sentiment toward antifascism. With solid support from the American

League Against War and Fascism, the PCDE waged a lively "Hands Off Ethiopia" united front campaign in several black communities across the country. However, the Party's efforts were weakened by its opposition to the idea of recruiting African Americans for the Ethiopian army and by the Soviet Union's weak stand vis-à-vis the invasion. During a League of Nations meeting in April 1935, months after Emperor Selassie appealed to the League to keep Italy's encroachments on Ethiopian soil at bay, Soviet delegate Maxim Litvinov did not condemn Italian aggression. To make matters worse, the *New York Times* ran an article in September claiming that the USSR had sold coal, tar, wheat, and oil to Italy at below market price. Both events outraged black supporters of the "Hands off Ethiopia" campaign.[17]

The Soviets' initial vacillation resulted in a loss of confidence in the PCDE, and a few organizations, such as the Ethiopian World Federation, were created expressly to counter Communist influence. But the majority of African Americans who had supported the "Hands off Ethiopia" campaign learned to distinguish between Soviet interests and the genuine antifascist politics of rank-and-file Communists. Besides, black Communists adopted a slightly different view of Ethiopia from their black nationalist counterparts. While "race" scholars praised Abyssinia for its ancient civilizations, its written language, its rulers' proud claim of direct lineage from Solomon and the Queen of Sheba, African American leftists viewed the African nation as a mountainous peasant region ruled by a dying monarchy that did not believe in land reform. Indeed, it was one of the few regions on earth where slavery persisted well into the early 1930s. In 1931, black Communist George Padmore (aka Malcolm Nurse) described Abyssinia as a feudal oligarchy under a reactionary emperor and called for an internal revolution against "the reactionary religious hierarchy and the feudal system." Soon after the invasion, black Communist leader James Ford similarly characterized Africa's only independent nation as "a feudal state, under the rule of powerful native feudal lords," but insisted that the "the war of Ethiopia against Italian aggression must be regarded as a national (liberation) war. . . . The international proletariat must regard the struggle of Ethiopia as a just war, as a national defensive war, and support the Ethiopian people." This is a critical observation, for it helps us understand why the Comintern never deployed International Brigades to Ethiopia. At the same time, in the eyes of African Americans in and out of the Communist movement, the "backwardness" of Ethiopia was not enough to justify not coming to its defense.[18]

When Franco began his assault on the Spanish Republic in 1936, the Communist International showed less signs of ambivalence in its opposition to fascism. In one sense, the tables were turned: the Comintern was now calling on African Americans to join in the defense of Spain. By early 1937, the Communist Party had adopted the slogan "Ethiopia's fate is at stake on the battlefields of Spain" and asked that material aid that had been collected for Ethiopia be passed on to Spain after the Ethiopian government could no longer receive shipments of supplies. While many nationalist leaders attacked the slogan and fiercely rejected the idea that Spain and Ethiopia were part of the same battle, a number of black intellectuals and artists adopted the Spanish cause as their own. Black newspapers, most notably the Pittsburgh *Courier*, the Baltimore *Afro-American*, the Atlanta *Daily World*, and the Chicago *Defender* unequivocally sided with the Spanish Republic and occasionally carried feature articles about black participation in the Lincoln Brigade. Several black medical personnel from the United Aid for Ethiopia (UAE) offered medical supplies and raised money in Harlem; black churches and professional organizations sponsored rallies in behalf of the Spanish Republic; black relief workers and doctors raised enough money to purchase a fully equipped ambulance for use in Spain; and some of Harlem's greatest musicians, including Cab Calloway, Fats Waller, Count Basie, W. C. Handy, Jimmy Lunceford, Noble Sissle, and Eubie Blake, gave benefit concerts sponsored by the Harlem Musicians' Committee for Spanish Democracy and the Spanish Children's Milk Fund.

Besides the few who volunteered for service or helped collect money and supplies, the Civil War itself attracted a number of prominent contemporary cultural figures. Paul Robeson, the great black renaissance man of modern times, actually visited Spain during the height of the war. So moved was Robeson by the black men of the Lincoln Brigade, that he planned to make a film about war hero Oliver Law, though he was unable to obtain sufficient backing. Poet Langston Hughes, who was also deeply touched by the black men he had met at the front, had intended to publish a book of essays entitled "Negroes in Spain." The war even gripped the imagination of a 12-year-old Harlem boy named James Baldwin, whose first published essay was "a short story I had written about the Spanish Revolution" which appeared in a local church newspaper. Although Baldwin could not later remember the story's contents, he did recall vividly that it had been "censored by the lady editor."[19]

Among the nurses and doctors who had turned their efforts from Ethiopian relief to Spanish relief, two actually went to Spain as part of the American Medical Bureau. Caribbean-born Arnold Donawa, a graduate of Harvard University and former dean of Howard University's dental school, had developed a reputation as a brilliant oral surgeon. In Spain, Donawa became the head of Oral Surgery in the Medical Corps. Although it is not clear where he stood on the political spectrum, especially in relation to the Communist Party, he had been among the first UAE members to redirect relief efforts to Spain. He also persuaded a young nurse from Harlem Hospital, Salaria Kee, to volunteer for service in Spain. Originally from Ohio, Kee was a recent graduate of the Harlem Hospital Training School—not the school of her choice, but the only one that would accept blacks into the nursing program. Upon completing her training in 1934, she was given an undesirable position as head nurse in a tuberculosis ward. Soon thereafter she found herself working with a group of Harlem nurses who collected medical supplies and helped organize a 75-bed field hospital for Ethiopia's troops. After talking with Dr. Donawa and reading bits and pieces of information about the Spanish Civil War, she tried to volunteer through the Red Cross, but they made it absolutely clear to her that they would not accept black nurses. The International Brigades, however, gladly accepted her, and so she set sail for Spain on March 27, 1937.[20]

African Americans who went to Spain shared with black nationalists the kind of moral and political obligation that persuaded them to come first to Ethiopia's defense. Although the Spanish Civil War gave African American brigade members a chance to get back at the fascists for the invasion of Ethiopia, black Lincolns also knew that Spain was a very different place. It was a nation experimenting in a radical democracy, where peasants, workers, and women had the right to vote, where Socialists and Communists held positions of power in government. More importantly, Spain was one of the few examples of the Popular Front in practice.

War and Its Discontents

Though their motivations were as diverse as their ranks, the Lincoln Brigade went to Spain primarily to fight the fascist threat. The more observant volunteers, as well as most perceptive historians, have come to realize that the conflict that they were joining was, in fact, much more than a struggle against fascism; it was several wars rolled up in one. The roots of the Civil War can be found in time-honored battles between the Church and anticlericalists, between ethnic regionalists from Catalonia and the Basque provinces and Castilian centralists, between urban workers and Spain's few capitalists, and most importantly, between landless peasants and the old agrarian ruling class. Peasants on the huge landed estates in the South fought fiercely for land reform, and agricultural laborers demanded better wages. Big landholders turned increasingly to conservative Catholic political organizations and relied on legal and extralegal terrorist activities to keep their estates intact.[21]

Meanwhile, the military had become a powerful influence in Spain's political life. Frustrated by peasant insurrections, military losses in Morocco, working-class radicalism, the militancy of Basque and Catalanist movements for autonomy, and the overall inability of liberals to build a meaningful political alliance, a military junta under the leadership of General Primo de Rivera seized power in 1923 with the encouragement of King Alfonso XIII. As dictator, Primo set out to resolve the political crises which had plagued Spain since the end of World War I, but the experiment was a dismal failure. After seven years of mass strikes from students and workers and small mutinies within the army, the King had no choice but to succumb to mass pressure and dismiss de Rivera. When municipal elections were finally held on April 12, 1931, a coalition of liberal and socialist parties defeated the monarchists, thus paving the way for the creation of the Second Republic.[22]

The new constitution declared the government "a republic of workers of all classes." But few agreed as to what the Republic should look like. Initially, some of the changes marked a dramatic break from the past. In addition to granting Catalonia and the Basque provinces limited autonomy, the Republic took a few halting steps toward social and economic reform, but Republican initiatives fell far short of peasants' expectations. Moreover, the new government's efforts at secularizing education and minimizing the power of the Church and army eventually led to a revolt of high-ranking officers in August 1932. Although the government easily suppressed the uprising, it was a foreshadowing of things to come.

After two years, popular support for the Republican government had begun to diminish. Riding the crest of clerical reaction, an electoral alliance of right-wing groups narrowly defeated the Left, and promptly dismantled social and economic reforms: wages were reduced, clerical control over schools was reinstated, land reform came to a standstill, and the central government in Madrid began to whittle away at Catalan autonomy. Thousands of urban industrial workers, already outraged by cutbacks in wages and benefits, were poised for a showdown.

Led by Socialists, Left Republicans, Communists, and a few anarchists, workers attempted a general strike in October 1934, which quickly turned into an insurrection in Barcelona and Asturias. Workers proclaimed a socialist republic in Asturias, ran mines and factories by council, and established a "red army" militia. The workers did not know it then, but the Asturian uprising (also known as Spain's October Revolution) was a dress rehearsal for the Civil War that was to follow. Acting on the advice of General Francisco Franco, the state used the Foreign Legion and Moroccan troops rather than Spanish conscripts to crush Asturian resistance. Hundreds were massacred, about 40,000 people were imprisoned, and whatever autonomy Catalonia still enjoyed was suspended.[23] The vicious suppression of the October Revolution and the reversal of social and economic reforms created another political crisis in 1935. The Left responded by building a Popular Front coalition which defeated the right wing in the 1936 elections.[24]

The Popular Front government could hardly be called radical. The new government had intended merely to continue some of the mild reforms implemented during first two years of the Second Republic. But, for the conservatives—especially in the military—the Popular Front constituted a considerable threat. Soon after the elections, a group of army officers calling themselves the Unión Militar Española denounced the Popular Front as a Communist-controlled government and set out to rid the country of the red menace, restore law and order, and save the Catholic church from ruin. Led by Franco and General Emilio Mola, a handful of junior officers stationed in Morocco revolted against the Republican government on July 17–18, 1936.[25]

The Civil War soon became an international ordeal. Franco's forces might have been easily defeated at the very outset had it not been for military support from Germany, Italy, and Portugal.[26] While the Nationalist insurrection led by Franco enjoyed massive assistance from fascist countries, the legally elected Republican government was literally abandoned by the leading Western capitalist nations. The governments of the United States and Britain invoked the argument of nonintervention to justify their refusal to sell arms to the Loyalists.[27] (Although U.S. companies did not follow suit: Texas Oil Company extended long-term credit to the Nationalists.) The American and British stand compelled the French Popular Front government under Socialist Léon Blum to place a ban on the sale and supply of all war materials to Spain in August 1936. While sympathetic to the Republicans, Blum did not wish to ruin relations with Britain, especially since Nazi expansion across the Rhine threatened France's security. Nonetheless, Blum did try to neutralize outside support for Franco. His efforts eventually led to the Nonintervention agreement requiring all foreign powers to withdraw military support and supplies.[28] The USSR initially abided by the decisions of the nonintervention committee, offering only food and other nonmilitary supplies to the Republic. But when it became evident that Italy and Germany would continue to arm the Nationalists, the Soviet Union and the Communist International came to the defense of Spain.[29]

The Road to Barcelona

The Communist International called for volunteers throughout the world to make "Spain the grave of European fascism." Altogether, an estimated 35,000 people from over fifty countries and colonies volunteered for the International Brigades.[30] The first contingent of U.S. volunteers left New York harbor on the day after Christmas, 1936, aboard the SS *Normandie* bound for Le Havre, France. Among this first group of ninety-six were two black Communists—Alonzo Watson, an artist from New York, and Edward White of Philadelphia. For

Watson, Spain, specifically the battlefields of Jarama, would be his fi-nal destination. These men knew full well that their chances of re-turning home in one piece were rather slim. And yet they continued to come. Within a month, the next few shipments of volunteers in-cluded Walter Garland, Oscar Hunter, James Roberson, Tomás Díaz Collado, Tom Trent, Oliver Law, and Douglas Roach. By late summer of 1937, nearly eighty black men had arrived in Spain, anxious to confront fascist troops on the battlefield.

Just getting to Spain, these men soon found out, was a battle in and of itself. First, enlisting in the International Brigades was made difficult by bureaucratic hurdles, security screenings, and the Com-munists' genuine fear that working-class struggles in the United States would suffer if too many of its members volunteered. Some ex-cellent organizers were turned down because they were considered indispensable to the CPUSA and/or the labor movement. The num-ber of willing volunteers from both black and white communities far exceeded the number of participants accepted into the Lincoln's ranks. Besides, few women were allowed to volunteer unless they were part of a medical unit, and none was allowed to fight. When a volunteer was accepted into the ranks, he usually had to come up with the money to pay his passage and purchase equipment. As his-torian and Brigade veteran Arthur Landis noted, "During this period, and in the months to follow, there was to be quite a run in New York [Army-Navy surplus] stores on sheepskin coats, heavy boots, khaki shirts, pants, army blankets, ammunition belts, and any serviceable equipment that could be packed in a simple suitcase." Given the fact that most of the volunteers were industrial workers, many of them unemployed or Works Progress Administration (WPA) workers, rais-ing money to go to Spain was no easy task.[31]

Once a volunteer obtained a passport and secured passage to France, he or she faced a difficult ordeal just to get into Spain. The U.S. government was not only prepared to punish volunteers for vio-lating the federal statute of 1818, which made it unlawful for any U.S. citizen to enlist in a foreign army, but it placed restrictions on travel to Spain soon after the State Department discovered that Americans were joining the brigades. After March 4, 1937, all U.S. passports were stamped "NOT VALID FOR TRAVEL IN SPAIN." Thus, in order to enter Spain, volunteers had to pass through France and embark upon a treacherous climb over the Pyrenees mountains, whose steep and rugged slopes challenged even the most physically fit. More often than not, the men had to drop their "knapsacks, coats, blankets; anything to lighten the load. They even took off their socks and flung them into the darkness." As if the ascent was not arduous enough, most volunteers had to climb by night in order to avoid being arrested or shot by the French border patrol.[32]

Black men survived the climb and the bureaucratic hurdles with a determination reminiscent of Southern slaves struggling to get to Union lines during the Civil War. In some ways their mission was similar. Spain offered black men what the Union army had offered them over seventy years earlier: guns, ammunition, and an opportunity to fight their oppressors. For Oscar Hunter, the war finally gave him "a chance to at least not have a god damn cop on a picket line, you know but that I'd have a gun against a gun." Crawford Morgan felt the same way: "I got a chance to fight [fascism] there with bullets and I went there and fought it with bullets. If I get a chance to fight it with bullets again, I will fight it with bullets again." Walter Garland viewed Spain as a rare and historic opportunity for black men to fight back and regain their manhood: "You know, in a measure, we Negroes who have been in Spain are a great deal luckier than those back in America. Here we have been able to strike back, in a way that hurts, at those who for years have pushed us from pillar to post. I mean this— actually strike back at the counterparts of those who have been grinding us down back home." Of course they were not literally fighting American landlords, policemen, and industrialists on Spanish soil, but like their emancipated ancestors who saw the entire Confederate army rather than their individual masters as the embodiment of the slave system, black volunteers regarded Franco, Mussolini, and Hitler as representative of their oppressors back home.[33]

After crossing the border into "España," the volunteers were shuttled from the Catalan town of Figueras, through Barcelona and Valencia, to the International Brigade headquarters at Albacete. Here they enjoyed a rare opportunity to shower, received mismatched uniforms and whatever supplies were on hand, filled out questionnaires, and were given assignments based on previous military experience and special skills. Because virtually all newly arrived volunteers wanted to get into the action, those who received noncombatant assignments were often disappointed. James Yates served in the motor pool; fifty-two-year-old Council Gibson Carter, a native of Carbonville, Utah, apparently too old for combat duty, was assigned to an ambulance, as was Howard University medical student Thaddeus Battle; Knute Frankson, a black auto worker from Detroit, was appointed chief mechanic at the Auto Park for the International Brigades; and Bert Jackson's knowledge of maps and artistic talent landed him a job as topographer for the Brigade Commissariat.

The International Brigades even attracted three black pilots, James Peck, Paul Williams, and Patrick Roosevelt. Their presence in Spain was remarkable in light of the fact that, less than eight years earlier, there were only five licensed black pilots in the United States. Williams was an aviation engineer with considerable flying time, and Peck, who had studied two years at the University of Pittsburgh, learned to fly privately after he was denied entrance to both the air corps and navy flying schools. Both men were among the last American pilots to serve in the Spanish Air Force, and Peck was decorated for heroism. The third black airman, Patrick Roosevelt, never had the opportunity to fly. His day-to-day confrontation with racism as a commercial pilot in New York led him to the Communist Party and to the struggle in Spain. He eventually served in the infantry and lost a leg during a battle in the hills of Sierra Cabals.[34]

Newly arrived volunteers could not help but notice the multinational character of the International Brigades. As soon as they reached Albacete they met volunteers from all over the world, including Germans in the Thaelmann battalion and Italians in the Garibaldi battalion who had fled fascism in their own countries. African American brigadists, whose Pan-African sensibilities contributed to their decision to come to Spain, were especially inspired by the presence of Africans and other people of African descent. In addition to a handful of Africans from Spain's colonies, one Ugandan, black volunteers from England, Latin America, and at least five black Cubans who were attached to the 15th Brigade, about a dozen Ethiopians made their way across the Pyrenees to re-engage with Mussolini. Most, like the son of Ras Imru, a member of the royal family, were the European-educated children of the ruling class. Realizing that Ethiopia was in no position to defeat Italy, he chose to enlist in the People's Army of the Republic as a rank-and-file soldier. "Madrid is not Addis

Ababa. There we had nothing but our justified hatred. Here we have guns, tanks, and aeroplanes." Overall, we do not know how many Africans and people of African descent participated in the war, but the presence of a Pan-African force within the International Brigades marked a historical moment in the history of the black world that deserves further examination.[35]

Building a volunteer army among American radicals was no easy task. First, most of the recruits had never even shot a gun before coming to Spain, and only a very tiny minority had any military experience. Although the infantry received some training at a base in Tarazona, so few weapons, so little ammunition, and so little time made proper training impossible. Some recruits had only fired their weapon four or five times before going into battle. To make matters worse, the Russian and Mexican-made rifles the Loyalists relied on periodically jammed, and few volunteers knew how to remedy the problem.[36] Second, the Communists and independent radicals were unaccustomed to, even disdainful of, military life. The deference that accompanies the salute and the hierarchical relationship between officers and men of lower rank resembled the class system they had grown to hate. Nonetheless, thanks in part to a system of commissars whose purpose was presumably to explain the political significance of important military decisions, and a conscious effort to play down differences by rank, this tension was not nearly as evident among the International Brigades as it was among the Spanish anarchists or combatants in the anti-Stalinist POUM (Workers' Party of Marxist Unification).[37]

The Lincoln battalion had its first and most bitter taste of war in the Jarama Valley in the spring of 1937. At Jarama the poorly trained, poorly equipped American volunteers paid a heavy price for their role in the defense of Madrid. Of the 400 American troops, 127 were killed (including Alonzo Watson) and over 200 were wounded. For the early black volunteers, Jarama was more than a baptism by fire; it was a test of courage and endurance which most passed with flying colors. Oliver Law, who commanded a machine gun crew under 120 days of heavy fire, was promoted to captain and subsequently rose to the rank of battalion commander, becoming the first African American in history to command a predominantly white military unit. Because of Walter Garland's performance, he was promoted to machine gun company commander and earned the rank of lieutenant. Two lesser-known black heroes at Jarama were Doug Roach and Oscar Hunter of the Tom Mooney machine gun company. Roach, a native of Provincetown, Massachusetts, and graduate of Massachusetts Agricultural College where he lettered in wrestling and football, was barely five feet tall. Having been a member of the Communist Party since 1932, he was among the first volunteers. Together, Roach and Hunter dug trenches and directed a barrage of fire at the enemy—not an easy task for machine gunners whose machine gun was inoperable. "The way Doug and I solved our problem," Hunter recalled, "was, as people died, we took their rifles . . . we had about ten guns and we just kept loading them and firing them."38

The Lincoln battalion, now under Oliver Law's command, had barely rested up before they were ordered to take part in the Brunete offensive in July. The purpose was to divert Franco's forces away from the northern front in order to mitigate pressure on Madrid. The American volunteers were infused with fresh arrivals from the States who comprised the newly formed George Washington battalion. Altogether, each of the battalions consisted of about 500 men, which included a handful of Canadian, Cuban, and Irish volunteers. Both groups were practically annihilated during the Brunete offensive, however, and the survivors (numbering little more than 250) ended up merging into one battalion as part of the 15th International Brigade. Most of the black recruits at Brunete were injured, including Roach and Garland, and their new commander, Oliver Law, was killed leading an assault up the hills of Villanueva del Pardillo.39

The high rate of casualties and the increasing number of wounded men (most of whom recuperated at overcrowded military hospitals perpetually short of supplies) did not deter the flow of American volunteers to Spain. Nor did the horrors of war keep the 15th Brigade out of the critical battles. A month after the Brunete offensive, the Lincolns fought Franco's forces street by street, house by house, in order to take Quinto and Belchite. During the unbearable winter of 1937–38, they battled both the enemy and the elements in the hills of Teruel, until rebel artillery and aerial bombs forced them to retreat to Belchite. When they discovered that Belchite was also under seige, they had to endure a longer, more difficult retreat under fire. Among the Lincolns captured by enemy forces were Edward Johnson and Claude Pringle, two African Americans who, at ages forty-seven and forty-four, respectively, were among the oldest volunteers at the front. (Coincidentally, both men were born in Virginia, served in World War I, and moved to Ohio where they became involved in radical politics.) By the time the Lincolns regrouped at Mora la Nueva in April 1938, their numbers had dwindled from 500, when the retreat began, to 100.[40]

African American volunteers took part in all of these battles, and many distinguished themselves under fire. Commander Milt Wolf witnessed several remarkable instances of black courage at the front:

> [Walter] Garland pulling the wounded Leo Kaufman off a hill and himself being wounded in the process, is a scene burned into my memory; him shouting for us to take cover as he lifted the frail Kaufman in his arms, a sniper peppering the exposed crest, bringing Leo safely into the waiting arms of Sanidad and then Walter tying a handkerchief around his own wound and leading us on.

In a letter home, volunteer Leo Gordon praised Milton Herndon for not even hesitating when he was ordered to lead his gun crew "thru a hail of fire up a slope in front of the enemy trenches." Gordon was also awed by Otto Reeves, a black Young Communist League (YCL) organizer from Los Angeles who "rode atop our tanks up to the enemy lines. With a bullet thru his arm, he managed to drag a wounded comrade two kilometers back to a first aid station."[41]

The endless stories of black courage and heroism were told over and over again in letters, speeches, and journalistic observations from the front, which the black press seized upon with enthusiasm. A few white observers from the United States were genuinely surprised, for no matter how progressive and antiracist they might have been, they were raised to believe that cowardice and mental inferiority were part of the Negro's genetic makeup. The performance of black volunteers proved how ridiculous it was for the United States to segregate its armed services and limit African Americans to noncombat duties. During a tour of the front, black Party member and International Workers' Order secretary, Louise Thompson, emphasized this point during a radio broadcast from Madrid. "These Negro soldiers are not in the work battalions, as was the case of the Negroes who fought in France during the World War. They occupy any military position for which they are qualified." Although Thompson's remarks are a slightly overstated, given the numerous examples of distinguished black combat service in previous U.S. wars,[42] her observations accurately describe the experiences of *most* African American servicemen, particularly those who had served in the armed forces before joining the Lincoln Brigade. While visiting the front with her husband Paul, Eslanda Goode Robeson jotted down a revealing conversation between Oliver Law and a Southern colonel from the U.S. Army who was visiting Spain. The somewhat puzzled colonel asked Law why he was wearing a captain's uniform, to which he responded "because I am a Captain. In America, in your army, I could only rise as high as corporal, but here people feel differently about race and I can rise according to my worth, not according to my color!"[43]

Although Party publications and the black press waged a noble propaganda effort, African American volunteers were not always heroes. Like other brigadists, they exhibited moments of cowardice, fear, and incompetence. Some cracked under pressure, and there is evidence that at least one deserted. Perhaps the least respected black officer was Harry Haywood, who earned the rank of political commissar largely because he was a leading member of the Communist Party. In addition to having personal conflicts with Brigade commanders, Haywood had had numerous run-ins with other black volunteers during his brief stay in Spain. Although we may never know the details of Haywood's experiences in Spain, his memoirs tell us that his biting criticism of the 15th Brigade's high command was the cause of his difficulties and the reason for his early withdrawal. But some of his black comrades tell a very different story. Mississippi-born Communist and brigade member, Eluard Luchell McDaniel, had a very clear image of Haywood in Spain: "He spent most of his time around women and dressed up and stuff like that." Oscar Hunter will never forget the day Haywood came to Jarama "with a pretty little suit on." When enemy fire became too heavy, "he got the hell out of there real quick . . . he was a real mess for us blacks up there." A few weeks after Haywood returned to the United States, Hunter and his comrades were dumbfounded when they received the most recent *Daily Worker* and discovered a photograph of Haywood at "Madison Square Garden, dressed up in this natty god damn uniform. You should have heard the roar all along that god damn line."[44]

Like their white compatriots, black troops at the front did not always follow the rules. Occasionally they might have faced charges of insubordination, but in most instances their tiny acts of rebellion were ad hoc responses to helpless situations, which occasionally made for some light-hearted moments. More than one black volunteer relied on cunning and wit to get himself out of a jam—a practice that we might well argue had been inherited from their enslaved ancestors. Leo Gordon described with admiration and humor Milton Herndon's problem-solving abilities when food and supplies were running low:

> There's a Negro section leader in my company who is very popular. Very intelligent . . . and a born leader. Once while marching down a road we passed a vineyard. All the fellows looked at the grapes longingly but in vain. There are certain restrictions about picking fruit. Sort of protect property if you know what I mean. Coming back we walked thru the same field. Suddenly Milt blew his whistle—an airplane signal! The entire mob dived into the bushes out of sight. Presently we heard the recall signal. Everybody emerged grinning widely—with peculiar bumps protruding out of their shirts.

In a similar fashion, Doug Roach, along with three other machine gunners, decided to "organize" a horse during the Brunete offensive. When Commissar Steve Nelson discovered the horse and found out how it had been obtained, he administered a well-deserved tongue lashing. "Don't you know this is no way to act in a Republican army—stealing horses?" They apologized but kept the horse.[45]

The Lincolns went to Spain exclusively to fight fascists, but very few could have remained oblivious to the workers' and peasants' revolution taking place around them. Anarchists, POUMists, and rank-and-file trade union members had begun to seize land, run factories by council, dismantle churches, and re-organize local politics—in short, they were attempting to revolutionize Spanish society in the midst of war. The Communist Party of Spain, the Communist International, and the majority of Spanish Socialists and liberals, on the other hand, decided that the military conflict had to take precedence over the revolution. The only way to win, they argued, was to defend the bourgeois republic and fight a very conventional war. Indeed, on a few occasions the Loyalist government outright suppressed the revolutionary process.[46]

African American volunteers generally supported the "war first" policy, but they were also impressed with the social and economic transformations taking place around them, particularly in the Spanish countryside. They had come to Spain armed with an unusually broad interpretation of fascism that included all forms of racist and class oppression. The American system of sharecropping and tenant farming, for example, was often described as fascist since it not only exploited rural folk economically but denied Southern blacks their civil rights and used extralegal violence to punish those who stepped out of line. Walter Garland once said, "We can't forget for one minute that the oppression of the Negro is nothing more than a very concrete form, the clearest expression, of fascism. . . . In other words, we saw in Spain . . . those who chain us in America to cotton fields and brooms." The analogy was extended to the deep South, in particular. After reading about a lynching in the *Daily Worker* during a lull in the fighting, one American volunteer observed, "Hitler uses bombs to destroy the people of Spain; Our Dixie Hitler's [*sic*] use rope."[47]

Even if a black volunteer knew virtually nothing about the revolution taking place around him, he certainly noticed the difference in the way he was treated by the Spanish people. There were no Jim Crow laws or racial barriers; not even restrictions on dating Spanish women. Visiting celebrities Paul Robeson and Langston Hughes repeatedly remarked on how the Spanish "lack all sense of color prejudice." "Spain was the first time in my life," recalled company sergeant Tom Page, "I was treated as a person. . . . I was a man! A person!" Having grown up in the South, Crawford Morgan was not used to living in a country where practically everyone he came in contact with treated him as an equal: "I felt like a human being, like a man. People didn't look at me with hatred in their eyes because I was black, and I wasn't refused this or refused that, because I was black." Nevertheless, while Spaniards might not have looked with hatred, they *did* look, especially if one had dark skin. African Americans were sometimes treated as curiosities. Eluard Luchell McDaniel remembers always being at "the center of attraction," and whenever Doug Roach entered a Spanish village, "the children would crowd around Doug, attracted by his dark color."[48]

Because African Americans were treated better in Spain than they were back home does not mean that Spaniards were free of racism.

What many black Lincolns failed to realize was that the respect and admiration bestowed upon them had more to do with their status as a volunteer than anything else. These same Spanish Loyalists felt utter hatred for the Moroccans fighting on Franco's side—a hatred whose roots go back at least a millennium. All Spanish schoolchildren learned about the age of "Moorish domination," when Muslims from North Africa ruled Spain from the eighth century until the fifteenth century. As the lessons had it, only the Christian crusades saved Spain and the rest of Europe from this heathen menace to civilization. Moreover, Spanish society had been shaped immeasurably by the trans-Atlantic slave trade, the exploitation of black labor on plantations in the so-called "New World," colonialism in Africa, and the Rif wars in Morocco in 1921, in which the army's defeats at the hands of the Rif people weakened Spain's rule in North Africa. Race, as well as a thousand years of history, undeniably complicated the way in which Republican Spain viewed Franco's Army of Africa.

According to historian Allen Guttman, North African troops fighting for Franco were "usually shown in Loyalist posters as very black," thus distorting their image in order to portray the "Moors" as an evil race of people. In fact, a tiny minority within the African American community were hesitant to support the Republic because Loyalist propaganda directed at North African troops was so venomous that it was interpreted as racism, pure and simple. Given these racial dynamics, being black in Spain complicated matters. On numerous occasions African Americans were shot at by Loyalists who had mistaken them for "Moors." Eluard Luchell McDaniel had to take precautions in certain sections of Spain in order to defuse any hostility from the crowd: "When we went in a town, I was called upon to make a speech . . . so they could see me. So I'm not a Moor. Black yes, Moor no. I'm a friend of theirs."[49]

Franco's use of Moroccan troops was disheartening to black volunteers whose Pan-Africanist and pro-Ethiopian sentiments brought them to Spain in the first place. Why would their darker brethren, laboring under the yoke of colonial oppression, fight on behalf of the fascists? Black novelist Richard Wright summed it up this way: "the fascists have duped and defrauded a terribly exploited people." Langston Hughes, who probably devoted more energy to understanding the role of North Africans in the conflict than any other contemporary observer, agreed with Wright and further noted the irony of Franco sending Muslim troops on a crusade to rid Christian Spain of "communism." Yet, he was most interested in the dilemma of blacks fighting on both sides. In fact, part of his rationale for going to Spain as a correspondent was to explore this relationship:

> I knew that Spain once belonged to the Moors, a colored people ranging from light dark to dark white. Now the Moors have come again to Spain with the fascist armies as cannon fodder for Franco. But on the loyalist side, there are many Negroes of various nationalities in the International Brigades. I want to write about both Moors and Negroes.

Although his investigative reporting offered more questions than answers, Hughes beautifully captured the confusion many black brigadists felt in a poem entitled "Letter from Spain":

> We captured a wounded Moor today.
> He was just as dark as me.
> I said, Boy, what you been doin' here
> Fightin' against the free?

Of course, the problem was much more complicated. Some radicals called on the Republican government to grant independence to North Africans under Spanish rule, arguing that such a measure not only had political merit but would, in effect, undercut Franco's forces. However, Prime Minister Largo Caballero and his predecessor, Juan Negrín, would not even consider it. On the contrary, the Caballero government went so far as to offer territorial concessions to France and Britain in exchange for Western support. "Its desire not to offend the Western powers," wrote historians Pierre Broue and Emile Temime, "now led it deliberately to renounce, not only the principle of self-determination for colonial peoples, but also a real chance to strike at the heart of Franco's power." The Communist Party of Spain, while supporting this policy, tried to improve relations by helping to bring about the Hispano Moroccan Anti-Fascist Association. Its purpose was to win North African support for the Republic and educate Spaniards about racism and colonial oppression, but it failed miserably to win large numbers of Moroccans to the Republican side.[50]

Not only did African American volunteers rarely experience discrimination from their Spanish hosts, but also blatant and conscious acts of racism within their own ranks were very rare. The majority of white volunteers had come out of movements in which racism was simply not tolerated. Still, American volunteers, whites as well as blacks, tended to overestimate the level of interethnic harmony and cultural integration within the International Brigades. Black Lincolns always remained a very small minority within their own battalion, and a miniscule presence among tens of thousands of International brigadists and millions of Spaniards. Though they certainly felt a strong sense of camaraderie with other Lincolns, black volunteers occasionally felt a tinge of alienation from the social and cultural life of the brigade.

James Yates's ruminations of life as a volunteer are revealing. He recalls, for example, the joy of "humming tunes I did not know," and yet never comments on the fact that everyone around him knew these songs. (Perhaps there is significance in the fact that, as black sergeant Joe Taylor was being carried away on a stretcher with a bullet lodged in his shoulder, he "hummed an old Negro folksong, 'The Preacher Went Down to the River to Pray'" rather than a standard International Brigade song.) Even more revealing is Yates's experience as a chauffer for Ernest Hemingway and two other white journalists from Britain and the United States, respectively. These three men had begun conversing among themselves about the war and never thought to ask Yates, a participant, his opinion. Volunteer Ramón Durem probably understood this sort of invisibility better than anyone. A native of Seattle, Washington, born of mixed parentage, Durem was twenty-two when he boarded the SS *Aquitania* bound for Spain. What enhanced Durem's invisibility was his skin color and features—he easily passed for white. "For this reason," he later wrote, "white people in the United States (and they are all racists in varying degrees) talk and act very freely in front of me, thus giving me an insight into their mentality seldom achieved by a dark negro who puts them on their guard." One cannot help but wonder if Durem was treated any differently by his comrades in the International Brigades. Did they know he was black? Had he been singled out like the rest as an exemplar of racial integration? How was he looked upon by his fellow African American brigadists?[51]

Although we know virtually nothing about the social and cultural life of black volunteers, it is possible that they developed a special sense of camaraderie among themselves alongside their strong feelings of international solidarity. As we have seen, most black volunteers came out of a Communist/nationalist political culture which discouraged separatism on the one hand, but encouraged members to gravitate toward issues affecting the African American community and anchor themselves in local community institutions, on the other. If such a community existed in Spain, few black volunteers would have admitted it; indeed, few would have been conscious of this kind of cultural bonding. It is fitting, even ironic, that the people who recognized a sense of community among African American volunteers would have been the individuals who felt alienated from such a community. Eluard Luchell McDaniel, for instance, felt like an outsider in relation to other black Lincolns. Although he was a preacher's son born in Lumberton, Mississippi, he ran away from home at a very young age (seven, he claims) and was raised in California by radical photographer Constance Kanga, who literally discovered him roaming along the beach. "I hadn't been used to associating with too many Negroes," McDaniel admitted. When he began associating with black brigadists in Spain he "seemed a little out of place" since he lacked "all the habits that the rest of them have. . . . I couldn't . . . sound like a Negro."[52]

If McDaniel felt out of place among fellow African Americans, how did African Americans feel among their fellow white Americans, particularly in a social setting? For that matter, how comfortable were they with other white brigadists for whom language served as a major barrier? To what extent were they treated as objects (i.e., representatives of a race and examples of an ideal) as opposed to thinking, feeling subjects? Only future scholarship will answer these and other questions about the lives of black Lincoln Brigade members. Such answers are crucial since, as we have already seen, African Americans did not necessarily take the same road to Spain as their white comrades. And as we shall see below, neither did they take the same road back home.

Coming Home

By the spring of 1938, the collapse of the Aragon front and the ensuing nightmare of a retreat left the Lincoln Brigade in shambles. "They were unshaven and filthy," writes historian Robert Rosenstone, "their clothes torn, their bodies full of lice, their feet swollen and blood-stained. Command had broken down, and for several days the Americans were less a military unit than a mob of homeless men." The combined forces of Mussolini, Hitler, and Franco had overwhelmed the Republican armies. The Lincolns alone had lost 70 percent of their men to fatal wounds, Franco's prisons, and desertion. Meanwhile, in March, France and England watched silently as Hitler's tanks rolled into Austria and formally annexed it to the German Reich. By this time, most Lincolns believed defeat was inevitable. Their wounds, fatigue, and hunger pains told them that fascist forces were militarily superior and the inaction of Western powers had sentenced the Spanish Republic to death. Except for the most recent arrivals and a handful of zealots, the Lincolns longed to go home.[53]

On September 21, Prime Minister Juan Negrín announced before the League of Nations that the Spanish government would withdraw all foreign volunteers. Negrín had hoped that international pressure might force Franco to withdraw Italian and German troops, and compel members of the Non-Intervention Committee to lift the embargo on war materials. Negrín's act of diplomatic goodwill was to no avail, however: nine days later the French and British signed the Munich agreement, giving Hitler the green light to invade Czechoslovakia. In view of this policy of "appeasement" to Hitler, few could have expected the West to defend Spain—a relatively insignificant player in the political landscape of Europe. On December 23, 1938, Franco invaded Catalonia, crushing the Republican army in the process. Barcelona fell on January 26, 1939, and two months later a coup led by Republican colonel López Casado and moderate socialist Julián Besteiro gave General Francisco Franco what he wanted—an unconditional surrender.[54]

Those who survived, and could still walk, received an emotional farewell from the Spanish people on October 29, 1938. They marched through the streets of Barcelona in the crisp autumn weather with mixed emotions, saddened by the defeat, burdened with a guilt-laden sense of abandonment, and ecstatic that they were finally going home. By December most of the Americans were well on their way, except for a handful still caught behind enemy lines rotting in Franco's prisons. Among the last group of Lincolns to make it back to the States were four African Americans—Kansas native Tom Brown and three Ohio residents, Abe Lewis, Claude Pringle, and Edward Johnson. Lewis arrived home in early February 1939, but Brown, Pringle, and Johnson were not released from Franco's prisons until April of that year. Otherwise, most of the black volunteers either found themselves on the SS *Paris* or the SS *Ausonia*, bound for home in time for Christmas.[55]

As these men gathered in small groups on deck, the chilly wind off the Atlantic Ocean underscoring the fact of their return home, we can only wonder what was going on in their minds. Of course they had grown weary of life in the trenches and were anxious to see loved ones, sleep in a warm bed, communicate in a language they knew, and enjoy some "down home" cuisine. But they were coming back to second-class citizenship, racist epithets, Jim Crow lines, and liberal condescension. Their struggle against fascism hadn't changed America, and they knew it. Several African American volunteers showed little interest in returning home. War hero Tom Page "hated to come back here [to the United States]." Luchell McDaniel wrote from the front, "I would rather die here than be slaved any more." Alpheus Prowell, who *did* die in Spain, had once written, "I was miserable in L.A. Here I'm happy."[56] Most of the returning black veterans probably had the same immediate experience as James Yates—a war hero's welcome from the American Left, followed by a slap in the face by American racists. On his first night home in New York, buoyed by the kisses and handshakes he received at the docks, Yates was denied a room at the hotel his comrades had planned to stay in. Although the white veterans checked in without a problem, when Yates stood before the registrar, the clerk simply looked at him and said "No Vacancy":

> Inwardly I winced. So soon? I had hardly left the boat and here it was. After having experienced being welcomed in cafes and hotels in Spain and France, I was doubly shocked to be hit so quickly. The pain went as deeply as any bullet could have done [sic]. I had the dizzy feeling I was back in the trenches again. But this was another front. I was home.

His comrades promptly gave up their accommodations and moved on.[57]

The transition to civilian life was not easy for the veterans, black or white. Even before touching U.S. soil, many Lincolns were harassed by the FBI and had their passport privileges revoked. Furthermore, they came home in dire need of medical attention, a place to stay, and employment of some kind. But in 1939, the United States was still in the throes of depression and jobs were scarce. Although a number of black veterans resumed their activities on behalf of the CP, very few (e.g., Harry Haywood) could expect sufficient financial support from the Party. In lieu of a Veterans Administration, they turned to the newly created Friends of the Abraham Lincoln Brigade. Composed of ex-Lincolns and their supporters, the FALB raised money to bring some volunteers back to the United States, provide small stipends to unemployed veterans during the winter of 1938–39, pay medical bills, and assist in any way it could to rehabilitate returning veterans. The FALB, for example, provided Crawford Morgan with a pair of eye-glasses and a new suit, and paid for a medical examination and minor dental work. Oscar Hunter was particularly useful to the FALB by making arrangements with the Cook County Hospital in Chicago to provide beds for incoming wounded.[58]

Nevertheless, despite personal hardships, most black veterans re-tained their enthusiasm for the "good fight." They returned to the burgeoning trade union movement, organized WPA workers, partici-pated in antifascist demonstrations, and spoke to anyone who would listen about the Spanish tragedy. This sort of collective action led to the formation of the Veterans of the Abraham Lincoln Brigade. More than a radical version of the American Legion, the VALB was con-ceived as an activist organization to protest fascism and other forms of injustice in the United States as well as the rest of the world. But be-cause the VALB was labeled a Communist front, it also had to fight for its very existence. It not only made Congressman Martin Dies's Un-American Activities hit list but it came under attack from liberals and anti-Stalinist leftists when the veterans joined the Communist Party in supporting the Nazi-Soviet Pact.

Signed in August of 1939, this nonaggression pact cleared the way for the Nazi invasion of Poland and simultaneously enabled Russia to invade Finland. Almost overnight Spanish Civil War veterans who supported the agreement dropped the old antifascist slogans and launched a campaign to keep America out of the "imperialist war." The Soviets' action was undoubtedly embarrassing and dishearten-ing, but from the veterans' perspective, their experiences in Spain in-dicated that, had Germany invaded the Soviet Union, the Western capitalist nations were likely to have done nothing. Stalin's compromise could not be compared with the Munich agreement or the Non-Intervention Committee, since he at least tried to fight fascism on Spanish soil.[59]

The VALB's political isolation came to an end when Germany invaded the Soviet Union, breaking the nonaggression pact. Three years after returning from Spain, most of the physically able veterans were anxious to engage the fascists once again in World War II. Soon after Japan's attack on Pearl Harbor, VALB executive secretary Jack Bjoze wrote President Franklin Roosevelt and offered the services of the Lincoln Brigade as a unit of experienced combatants. Roosevelt declined the offer, of course, but many veterans enlisted in the armed forces anyway. Within a few months an estimated 500 were back in uniform. Despite their combat experience and willingness to put their lives on the line, some of these "premature antifascists" were hounded by military intelligence and punished by their superior officers because they had gone to Spain. Black Lincolns who enlisted faced the double burden of regular military racism as well as anti-Communist persecution. All branches of the U.S. armed services enforced racial segregation, denied African Americans combat duty until 1944, relegated black servicemen and women to menial tasks, and banned black newspapers from military posts until 1943, to name but a few of the federally sanctioned indignities black soldiers had to live with. To add insult to injury, physical and verbal assaults by racist white servicemen were almost commonplace, and in several instances black soldiers in the United States were treated worse than German and Italian war prisoners.[60]

Lincoln veteran James Peck, an experienced pilot who had fought Hitler's Luftwaffe in Spanish skies, vainly offered his services to the U.S. Army Air Corps. He was not only turned down for combat duty but rejected as a possible instructor at the segregated aviation training program for black cadets at Tuskegee despite the fact that he was better qualified than many of the other instructors. Crawford Morgan, who had reached the rank of sergeant in the U.S. Army, witnessed racism and violence against black soldiers firsthand. "Not only were we Jim Crowed . . . but all of the nasty jobs, all of the worst jobs were handed to the majority of the Negroes." While stationed in Mississippi, he complained, "the 'Crackers' shot us up, and never did the Government do nothing about it." Is it possible that his efforts to make the "Government" do something about conditions in the army could have led to Morgan's demotion to corporal? Was he regarded as a greater threat than other black soldiers because of his Spanish Civil War background? James Yates enlisted in the Signal Corps, but for some strange reason he was pulled from his unit just before they were about to go overseas. He was then placed "in charge of a unit doing dirty work for the medics" at Bushnell Hospital in Utah. Soon thereafter, the Spanish Civil War veteran contracted an infection during a routine tooth extraction and had to be hospitalized for three months. He, like many other black veterans, accepted an honorable discharge and finished out the war as a civilian.[61]

The veterans who did not enlist in the military joined the upsurge of black protest during the war, embodied in the "Double V" slogan: victory against racism and fascism at home and abroad. Ironically, wartime black militancy and the "Double V" slogan created a dilemma for black Lincoln Brigade veterans who were still members of, or close to, the Communist Party. The CP essentially opposed the Double V campaign, arguing that too much black militancy could undermine the war effort. Yet, the Party's "war first" policy did not mean giving up the black struggle entirely. Rank-and-file Communists as well as Lincoln veterans continued to fight on the civil rights front throughout the war. In fact, the VALB was at the forefront of a campaign to create a mixed combat unit bearing the name "the Crispus Attucks Brigade," and Adam Clayton Powell, Jr., frequently pointed to the Lincolns as an example *par excellence* of a successful integrated military unit. Nevertheless, in spite of these measures, the Party's opposition to the "Double V" slogan left many African Americans feeling that it had abandoned them for the sake of the war.[62]

The VALB's decision to adopt the policy that the war take precedence over the "Negro Revolution" probably embittered a few of the more nationalist-inclined black veterans. This seems to be the case with Ramón Durem, who had once "hoped that by building left-wing organizations without respect of colour, we could do away with the rank injustice in the United States. At the end of World War Two, I discovered that even the white radicals were not interested in a radical solution to the Negro Question." Durem's shift to black nationalism does not seem to have dampened the internationalist outlook that had brought many black radicals to Spain in the first place, though for him it was internationalism limited to Third World solidarity. As early as 1962, he had anticipated the rise of urban black nationalism as "part of the general world colonial revolution."[63] His poem, "Hipping the hip" is even more telling. A critique of the Beat generation and its false claim to radicalism, he suggests looking to Africa and China for possible alternatives:

> Juice [alcohol]
> is no use
> and H [heroin]
> don't pay
>
> I guess revolution
> is the only way
>
> Blues—is a tear
> bop—a fear
> of reality.
> There's no place to hide
> in a horn
>
> Chinese may be lame
> but they ain't tame
>
> Mau Mau only got a five-tone scale
> but when it comes to Freedom, Jim—
> they wail!
>
> dig?[64]

Oscar Hunter, who was kept out of the war because of hypertension, had his own problems with the CP over the issue of race. During the immediate postwar period, Hunter became wedded to the underground world of bebop, the music and counterculture that represented the latest anthem of black urban militancy. His attachment to this cultural world—a world few white Communists were familiar with—eventually led to his break with the Party. One Chicago club owner, whom Hunter claimed was a gangster, occasionally helped him raise money for the Party by having small jazz concerts and running "gambling games." Hunter's alleged gangster friend never knew "what the hell I was up to but that there was a lot of good music and a lot of beautiful broads. . . . But that didn't satisfy the party." He eventually faced disciplinary action as a result of his lifestyle, but before the Chicago cadre had a chance to expel him, he quit.[65]

Most black veterans, however, remained staunch supporters of the VALB and held fast to their radical convictions, even at the height of McCarthyite repression. Some veterans were dismissed from their jobs because of their politics, hounded by the FBI, and barred from unions they had helped to build. Of the ex-Lincolns subpoenaed by the House Un-American Activities Committee and, later, by the Subversive Activities Control Board, only one witness, veteran Robert Gladnick, willingly cooperated with the government. Indeed, not one single black ex-Lincoln brought before the HUAC or the SACB turned informant. Some, like black Philadelphia Communist Sterling Rochester, refused to answer almost every question. Others, such as Crawford Morgan and Admiral Kilpatrick, brilliantly turned these "inquisitions" into a forum to indict U.S. foreign policy abroad and domestic racism at home. When asked by the Subversive Activities Control Board what the VALB's policy was with respect to U.S. recognition of Franco, Crawford had this to say:

> Well, we thought it was one of the most terrible things our government had ever done for the simple reason [that] we were the first Americans that felt fascism and later on a great section of the world was fighting it, including America. Thousands of our sons and daughters died over on the other side fighting fascism, and now our government is embracing it, and because we don't want to embrace it with them they are persecuting us for it.

As a former Wobbly who had survived the Palmer raids in 1919, Admiral Kilpatrick was no neophyte when it came to government repression. "In the class struggle," he reflected, "you can't stay in it when it's good and jump out and leave it when it's bad. You go all the way." When he testified before HUAC, he neither cooperated with the committee nor took the First or Fifth amendments. "I didn't take no Fifth Amendment. What the hell am I going to take the Fifth? They knew who I was, I didn't give a damn. . . . I've been trying to take the 13th, 14th, and 15th Amendment all my damn life and got nowhere."[66]

Black veterans emerged from the postwar Red Scare as militant and committed as ever, although the struggles they chose to engage in were as diverse as they were. Abe Lewis remained a leading Communist in Cleveland until his untimely death in 1949. Together, Bert Jackson and Walter Garland formed the United Negro Allied Veterans of America and fought tirelessly for the rights of African American vets. James Yates was elected president of the Greenwich Village–Chelsea chapter of the NAACP in the early sixties and raised money for civil rights activists in Mississippi. Oscar Hunter joined most of the surviving vets in their demonstration against the Vietnam War. Ramón Durem became a militant nationalist whose ideas, articulated in poetry published in the late 1940s and early 1950s, anticipated positions Malcolm X would espouse nearly a decade later. Like Malcolm, Durem had forseen the black power movement of the late sixties but did not live long enough to see the end result. He died of cancer on December 17, 1963. Not surprisingly, Admiral Kilpatrick remained a committed Marxist—so committed that he insists he was expelled from the CPUSA "because I wasn't going to go along with the fact [that] now all of a sudden you can build a Party with all classes." His problems with Party leadership had begun during the Popular Front. The very idea that the Party "was carrying on the traditions of Lincoln, Jefferson, and Douglass," in Kilpatrick's opinion, was "a lot of bull."[67]

That these men turned out to be "long distance runners" in the struggle against racism and injustice has a lot to do with their experiences in Spain. It was one of the few places on earth where black and white, Jew and gentile, could use guns to battle forces that threatened their individual and collective security, though they paid a dear price for this opportunity. More importantly, the particular historical road that African Americans had to travel before arriving on Spanish soil gave them a unique vantage point. Black Lincolns knew class oppression and racism; shared with each other a dual identity rooted in an African and an American past; and were willing to put their lives on the line in Spain partly to revenge the pillage of Ethiopia. Of course, not every African American volunteer was a Communist, but all of them accepted the Communists' vision of internationalism and interracial unity—a vision that allowed them to retain their nationalism and to transcend it.

Yet, the war itself was a transformative experience. The volunteers had no regrets. As Oscar Hunter put it:

We fought in Spain because it would benefit ordinary human beings everywhere. For all the errors, dogmas, harshness, petty or grand betrayals, the war in Spain was truly a war between right and wrong, between the exploited and the exploiters, between democrats and fascists. And while there were some terrible leaders and some cowardly individuals on our side, by and large it was certainly the most beautiful expression of the commitment to humanity by ordinary humans that I have ever read about or experienced.[68]

These words are a fitting summary of what Spain meant to all members of the Abraham Lincoln Brigade, irrespective of color. And they were uttered by a man whose entire life embodied the mosaic of experiences and emotions that brought a tiny band of black folk to the Iberian peninsula in the late 1930s. In many ways Hunter typified the African American volunteer. He was a worker and an intellectual; he knew class oppression and racism; he insisted on defending Spain and Ethiopia; and in the midst of battle, he showed signs of courage and fear, laughter and pain, clear thinking and confusion. The Oscar Hunters, Oliver Laws, James Yates's, Walter Garlands, and Salaria Kees were not simply fighting *the* "good fight" but several "good fights" all rolled up in one. Like Crispus Attucks in the American Revolution, or Martin Delany in the American Civil War, African Americans in the Lincoln Brigade believed their people's struggles were inextricably intertwined with the larger conflict. Neither patriotism nor a desire to "save the union" brought ex-slaves and the sons of slaves into the Union Army during the U.S. Civil War; rather, they put their lives on the line with the intention of destroying the system of slavery once and for all.

But this is where the analogy ends. Whereas black Union troops fought in segregated units under white command, often accompanied by indifferent or confused white men, the Lincolns waged war in an army that did not divide troops by skin color, whose members shared for the most part a singularity of purpose, and whose principal commander for a brief moment was a black man from Southside Chicago.

PART III

REBELS WITHOUT A CAUSE?

How do you know where I'm at
When you haven't been where I've been?
Understand where I'm coming from?

—CYPRESS HILL, "How I Could Just Kill a Man"[1]

Chapter 7

The Riddle of the Zoot

Malcolm Little and Black Cultural Politics During World War II

But there is rhythm here. Its own special substance:
I hear Billie sing, no good man, and dig Prez, wearing
    the Zoot
suit of life, the pork-pie hat tilted at the correct angle,
through the Harlem smoke of beer and whiskey, I
    understand the
mystery of the signifying monkey,
in a blue haze of inspiration, I reach to the totality
    of Being.
I am at the center of a swirl of events. War and death.
rhythm. hot women. I think life a commodity
    bargained for
across the bar in Small's.
I perceive the echoes of Bird and there is a gnawing in
    the maw
of my emotions.

—LARRY NEAL, "Malcolm X—An Autobiography"[1]

Much in Negro life remains a mystery; perhaps the zoot suit conceals profound political meaning; perhaps the symmetrical frenzy of the Lindy Hop conceals clues to great potential power—if only Negro leaders would solve this riddle.

—RALPH ELLISON, 1943[2]

"Like hundreds of thousands of country-bred Negroes who had come to the Northern black ghetto before me, and had come since," Malcolm X recalled in his autobiography, "I'd also acquired all the other fashionable ghetto adornments—the zoot suits and conk that I have described, the liquor, cigarettes, the reefers—all to erase my embarrassing background."[3] His narrative is familiar: the story of a rural migrant in the big city who eventually finds social acceptance by shedding his country ways and adopting the corrupt lifestyles of urban America. The big city stripped him of his naiveté, ultimately paving the way for his downward descent from hipster to hustler to criminal. As Malcolm tells the story, this period in his life was, if anything, a fascinating but destructive detour on the road to self-consciousness and political enlightenment.

But Malcolm's narrative of his teenage years should also be read as a literary construction, a cliché that obscures more than it reveals.[4] The story is tragically dehistoricized, torn from the sociopolitical context that rendered the zoot suit, the conk, the lindy hop, and the language of the "hep cat" signifiers of a culture of opposition among black, mostly male, youth. According to Malcolm's reconstructed memory, these signifiers were merely "ghetto adornments," no different from the endless array of commodities black migrants were introduced to at any given time. Of course, Malcolm tells his story from the vantage point of the civil rights movement and a resurgent Pan-Africanism, the early 1960s when the conk had been abandoned for closely cropped hairstyles, when the zoot had been replaced with the respectable jacket and tie of middle-class America (dashikis and Afros from our reinvented mother country were not yet born), and when the sons and daughters of middle-class African Americans, many of whom were themselves college students taking a detour on the road to respectability to fight for integration and equality, were at the forefront of struggle. Like the movement itself, Malcolm had reached a period of his life when opposition could only be conceived of as uncompromising and unambiguous.

The didactic and rhetorical character of Malcolm's *Autobiography*—shaped by presentist political concerns of the early 1960s and told through the cultural prism of Islam—obscures the oppositional meanings embedded in wartime black youth culture. And none of Malcolm's biographers since have sought to understand the history and political character of the subculture to which he belonged.[5] The purpose of this chapter is to rethink Malcolm's early life, to reexamine the hipster subculture and its relation to wartime social, political, economic, and ideological transformations.

World War II was a critical turning point not only for Malcolm but for many young African Americans and Latinos in the United States. Indeed, it was precisely the cultural world into which Malcolm stepped that prompted future novelist Ralph Ellison to reflect on the political significance of the dance styles and attire of black youth. Ironically, one would think that Malcolm, himself a product of wartime black youth culture, was uniquely situated to solve the riddle posed by Ellison in 1943. Nevertheless, whether or not Malcolm acknowledged the political importance of that era on his own thinking, it is my contention that his participation in the underground subculture of black working-class youth during the war was not a detour on the road to political consciousness but rather an essential element of his radicalization. The zoot suiters and hipsters who sought alternatives to wage work and found pleasure in the new music, clothes, and dance styles of the period were "race rebels" of sorts, challenging middle-class ethics and expectations, carving out a distinct generational and ethnic identity, and refusing to be good proletarians. But in their efforts to escape or minimize exploitation, Malcolm and his homies became exploiters themselves.

"I Am at the Center of a Swirl of Events"

The gangly, red-haired young man from Lansing looked a lot older than fifteen when he moved in with his half-sister Ella, who owned a modest home in the Roxbury section of Boston. Little did he know how much the world around him was about to change. The bombing of Pearl Harbor was still several months away, but the country's economy was already geared up for war. By the time U.S. troops were finally dispatched to Europe, Asia, and North Africa, many in the black community restrained their enthusiasm, for they shared a collective memory of the unfulfilled promises of democracy generated by the First World War. Hence, the Double V campaign, embodied in A. Philip Randolph's threatened march on Washington to protest racial discrimination in employment and the military, partly articulated the sense of hope and pessimism, support and detachment, that dominated a good deal of daily conversation. This time around, a victory abroad without annihilating racism at home was unacceptable. As journalist Roi Ottley observed during the early years of the war, one could not walk the streets of Harlem and not notice a profound change. "Listen to the way Negroes are talking these days! . . . [B]lack men have become noisy, aggressive, and sometimes defiant."[6]

The defiant ones included newly arrived migrants from the South who had flooded America's Northeastern and Midwestern metropolises. Hoping to take advantage of opportunities created by the nascent wartime economy, most found only frustration and disappointment because a comparatively small proportion of African Americans gained access to industrial jobs and training programs. By March of 1942, black workers constituted only 2.5 to 3 percent of all war production workers, most of whom were relegated to low-skill, low-wage positions. The employment situation improved more rapidly after 1942: by April of 1944, blacks made up 8 percent of the nation's war production workers. But everyone in the African American community did not benefit equally. For example, the United Negro College Fund was established in 1943 to assist African Americans attending historically black colleges, but during the school year of 1945–46, undergraduate enrollment in those institutions amounted to less than 44,000. On the other hand, the number of black workers in trade unions increased from 150,000 in 1935 to 1.25 million by the war's end. The Congress of Industrial Organizations' (CIO) organizing drives ultimately had the effect of raising wages and improving working conditions for these black workers, though nonunion workers, who made up roughly 80 percent of the black working class, could not take advantage of the gains. The upgrading of unionized black workers did not take place without a struggle; throughout the war white workers waged "hate strikes" to protest the promotion of blacks, and black workers frequently retaliated with their own wildcat strikes to resist racism.[7]

In short, wartime integration of black workers into the industrial economy proceeded unevenly; by the war's end most African Americans still held unskilled, menial jobs. As cities burgeoned with working people, often living in close quarters or doubling up as a result of housing shortages, the chasm between middle-class and skilled working-class blacks, on the one hand, and the unemployed and working poor, on the other, began to widen. Intraracial class divisions were exacerbated by cultural conflicts between established urban residents and the newly arrived rural folk. In other words, demographic and economic transformations caused by the war not only intensified racial conflict but led to heightened class tensions within urban black communities.[8] For Malcolm, the zoot suit, the lindy hop, and the distinctive lingo of the hep cat simultaneously embodied these class, racial, and cultural tensions. This unique subculture enabled him to negotiate an identity that resisted the hegemonic culture and its attendant racism and patriotism, the rural folkways (for many, the "parent culture") which still survived in most black urban households, and the class-conscious, integrationist attitudes of middle-class blacks.

"The Zoot Suit of Life"

Almost as soon as Malcolm settled into Boston, he found he had little tolerance for the class pretensions of his neighbors, particularly his peers. Besides, his own limited wardrobe and visible "country" background rendered him an outsider. He began hanging out at a local pool hall in the poorer section of Roxbury. Here, in this dank, smoky room, surrounded by the cracking sounds of cue balls and the stench of alcohol, Malcolm discovered the black subculture which would ultimately form a crucial component of his identity. An employee of the poolroom, whom Malcolm called "Shorty" (most likely a composite figure based on several acquaintances, including his close friend Malcolm Jarvis), became his running partner and initiated him into the cool world of the hep cat.[9]

In addition to teaching young Malcolm the pleasures, practices, and possibilities of hipster culture, Shorty had to make sure his homeboy wore the right uniform in this emerging bebop army. When Malcolm put on his very first zoot suit, he realized immediately that the wild sky-blue outfit, the baggy punjab pants tapered to the ankles, the matching hat, gold watch chain, and monogrammed belt were more than a suit of clothes. As he left the department store he could not contain his enthusiasm for his new identity. "I took three of those twenty-five-cent sepia-toned, while-you-wait pictures of myself, posed the way 'hipsters' wearing their zoots would 'cool it'—hat dangled, knees drawn close together, feet wide apart, both index fingers jabbed toward the floor." The combination of his suit and body language encoded a culture that celebrated a specific racial, class, spatial, gender, and generational identity. East Coast zoot suiters during the war were primarily young black (and Latino) working-class males whose living spaces and social world were confined to Northeastern ghettos, and the suit reflected a struggle to negotiate these multiple identities in opposition to the dominant culture. Of course, the style itself did not represent a complete break with the dominant fashion trends; zoot suiters appropriated, even mocked, existing styles and reinscribed them with new meanings drawn from shared memory and experiences.[10]

While the suit itself was not meant as a direct political statement, the social context in which it was created and worn rendered it so. The language and culture of zoot suiters represented a subversive refusal to be subservient. Young black males created a fast-paced, improvisational language which sharply contrasted with the passive stereotype of the stuttering, tongue-tied Sambo; in a world where whites commonly addressed them as "boy," zoot suiters made a fetish of calling each other "man." Moreover, within months of Malcolm's first zoot, the political and social context of war had added an explicit dimension to the implicit oppositional meaning of the suit; it had become an explicitly un-American style. By March 1942, because fabric rationing regulations instituted by the War Productions Board forbade the sale and manufacturing of zoot suits, wearing the suit (which had to be purchased through informal networks) was seen by white servicemen as a pernicious act of anti-Americanism—a view compounded by the fact that most zoot suiters were able-bodied men who refused to enlist or found ways to dodge the draft. Thus when Malcolm donned his "killer-diller coat with a drape-shape, reat-pleats and shoulders padded like a lunatic's cell," his lean body became a dual signifier of opposition—a rejection of both black petit bourgeois respectability and American patriotism.[11]

The urban youth culture was also born of heightened interracial violence and everyday acts of police brutality. Both Detroit and Harlem, two cities in which Malcolm spent considerable time, erupted in massive violence during the summer of 1943. And in both cases riots were sparked by incidents of racial injustice.[12] The zoot suiters, many of whom participated in the looting and acts of random violence, were also victims of, or witnesses to, acts of outright police brutality. In a description of the Harlem Riot, an anonymous zoot suiter expresses both disdain for and defiance toward police practices:

> A cop was runnin' along whippin' the hell outa [sic] colored man like they do in [the] slaughter pen. Throwin' him into the police car, or struggle-buggy, marchin' him off to the jail. That's that! Strange as it may seem, ass-whippin' is not to be played with. So as I close my little letter of introduction, I leave this thought with thee:
>
> Yea, so it be
> I leave this thought with thee
> Do not attempt to fuck with me.[13]

The hipster subculture permeated far more than just sartorial style. Getting one's hair straightened (the "conk" hairdo) was also required. For Malcolm, reflecting backward through the prism of the Nation of Islam and Pan-Africanism, the conk was the most degrading aspect of the hipster subculture. In his words, it was little more than an effort to make his hair "as straight as any white man's."

> This was my first really big step toward self-degradation: when I endured all of that pain, literally burning my flesh to have it look like a white man's hair. I had joined that multitude of Negro men and women in America who are brainwashed into believing that the black people are "inferior"—and white people "superior"—that they will even violate and mutilate their God-created bodies to try to look "pretty" by white standards.[14]

Malcolm's interpretation of the conk, however, conveniently separates the hairstyle from the subculture of which it was a part, and the social context in which such cultural forms were created. The conk was a "refusal" to look like either the dominant, stereotyped image of the Southern migrant or the black bourgeoisie, whose "conks" were closer to mimicking white styles than those of the zoot suiters. Besides, to claim that black working-class males who conked their hair were merely parroting whites ignores the fact that specific stylizations created by black youth emphasized difference—the ducktail down the back of the neck, the smooth, even stiff look created by Murray's Pomade (a very thick hair grease marketed specifically to African Americans), the neat side parts angling toward the center of the back of the head.

More importantly, once we contextualize the conk, considering the social practices of young hep cats, the totality of ethnic signifiers from the baggy pants to the coded language, their opposition to war, and emphasis on pleasure over waged labor, we cannot help but view the conk as part of a larger process by which black youth appropriated, transformed, and reinscribed coded oppositional meanings onto styles derived from the dominant culture. For

> the conk was conceived in a subaltern culture, dominated and hedged in by a capitalist master culture, yet operating in an "underground" manner to subvert given elements by creolizing stylization. Style encoded political "messages" to those in the know which were otherwise unintelligible to white society by virtue of their ambiguous accentuation and intonation.[15]

"But There Is Rhythm Here"

Once properly attired ("togged to the bricks," as his contemporaries would have said), sixteen-year-old Malcolm discovered the lindy hop, and in the process expanded both his social circle and his politics. The Roseland Ballroom in Boston, and in some respects the Savoy in Harlem, constituted social spaces of pleasure free of the bourgeois pretensions of "better-class Negroes." His day job as a soda fountain clerk in the elite section of black Roxbury became increasingly annoying to him as he endured listening to the sons and daughters of the "Hill Negroes," "penny-ante squares who came in there putting on their millionaires' airs." Home (his sister Ella's household) and spaces of leisure (the Roseland Ballroom) suddenly took on new significance, for they represented the negation of black bourgeois culture and a reaffirmation of a subaltern culture that emphasized pleasure, rejected work, and celebrated a working-class racial identity. "I couldn't wait for eight o'clock to get home to eat out of those soul-food pots of Ella's, then get dressed in my zoot and head for some of my friends' places in town, to lindy-hop and get high, or something, for relief from those Hill clowns."[16]

For Malcolm and his peers, Boston's Roseland Ballroom and, later, Harlem's Savoy, afforded the opportunity to become something other than workers. In a world where clothes constituted signifiers of identity and status, "dressing up" was a way of escaping the degradation of work and collapsing status distinctions between themselves and their oppressors. In Malcolm's narrative, he always seemed to be shedding his work clothes, whether it was the apron of a soda jerk or the uniform of a railroad sandwich peddler, in favor of his zoot suit. At the end of his first run to New York on the Yankee Clipper rail line, he admitted to having donned his "zoot suit before the first passenger got off." Seeing oneself and others "dressed up" was enormously important in terms of constructing a collective identity based on something other than wage work, presenting a public challenge to the dominant stereotypes of the black body, and reinforcing a sense of dignity that was perpetually being assaulted. Malcolm's images of the Roseland were quite vivid in this respect: "They'd jampack that ballroom, the black girls in wayout silk and satin dresses and shoes, their hair done in all kinds of styles, the men sharp in their zoot suits and crazy conks, and everybody grinning and greased and gassed."[17]

For many working-class men and women who daily endured backbreaking wage work, low income, long hours, and pervasive racism, as we have shown in chapter 2, these urban dance halls were places to recuperate, to take back their bodies. Despite opposition from black religious leaders and segments of the petite bourgeoisie, black working people took the opportunity to do what they wished with their own bodies. The sight of hundreds moving in unison on a hardwood dance floor unmistakably reinforced a sense of collectivity as well as individuality, as dancers improvised on the standard lindy hop moves in friendly competition, like the "cutting sessions" of jazz musicians or the verbal duels known as "the dozens." Practically every Friday and Saturday night, young Malcolm experienced the dual sense of community and individuality, improvisation and collective call and response:

> The band, the spectators and the dancers, would be making the Roseland Ballroom feel like a big rocking ship. The spotlight would be turning, pink, yellow, green, and blue, picking up the couples lindy-hopping as if they had gone mad. "*Wail, man, wail!*" people would be shouting at the

band; and it *would* be wailing, until first one and then another couple just ran out of strength and stumbled off toward the crowd, exhausted and soaked with sweat.[18]

It should be noted that the music itself was undergoing a revolution during the war. Growing partly out of black musicians' rebellion against white-dominated swing bands, and partly out of the heightened militancy of black urban youth—expressed by their improvisational language and dress styles, as well as by the violence and looting we now call the Harlem Riot of 1943—the music that came to be known as "bebop" was born amid dramatic political and social transformations. At Minton's Playhouse and Monroe's Uptown a number of styles converged; the most discerning recognized the wonderful collision and reconstitution of Kansas City big band blues, East Coast swing music, and the secular as well as religious sounds of the black South. The horns, fingers, ideas, and memories of *young* black folk (most, keep in mind, were only in their early twenties) like Charlie Parker, Thelonius Monk, Dizzy Gillespie, Mary Lou Williams, Kenny Clarke, Oscar Pettiford, Tadd Dameron, Bud Powell, and a baby-faced Miles Davis, to name only a few, gave birth to what would soon be called "bebop."

Bebop was characterized by complex and implied rhythms frequently played at blinding tempos, dissonant chord structures, and a pre-electronic form of musical "sampling" in which the chord changes for popular Tin Pan Alley songs were appropriated, altered, and used in conjunction with new melodies. While the music was not intended to be dance music, some African American youth found a way to lindy hop to some remarkably fast tempos, and in the process invented new dances such as the "apple jack."

Although the real explosion in bebop occurred after Malcolm began his stay at Charleston State Penitentiary, no hip Harlemite during the war could have ignored the dramatic changes in the music or the musicians. Even the fairly conservative band leader Lionel Hampton, a close friend of Malcolm's during this period, linked bebop with oppositional black politics. Speaking of his own music in 1946, he told an interviewer, "Whenever I see any injustice or any unfair action against my own race or any other minority groups 'Hey Pa Pa Rebop' stimulates the desire to destroy such prejudice and discrimination."[19]

Moreover, as I suggest in chapter 2, while neither the lindy hop nor the apple jack carried intrinsic political meanings, the social act of dancing was nonetheless resistive—at least with respect to the work ethic.[20]

"War and Death"

From the standpoint of most hep cats, the Selective Service was an ever-present obstacle to "the pursuit of leisure and pleasure." As soon as war broke out, Malcolm's homeboys did everything possible to evade the draft (Malcolm was only sixteen when Pearl Harbor was attacked, so he hadn't yet reached draft age). His partner Shorty, a budding musician hoping to make a name for himself stateside, was "worried sick" about the draft. Like literally dozens of young black musicians (most of whom were drawn to the dissonant, rapid fire, underground styles of bebop), Shorty succeeded in obtaining 4F status by ingesting something which made "your heart sound defective to the draft board's doctors"—most likely a mixture of benzadrine nasal spray and coke.[21] When Malcolm received notice from the draft board in October of 1943, he employed a variety of tactics in order to attain a 4F classification. "I started noising around that I was frantic to join . . . the Japanese Army. When I sensed that I had the ears of the spies, I would talk and act high and crazy. . . . The day I went down there, I costumed like an actor. With my wild zoot suit I wore the yellow knob-toed shoes, and I frizzled my hair up into a reddish bush conk." His interview with the army psychiatrist was the icing on the cake. In a low, conspiratorial tone, he admitted to the doctor, "Daddy-o, now you and me, we're from up North here, so don't you tell nobody. . . . I want to get sent down South. Organize them nigger soldiers, you dig? Steal us some guns and kill up crackers [*sic*]!" Malcolm's tactic was hardly unique, however. Trumpeter John "Dizzy" Gillespie, a pioneer of bebop, secured 4F status and practically paralyzed his army recruitment officer with the following story:

> Well, look, at this time, at this stage in my life here in the United States whose foot has been in my ass? The white man's foot has been in my ass hole buried up to his knee in my ass hole! . . . Now you're speaking of the enemy. You're telling me the German is the enemy. At this point, I

can never even remember having met a German. So if you put me out there with a gun in my hand and tell me to shoot at the enemy, I'm liable to create a case of "mistaken identity," of who I might shoot.[22]

Although these kinds of "confessions" were intended to shake up military officials and avoid serving, both Malcolm and Dizzy were articulating the feelings of a great majority of men who shared their inner cultural circle—feelings with which a surprisingly large number of African Americans identified. The hundreds, perhaps thousands, of zoot suiters and musicians who dodged the draft were not merely evading responsibility. They opposed the war altogether, insisting that African Americans could not afford to invest their blood in another "white man's war." "Whitey owns everything," Shorty explained to Malcolm. "He wants us to go and bleed? Let him fight." Likewise, a Harlem zoot suiter interviewed by black social psychologist Kenneth Clark made the following declaration to the scholarly audience for whom the research was intended: "By [the] time you read this I will be fighting for Uncle Sam, the bitches, and I do not like it worth a dam [sic]. I'm not a spy or a saboteur, but I don't like goin' over there fightin' for the white man—so be it."[23] We can never know how many black men used subterfuge to obtain a 4F status, or how many men—like Kenneth Clark's informant—complied with draft orders but did so reluctantly. Nevertheless, what evidence we do possess suggests that black resistance to the draft was more pervasive than we might have imagined. By late 1943, African Americans comprised 35 percent of the nation's delinquent registrants, and between 1941 and 1946, over 2,000 black men were imprisoned for not complying with the provisions of the Selective Service Act.[24]

While some might argue that draft dodging by black hipsters hardly qualifies as protest politics, the press, police, and white servicemen thought otherwise. The white press, and to a lesser degree the black press, cast practically all young men sporting the "drape shape" (zoot suit) as unpatriotic "dandies."[25] And the hep cats who could not escape the draft and refused to either submerge their distaste for the war or discard their slang faced a living nightmare in the armed forces. Zoot suiters and jazz musicians, in particular, were the subject of ridicule, severe punishment, and even beatings. Civilian hipsters fared no better. That black and Latino youth exhibited a cool, measured indifference to the war, as well as an increasingly defiant posture toward whites in general, annoyed white servicemen to no end. Tensions between zoot suiters and servicemen consequently erupted in violence; in June 1943, Los Angeles became the site of racist attacks on black and Chicano youth, during which white soldiers engaged in what amounted to a ritualized stripping of the zoot. Such tensions were also evident in Malcolm's relations with white servicemen. During a rather short stint as a sandwich peddler on the Yankee Clipper train, Malcolm was frequently embroiled in arguments with white soldiers, and on occasion came close to exchanging blows.[26]

"I Think Life a Commodity Bargained For"

Part of what annoyed white servicemen was the hipsters' laissez-faire attitude toward work and their privileging of the "pursuit of leisure and pleasure." Holding to the view that one should work to live rather than live to work, Malcolm decided to turn the pursuit of leisure and pleasure into a career. Thus after "studying" under the tutelage of some of Harlem's better-known pimps, gangsters, and crooks who patronized the popular local bar Small's Paradise, Malcolm eventually graduated to full-fledged "hustler."

   Bruce Perry and other biographers who assert that, because Malcolm engaged in the illicit economy while good jobs were allegedly "a dime a dozen," we should therefore look to psychological explanations for his criminality, betray a profound ignorance of the wartime political economy and black working-class consciousness.[27] First, in most Northeastern cities during the war, African Americans were still faced with job discrimination, and employment opportunities for blacks tended to be low-wage, menial positions. In New York, for example, the proportion of blacks receiving home relief *increased* from 22 percent in 1936 to 26 percent in 1942, and when the Works Progress Administration shut down in 1943, the percentage of African Americans employed by the New York WPA was higher than it had been during the entire depression.[28] Second, it was hard for black working people not to juxtapose the wartime rhetoric of equal opportunity and the apparent availability of well-paying jobs for whites with the reality of racist discrimination in the labor market. Of the many jobs Malcolm held during the war, none can be said to have been well-paying and/or fulfilling. Third, any attempt to understand the relationship between certain forms of crime and resistance must begin by questioning the dominant view of criminal behavior as social deviance. As a number of criminologists and urban anthropologists have suggested, "hustling" or similar kinds of informal/illicit economic strategies should be regarded as efforts to escape dependency on low-wage, alienating labor.[29]

The zoot suiters' collective hostility to wage labor became evident to young Malcolm during his first conversation with Shorty, who promptly introduced the word "slave" into his nascent hipster vocabulary. A popular slang expression for a job, "slave" not only encapsulated their understanding of wage work as exploitative, alienating, and unfulfilling, but it implies a refusal to allow *work* to become the primary signifier of identity. (This is not to say that hustlers adamantly refused wage labor; on the contrary, certain places of employment were frequently central loci for operations.) Implied, too, is a rejection of a work ethic, a privileging of leisure, and an emphasis on "fast money" with little or no physical labor. Even Shorty chastised Malcolm for saving money to purchase his first zoot suit rather than taking advantage of credit.[30]

Malcolm's apprenticeship in Boston's shoeshine trade introduced him to the illicit economy, the margins of capitalism where commodity relations tended to be raw, demystified, and sometimes quite brutal. Success here required that one adopt the sorts of monopolist strategies usually associated with America's most celebrated entrepreneuers. Yet, unlike mainstream entrepreneurs, most of the hustlers with whom Malcolm was associated believed in an antiwork, anti-accumulation ethic. Possessing "capital" was not the ultimate goal; rather, money was primarily a means by which hustlers could avoid wage work and negotiate status through the purchase of prestigious commodities. Moreover, it seems that many hustlers of the 1940s shared a very limited culture of mutuality that militated against accumulation. On more than one occasion, Malcolm gave away or loaned money to friends when he himself was short of cash, and in at least one case "he pawned his suit for a friend who had pawned a watch for him when he had needed a loan."[31]

Nevertheless, acts of mutuality hardly translated into a radical collective identity; hustling by nature was a predatory act which did not discriminate by color. Moreover, their culture of mutuality was a male-identified culture limited to the men of their inner circle, for, as Malcolm put it, the hustler cannot afford to "trust anybody." Women were merely objects through which hustling men sought leisure and pleasure; prey for financial and sexual exploitation. "I believed that a man should do anything that he was slick enough, or bad and bold enough, to do and that a woman was nothing but another commodity." Even women's sexuality was a commodity to be bought and sold, though for Malcolm and his homeboys selling made more sense than buying. (In fact, Bruce Perry suggests that Malcolm pimped gay men and occasionally sold his own body to homosexuals.)[32]

At least two recent biographies suggest that the detached, sometimes brutal manner with which Malcolm treated women during his hipster days can be traced to his relationship with his mother.[33] While such an argument might carry some validity, it essentially ignores the gendered ideologies, power relationships, and popular culture which bound black hipsters together into a distinct, identifiable community. Resistance to wage labor for the hep cat frequently meant increased oppression and exploitation of women, particularly black women. The hipsters of Malcolm's generation and after took pride in their ability to establish parasitical relationships with women wage earners or sex workers. And jazz musicians of the 1940s spoke quite often of living off women, which in many cases translated into outright pimping.[34] Indeed, consider Tiny Grimes's popular 1944 recording featuring Charlie Parker on alto:

> Romance without finance is a nuisance,
> Mama, mama, please give up that gold.
> Romance without finance just don't make sense,
> Baby, please give up that gold.
>
> You're so great and you're so fine,
> You ain't got no money, you can't be mine,
> It ain't no joke to be stone broke,
> Honey you know I ain't lyin'.[35]

Furthermore, the hustler ethic demanded a public front of emotional detachment. Remaining "cool" toward women was crucial to one's public reputation and essential in a "business" which depended on the control and brutal exploitation of female bodies. In the words of black America's most noted pimp scribe, Iceberg Slim, "the best pimps keep a steel lid on their emotions."[36]

These gendered identities, social practices, and the discursive arena in which pimping and hustling took place were complicated by race. As in the rest of society, black and white women did not occupy the same position; white women, especially those with money, ranked higher. Once Malcolm began going out with Sophia, his status among the local hipsters and hustlers rose enormously:

> Up to then I had been just another among all the conked and zooted youngsters. But now, with the best-looking white woman who ever walked in those bars and clubs, and with her giving me the money I spent, too, even the big important black hustlers and "smart boys" . . . were clapping me on the back, setting us up to drinks at special tables, and calling me "Red."[37]

As far as Malcolm and his admirers were concerned, "Detroit Red" conquered and seized what he was not supposed to have—a white woman. Although some scholars and ordinary folk might view Malcolm's dangerous liaison as an early case of self-hatred, the race/gender politics of the hustling community and the equally cool, detached manner with which they treated white women suggests other dynamics were operating as well. White women, like virtually all women (save one's mama), were merely property to be possessed, sported, used, and tossed out. But unlike black women, they belonged to "Charlie," the "Man," "whitey," and were theoretically off limits. Thus, in a world where most relationships were "commodified," white women, in the eyes of hustlers at least, were regarded as stolen property, booty seized from the ultimate hustle.

Hustling not only permitted Malcolm to resist wage labor, pursue leisure, and demystify the work ethic myth, but in a strange way the kinds of games he pulled compelled him to "study" the psychology of white racism. Despite the fact that members of this subaltern culture constructed a collective identity in defiance of dominant racist images of African Americans, the work of hustling "white folks" often required that those same dominant images be resurrected and employed as discursive strategies. As a shoeshine boy, for example, Malcolm learned that extra money could be made if one chose to "Uncle Tom a little," smiling, grinning, and making snapping gestures with a polishing rag to give the impression of hard work. Although it was nothing more than a "jive noise," he quickly learned that "cats tip better, they figure you're knocking yourself out." The potential power blacks possessed to manipulate white racial ideologies for their own advantage was made even clearer during his brief stint as a sandwich salesman on the Yankee Clipper commuter train:

> It didn't take me a week to learn that all you had to do was give white people a show and they'd buy anything you offered them. . . . We were in that world of Negroes who are both servants and psychologists, aware that white people are so obsessed with their own importance that they will pay liberally, even dearly, for the impression of being catered to and entertained.

Nevertheless, while Malcolm's performance enabled him to squeeze nickels and dimes from white men who longed for a mythic plantation past where darkeys lived to serve, he also played the part of the model Negro in the watchful eye of white authority, a law-abiding citizen satisfied with his "shoeshine boy" status. It was the perfect cover for selling illegal drugs, acting as a go-between for prostitutes and "Johns," and a variety of other petty crimes and misdemeanors.[38]

In some respects, his initial introduction to the hustling society illumined the power of the trickster figure or the signifying monkey, whose success depended not only on cunning and wiles, but on knowing what and how the powerful thought. Yet the very subculture which drew Malcolm to the hustling world in the first place created enormous tension, as he tried to navigate between Sambo and militant, image and reality. After all, one of the central attractions of the zoot suiters was their collective refusal to be subservient. As Malcolm grew increasingly wary of deferential, obsequious behavior as a hustling strategy, he became, in his words, an "uncouth, wild young Negro. Profanity had become my language." He cursed customers, took drugs with greater frequency, came to work high, and copped an attitude which even his co-workers found unbecoming. By the war's end, burglary became an avenue through which he could escape the mask of petty hustling, the grinning and Tomming so necessary to cover certain kinds of illicit activities. Although burglary was no less difficult and far more dangerous than pulling on-the-job hustles, he chose the time, place, and frequency of his capers, had no bosses or foremen to contend with, and did not have to submit to time clocks and industrial discipline. Furthermore, theft implied a refusal to recognize the sanctity of private property.

Malcolm's increasingly active opposition to wage labor and dependence upon the illicit economy "schooled" him to a degree in how capitalism worked. He knew the system well enough to find ways to carve out more leisure time and autonomy. But at the same time it led to a physically deleterious lifestyle, reinforced his brutal exploitation of women, and ensured his downward descent and subsequent prison sentence. Nevertheless, Malcolm's engagement with the illicit economy offered important lessons that ultimately shaped his later political perspectives. Unlike nearly all of his contemporaries during the 1960s, he was fond of comparing capitalism with organized crime and refused to characterize looting by black working people as criminal acts—lessons he clearly did not learn in the Nation of Islam. Just five days before his assassination, he railed against the mainstream press's coverage of the 1964 Harlem riot for depicting "the rioters as hoodlums, criminals, thieves, because they were abducting some property." Indeed, Malcolm insisted that dominant notions of criminality and private property only obscure the real nature of social relations: "Instead of the sociologists analyzing it as it actually is . . . again they cover up the real issue, and they use the press to make it appear that these people are thieves, hoodlums. No! They are the victims of organized thievery."[39]

"In a Blue Haze of Inspiration, I Reach the Totality of Being"

Recalling his appearance as a teenager in the 1940s, Malcolm dismissively observed, "I was really a clown, but my ignorance made me think I was 'sharp.'" Forgetting for the moment the integrationist dilemmas of the black bourgeoisie, Malcolm could reflect:

> I don't know which kind of self-defacing conk is the greater shame—the one you'll see on the heads of the black so-called "middle class" and "up-

per class," who ought to know better, or the one you'll see on the heads of the poorest, most downtrodden, ignorant black men. I mean the legal-minimum-wage ghetto-dwelling kind of Negro, as I was when I got my first one.[40]

Despite Malcolm's sincere efforts to grapple with the meaning(s) of "ghetto" subculture, to comprehend the logic behind the conk, the reat pleat, and the lindy hop, he ultimately failed to solve Ralph Ellison's riddle. In some ways this is surprising, for who is better suited to solve the riddle than a former zoot suiter who rose to become one of America's most insightful social critics of the century?

When it came to thinking about the significance of *his own* life, the astute critic tended to reduce a panoply of discursive practices and cultural forms to dichotomous categories—militancy versus self-degradation, consciousness versus unconsciousness. The sort of narrow, rigid criteria Malcolm used to judge the political meaning of his life left him ill-equipped to capture the significance of his youthful struggles to carve out more time for leisure and pleasure, free himself from alienating wage labor, survive and transcend the racial and economic boundaries he confronted in everyday life. Instead, "Detroit Red" in Malcolm's narrative is a lost soul devoid of an identity, numbed to the beauty and complexity of lived experience, unable to see beyond the dominant culture he mimics.

This is not at all to suggest that Malcolm's narrative is purposely misleading. On the contrary, precisely because his life as a pimp, prostitute, exploiter, addict, pusher, and all-purpose crook loomed so large in his memory of the 1940s, the thought of recuperating the oppositional meanings embedded in the expressive black youth cultures of his era probably never crossed his mind. Indeed, as a devout Muslim recalling an illicit, sinful past, he was probably more concerned with erasing his hustling years than reconstructing them. As bell hooks surmises, Malcolm's decision to remain celibate for twelve years probably stems from a desire to "suppress and deny those earlier years of hedonistic sexual practice, the memory of which clearly evoked shame and guilt. Celibacy alongside rigid standards for sexual behavior may have been Malcolm's way of erasing all trace of that sexual past."[41]

In the end, Malcolm did not need to understand what the zoot suit, bebop, lindy, or even hustling signified for black working-class politics during the war. Yet his hipster past continued to follow him, even as he ridiculed his knob-toed shoes and conked hair. His simple but colorful speaking style relied on an arsenal of words, gestures, and metaphors drawn in part from his streetcorner days. And when he lampooned the black bourgeoisie before black working-class audiences, he might as well have donned an imaginary zoot suit, for his position had not changed dramatically since he first grew wary of the "Hill Negroes" and began hanging out in Roxbury's ghetto in search of "Negroes who were being their natural selves and not putting on airs."[42] There, among the folks today's child gangstas might have called "real niggaz," fifteen-year-old Malcolm Little found the uniform, the language, the culture which enabled him to express a specific constellation of class, racial, generational, and gendered identities.

What Malcolm's narrative shows us (unintentionally, at least) is the capacity of cultural politics, particularly for African American urban working-class youth, to both contest dominant meanings ascribed to their experiences and seize spaces for leisure, pleasure, and recuperation. Intellectuals and political leaders who continue to see empowerment solely in terms of "black" control over political and economic institutions, or who belittle or ignore class distinctions within black communities, or who insist on trying to find ways to quantify oppression, need to confront Ellison's riddle of the zoot suit. Once we situate Malcolm Little's teenage years squarely within the context of wartime cultural politics, it is hard to ignore the sense of empowerment and even freedom thousands of black youth discovered when they stepped onto the dance floor at the Savoy or Roseland ballrooms, or the pleasure young working-class black men experienced when they were "togged to the bricks" in their wild zoot suits, strolling down the avenue "doin' the streets up brown."

Whatever academicians and self-styled nationalist intellectuals might think about Malcolm Little's teenage years, the youth today, particularly the hip hop community, are reluctant to separate the hipster from the minister. Consider, for example, W.C. and the MAAD Circle's sampling of Malcolm's voice to open their lyrical recasting of the political economy of crime, "If You Don't Work, U Don't Eat," in which Los Angeles rapper Coolio asserts, "A hustle is a hustle, and a meal is a meal/that's why I'm real, and I ain't afraid to steal." Or consider Gangstarr's video, "Manifest," in which the lead rapper, "Guru," shifts easily between playing Malcolm—suit, rimmed glasses, and all—rapping behind a podium before a mosque full of followers, to rollin' with his homeboys, physically occupying an abandoned, deteriorating building which could have easily been a decaying Roseland Ballroom. Not coincidentally, beneath his understated tenor voice switching back and forth between sexual boasting and racial politics, one hears the bass line from Dizzy Gillespie's bebop classic, "A Night in Tunisia." Through an uncanny selection of music, an eclectic mix of lyrics, and a visual juxtaposing of young black men "hanging out" against Malcolm the minister, Guru and D. J. Premier are able to invoke two Malcolms, both operating in different social spaces but sharing the same time—or, rather, timelessness. While some might find this collapsing of Malcolm's life politically and intellectually disingenuous, it does offer a vehicle for black (male) youth to further negotiate between culture as politics and culture as pleasure.

But "collapsing" the divisions Malcolm erected to separate his enlightened years from his preprison "ignorance" also compels us to see him as the product of a *totality of lived experiences*. As I have tried to suggest, aspects of Malcolm's politics must be sought in the riddle of the zoot suit, in the style politics of the 1940s which he himself later dismissed as stupidity and self-degradation. This realization is crucial for our own understanding of the current crisis of black working-class youth in urban America. For if we look deep into the interstices of the postindustrial city, we are bound to find millions of Malcolm Littles, male and female, whose social locations have allowed them to demystify aspects of the hegemonic ideology while reinforcing their ties to it. But to understand the elusive cultural politics of contemporary black urban America requires that we return to Ellison's riddle posed a half century ago and search for meaning in the language, dress, music, and dance styles rising out of today's ghettos, as well as the social and economic context in which styles are created, contested, and reaccented. Once we abandon decontextualized labels like "nihilism" or "outlaw culture" we might discover a lot more Malcolm X's—indeed, more El Hajj Malik El Shabazz's—hiding beneath hoods and baggy pants, Dolphin earrings and heavy lipstick, Raiders' caps and biker shorts, than we might have ever imagined.

Chapter 8

Kickin' Reality, Kickin' Ballistics

"Gangsta Rap" and Postindustrial Los Angeles

In ways that we do not easily or willingly define, the gangster speaks for us, expressing that part of the American psyche which rejects the qualities and the demands of modern life, which rejects "Americanism" itself.

—Robert Warshow, "The Gangster as a Tragic Hero"[1]

Oppressed peoples cannot avoid admiring their own nihilists, who are the ones dramatically saying "No!" and reminding others that there are worse things than death.

—Eugene Genovese, *Roll, Jordan, Roll*[2]

foreWORD: South Central Los Angeles, April 29, 1992

Believe it or not, I began working on this chapter well over a year before the Los Angeles Rebellion of 1992, and at least two or three months before Rodney King was turned into a martyr by several police officers and a video camera.[3] Of course, the rebellion both enriched and complicated my efforts to make sense of gangsta rap in late twentieth-century Los Angeles. West Coast gangsta-flavored hip hop—especially in its formative stage—was, in some ways, a foreboding of the insurrection. The previous two years of "research" I spent rocking, bopping, and wincing to gangsta narratives of everyday life

183

were (if I may sample Mike Davis) very much like "excavating the future in Los Angeles." Ice T, truly the "OG" (Original Gangster) of L.A. gangsta rap, summed it up best in a recent *Rolling Stone* interview:

> When rap came out of L.A., what you heard initially was my voice yelling about South Central. People thought, "That shit's crazy," and ignored it. Then NWA [the rap group Niggas With Attitude] came and yelled, Ice Cube yelled about it. People said, "Oh, that's just kids making a buck." They didn't realize how many niggas with attitude there are out on the street. Now you see them.[4]

Indeed, though the media believes that the riots began with the shock of the beating of Rodney King, neither the hip hop community nor residents of South Central Los Angeles were really surprised by the videotape. Countless numbers of black Angelenos had experienced or witnessed this sort of terror before. When L.A. rapper Ice Cube was asked about the King incident on MTV, he responded simply, "It's been happening to us for years. It's just we didn't have a camcorder every time it happened." (Subsequently, Cube recorded "Who Got the Camera," a hilarious track in which he asks the police brutalizing him to hit him once more in order to get the event on film.)[5]

Few black Angelenos could forget the 1979 killing of Eula Mae Love, a five-feet four-inch, thirty-nine-year-old widow who was shot a dozen times by two LAPD officers. Police were called after she tried to stop a gas maintenance man from turning off her gas. When they arrived she was armed with a kitchen knife, but the only thing she stabbed was a tree in her yard. Nor could anyone ignore the fifteen deaths caused by LAPD chokeholds in the early eighties, or Chief Darryl Gates's infamous explanation: "We may be finding that in some blacks when [the chokehold] is applied the veins or arteries do not open up as fast as they do on normal people." And then there were the numerous lesser-known incidents for which no officers were punished. Virtually every South Central resident has experienced routine stops, if not outright harassment, and thousands of African American and Latino youth have had their names and addresses logged in the LAPD antigang task force data base—ironically, called a "rap sheet"—whether they were gang members or not.[6]

The L.A. rebellion merely underscores the fact that a good deal of gangsta rap is (aside from often very funky music to drive to) a window into, and critique of, the criminalization of black youth. Of course, this is not unique to gangsta rap; all kinds of "B-boys" and "B-girls"—rappers, graffiti artists, break dancers—have been dealing with and challenging police repression, the media's criminalization of inner-city youths, and the "just-us" system from the get-go. Like the economy and the city itself, the criminal justice system changed just when hip hop was born. Prisons were no longer just places to discipline; they became dumping grounds to corral bodies labeled a menace to society. Policing in the late twentieth century was designed not to stop or reduce crime in inner-city communities but to manage it.[7] Economic restructuring resulting in massive unemployment has created criminals out of black youth, which is what gangsta rappers acknowledge. But rather than apologize or preach, most attempt to rationalize and explain. Virtually all gangsta rappers write lyrics attacking law enforcement agencies, their denial of unfettered access to public space, and the media's complicity in equating black youth with criminals. Yet, the rappers' own stereotypes of the ghetto as "war zone" and the black youth as "criminal," as well as their adolescent expressions of masculinity and sexuality, in turn structure and constrain their efforts to create a counternarrative of life in the inner city.

Indeed, its masculinist emphasis and pimp-inspired vitriol toward women are central to gangsta rap. While its misogynistic narratives are not supposed to be descriptions of everyday reality, they are offensive and chilling nonetheless. Of course, it can be argued that much of this adolescent misogyny is characteristic of most male youth cultures, since male status is defined in part through heterosexual conquest and domination over women. Part of what distinguishes gangsta rap from "locker room" braggadocio is that it is circulated on compact discs, digital tapes, and radio airwaves. But the story is so much more complicated than this. In order to make sense of the pervasiveness and appeal of the genre's misogyny, I also explore the traditions of sexism in black vernacular culture as well as the specific socioeconomic conditions in which young, urban African American males must negotiate their masculine identities.

Lest we get too sociological here, we must bear in mind that hip hop, irrespective of its particular "flavor," is music. Few doubt it has a message, whether they interpret it as straight-up nihilism or the words of "primitive rebels." Not many pay attention to rap as art—the musical art of, for example, mixing "break beats" (the part of a song where the drums, bass, or guitar are isolated and extended via two turntables or electronic mixers); the verbal art of appropriating old-school "hustler's toasts"; or the art simply trying to be funny. Although what follows admittedly emphasizes lyrics, it also tries to deal with form, style, and aesthetics. As Tricia Rose puts it, "Without historical contextualization, aesthetics are naturalized, and certain cultural practices are made to appear essential to a given group of people. On the other hand, without aesthetic considerations, Black cultural practices are reduced to extensions of sociohistorical circumstances."[8]

Heeding Rose's call for a more multilayered interpretation of cultural forms that takes account of context *and* aesthetics, politics *and* pleasure, I will explore the politics of gangsta rap—its lyrics, music, styles, roots, contradictions, and consistencies—and the place where it seems to have maintained its deepest roots: Los Angeles and its black environs. To do this right we need a historical perspective. We need to go back . . . way back, to the dayz of the O[riginal] G[angster]s. This, then, is a tale of very recent and slightly less recent urban race rebels, a tale that cannot be totally separated from black workers' sabotage in the Jim Crow South or young black passengers' "acting up" on streetcars in wartime Birmingham. Still, these more recent tales of rebellion, which highlight the problems of gangsta rappers against a background of racial "progress," reveal that the black working class of the late twentieth-century city faces a fundamentally different reality—the postindustrial city.

OGs in Postindustrial Los Angeles: Evolution of a Style

L.A. might be the self-proclaimed home of gangsta rap, but black Angelenos didn't put the gangsta into hip hop. Gangsta lyrics and style were part of the whole hip hop scene from its origins in the South Bronx during the mid-1970s. In Charlie Ahearn's classic 1982 film *Wild Style* about the early hip hop scene in New York, the rap duo Double Trouble stepped on stage decked out in white "pimp-style" suits, matching hats, and guns galore. Others in the film are "strapped" (armed) as well, waving real guns as part of the act. The scene seems so contemporary, and yet it was shot over a decade before the media paid attention to such rap songs as Onyx's "Throw Ya Guns in the Air."[9]

But to find the roots of gangsta rap's violent images, explicit language, and outright irreverence, we need to go back even further. Back before Lightin' Rod (aka Jalal Uridin of the Last Poets) performed toasts (narrative poetry from the black oral tradition) over live music on a popular album called *Hustlers' Convention* in 1973; before Lloyd Price recorded the classic black baaadman narrative, "Stagger Lee," in 1958; even before Screamin' Jay Hawkins recorded his explicitly sexual comedy "rap" "Alligator Wine." Indeed, in 1938 folklorist Alan Lomax recorded Jelly Roll Morton performing a number of profane and violent songs out of the black vernacular, including "The Murder Ballad" and "Make Me a Pallet on the Floor." Morton's lyrics rival the worst of today's gangsta rappers: "Come here you sweet bitch, give me that pussy, let me get in your drawers/I'm gonna make you think you fuckin' with Santa Claus." In other words, we need to go back to the blues, to the baaadman tales of the late nineteenth century, and to the age-old tradition of "signifying" if we want to discover the roots of the "gangsta" aesthetic in hip hop. Irreverence has been a central component of black expressive vernacular culture, which is why violence and sex have been as important to toasting and signifying as playfulness with language. Many of these narratives are about power. Both the baaadman and the trickster embody a challenge to virtually *all* authority (which makes sense to people for whom justice is a rare thing), creates an imaginary upside-down world where the oppressed are the powerful, and it reveals to listeners the pleasures and price of reckless abandon. And in a world where male public powerlessness is often turned inward on women and children, misogyny and stories of sexual conflict are very old examples of the "price" of being baaad.[10]

Nevertheless, while gangsta rap's roots are very old, it does have an identifiable style of its own, and in some respects it is a particular product of the mid-1980s. The inspiration for the specific style we now call gangsta rap seems to have come from Philadelphia's Schooly D, who made *Smoke Some Kill*, and the Bronx-based rapper KRS 1 and Scott La Rock of Boogie Down Productions, who released *Criminal Minded*. Although both albums appeared in 1987, these rappers had been developing an East Coast gangsta style for some time. Ice T, who started out with the technopop wave associated with Radio and Uncle Jam's Army (recording his first single, "The Coldest Rap," in 1981), moved gangsta rap to the West Coast when he recorded "6 in the Mornin'" in 1986. Less than a year later, he released his debut album, *Rhyme Pays*.[11]

Ice T was not only the first West Coast gangsta-style rapper on wax, but he was himself an experienced OG whose narratives were occasionally semi-autobiographical or drawn from things he had witnessed or heard on the street. A native of New Jersey who moved to Los Angeles as a child, "T" (Tracy Marrow) joined a gang while at Crenshaw High School and began a very short career as a criminal. He eventually graduated from Crenshaw, attended a junior college, and, with practically no job prospects, turned to the armed services. After four years in the service, he pursued his high school dream to become a rapper and starred in a documentary film called "Breaking and Entering," which captured the West Coast break dance scene. When Hollywood made a fictionalized version of the film called "Breakin'," Ice T also made an appearance. Although Ice T's early lyrics ranged from humorous boasts and tales of crime and violence to outright misogyny, they were clearly as much fact as fiction. In "Squeeze the Trigger" he leads off with a brief autobiographical, composite sketch of his gangsta background, insisting all along that he is merely a product of a callous, brutal society.[12]

Even before *Rhyme Pays* hit the record stores (though banned on the radio because of its explicit lyrics), an underground hip hop community was forming in Compton, a predominantly black and Latino city south of Los Angeles, that would play a pivotal role in the early history of gangsta rap. Among the participants was Eric Wright—better known as Eazy E—who subsequently launched an independent label known as Ruthless Records. He eventually teamed up with Dr. Dre and Yella, both of whom had left the rap group World Class Wreckin Cru, and Ice Cube, who was formerly a member of a group called The CIA. Together they formed Niggas With Attitude and moved gangsta rap to another level. Between 1987 and 1988, Ruthless produced a string of records, beginning with their twelve-inch *NWA and the Posse*, Eazy E's solo album, *Eazy Duz It*, and the album which put NWA on the map, *Straight Outta Compton*.[13] Dr. Dre's brilliance as a producer—his introduction of hard, menacing beats, sparse drum tracks, and heavy bass with slower tempos—and Ice Cube's genius as a lyricist, made NWA one of the most compelling groups on the hip hop scene in years.

A distinctive West Coast style of gangsta rap, known for its rich descriptive storytelling laid over heavy funk samples[14] from the likes of George Clinton and the whole Parliament-Funkadelic family, Sly Stone, Rick James, Ohio Players, Average White Band, Cameo, Zapp and, of course, the Godfather himself—James Brown—evolved and proliferated rapidly soon after the appearance of Ice T and NWA. The frequent use of Parliament-Funkadelic samples led one critic to dub the music "G-Funk (gangsta attitude over P-Funk beats)."[15] Within three years, dozens of Los Angeles-based groups came onto the scene, many produced by either Eazy E's Ruthless Records, Ice T and Afrika Islam's Rhyme Syndicate Productions, Ice Cube's post-NWA project, Street Knowledge Productions, or Dr. Dre's Deathrow Records. The list of West Coast gangsta rappers includes Above the Law, Mob Style, Compton's Most Wanted, King Tee, The Rhyme Syndicate, Snoop Doggy Dogg, (Lady of) Rage, Poison Clan, Capital Punishment Organization (CPO), the predominantly Samoan Boo-Yaa Tribe, the DOC, DJ Quick, AMG, Hi-C, Low Profile, Nu Niggaz on the Block, South Central Cartel, Compton Cartel, 2nd II None, W.C. and the MAAD (Minority Alliance of Anti-Discrimination) Circle, Cypress Hill, and Chicano rappers like Kid Frost and Proper Dos.

Although they shared much with the larger hip hop community, gangsta rappers drew both praise and ire from their colleagues. Indeed, gangsta rap has generated more debate both within and without the hip hop world than any other genre.[16] Unfortunately, much of this debate, especially in the media, has only disseminated misinformation. Thus, it is important to clarify what gangsta rap *is not*. First, gangsta rappers have never merely celebrated gang violence, nor have they taken a partisan position in favor of one gang over another. Gang bangin' (gang participation) itself has never even been a central theme in the music. Many of the violent lyrics are not intended to be literal. Rather, they are boasting raps in which the imagery of gang bangin' is used metaphorically to challenge competitors on the microphone—an element common to all hard-core hip hop. The mic becomes a Tech-9 or AK-47, imagined drive-bys occur from the stage, flowing lyrics become hollow-point shells. Classic examples are Ice Cube's "Jackin' for Beats," a humorous song that describes sampling other artists and producers as outright armed robbery, and Ice T's "Pulse of the Rhyme" or "Grand Larceny" (which brags about stealing a show), Capital Punishment Organization's aptly titled warning to other perpetrating rappers, "Homicide," NWA's "Real Niggaz," Dr. Dre's "Lyrical Gangbang," Ice Cube's, "Now I Gotta Wet'cha," Compton's Most Wanted's "Wanted" and "Straight Check N' Em." Sometimes, as in the case of Ice T's "I'm Your Pusher," an antidrug song that boasts of pushing "dope beats and lyrics/no beepers needed," gangsta rap lyrics have been misinterpreted by journalists and talk show hosts as advocating criminality and violence.[17]

This is not to say that all descriptions of violence are simply metaphors. Exaggerated and invented boasts of criminal acts should sometimes be regarded as part of a larger set of signifying practices. Performances like The Rhyme Syndicate's "My Word Is Bond" or J.D.'s storytelling between songs on Ice Cube's *AmeriKKKa's Most Wanted* are supposed to be humorous and, to a certain extent, unbelievable. Growing out of a much older set of cultural practices, these masculinist narratives are essentially verbal duels over who is the "baddest motherfucker around." They are not meant as literal descriptions of violence and aggression, but connote the playful use of language itself. So when J.D. boasts about how he used to "jack them motherfuckers for them Nissan trucks," the story is less about stealing per se than about the way in which he describes his bodaciousness.[18]

When gangsta rappers do write lyrics intended to convey a sense of social realism, their work loosely resembles a sort of street ethnography of racist institutions and social practices, but told more often than not in the first person. Whether gangsta rappers step into the character of a gang banger, hustler, or ordinary working person—that is, products and residents of the "'hood"—the important thing to remember is that they are stepping into character; it is for descriptive purposes rather than advocacy. In some ways, these descriptive narratives, under the guise of objective "street journalism," are no less polemical (hence political) than nineteenth-century slave narratives in defense of abolition. When Ice Cube was still with NWA he explained, "We call ourselves underground street reporters. We just tell it how we see it, nothing more, nothing less."[19]

It would be naive to claim that descriptive lyrics, as an echo of the city, do not, in turn, magnify what they describe—but to say so is a far cry from claiming that the purpose of rap is to advocate violence. And, of course, rappers' reality is hardly "objective" in the sense of being detached; their standpoint is that of the ghetto dweller, the criminal, the victim of police repression, the teenage father, the crack slanger, the gang banger, and the female dominator. Much like the old "baaadman" narratives that have played an important role in black vernacular folklore, the characters they create, at first glance, appear to be apolitical individuals only out for themselves; and like the protagonist in Melvin Van Peebles's cinematic classic, *Sweet Sweetback's Baaadass Song*, they are reluctant to trust anyone. It is hard not to miss the influences of urban toasts and "pimp narratives," which became popular during the late 1960s and early 1970s. In many instances the characters are almost identical, and on occasion rap artists pay tribute to black vernacular oral poetry by lyrically "sampling" these early pimp narratives.[20]

For other consumers of gangsta rap, such as middle-class white males, the genre unintentionally serves the same role as blaxploitation films of the 1970s or, for that matter, gangster films of any generation. It attracts listeners for whom the "ghetto" is a place of adventure, unbridled violence, erotic fantasy, and/or an imaginary alternative to suburban boredom. White music critic John Leland once praised NWA because they "dealt in evil as fantasy: killing cops, smoking hos, filling quiet nights with a flurry of senseless buckshot." This kind of voyeurism partly explains NWA's huge white following and why their album, *Efil4zaggin*, shot to the top of the charts as soon as it was released. As one critic put it, "In reality, NWA have more in common with a Charles Bronson movie than a PBS documentary on the plight of the inner-cities." And why should it be otherwise? After all, NWA members have even admitted that some of their recent songs were not representations of reality "in the hood" but inspired by popular films like *Innocent Man* starring Tom Selleck and *Tango and Cash* starring Sylvester Stallone and Kurt Russell.[21]

While I'm fully aware that some rappers are merely "studio gangstas," and that the *primary* purpose of this music is to produce "funky dope rhymes" for our listening pleasure, we cannot ignore the fact that West Coast gangsta rap originated in, and continues to maintain ties to, the streets of L.A.'s black working-class communities. The generation that came of age in the 1980s was the product of devastating structural changes in the urban economy that date back at least to the late 1960s. While the city as a whole experienced unprecedented growth, the communities of Watts and Compton faced increased economic displacement, factory closures, and an unprecedented deepening of poverty. The uneven development of L.A.'s postindustrial economy meant an expansion of high-tech firms like Aerospace and Lockheed, and the disappearance of rubber and steel manufacturing firms, many of which were located in or near Compton and Watts. Deindustrialization, in other words, led to the establishment of high-tech firms in less populated regions like Silicon Valley and Orange County. Developers and local governments helped the suburbanization process while simultaneously cutting back expenditures for parks, recreation, and affordable housing in inner-city communities. Thus since 1980 economic conditions in Watts deteriorated on a greater scale than in any other L.A. community, and by some estimates Watts is in worse shape now than in 1965. A 1982 report from the California Legislature revealed that South Central neighborhoods experienced a 50 percent rise in unemployment while purchasing power dropped by one-third. The median income for South Central L.A.'s residents was a paltry $5,900—$2,500 below the median income for the black population a few years earlier.

Youth were the hardest hit. For all of Los Angeles County, the unemployment rate of black youth remained at about 45 percent, but in areas with concentrated poverty the rate was even higher. As the composition of L.A.'s urban poor becomes increasingly younger, programs for inner-city youth are being wiped out at an alarming rate. Both the Neighborhood Youth Corps and the Comprehensive Employment and Training Act (CETA) have been dismantled, and the Jobs Corps and Los Angeles Summer Job Program have been cut back substantially.[22]

Thus, on the eve of crack cocaine's arrival on the urban landscape, the decline in employment opportunities and growing immizeration of black youth in L.A. led to a substantial rise in property crimes committed by juveniles and young adults. Even NWA recalls the precrack illicit economy in a song titled "The Dayz of Wayback," in which Dr. Dre and M. C. Ren wax nostalgic about the early to mid-1980s, when criminal activity consisted primarily of small-time muggings and rob-beries.[23] Because of its unusually high crime rate, L.A. had by that time gained the dubious distinction of having the largest urban prison population in the country. When the crack economy made its pres-ence felt in inner-city black communities, violence intensified as vari-ous gangs and groups of peddlers battled for control over markets. In spite of the violence and financial vulnerability that went along with peddling crack, for many black youngsters it was the most viable eco-nomic option.[24]

While the rise in crime and the ascendance of the crack economy might have put money into some people's pockets, for the majority it meant greater police repression. Watts, Compton, Northwest Pasade-na, Carson, North Long Beach, and several other black working-class communities were turned into war zones during the mid- to late 1980s. Police helicopters, complex electronic surveillance, even small tanks armed with battering rams became part of this increasingly mili-tarized urban landscape. During this same period, housing projects, such as Imperial Courts, were renovated along the lines of minimum security prisons and equipped with fortified fencing and an LAPD substation. Imperial Court residents were now required to carry iden-tity cards and visitors were routinely searched. As popular media cov-erage of the inner city associated drugs and violence with black youth, young African Americans by virtue of being residents in South Central L.A. and Compton were subject to police harassment and, in some cases, feared by older residents.[25]

All of these problems generated penetrating critiques by gangsta rappers. M. C. Ren, for example, blamed "the people who are holding the dollars in the city" for the expansion of gang violence and crime, arguing that if black youth had decent jobs, they would not need to participate in the illicit economy. "It's their fault simply because they refused to employ black people. How would you feel if you went for job after job and each time, for no good reason, you're turned down?"[26] Ice T blames capitalism entirely, which he defines as much more than alienating wage labor; the marketplace itself as well as a va-riety of social institutions are intended to exercise social control over African Americans. "Capitalism says you must have an upper class, a middle class, and a lower class. . . . Now the only way to guarantee a lower class, is to keep y'all uneducated and as high as possible."[27] According to Ice T, the ghetto is, at worst, the product of deliberately oppressive policies, at best, the result of racist neglect. Nowhere is this clearer than in his song "Escape from the Killing Fields," which uses the title of a recent film about the conflict in Cambodia as a metaphor for the warlike conditions in today's ghettos.[28]

Gangsta rappers construct a variety of first-person narratives to illustrate how social and economic realities in late capitalist L.A. affect young black men. Although the use of first-person narratives is rooted in a long tradition of black aesthetic practices,[29] the use of "I" to signify both personal and collective experiences also enables gangsta rappers to navigate a complicated course between what social scientists call "structure" and "agency." In gangsta rap there is almost always a relationship between the conditions in which these characters live and the decisions they make. Some gangsta rappers—Ice Cube in particular—are especially brilliant at showing how, if I may paraphrase Marx, young urban black men make their own history but not under circumstances of their own choosing.

"Broke Niggas Make the Best Crooks"[30]

The press is used to make the victim look like the criminal
and make the criminal look like the victim.
—MALCOLM X, "Not Just an American Problem"[31]

In an era when popular media, conservative policy specialists, and some social scientists are claiming that the increase in street crime can be explained by some pathological culture of violence bereft of the moderating influences of a black middle class (who only recently fled to the suburbs), L.A.'s gangsta rappers keep returning to the idea that joblessness and crime are directly related.[32] Consider W.C. and the MAAD Circle's manifesto on the roots of inner-city crime. Its title, "If You Don't Work, U Don't Eat," appropriates Bobby Byrd's late 1960s' hit song of the same title (it, too, is sampled), and replicates a very popular Old Left adage. Describing the song in a recent interview, W.C. explained the context in which it was conceived: "I've got to feed a family. Because I don't have [job] skills I have no alternative but to turn this way. My little girl don't take no for an answer, my little boy don't take no for an answer, my woman's not going to take no for an answer, so I gotta go out and make my money."[33] In the song, members from his own crew as well as guest artists (M. C. Eiht from Compton's Most Wanted [CMW] and J.D. from Ice Cube's posse, Da Lench Mob) each give their own personal perspective on how they (or their character) became criminals. For MAAD Circle rapper Coolio, crime is clearly a means of survival, though he is fully cognizant that each job he pulls might lead to death or incarceration.[34] M. C. Eiht (pronounced "eight") of CMW openly declares that crime is his way of resisting wage labor ("I ain't punchin' a clock"), but admits with some remorse that his victims are usually regular black folk in the hood. Unless conditions change, he insists, neighborhood crime will continue to be a way of life.[35]

Ice Cube's "A Bird in the Hand," from his controversial album *Death Certificate*, is about the making of a young drug peddler. In this narrative, Cube plays a working-class black man just out of high school who can't afford college and is consistently turned down for medium-wage service-sector jobs. Because he is also a father trying to provide financial support for his girlfriend and their baby, he decides to take the only "slave" (job) available—at McDonald's. As the bass line is thumpin' over well-placed samples of screaming babies in the background, Ice Cube looks for another way out. It does not take much reflection for him to realize that the drug dealers are the only people in his neighborhood making decent money. Although his immediate material conditions improve, he now must face constant hounding from police and the mass media: "Now you put the feds against me/ Cause I couldn't follow the plan of the presidency/ I'm never gettin' love again/ But blacks are too fuckin' broke to be Republican." In the end, the blame for the rapid expansion of crack is placed squarely on the Bush administration. "Sorry, but this is our only room to walk/ Cause we don't want to drug push/ But a bird in the hand, is worth more than a Bush."[36]

The characters in gangsta narratives defy our attempts to define them as Robin Hoods or "criminal-criminals."[37] The very same voices we hear "jackin'" (robbing) other brothers and sisters occasionally call on male gangsters to turn their talents against the state. In "Get up off that Funk," W.C. and the MAAD Circle take a sort of Robin Hood stand, declaring that their own agenda includes jackin' the powerful and distributing the wealth. Rapping over a heavy bass and trap drum, reminiscent of the hardcore "go-go" music one hears in the darker side of the nation's capital, W.C. describes the Minority Alliance of Anti-Discrimination as an organization intent on stealing from the rich to give "to the poor folks in the slums."[38]

Ice Cube takes the Robin Hood metaphor a step further, calling for the "ultimate drive-by" to be aimed at the U.S. government. In a recent interview, he even suggested that gang bangers "are our warriors. . . . It's just they're fighting the wrong gang." The gang they ought to be fighting, he tells us, is "the government of the United States."[39] "I Wanna Kill Sam" on his album *Death Certificate* is his declaration of gang warfare on America. It begins with Cube loading up his "gat" in anticipation of taking out the elusive Uncle Sam. Following a brief interlude—a fictional public service announcement on behalf of the Armed Services—Cube gives us his own version of American history in which the slave trade, forced labor in the era of freedom, and army recruitment are all collapsed into a single narrative of racist repression and exploitation. He then connects the "pasts" to the present, suggesting that while the same old racism still lingers, the victims are unwilling to accept the terms of order. Instead of retreats and nonviolent protests, there will be straight jackin', gangsta style. Da Lench Mob's "Guerrillas in tha Midst" takes its title from an infamous LAPD term describing African Americans in the vicinity, which itself puns on the popular film set in Africa titled *Gorillas in the Mist*. But for Da Lench Mob, the "gorillas" are America's nightmare, organized and armed gangstas ready for the Big Payback.[40]

Of course, the idea of street gangs like the Crips and Bloods becoming a revolutionary guerrilla army seems ludicrous, especially given the role street gangs have assumed as protectors of the illicit economy. Consider the words of a Chicano gang member from Los Angeles: "I act like they do in the big time, no different. There ain't no corporation that acts with morals and that ethics shit and I ain't about to either. As they say, if it's good for General Motors, it's good enough for me."[41] Hardly the stuff one would expect from an inner-city rebel. Nevertheless, we need to keep in mind that the hip hop generation consumed movies like *The Spook Who Sat by the Door*, a film version of Sam Greenlee's novel about a former black CIA agent who uses his training to turn gang members into a revolutionary army. *The Autobiography of Malcolm X* convinced unknown numbers of kids that even second-rate gangsters can become political radicals. It's possible that a few black Angelenos absorbed some OG oral history about the gang roots of the Black Panther Party. L.A. Panther leaders Bunchy Carter and John Huggins were former members of the Slausons gang, and their fellow banger, Brother Crook (aka Ron Wilkins), founded the Community Alert Patrol to challenge police brutality in the late 1960s. And the postrebellion role of gang leaders in drafting and proposing the first viable plan of action to rebuild South Central Los Angeles cannot be overlooked. Indeed, much like today, both the presence of the Nation of Islam and the rise in police brutality played pivotal roles in politicizing individual gang members.[42]

By treating crime as a mode of survival and as a form of rebellion, gangsta rappers partly serve to idealize criminal activity. However, they also use the same narrative strategies—the use of first-person autobiographical accounts or the ostensibly more objective "street journalism"—to criticize inner-city crime and violence. Songs like Ice T's "Pain," "6 in the Mornin,'" "Colors," "New Jack Hustler," and "High Rollers"; Ice Cube's "Dead Homiez" and "Color Blind"; NWA's "Alwayz into Somethin'"; Cypress Hill's "Hand on the Pump" and "Hole in the Head"; and the gangsta groups that participated in making "We're All in the Same Gang" express clear messages that gang banging and jackin' for a living usually ends in death or incarceration—that is, if you're caught.[43] CPO's "The Wall" (as well as "The Movement," and sections from "Gangsta Melody"), performed by their quick-tongued lead lyricist Lil Nation, rail against drive-by shootings, the rising rate of black-on-black homicide, and brothers who try to escape reality by "Cold drinkin' 8-ball." Lil Nation even breaks with the majority of his fellow gangsta rappers by announcing that black youth today need more religion, a better set of values, and a radical social movement.[44]

Most gangsta rappers, however, are not so quick to criticize violence, arguing that it is the way of the street. This reticence is certainly evident in Ice Cube's advice that "if you is or ain't a gang banger/ keep one in the chamber" as well as his tongue-in-cheek call to replace guard dogs with guns ("A Man's Best Friend"). Even his anti-gang song, "Color Blind," implies that inner-city residents should be armed and ready in the event of a shoot-out or attempted robbery.

Likewise, MAAD Circle rappers Coolio and W.C. emphasize the need for protection. Although they both agree that gang banging will ultimately lead to death or prison, they also realize that "rolling with a crew" serves the same purpose as carrying a gun. As Coolio points out, "They say on the radio and TV that you have a choice, but it's bullshit. If you're getting your ass whipped everyday, you've got to have some protection."[45]

The gendering of crime also helps explain why gangsta rappers are reluctant to denounce violence, why the criminals in their narratives are almost always men, and why, in part, violence against women appears consistently in the music of many gangsta groups. As criminologist James Messerschmidt reminds us, "Throughout our society . . . violence is associated with power and males, and for some youth this association is reinforced as part of family life. As a result, most young males come to identify the connection between masculinity-power-aggression-violence as part of their own developing male identities." Being a man, therefore, means not "taking any shit" from anyone, which is why the characters in gangsta rap prefer to use a gat rather than flee the scene, and why drive-by shootings are often incited by public humiliations. Second, although it might be argued that men dominate these narratives because they construct them, it is also true that the preponderance of street crime is committed by marginalized males. The matter is far too complicated to discuss in detail here, but several scholars attribute these patterns to higher rates of male unemployment, greater freedom from the restraints of the household compared to females (i.e., more opportunities to engage in criminal activity), and a patriarchal culture that makes earning power a measure of manhood.[46]

The misogyny of gangsta rap is deeply ingrained. Most gangsta rappers take violence against women for granted. It is primarily the dark, nasty side of *male-on-male* street violence that they attempt to illustrate. Sir Jinx's use of documentary-style recordings of simulated drive-by's and fights that escalate into gun battles are intended to deromanticize gang violence.[47] A much more clear-cut example is CMW's "Drive By Miss Daisy," a powerful, complex depiction of the ways in which ordinary bystanders can become victims of intergang warfare. The story begins with a young man assigned to assassinate a rival gangbanger who had just killed his homie. Afraid and intimidated, he decides to get drunk before calling his posse together for the drive-by. When they finally pull up in front of the house, he is apparently unaware that the boy's mother is in the kitchen cooking dinner. Just before he pulls the trigger his conscience intervenes for a second and he questions the morality of his actions. But because of gang loyalty, he does the deed just the same.

What makes the song so compelling is its music. Although CMW had already established a reputation among gangsta rappers for employing more laid-back jazz and quiet storm tracks than hardcore funk, their choice of music in "Drive By" was clearly intended to heighten the intensity rather than provide an understated backdrop for their lead rapper. Thus we hear straight-ahead modal jazz circa 1960s—heavy ride and crash cymbals and acoustic bass beneath the laid-back and strangely cartoonish, high-pitched voice of M. C. Eiht. The two instrumental interludes are even more powerful. The bass and cymbal combination is violently invaded by an acoustic piano playing strong, dissonant block chords very much in the vein of Don Pullen or Stanley Cowell. Mixed in are the sounds of automatic weapons, a looped sample of blood-curdling screams that has the effect of creating an echo without reverberation, and samples of would-be assassins hollering "you die motherfucker." This disturbing cacophony of sounds all at once captures the fragility of human life, the chaos of violent death, and the intensity of emotions young murderers and their victims must feel.[48]

Ice Cube's "Dead Homiez" uses a graveyard to reflect on the tragedy of inner-city homicide. An able storyteller, he is especially effective at painting a detailed picture of his homie's funeral, interrupting periodically with loving as well as frustrating memories of his dead friend. No matter how many forty-ounce bottles of malt liquor he downs, his friend's death continues to haunt him: "Still hear the screams from his mother/as my nigger lay dead in the gutter." The anger, pain, confusion, and fear of those left behind are all inscribed in the ritual of mourning.[49]

Drug dealers have been a common target of gangsta rap from the beginning. One of NWA's very first releases, "Dope Man," offers some brutal insights into the effects of the rising crack cocaine economy. Screamed over electronic drum tracks and a Middle Eastern–sounding reed instrument, Dr. Dre first declares that "If you smoke 'caine you a stupid motherfucker" and then goes on to describe some name-less "crackhead" whose habit forced him into a life of crime.[50] CPO's "The Movement" and "The Wall" wage frontal attacks on all pushers, whom he accuses of committing genocide against black people; he advocates a social movement to wipe them out, since law enforcement is half-hearted and the justice system both inept and corrupt.[51]

Because most gangsta rappers simultaneously try to explain why people turn to drug dealing and other assorted crimes, and vehemently attack drug dealers for the damage they do to poor black communities, they have often been accused of being inconsistent, contradictory, or even schizophrenic. For example, on the same album with "A Bird in the Hand," Ice Cube includes an uncompromising attack on drug dealers, calling them "killers" and insisting that they exploit black people "like the caucasians did."[52] That Cube finds nothing redeeming in the activities of crack peddlers underscores the point that his descriptions are not intended as advocacy. His effort to explain why the drug trade is so appealing to some inner-city residents is not an uncritical acceptance of it. Indeed, "My Summer Vacation," a third song on his *Death Certificate* album about the crack economy, not only reveals the immense violence that goes along with carving out new markets, but borrows from typical images of legitimate entrepreneurship to argue that legal and illicit capitalism are two sides of the same coin—both are ruthless, exploitative, and often produce violence. The point is certainly not to glorify violence. Similarly, Ice T, in "New Jack Hustler," not only suffers from a "capitalist migraine" but asks if the luxury he enjoys as a big-time drug dealer is "a nightmare, or the American dream?" His implication is clear, for this particular enterprise leads to death, destruction, and violence rather than accumulation and development.[53]

Let me not overstate my case, for these economic critiques resist labels. The recasting of capitalism as gangsterism is not simply intended to legitimate the illicit economy or de-legitimate capitalist exploitation. Gangsta rappers discuss capitalism in varying contexts, and to portray them as uniformly or consistently anticapitalist would certainly misrepresent them. All groups emphasize getting paid and, in real life, the more successful artists invest in their own production companies. They understand better than their audiences that music is a business and rapping is a job. At the same time, being paid for their work does not mean they accept the current economic arrangements or think their music lacks integrity. On the contrary, for many black and Latino working-class youth who turned to hip hop music, rapping, deejaying, or producing is a means to avoid low-wage labor or, possibly, incarceration. As Cube said of his own crew, "You can either sell dope or get your ass a job/ I'd rather roll with the Lench Mob."[54]

Their ambivalence toward capitalism notwithstanding, gangsta rappers are consistent about tracing criminal behavior and vicious individualism to mainstream American culture. Contrary to the new "culture of poverty" theorists who claim that the lifestyles of the so-called black "underclass" constitute a significant deviation from mainstream values, most gangsta rappers insist that the characters they rap about epitomize what America has been and continues to be. In challenging the equation of criminality with some sort of "underclass" culture, Ice T retorts, "America stole from the Indians, sure and prove/What's that? A straight up nigga move!" Similarly, in "AmeriKKKa's Most Wanted," Ice Cube considers crime as American as apple pie: "It's the American way/ I'm a G-A-N-G-S-T-A." He even takes a swipe at the purest of American popular heroes, Superman. The man who stands for Truth, Justice, and the American Way is appropriated and then inverted as Public Enemy Number 1. From Ice Cube's perspective, Superman is a hero because the Americanism he represents is nothing but gangsterism. Donning the cape himself, Cube declares, "I'm not a rebel or a renegade on a quest, I'm a Nigga with an 'S'/So in case you get the kryptonite/I'm gonna rip tonight cause I'm scaring ya/ Wanted by America."[55]

These artists are even less ambiguous when applying the gangster metaphor to the people and institutions that control their lives—especially politicians, the state, and police departments. Ice T's "Street Killer," for example, is a brief monologue that sounds like the boasts of a heartless gangbanger but turns out to be a cop. In a recent interview, Coolio and W.C. of the MAAD Circle reverse the dominant discourse about criminals, insisting that the powerful, not powerless, ghetto dwellers, are the real gangsters:

COOLIO: Who's the real gangsta, the brotha with the khakis on, the brotha with the Levis on or the muthafucka in the suit? Who's the real gangsta?

W.C.: Well, the suit is running the world, that's the real gangsta right there.[56]

Dozens of rap artists, both inside and outside L.A., indict "America" for stealing land, facilitating the drug trade either through inaction or active participation of the CIA and friendly dictators, and waging large-scale "drive-by shootings" against little countries such as Panama and Iraq. In the aftermath of the L.A. uprising, while politicians and media spokespersons called black participants "criminals" and "animals," Ice Cube reminded whoever would listen that, "The looting . . . in South-Central was nothing like the looting done by the savings and loans." Cube's video for "Who's the Mack," which reveals a photo of George Bush playing golf over the caption "President Mack" and a graffiti American flag with skull and crossbones replacing the stars, further underscored the argument that violence and gangsterism are best exemplified by the state, not young inner-city residents.[57]

Police repression remains gangsta rap's primary target. We must bear in mind that this subgenre was born amidst the militarization of Compton, Watts, and other black communities like Southgate, Carson, Northwest Pasadena, Paramount, and North Long Beach, which became the battlefields of the so-called "war on drugs" in L.A. The recasting of South Central as an American war zone was brought to us on NBC Nightly News, in Dan Rather's special report "48 Hours: On Gang Street," and in Hollywood films like *Colors* and *Boyz in the Hood*. *Straight Outta Compton*, for example, was released about the time Chief Darryl Gates implemented "Operation HAMMER," when almost 1,500 black youth in South Central were picked up for merely "looking suspicious." While most were charged with minor offenses like curfew and traffic violations, some were not charged at all but simply had their names and addresses logged in the LAPD antigang task force data base.[58] In this context NWA released their now classic anthem, "F——Tha Police." Opening with a mock trial in which NWA is the judge and jury and the police are the defendants, each member of the group offers his own testimony. After promising to tell "the whole truth and nothing but the truth," Ice Cube takes the stand and explodes with an indictment against racism, repression, and the common practice of criminalizing all black youth. NWA emphasizes the fact that police repression is no longer a simple matter of white racists with a badge, for black cops are just as bad, if not worse, than white cops.[59]

L.A. rappers have since expanded their critique of the relationship between police repression and their own political and economic powerlessness. Ice Cube's solo effort, NWA's most recent album, and groups like Compton's Most Wanted ("They Still Gafflin"), Cypress Hill ("Pigs" and "How I Could Just Kill a Man"), Kid Frost ("I Got Pulled Over" and "Penitentiary") to name but a few, try to place their descriptions of police repression within a broader context of social control.[60] "One Time's" or "Five-O's," as the police are called in L.A., are portrayed as part of a larger system of racist and class domination that includes black officers. For W.C. and the MAAD Circle, policing as a form of racial and class oppression is part of a longer historical tradition etched in the collective memory of African Americans. "Behind Closed Doors" begins with lead rapper W.C. writing a letter of complaint to the chief of police describing an incident in which he was beaten and subsequently shot by officers with no provocation. In just a few lines, W.C. links antebellum slavery and depression-era fascism to the more recent police beating of Rodney King.[61]

Mirroring much current political discourse in urban black America, some gangsta rappers implicitly or explicitly suggest that police repression is a genocidal war against black men.[62] "Real Niggaz Don't Die," which samples the Last Poets' live performance of "Die Nigger," and Ice Cube's "Endangered Species (Tales from the Darkside)" construct black males as the prey of vicious, racist police officers. Cube's lyrics underscore the point that the role of law enforcement is to protect the status quo and keep black folks in check:

Every cop killer goes ignored,
They just send another nigger to the morgue.
A point scored. They could give a fuck about us.
They'd rather catch us with guns and white powder.

They'll kill ten of me to get the job correct
To serve, protect, and break a nigga's neck[63]

In the title track of *AmeriKKKa's Most Wanted*, in which Ice Cube assumes the role of an inner-city criminal who ventures into the suburbs, he closes the song having learned a valuable lesson about community differences in policing: "I think back when I was robbing my own kind/The police didn't pay it no mind/But when I started robbing the white folks/Now I'm in the pen with the soap on the rope."

"Behind Closed Doors" by W.C. and the MAAD Circle speaks to the less dramatic incidents of police repression that frequently have greater resonance among black youth. In one of the stories, Circle rapper Coolio is a recently discharged ex-convict working hard to survive legitimately, until he is stopped and harassed for no apparent reason by "the same crooked cop from a long time ago/ Who planted an ounce in my homie's El Camino." He and the cop exchange blows, but instead of taking him into custody the officer and his partner decide to drop him off in hostile gang territory in order to incite violence. Coolio's narrative is more than plausible: among the tactics adopted by Chief Darryl Gates in his antigang sweeps was to draw out gang bangers by "leaving suspects on enemy turfs, writing over Crip graffiti with Blood colors (or vice versa) and spreading incendiary rumors."[64]

Even more common to the collective experience of young black residents of L.A.'s inner city was the police policy of identifying presumably suspicious characters on the basis of clothing styles. Indeed, officers who were part of the Gang Related Active Trafficker Suppression program were told to "interrogate anyone who they suspect is a gang member, basing their assumptions on their dress or their use of gang hand signals."[65] Opposition to this kind of marking, along the lines of a battle for the right to free expression and unfettered mobility in public spaces, has been a central subtheme in gangsta rap's discursive war of position against police repression. In CMW's cut "Still Gafflin," lead rapper M. C. Eiht complains that the police are "on my dick trying to jack me/ I guess because I sport a hat and the khakis." Perhaps the sharpest critique is W.C. and the MAAD Circle's "Dress Code." Directed at ordinary white citizens, club owners, as well as police officers, the Circle tell stories of being stereotyped as common criminals or gang bangers by complete strangers, all of whom presume that "If you dress like me, you gotta run with a crew." Clothing also signifies status, as is evident in the way W.C. is treated when he tries to get into a club: "Got a wear a silk shirt/ just to dance to a funky song." Nevertheless, he and his crew not only refuse to apologize for their appearance, insisting all along that young working-class black men have the right to dress as they please without being treated with fear or contempt, but W.C. also attributes his style to his class position. Because he "can't afford to shop at Macy's or Penney's . . . its off to the swap meet for a fresh pair of dicky's [khaki pants]."[66]

Of course, style politics are much more complicated. Even the most impoverished black youth do not choose styles solely on the basis of what is affordable. Young men wear the starter jackets, hoodies, L.A. Raiders caps, baggy khaki pants, and occasionally gold chains not only because they are in style, but because it enables them to create their own identity—one that defines them as rebels. While clothes are not intrinsically rebellious, young people give them what Dick Hebdige identifies as "'secret' meanings: meanings which express, in code, a form of resistance to the order which guarantees their continued subordination."[67] It is naive to believe, for example, that black youth merely sport Raiders paraphernalia because they are all hardcore fans. Besides, as soon as NWA and more recent L.A. groups came on the scene sporting Raiders caps, the style became even more directly associated with the gangsta rappers than with the team itself, and the police regarded the caps, beanies, hoods, and starter jackets as gang attire.

What we need always to keep in mind is the degree of self-consciousness with which black urban youth—most of whom neither are gang members nor engage in violent crime—insist on wearing the styles that tend to draw police attention. By associating certain black youth styles with criminality, violence, and (indirectly) police repression, the dominant media unintentionally popularize these styles among young men who reinterpret these images as acts of rebellion or outright racist terror.[68] The styles also suggest an implicit acceptance of an "outlaw" status that capitalist transformation and the militarization of black Los Angeles have brought about. Hence the adoption and recasting of "G" as a friendly form of address used by young African American men and, to a lesser degree, women. While the origins of "G" apparently go back to the Five-Percent Nation (a fairly unorthodox Black Muslim youth group) on the East Coast where it was an abbreviation for "God," among youth in California and elsewhere it currently stands for "gangsta."[69] Finally, my own discussions with black youth in L.A. reveal that the black and silver Los

Angeles Kings caps, associated with artists like King Tee, NWA, and other gangsta groups, have become even more popular following the King beating and the subsequent uprising—and hockey clearly has nothing to do with it. These caps signify very powerfully that all young African Americans are potential "L.A. [Rodney] Kings."[70]

In the streets of Los Angeles, as well as in other cities across the country, hip hop's challenge to police brutality sometimes moves beyond the discursive arena. Their music and expressive styles have literally become weapons in a battle over the right to occupy public space. Frequently employing high-decibel car stereos and boom boxes, black youth not only "pump up the volume" for their own listening pleasure, but also as part of an indirect, ad hoc war of position. The "noise" constitutes a form of cultural resistance that should not be ignored, especially when we add those resistive lyrics about destroying the state or retaliating against the police. Imagine a convertible Impala or a Suzuki pulling up alongside a "black and white," pumping the revenge fantasy segment of Ice Cube's "The Wrong Nigga to F——Wit" which promises to break Chief Darryl Gates's "spine like a jelly fish" or Cypress Hill vowing to turn "pigs" into "sausage."[71] Hip hop producers have increased the stakes by pioneering technologies that extend and "fatten" the bass in order to improve clarity at higher volume (appropriately called "jeep beats"). We cannot easily dismiss Ice Cube when he declares, "I'm the one with a trunk of funk/ and 'Fuck the Police' in the tape deck."[72]

For gangsta rappers, and black urban youth more generally, the police are a small part of an oppressive criminal justice system. The fact that, in 1989, 23 percent of black males ages twenty to twenty-nine were either behind bars or on legal probation or parole, has been a central political issue in the hip hop community. The combination of rising crime rates and longer sentencing has led to a rapid increase in the black prison population in the United States, and there is substantial evidence that racial bias is partly responsible; studies have shown, for example, that black men convicted of the same crime as whites receive longer sentences on average. The racial inequities were even more pronounced for juvenile offenders; during the last two decades, whereas most African American juveniles ended up in prisonlike public detention centers, white youths were more likely to end up in private institutions (halfway houses, shelters, group homes, etc.) that encouraged rehabilitation, skill development, and family interaction.[73]

With rising rates of incarceration for young black males, life behind bars has become a major theme in gangsta narratives. Through thick descriptions of prison life and samples of the actual voices of convicts (e.g., Ice T's "The Tower," W.C. and the MAAD Circle's "Out on a Furlough," and Kid Frost's "The Penitentiary") gangsta rappers come close to providing what Michel Foucault calls a "counter-discourse of prisoners." As Foucault explains, "when prisoners began to speak, they possessed an individual theory of prisons, the penal system, and justice. It is this form of discourse which ultimately matters, a discourse against power, the counter-discourse of prisoners and those we call delinquents—and not a theory *about* delinquency."[74] Most rappers—especially gangsta rappers—treat prisons as virtual fascist institutions. At the end of his *OG* album, Ice T suggests that prisons constitute a form of modern-day bondage. "They say slavery has been abolished except for the convicted felon." Moreover, mirroring the sentiments of a significant segment of the black community, several rappers suggest that the high incarceration rate of black males is part of a conspiracy. In "The Nigga Ya Love to Hate," Ice Cube asks aloud, "why [are] there more niggas in the pen than in college?"[75] He even suggests in "The Product" that prison is the inevitable outcome for young black men who fail or refuse to conform to the dominant culture. Inmates, he argues, are "products" of joblessness, police repression, and an inferior and racist educational system.[76]

Gangsta rappers tend toward a kind of "scared straight" approach to describing actual prison life. But unlike, say, the "Lifer's Group," their descriptions of prison are not intended merely to deter black youth from crime, for that would imply an acceptance of prisons as primarily institutions to punish and reform "criminals." Instead, their descriptions of prison life essentially reverse the popular image of black prisoners as "Willie Horton" and paint a richer portrait of inmates as real human beings trying to survive under inhuman conditions. While they do not ignore the physical and sexual violence[77] between prisoners, they do suggest that prison conditions are at the root of such behavior. Again, we return to "The Product":

Livin' in a concrete ho house,
Where all the products go, no doubt.
Yo, momma, I got to do eleven,
Livin' in a five by seven.
Dear babe, your man's gettin worn out
Seeing young boys gettin' their assholes torn out.

It's driving me batty,
Cause my little boy is missing daddy.
I'm ashamed but the fact is,
I wish pops let me off on the mattress [i.e., wishes he
was never conceived.]
Or should I just hang from the top bunk?
But that's going out like a punk.
My life is fucked. But it ain't my fault
Cause I'm a motherfuckin' product.

Ice T's "The Tower" suggests that violence between inmates, especially racial conflict, is permitted if not instigated by guards and adminis-
trators as a means of controlling "the yard." The song consists of
several first-person anecdotes rapped over a haunting synthesized cel-
lo track and punctuated by "audio verité" samples of presumably authentic prisoners telling their own stories of violence in the pen. By
focusing on prison architecture rather than the inmates themselves,
the video for "The Tower" emphasizes how the structural and spatial
arrangements themselves reproduce the prisoners' powerlessness. After each verse, Ice T asks "who had the power?/ The whites, the
blacks, or just the gun tower?"[78]

The criminalization, surveillance, incarceration, and immizeration
of black youth in the postindustrial city have been the central theme
in gangsta rap, and at the same time, sadly, constitute the primary experiences from which their identities are constructed. Whereas Afrocentric rappers build an imagined community by invoking images of
ancient African civilizations, gangsta rappers are more prone to follow
Eric B. and Rakim's dictum, "It ain't where you're from, it's where
you're at." When they are not describing prison or death, they describe daily life in the "ghetto"—an overcrowded world of deteriorating tenement apartments or tiny cement block, prisonlike "projects,"

streets filthy from the lack of city services, liquor stores and billboards selling malt liquor and cigarettes. The construction of the "ghetto" as a living nightmare and "gangstas" as products of that nightmare has given rise to what I call a new "Ghettocentric" identity in which the specific class, race, and gendered experiences in late capitalist urban centers coalesce to create a new identity—"Nigga."

Niggas in Post–Civil Rights America

I'm a nigger, not a colored man or a black
    or a Negro or an Afro-American—I'm all that
Yes, I was born in America too.
But does South Central look like America to you?
—ICE T, "Straight Up Nigga"[79]

Perhaps the most soulful word in the world is "nigger."
—CLAUDE BROWN, "The Language of Soul"[80]

Gangsta rappers have drawn a lot of fire for their persistent use of "Nigga." Even the *New York Times* and popular magazines like *Emerge* have entered the debate, carrying articles about the growing popularity of the "N" word among young people. Rap artists are accused of inculcating self-hatred and playing into white racism. Yet those who insist that the use of "Nigga" in rap demonstrates self-hatred and ignorance of African American history do not generally impose the same race-conscious litmus test to black folklore, oral histories, ordinary vernacular speech, or other cultural traditions where "nigger" is used as a neutral or even friendly appellation. In these latter circumstances, "nigger" was/is uttered and interpreted among black folk within a specific, clearly defined context, tone, and set of "codes" rooted in black vernacular language. As anthropologist Claudia Mitchell-Kernan explained, "the use of 'nigger' with other black English markers has the effect of 'smiling when you say that.' The use of standard English with 'nigger,' in the words of an informant, is 'the wrong tone of voice' and may be taken as abusive." Very few African Americans would point to such dialogues as examples of "self-hatred." This is what Ice Cube was trying to get at in an interview: "Look, when we call each other nigger it means no harm, in fact, in

Compton, it's a friendly word. But if a white person uses it, it's something different, it's a racist word."[81]

To comprehend the politics of Ghettocentricity, we must understand the myriad ways in which the most Ghettocentric segments of the West Coast hip hop community have employed the term "Nigga." Gangsta rappers, in particular, are struggling to ascribe new, potentially empowering meanings to the word. Indeed, the increasingly common practice of spelling it "N-i-g-g-a" suggests a revisioning. For example, Bay Area rapper and former Digital Underground member, 2Pac (Tupac Shakur), insists in his first album that Nigga stands for "Never Ignorant, Getting Goals Accomplished."[82] More common, however, is the use of "Nigga" to describe a condition rather than skin color or culture. Above all, Nigga speaks to a collective identity shaped by class consciousness, the character of inner-city space, police repression, poverty, and the constant threat of intraracial violence. Part of NWA's "Niggaz4Life," for instance, uses "Nigga" almost as a synonym for oppressed.[83]

In other words, Nigga is not merely *another* word for black. Products of the postindustrial ghetto, the characters in gangsta rap constantly remind listeners that they are still second-class citizens—"Niggaz"—whose collective experiences suggest that nothing has changed *for them* as opposed to the black middle class. In fact, Nigga is frequently employed to distinguish urban black working-class males from the black bourgeoisie and African Americans in positions of institutional authority. Their point is simple: the experiences of young black men in the inner city are not universal to all black people, and, in fact, they recognize that some African Americans play a role in perpetuating their oppression. To be a "real nigga" is to be a product of the ghetto. By linking their identity to the "'hood" instead of simply skin color, gangsta rappers implicitly acknowledge the limitations of racial politics, including black middle-class reformism as well as black nationalism. Again, this is not new. "Nigger" as a signifier of class and race oppression has been a common part of black rural and working-class language throughout the twentieth century, if not longer. In fact, because of its power to distinguish the black urban poor from upwardly mobile middle-class blacks, "Nigger" made a huge comeback at the height of the Black Power movement. Robert DeCoy's infamous book, *The Nigger Bible*, published in 1967, distinguishes "Nigger" from "Negroes"—the latter a derogatory term for sellouts. DeCoy defined "Negro" as a "vulgar but accepted description of the Nigrite or Nigger. Referring to an American Nigger of decency and status. A White-Nigger. Or a brainwashed Black who would be Caucasian if possible . . ." And one Los Angeles–based black nationalist artist's collective, the Ashanti Art Service, launched a journal called *Nigger Uprising* in 1968.[84]

Perhaps not since the days of blues singer "Leadbelly" has the word "bourgeois" been so commonly used by black musicians. It has become common lingo among hip hop artists to refer to black-owned radio stations and, more generally, middle-class African Americans who exhibit disgust or indifference toward young, working-class blacks. For Ice T, living in the lap of luxury is not what renders the black bourgeoisie bankrupt, but rather their inability to understand the world of the ghetto, black youth culture, and rap music. In an interview a few years back he explained, "I don't think the negative propaganda about rap comes from the true black community—it comes from the bourgeois black community, which I hate. Those are the blacks who have an attitude that because I wear a hat and a gold chain, I'm a nigger and they're better than me." More recently, on his album *The Iceberg/Freedom of Speech . . . Just Watch What You Say*, he expressed similar sentiments: "I'm trying to save my community, but these bourgeois blacks keep on doggin' me. . . . You just a bunch of punk, bourgeois black suckers."[85] W.C. and the MAAD Circle level an even more sustained attack on those they call "bourgeois Negroes." Proclaiming that the Circle's sympathies lie with "poor folks in the slums," W.C. writes off suburban middle-class African Americans as turncoats and cowards.[86]

And to be fair, not only is there increasing intraracial class segregation with the suburbanization of the black middle class, but wealthy African Americans are often guilty of the kind of social labeling associated with white suburbanites and police. One need only visit predominantly black public spaces with considerable cross-class mixing (e.g., L.A.'s venerable Fox Hills Mall) to notice the considerable disdain many middle-class African Americans exhibit toward youth who are dressed a certain way or elect to walk in groups. Moreover, having come of age under a black mayor, black police officers, and a city council and legislature with a small but significant black presence,

L.A. gangsta rappers blame black politicians and authority figures as much as their white counterparts for the conditions that prevail in poor communities.[87]

L.A. gangsta rappers are frequent critics of black nationalists as well. They contend that the nationalists' focus on Africa—both past and present—obscures the daily battles poor black folk have to wage in contemporary America. In what proved to be a highly controversial statement, Eazy E declared: "Fuck that black power shit: we don't give a fuck. Free South Africa: we don't give a fuck. I bet there ain't nobody in South Africa wearing a button saying 'Free Compton' or 'Free California.'"[88] Ice Cube poses the same issue in "Endangered Species (Tales from the Darkside)," but in a less dismissive and more meaningful manner:

> You want to free Africa,
> I'll stare at ya'
> Cause we ain't got it too good in America.
> I can't fuck with 'em overseas
> My homeboy died over kee's [kilos of cocaine][89]

To say that gangsta rappers are *anti*nationalist overstates the case. Groups like CPO and, more recently, Ice Cube express some explicitly nationalist positions, though L.A. groups have shown less inclination than their East Coast counterparts to openly support the Nation of Islam or the Five-Percent Nation. West Coast gangsta groups tend to be more wary of nationalism given the real divisions that exist among African Americans, the Afrocentric celebration of a past which, to them, has no direct bearing on the present, and the hypocrisy and inconsistency exhibited by individual black nationalists. The last point is the subject of W.C. and the MAAD Circle's "Caught N' a Fad," wherein they tell the story of a hustler who joined the Nation and wore African garb because it was in style but never changed his ways. He was "popping that 'too black, too strong/ But he was the first to get the dice game going on." Likewise, in "The Nigga Ya Love to Hate" Ice Cube takes a swipe at the Afrocentrists who speak of returning to Africa: "All those motherfuckers who say they're too black/ Put 'em overseas, they be beggin' to come back."[90]

For all of its rebelliousness, Ghettocentricity, like Afrocentricity, draws its arsenal from the dominant ideology. As products of sustained violence, the characters in gangsta rap are constantly prepared to retaliate with violence, whether it's against a cop or another brother; those unwilling are considered "cowards," "punks," or as Ice T would say, "bitches." In other words, "real Niggaz" are not only victims of race and class domination but agents—dangerous agents, nightmarish caricatures of the worst of the dispossessed. What is most striking about gangsta rappers' construction of "Nigga" as the embodiment of violence is the extent to which this highly masculinist imagery draws from existing stereotypes. Once again, we find black youth subculture reconstructing dominant representations of who they are in order to "remake" their image in popular discourse.[91] Negative stereotypes of black men as violent, pathological, and lazy are recontextualized: criminal acts are turned into brilliant capers and a way to *avoid* work; white fears of black male violence become evidence of black power; fearlessness is treated as a measure of masculinity. A large part of Eazy E's repertoire has him proving his manhood and authenticity as a "real nigga" by bustin' caps on anyone who stands in his way.[92]

Following a long tradition of black humor, both Ice T and Eazy E appropriate and recast stereotypes of black men as hypersexual beings with large penises. Eazy explains that one of the reasons why he calls *himself* a "Nigga" is because he "can reach in my draws and pull out a bigger dick." Ice T, who refers to himself as a "White woman's dream/ Big dick straight up Nigger," combines several stereotypes in the following passage:

> I'm loud and proud,
> Well endowed with the big beef.
> Out on the corner,
> I hang out like a horse thief.
> So you can call me dumb or crazy,
> Ignorant, stupid, inferior, or lazy,
> Silly or foolish,
> But I'm badder and bigger,
> And most of all
> I'm a straight up Nigga.[93]

While the meanings of these appropriations and reversals of racial stereotypes constantly shift with different contexts, in many cases they ultimately reinforce dominant images of African Americans. Moreover, the kinds of stereotypes they choose to appropriate—hypermasculinity, sexual power, and violence as a "natural" response— not only reproduce male domination over women, but often do so in an especially brutal manner.

"Pimpin' Ain't Easy": Women in the Male Gangsta Imagination

To me, all bitches are the same: money-hungry, scandalous, groupie hos that's always riding on a nigger's dick, always in a nigger's pocket.

—EAZY E, "One Less Bitch"[94]

While young African American males are both products of and sometimes active participants in the creation of a new masculinist, antifeminist cultural current, we cannot be too quick to interpret sexist and misogynist lyrics as a peculiarly modern product. African American vernacular culture has a very long and ignoble tradition of sexism evidenced in daily language and other more formal variants such as "the dozens," "toasts," and the age-old "baaadman narratives." A word like "bitch," for example, was not suddenly imported into African American male vocabulary by rap music. In the late 1950s, it was such a common reference to women that folklorist Roger Abrahams, in his study of black oral culture in Philadelphia, added it to his glossary of terms as "Any woman. As used here, usually without usual pejorative connotations."[95] While his claim that the term was usually not pejorative is highly suspect, the pervasiveness of the term is clearly longstanding. Some of the toasts that are at least a few decades old are more venomous than much of what we find today in Hip Hop. In 1966, Bruce Jackson recorded a toast titled "The Lame and the Whore" in which a veteran pimp teaches a "weak" mack daddy how to treat his women:

Say, you got to rule that bitch,
you got to school that bitch,
you got to teach her the Golden Rule,
you got to stomp that bitch,
you got to tromp that bitch,

and use her like you would a tool.
You got to drive that bitch
and got to ride that bitch
like you would a motherfucken mule.

Then take the bitch out on the highway and drag her
until she's damn near dead.
Then take your pistol and shoot her
right through her motherfucken head.[96]

Aside from narratives that have been recovered by historians and folk-lorists, I personally remember having learned by heart "Imp the Skimp, the Tennis Shoe Pimp," a long first-person narrative in which we bragged incessantly of being "the baby maker/ the booty taker." "Imp" became part of my verbal repertoire around 1971; I was nine years old. Unlike rap music, however, our sexist and misogynist street rhymes were never discussed on Ted Koppel's *Nightline* because they never made it to wax; they remained where our mamas said they should—in the streets.[97]

But the story is a bit more complicated than black youth recording and distributing an oral tradition of "hustler poetry." During the late 1960s and early 1970s, as America became an increasingly "sexual-ized society," we witnessed an explosion of recorded sexually explicit comedy routines by black comics like Rudy Ray Moore, Redd Foxx, and Richard Pryor, as well as the publication and popularization of so-called genuine "pimp narratives." The *Pimp*, not just any "baaad-man," became an emblematic figure of the period, elevated to the sta-tus of hero and invoked by Hollywood as well as in the writings of black nationalist militants like H. Rap Brown, Eldridge Cleaver, Bobby Seale, and Huey P. Newton. Aside from film and popular literature, the Pimp appeared in a proliferation of sensationalist autobiogra-phies, scholarly ethnographies, and "urban folklore" collections of in-carcerated hustlers.[98]

Old school rappers like Ice T and Philly's Schooly D were strongly influenced by some of these published reminiscences of hustlers. Ice T recalls, "I used to read books by Iceberg Slim. . . . He would talk in rhyme—hustler-like stuff—and I would memorize lines." The classic recording of *Hustlers' Convention* in 1973 by an ex-prisoner who would eventually help found the Last Poets, and the celebrated status of the pimp in blaxploitation films also had a profound impact on gangsta rap.[99] In fact, the word "gangsta" is frequently used interchangeably with terms like "Pimp," "Mack Daddy," "Daddy Mack," and "Hustler." One can hear the influence of the pimp narratives and black comedians on several Ice T cuts, especially "Somebody's Gotta Do It [Pimpin' Ain't Easy]," "I Love Ladies," and "Sex," which were recorded on his first album, *Rhyme Pays*. Boasting about his ability to please women sexually, the number of women he sleeps with, and the money he is making in the process, these kinds of rhymes are not descriptions of social reality but recorded versions of what anthropologist Ulf Hannerz calls "streetcorner mythmaking" or what hip hop critic Dan Charnas simply calls "bullshit, schoolboy humor."[100]

The critical question, it seems to me, is why has the pimp returned to an exalted status in black male popular culture in the 1990s? Or more broadly, why has the pimp figured so prominently in the late 1960s/early 1970s and the late 1980s/early 1990s, periods of rising black nationalism and male backlash? I have to believe that the celebration of the pimp in popular culture during the Black Power era is in part a response to the image of black female dominance created by the Moynihan report. Perhaps young black men identified with the pimp because he represented the ultimate dominator, turning matriarchy on its head. Perhaps the valorization of the pimp was just another example of black militants celebrating a "lumpen" lifestyle.

As for the present, the pimp may have made such a strong return via gangsta rap because the dominant discourse—from conservatives to African American nationalists—demands the restoration of the patriarchal family. But why do gangsta rappers (not unlike other male hip hop performers) exhibit a profound fear of black female sexuality, which manifests itself as open distrust or, in some cases, an aggressive hatred, of women?[101]

Given the central place that misogyny occupies in the gangsta/ baaadman aesthetic, it would be hard to trust a straight sociological answer to this question. Furthermore, I do not believe rap music can or ever intended to represent the true and complex character of male/female relations among black urban youth. Too many critics have taken the easy way out by reading rap lyrics literally rather than developing a nuanced understanding of actual social relations among young people, in all of their diversity and complexity. And there is no reason in the world to believe that any music constitutes a mirror of social relations that can be generalized for entire groups of people.

Nevertheless, I do think that there is a specific social context that provides some insights into the *popularity* of gangsta rap and the particular forms its misogyny takes. For example, although the "traditional" family itself might be fading, neither the ideology of male dominance nor the kinds of economic negotiations that have always been a part of intrafamily conflict have disappeared. As is evident in both contemporary popular culture and current policy debates, the last decade or so has witnessed a reassertion of masculinity and the increasing commodification of sexual relations. Moreover, gangsta rappers, the mass media, and mainstream black leadership commonly cast the problems of the inner city as a problem of black males, even if their interpretations differ. Some intellectuals and politicians propose saving the "underclass" by eliminating welfare, retraining young black men in all-male schools, and reinstituting the nuclear family, implying, of course, that the cause of the current crisis lies not in economic decline but in the collapse of the male-headed family.[102]

But apparently it is not just men who are to blame: young working-class African American women are often portrayed as welfare queens making babies merely to stay on public assistance, or "gold diggers" who use their sexuality to take black men's meager earnings. Of course, this image is hardly new. But it has become an increasingly prominent theme in hip hop over the last ten years or so. In a "tongue-in-cheek" verbal duel with female rapper Yo Yo, Ice Cube offers some lyrics that are partly meant in jest but nonetheless reflect the thinking of many of his black male compatriots: "I hear females always talking 'bout women's lib/Then get your own crib, and stay there/Instead of having more babies for the welfare/Cause if you don't I'll label you a gold digger."[103]

Part of the attack has to do with what these rappers feel are overly high expectations of black men held by young black women. Thinking back to their pre-celebrity days when they were reportedly jobless or worked for minimum wages, a number of male rappers criticize women who wanted to go out only with men who were stable or fairly well-off financially. Given the lack of employment opportunities available to young black women, and the still dominant notion that males ought to be the primary wage earners, these expectations could hardly be considered unreasonable. Yet, in interviews and in their music, most gangsta rappers label such women "bitches," "hos," or "skeezers." W.C. of the MAAD Circle, who is unique for avoiding these epithets on his debut album, tries to be slightly more conscientious by blaming "society" for inculcating women with materialistic values. Nevertheless, he throws up a weak argument for the use of the term "bitch": "Well, society has us all believing that if you don't fit up to their standard, then you're not shit. . . . If you have that attitude, then W.C. is calling you a bitch. But I'll never call a *woman* a bitch, because a real woman doesn't think with that mentality. This society has us believing that if you don't drive a brand new car, if you drive a bucket, you're not shit."[104]

While W.C. reveals one dimension of the pain poverty causes, his response is nonetheless a weak attempt to shift the issue. Distinguishing "bad" women from "good" women (or, in W.C.'s case, "real" women) still justifies violence against women by devaluing them, like most gangsta rap.[105] The most obvious examples can be found on NWA's recent album *Efil4zaggin*. Songs like "One Less Bitch" and the audio-verité recording "To Kill a Hooker" justify outright brutality and murder by using labels intended to strip women of any humanity. Hardly the stuff of everyday life in the ghetto, these draconian fantasy performances are more akin to "snuff films" than the kind of ethnographic observations NWA claim as their raw material. And like violent pornography, NWA's misogynist narratives are essentially about the degradation and complete domination of women. On the one hand, like the vast array of cultural images, they reinforce existing forms of patriarchal power; on the other hand, they construct male fantasy scenes of uncontested domination. They are never resisted or held accountable for acts of violence against women. In "One Less Bitch," Dr. Dre assumes the role of a pimp who discovers that his prostitute is trying to "steal" from him by retaining some of the money she earned. Reminiscent of "The Lame and the Whore" (or a "snuff film"—take your pick), Dre orchestrates what is best described as a lynching:

> I tied her to the bed, I was thinking the worst
> But, yo, I had to let my niggers fuck her first

Yea, loaded up the .44
Yo, then I straight smoked the ho.

Each story of mayhem and murder is broken up with a chorus of the entire NWA crew chanting: "One Less, one less, one less bitch you gotta worry about."

Economic conflict and a reassertion of male dominance in response to shifting gender and family relations still does not fully explain misogyny. Another part of the answer can be found in Tricia Rose's provocative and compelling argument that misogynist lyrics in rap reflect black male fears of black women's sexuality. Unlike male utopian spaces like "playboy clubs" where women are paid to be packaged fantasies, young inner-city black men have to deal with black women with real voices, demands, expectations, and complaints—women with agency. In the everyday lives of young black men, sexuality is always a process of negotiation. Rose suggests that "many men are hostile toward women because the fulfillment of male heterosexual desire is significantly checked by women's capacity for sexual rejection and/or manipulation of men." Manipulation, in this context, refers to the perceived power of black women to obtain money and goods in exchange for sex.[106]

Pregnancy is one way women allegedly extract attention and financial support, as is depicted in Ice Cube's "You Can't Fade Me." The narrative opens with Cube's character, who is on the corner drinking with his homies, discovering that he might have fathered a child by a young woman with whom he had a one-night stand. His initial impulse, not surprisingly, is to blame *her* rather than take responsibility. As the story progresses he recounts that one fateful night in stark, unflattering terms stripped completely of sensuality or pleasure. Because he saw her as physically unattractive he felt compelled to sneak around in order to have sex with her while preserving his reputation. When they finally found a safe place to have intercourse—in the backseat of his "homie's Impala"—both the sex and the end of their "date" were anticlimactic:

I dropped her off man, and I'm knowing,
That I'm a hate myself in the morning.
I got drunk to help me forget,
Another day, another hit, shit, I'm getting faded.

But once he returns to the present and she's about to have the child, the character Cube plays turns all of his anger and frustration upon her, threatening to beat her down and perform an abortion himself. In the end, the baby turns out not to be his, but the whole ordeal illustrates the possible consequences of his actions, even if the character Cube plays failed to learn anything from it. Sex as an act of conquest can also degrade men. Moreover, the end result of sexual conquest might be pregnancy, leading to the very thing the "playboy" ethic tries to avoid: commitment. In short, like all forms of power, male domination not only produces its own limits but it is constantly contested.

While songs like "You Can't Fade Me" are decidedly sexist, Ice Cube was among the first L.A. gangsta rappers to incorporate women's voices that contested his own lyrics. On *AmeriKKKa's Most Wanted*, for example, we not only hear a young woman's voice disrupt "The Nigga You Love to Hate" with vehement protests over the use of the word "bitch," but Ice Cube invited Yo Yo, an extraordinary female rapper concerned with building a progressive movement of black women, to engage him in a verbal "battle of the sexes." "It's a Man's World" is the classic "dis" tune, a duet rooted in the "dozens" tradition and thus intended to be humorous. But it also reminds us that the discursive space in which young black men assert their masculinity and dominance over women is always highly contested terrain. After the song opens with literally dozens of sampled voices saying "bitch"—ranging from Richard Pryor, Eazy E, and controversial comedian Andrew "Dice" Clay—the machine-gunlike assault of sexist epithets closes with a lone male voice who responds, "don't talk about my mamma!" Ice Cube launches into what is ostensibly supposed to be monologue about what women are "good for," when suddenly Yo Yo seems to come out of nowhere and interrupts with, "What the hell you think you're talkin' about?" Because her initial intervention takes place away from the microphone in a sort of echo mode, her interruption is presented as an unexpected penetration into all-male space, reminding the "brothas" just how vulnerable "the circle" is to female invasion and disruption. From that point on, Yo Yo criticizes Cube's ability to rap, questions his manhood, and even makes fun of the size of his penis.[107]

Finally, I must caution against interpreting the misogyny in gangsta rap as merely a reflection of daily gender conflicts and negotiations among inner-city black youth. In many instances, their narratives are based on their lived experiences as *performers* whose status as cultural icons gives them an enormous amount of sexual power and freedom. The long version of Ice Cube's "Get Off My Dick Nigger—and Tell Yo' B—to Come Here," which is primarily an attack on male "groupies," simultaneously celebrates his new status and ridicules starstruck teenage women who ultimately become the prey of male performers. In a line that falls somewhere between masculinist boast and paternal warning, Cube tells these women "See for a fact, I do damage/ They think I'm a star, so I take advantage."[108] Several songs on NWA's *Efil4zaggin* assert both the newfound power the group holds over impressionable and sexually curious young female fans and the brutality that can result from such power. One of the more vicious segments in "She Swallowed It" is the story of a woman who "did the whole crew." As NWA tried to make the difficult shift from "street niggas" to fame and fortune, it became increasingly clear that they not only saw their newfound power as boundless but had no qualms about practicing what they "preach." Dr. Dre's assault on Dee Barnes, the host of the video show *Pump It Up* and member of the rap duo Body and Soul, is a case in point, as is Tupac Shakur's recent arrest for sexually assaulting a young woman whom he and his friends had imprisoned in a hotel room.[109]

Are there any potential cracks or ruptures in the gangsta rappers' constructions of women or in their efforts to reassert male power through violence and sexual domination? Occasionally there are, especially when rappers focus their attention on bad fathering and family violence. Indeed, Ice T's "The House" demands an end to violence against children within the family context, and W.C. and the MAAD Circle critiques domestic violence against women. The medium-tempo, hauntingly funky "Fuck My Daddy" shows the flip side of the world NWA raps about:

I'm giving peace to moms
Cause moms was the strongest.

Dad was a wino, as sick as a psycho.
I used to hide under the covers with my eyes closed.

Crying and hoping tonight that daddy didn't trip,
Cause mama already needs stitches in her top lip.

I used to pray and hope that daddy would die,
Cause over nothing mama suffered from a swole up
    black eye.
And at the end of my prayers cry myself to sleep.
All I could think about was "Fuck my daddy."[110]

While W.C.'s lyrics mark a significant break from earlier gangsta groups, by focusing on his own mother as victim he does not directly challenge the dichotomy between "good" and "bad" women.[111] Moreover, neither of these examples challenges male domination, and reflections on lived experience alone are unlikely to convince most young men—gangsta rapper or not—that the overthrow of patriarchy should be part of an emancipatory agenda. However, the introduction of new *discourses* can play an important role in shaping the politics of rap music, and has. Not only have black women rappers played a crucial role in reshaping the attitudes toward women among a substantial segment of the hip hop community, they are also largely responsible for raising the issue of sexism within rap. Insofar as recording technology has conveyed the voices of ghetto youth (or those who claim the "authenticity" of ghetto living) to a national audience, it has brought rappers face-to-face with other critical communities, including feminists, left-wing radicals, suburban white youth, and Christian fundamentalists. The heated debates surrounding rap music have found their way into mainstream media where rap is generally either misunderstood or gangsta rap is regarded as real descriptions of daily life in the "ghetto." More significantly, the mass media attack on sexism in hip hop has obscured or ignored the degree to which rappers merely represent an extreme version of sexism that pervades daily life, across race and class. The devaluation of women goes on constantly, in television and film, in the labor market, in the courts, in educational and religious institutions, in suburban tract homes and gentrified high-class row houses, even in the way children are raised. Sexism is very much a part of "mainstream" American culture, and yet it is very difficult to generate a national dialogue about how pervasive it is in our society without eliciting diatribes about "political correctness" or the hypersensitivity of females. The Anita Hill/Clarence Thomas hearings are a case in point. The attacks on rap music also imply that misogyny is the unique property of young black males. While black male sexism should certainly not be ignored, the particular class and racial cast these criticisms take ultimately diverts attention from the general sexism in American culture. Hence, black youths' use of the term "bitch" gets more publicity than male bias on the bench in rape cases or gender discrimination in wages.

On the other hand, although the dialogue itself is limited, public discussions about rap's sexism have disrupted or challenged the narrow and localized assumptions of young black males. In other words, if rap had never become a commodity but remained forever in the streets and house parties of urban America, derogatory terms like "bitch" and misogyny within black communities would probably not have been so widely debated with such force. By turning what is frequently "street talk" into a national discussion that crosses gender, class, and racial boundaries, new discourses have the potential of at least challenging misogyny and possibly enabling black youth to perhaps see the limitations of the ideology of male dominance.

afterWORD: A Genre Spent?

I don't like the trend toward so many gangster records in rap, but I am an art dealer and that's what is selling now.
—RUSSELL SIMMONS, CEO of Rush Communications[112]

After the National Guard leaves, there's still gonna be angry, psycho motherfuckers out there.
—B-REAL OF CYPRESS HILL[113]

Who is Snoop Doggy Dogg? He's the latest superstar addition to Dr. Dre's stable on Deathrow Records, a gangsta rapper from Long Beach with the coolest, slickest "Calabama"[114] voice I've ever heard. You know his name because his recent arrest for the fatal shooting of a young black man became national news. While his picture never made the post office, Snoop's face graced the cover of *Newsweek* and almost every major music magazine, and gained notoriety on a variety of television news programs. That Snoop's murder charges coincided with the release of his debut CD/album did not seem to hurt record sales one bit. On the contrary, the shooting simply confirmed his claims to be a "real" gangsta, to have committed more "dirt" than the next man. The hype around the man is clearly responsible for pushing *Doggy Style* to the top of the charts *before* it was released. Most of his lyrics represent nothing but senseless, banal nihilism. The misogyny is so dense that it sounds more like little kids discovering nasty words for the first time than some male pathos. It is pure profanity bereft of the rich storytelling and use of metaphor and simile that have been cornerstones of rap music since its origins.

Snoop Doggy Dogg is just the tip of the iceberg. Former NWA member Eazy E (aka Eric Wright) has either turned conservative or (more likely) found a new gimmick to sell records. Recently he donated money to the Republican Party and publicly defended one of the police officers accused of beating Rodney King. Not your typical gangsta posture. Furthermore, the current war between Dr. Dre and Eazy E has reduced gangsta rap to a battle over who has done the most dirt. According to Eazy, Dr. Dre and his new partners on Deathrow Records are just "studio gangstas" because they've committed little or no crimes.

While I still contend that most of the early gangsta rappers did not set out to glamorize crime, by the summer of 1993 gangsta rap had been reduced to "nihilism for nihilism's sake." For a moment, the hardest-core, most fantastic, misogynist, and nihilistic music outsold almost everything on the rap scene, burying the most politically correct. In some respects, this development should not be surprising. Hard-core gangsta rap has become so formulaic that capturing even a modicum of reality no longer seems to be a priority. Ironically, the massive popularity of gangsta rap coincided with a fairly substantial increase in white suburban consumers of rap. This is in spite of the post–L.A. rebellion political climate, when many commentators and cultural critics had hopes for a progressive turn in Ghettocentric music, and a militant backlash against gangsta rap specifically, and hip hop more generally (led mainly by middle-class male spokespersons like the Reverend Calvin Butts of Abyssinian Baptist Church in New York, African American feminist groups, and some black working-class communities concerned about violence in their midst). And, as I pointed out elsewhere in this chapter, some of the most vociferous critics of gangsta rap come from within the hip hop community itself.[115]

As I close this chapter, with just two weeks left in 1993, one cannot help but notice how rap music generally, and gangsta rap in particular, has become the scapegoat for some very serious problems facing urban America. Besieged communities who are truly drowning in poverty and violence, it seems, are reaching out for a straw. Spokespersons for these antirap movements invoke a mythic past in which middle-class values supposedly ruled. They point to a "golden age" of good behavior, when the young respected their elders, worked hard, did not live their lives for leisure, took education seriously, and respected their neighbor's property. But this has been the claim of every generation of black intellectuals and self-appointed leaders since the end of Reconstruction (see chapter 2). The critique of the middle class that was so powerful in some glimmers of early gangsta rap is now silenced, as is the critique of what the economy has done to people. The door is open, more so than ever, for more all-male schools, heavier discipline, more policing, censorship, dress codes— what amounts to an all-out war on African American youth. On the other hand, the money is still flowing for gangsta rappers, many of whom now live in the hills overlooking the ghetto. The tragedy of all this is that the gangsta rappers have gotten harder and harder, kicking more ballistics than "reality"; critics and opponents have become harder and more sweeping in their criticism, dismissing not only the gangsta stuff but the entire body of rap; and the very conditions they are concerned about remain the same.

Gangsta rap might be on its last legs, a completely spent genre that now exists in a cul-de-sac of posturing, adolescent misogyny and blood-and-guts narratives. But it would be a mistake to dismiss gangsta rap and other genres of hip hop as useless creations of the marketplace. If we want to know the political climate among urban youth, we should still listen to the music and, most importantly, to the young people who fill the deadened, congested spaces of the city with these sonic forces. And as we all probably realize, the world from which this music emerged, and to which it partially speaks, inevitably faces the further deterioration of already unlivable neighborhoods, more street crime, and increased police repression. To take their voices seriously, however, is not to suggest that they are progressive or correct, or that every word, gesture, or beat is dripping with social significance. More often than not, "G-boys" are simply out to get paid, making funky jeep music, practicing the ancient art of playing the dozens, trying to be funny, and giving the people what they want. And when they are addressing the problems of inner-city communities we have to keep in mind that their sharpest critiques of capitalist America are derived from the same social and economic contexts that led a lot of homies to distrust black women and each other. Nevertheless, if we learned anything from that fateful night of April 29, it is that, whether we like the message or not, we must read the graffiti on the walls and, as Ice T puts it, "check the pulse of the rhyme flow."

Kickin' Reality, Kickin' Ballistics (The "Race Rebel" Remix Version)

. . . A nice, neat ending to be sure, but I can't go out like that. To write about the "politics" of gangsta rap is only part of the story. Let's face it: listening to gangsta rap, or any hardcore hip hop, is not exactly like reading an alternative version of the Times *(New York or L.A.). Hip hop is first and foremost music, "noize" produced and purchased to drive to, rock to, chill to, drink to, and occasionally dance to. To the hardcore, how many people get fucked up in a song is less important than an MC's verbal facility on the mic, the creative and often hilarious use of puns, metaphors, similes, not to mention the ability to kick some serious slang and some serious ass on the microphone. A dope MC leaves a trail of victims to rot in body bags, perpetrators who had the audacity to front like they could flow. This is why I insisted from the get-go that gangsterism is integral to all hardcore hip hop, from EPMD to MC Lyte, from Big Daddy Kane to Nice n' Smooth, just as gangstas have been integral to all African American and, for that matter, black Atlantic oral traditions. Moreover, as microphone fiend Rakim might put it, hip hop ain't hip hop if you can't "move the crowd." In my book, the most politically correct rapper will never get my hard-earned duckets if they ain't kickin' some boomin' drum tracks, a phat bass line, a few well-placed JB-style guitar riffs, and some stupid, nasty turntable action. If it claims to be hip hop, it has to have, as Pete Rock says, "the breaks . . . the funky breaks . . . the funky breaks."*

I wrote this little refrain not to contradict my analysis but to go out with a dose of reality while giving a shout out to the hardcore. For all the implicit and explicit politics of rap lyrics, hip hop must be understood as a sonic force more than anything else. You simply can't just read about it; it has to be heard, volume pumping, bass in full effect, index finger in reach of the rewind button when a compelling sample, break beat, or lyric catches your attention. This is why, for all my left-wing politics, when you see me driving by in my Subaru wagon, windows wide open, digging in the seams with the gangsta lean, rearview mirror trembling from the sonic forces, I'll probably be rockin' to the likes of King Tee, Dr. Dre, Pete Rock and C. L. Smooth, Das EFX, The Pharcyde, Cypress Hill, Boss, Lords of the Underground, MC Lyte, Ice T, The Coup, Jeru da Damaja, Son of Bazerk, Gangstarr, and, yes, Ice Cube. Keep the crossover and save the "PC" morality rap for those who act like they don't know. I'm still rollin' with Da Lench Mob, kickin' it with the Rhyme Syndicate, hanging out in the Basement with Pete Rock and the rest, and, like Das EFX, I'm coming straight from the Sewer . . .

I'm out. . . . Peace.

Notes

Introduction

1. C.L.R. James, Grace Lee, and Pierre Chaulieu, *Facing Reality* (Detroit: Correspondence Publishing Co., 1958), 5.

2. I also worked at the McDonald's on Foothill Boulevard in East Pasadena, where my experience was quite different. The "crew" there was predominantly white and very efficient. They took the job so seriously that I was suspended for two weeks for not asking a customer (who turned out to be a manager from another store pretending to be a customer) if he wanted an apple pie. I didn't stick around to get my job back; two days later I got a job at In and Out, a drive-in hamburger stand with chain stores spread throughout California.

3. "Taylorism" refers to the system of scientific management developed by Frederick Winslow Taylor a century ago. His aim was to limit all decision making to managers and engineers, and restructure the labor process in order to reduce unnecessary movement, lower the level of skill needed to perform a task, and make production more efficient. For a thorough discussion of the Taylorizing of McDonald's, see Robin Leidner, *Fast Food, Fast Talk: Service Work and the Routinization of Everyday Life* (Berkeley and Los Angeles: University of California Press, 1993), especially 51–53, 67–69, 79–83, 129–34.

4. W.E.B. DuBois, *Black Reconstruction in America: An Essay toward a History of the Part Which Black Folk Played in the Attempt to Reconstruct Democracy in America, 1860–1880* (New York: Harcourt Brace, 1935); C.L.R. James, *Black Jacobins: Toussaint L'Ouverture and the San Domingo Revolution*, 2nd ed. (New York: Vintage Books, 1963). Another important work from that era was Herbert Aptheker's *American Negro Slave Revolts* (New York: International Publishers, 1943). He offered a rough but useful framework for studying the hidden and disguised struggles of slaves in North America. This important book not only

229

tries to identify acts of resistance and plans for rebellion among slaves, but demonstrates how small conflicts and the threat of revolt shaped all of Southern society. Also see his earlier essays and pamphlets which were intended for the kind of working-class audiences he had been organizing at the time: *Negro Slave Revolts in the United States, 1526–1860* (New York: International Publishers, 1939); *The Negro in the Civil War* (New York: International Publishers, 1938); Herbert Aptheker, "Maroons within the Present Limits of the United States," *Journal of Negro History* 24 (April 1939), 167–84. For an appraisal of *American Negro Slave Revolts* and a history of the various responses from the historical profession, see Herbert Shapiro, "The Impact of the Aptheker Thesis: A Retrospective View of *American Negro Slave Revolts*," *Science and Society*, 48 (Spring 1984), 52–73.

5. The seminal texts include E. P. Thompson, *The Making of the English Working Class* (New York: Vintage Books, 1963) and *Whigs and Hunters: The Origins of the Black Act* (London: Allen Lane, 1975); Eric Hobsbawm, *Primitive Rebels: Studies in Archaic Forms of Social Movements in the 19th and 20th Centuries.* 1959 reprint (New York: Norton, 1965); George Rudé, *The Crowd in History: A Study of Popular Disturbances in France and England, 1730–1848* (New York: Wiley, 1964); Herbert Gutman, *Work, Culture, and Society in Industrializing America: Essays in American Working-Class and Social History* (New York: Knopf, 1976); Eugene Genovese, *Roll, Jordan, Roll: The World the Slaves Made* (New York: Pantheon, 1974); David Montgomery, *Workers Control in America: Studies in the History of Work, Technology, and Labor Struggles* (Cambridge and New York: Cambridge University Press, 1979).

6. Some early examples of scholars attempting to examine African American working-class history "from below" include: Herbert Gutman, "The Negro and the United Mine Workers of America: The Career and Letters of Richard L. Davis and Something of Their Meaning, 1890–1900," in *The Negro and the American Labor Movement*, ed. Julius Jacobson (Garden City, N.Y.: Anchor Books, 1968), 49–127; Gutman, "Black Coal Miners and the Greenback-Labor Party in Redeemer, Alabama: 1878–1879," *Labor History* 10 (1969), 506–35; Nell Irvin Painter, *Exodusters: Black Migration to Kansas after Reconstruction* (New York: Knopf, 1976); Painter, *The Narrative of Hosea Hudson, His Life as a Negro Communist in the South* (Cambridge, Mass.: Harvard University Press, 1979); Peter J. Rachleff, *Black Labor in the South: Richmond, Virginia, 1865–1890* (Philadelphia: Temple University Press, 1984); Joe William Trotter, Jr., *Black Milwaukee: The Making of an Industrial Proletariat, 1915–1945* (Urbana: University of Illinois Press, 1985); Paul Worthman, "Working Class Mobility in Birmingham, Alabama, 1880–1914," in *Anonymous Americans: Explorations in Nineteenth–Century Social History*, ed. Tamara K. Hareven (Englewood Cliffs, N.J.: Prentice-Hall, 1971), 172–213; Paul Worthman and James Green, "Black Workers in the New South, 1865–1915," in *Key Issues in the Afro-American Experience*, eds. Nathan Huggins, Martin Kilson, and Daniel Fox (New York: Harcourt Brace Jovanovich, 1971), II, 47–69. Some more recent examples include Eric Arnesen, *Waterfront*

Workers of New Orleans: Race, Class, and Politics, 1863–1923 (New York: Oxford University Press, 1991); Michael Honey, *Southern Labor and Black Civil Rights: Organizing Memphis Workers* (Urbana: University of Illinois Press, 1993); Tera W. Hunter, "Household Workers in the Making: Afro-American Women in Atlanta and the New South, 1861–1920" (Ph.D. diss., Yale University, 1990); Robin D. G. Kelley, *Hammer and Hoe: Alabama Communists during the Great Depression* (Chapel Hill: University of North Carolina Press, 1990); Robert Korstad, "'Daybreak of Freedom': Tobacco Workers and the CIO, Winston-Salem, North Carolina, 1943–1950" (Ph.D. diss., University of North Carolina, Chapel Hill, 1987); Dolores Janiewski, *Sisterhood Denied: Race, Gender, and Class in a New South Community* (Philadelphia: Temple University Press, 1985); Jacqueline Jones, *Labor of Love, Labor of Sorrow: Black Women, Work and the Family, From Slavery to the Present* (New York: Basic Books, 1985); Earl Lewis, *In Their Own Interests: Race, Class, and Power in Twentieth Century Norfolk, Virginia* (Berkeley and Los Angeles: University of California Press, 1991); Bruce Nelson, "Class and Race in the Crescent City: The ILWU, from San Francisco to New Orleans," in *The CIO's Left-led Unions*, ed. Steven Rosswurm (New Brunswick, NJ: Rutgers University Press, 1992), 19–45; and Nelson, "Organized Labor and the Struggle for Black Equality in Mobile during World War II," *Journal of American History* 80, no. 3 (December 1993), 952–88; Joe William Trotter, Jr., *Coal, Class, and Color: Blacks in Southern West Virginia, 1915–1932* (Urbana: University of Illinois Press, 1990).

7. Painter, *Exodusters*, 15–16.

8. Gloria Wade-Gayles, *Pushed Back to Strength: A Black Woman's Journey Home* (Boston: Beacon Press, 1993), 5.

9. James C. Scott, *Domination and the Arts of Resistance: Hidden Transcripts* (New Haven: Yale University Press, 1990), quote from p. 183; see also James C. Scott, *Weapons of the Weak: Everyday Forms of Peasant Resistance* (New Haven: Yale University Press, 1985); James C. Scott, *The Moral Economy of the Peasant: Rebellion and Subsistence in Southeast Asia* (New Haven: Yale University Press, 1976); Rosalind O'Hanlon, "Recovering the Subject: *Subaltern Studies* and Histories of Resistance in Colonial South Asia," *Modern Asian Studies* 22 (February 1988), 189–224. The precursors of Scott's work include E. P. Thompson, *The Making of the English Working Class*; E. P. Thompson, "The Crime of Anonymity," in *Albion's Fatal Tree: Crime and Society in Eighteenth-Century England*, eds. Douglas Hay, Peter Linebaugh, John G. Rule, E. P. Thompson, and Cal Winslow (New York: Pantheon Books, 1975), 255–344; Michel de Certeau's *The Practice of Everyday Life*, trans. Steven Rendall (Berkeley and Los Angeles: University of California Press, 1984); Aptheker, *American Negro Slave Revolts*; Raymond A. Bauer and Alice H. Bauer, "Day to Day Resistance to Slavery," *Journal of Negro History*, 37 (October 1942), 388–419; Genovese, *Roll, Jordan, Roll*, 599–621; *see also* Peter Kolchin, *Unfree Labor: American Slavery and Russian Serfdom* (Cambridge, Mass.: Harvard University Press, 1987), 241–44; Alex Lichtenstein, "That Disposition to Theft, With Which They have been Branded:

Moral Economy, Slave Management, and the Law," *Journal of Social History* 22 (Spring 1988), 413–40; Sterling Stuckey, "Through the Prism of Folklore: The Black Ethos in Slavery," *Massachusetts Review* 9 (Summer 1968), 417–37.

10. Lila Abu-Lughod, "The Romance of Resistance: Tracing Transformations of Power through Bedouin Women," *American Ethnologist* 17, no. 1 (1990), 55. I'm grateful to Victoria Wolcott for bringing this source to my attention. For a more developed critique of Scott, see Robin D. G. Kelley, "An Archeology of Resistance," *American Quarterly* 44 (June 1992), 292–98; Timothy Mitchell, "Everyday Metaphors of Power," *Theory and Society* 19 (October 1990), 545–77; David Hunt, "From the Millennial to the Everyday: James Scott's Search for the Essence of Peasant Politics," *Radical History Review* 42 (Fall 1988), 155–72. For a general critique of the current misuses of hegemony, see Michael Denning, "The End of Mass Culture," *International Labor and Working-Class History* 37 (Spring 1990), 13–14.

11. My recasting of "the political" is inspired in part from my reading of Geoff Eley, "Labor History, Social History, *Alltagsgeschichte*: Experience, Culture, and the Politics of the Everyday—A New Direction for German Social History?" *Journal of Modern History* 61 (June 1989), 297–343.

Part I. "We Wear the Mask"

1. Paul Laurence Dunbar, "We Wear the Mask," in *The Complete Works of Paul Laurence Dunbar*, ed. W.D. Howells, (New York: Dodd, Mead, and Co., 1922), 71.

Chapter 1. Shiftless of the World Unite!

1. Daniel Bell, *Work and Its Discontents: The Cult of Efficiency in America* (Boston: Beacon, 1956), 15.

2. W.E.B. DuBois, *Black Reconstruction in America: An Essay toward a History of the Part Which Black Folk Played in the Attempt to Reconstruct Democracy, 1860–1880* (New York: Harcourt Brace, 1935), 40.

3. George Rawick, "Working-Class Self-Activity," *Radical America* 3 (March–April 1969), 145.

4. Tera W. Hunter, "Household Workers in the Making: Afro-American Women in Atlanta and the New South, 1861–1920" (Ph.D. diss., Yale University, 1990), 76–82; Jacqueline Jones, *Labor of Love, Labor of Sorrow: Black Women, Work and the Family, From Slavery to the Present* (New York: Basic Books, 1985), 132–33; Dolores Janiewski, "Sisters under Their Skins: Southern Working Women, 1880–1950," in *Sex, Race, and the Role of Women in the South*, eds. Joanne V. Hawks and Sheila L. Skemp (Jackson, 1983), 788; David Katzman, *Seven Days a Week: Women and Domestic Service in Industrializing America* (New York, 1978), 195–97.

5. Robert Korstad, "'Daybreak of Freedom': Tobacco Workers and the CIO, Winston-Salem, North Carolina, 1943–1950" (Ph.D. diss., University of

North Carolina, Chapel Hill, 1987), 101; Dolores Janiewski, *Sisterhood Denied: Race, Gender, and Class in a New South Community* (Philadelphia: Temple University Press, 1985), 98; Jones, *Labor of Love, Labor of Sorrow*, 140.

6. The obvious exceptions, of course, are slavery studies and the growing literature on domestic workers. In particular, slavery historians have imaginatively examined and interpreted this elusive but no less powerful form of resistance. See especially Eugene Genovese, *Roll, Jordan, Roll: The World the Slaves Made* (New York: Pantheon Books, 1974), 599–621; Peter Kolchin, *Unfree Labor: American Slavery and Russian Serfdom* (Cambridge, Mass.: Harvard University Press, 1987), 241–44; Alex Lichtenstein, "That Disposition to Theft, With Which They have been Branded: Moral Economy, Slave Management, and the Law," *Journal of Social History* 22 (Spring 1988), 413–40; and the pioneering contributions by Raymond A. Bauer and Alice H. Bauer, "Day to Day Resistance to Slavery," *Journal of Negro History* 37 (Oct. 1942), 388–419, and Herbert Aptheker, *American Negro Slave Revolts* (New York: International Publishers, 1943), 141–49; Edward L. Ayers, *Vengeance and Justice: Crime and Punishment in the 19th Century American South* (New York: Oxford University Press, 1984). The most sophisticated work on crime and resistance at the workplace continues to come from sociologists, radical criminologists, and historians of Europe and Africa. See, for example, Peter Linebaugh's brilliant book, *The London Hanged: Crime and Civil Society in the Eighteenth Century* (London: Allen Lane, The Penguin Press, 1991); Robin Cohen, "Resistance and Hidden Forms of Consciousness among African Workers," *Review of African Political Economy* 19 (1980), 8–22; Jeff Crisp, *The Story of an African Working Class: Ghanaian Miners' Struggles, 1870–1980* (London: Zed Books, 1984), 18, 26, 44–45, 68, 78; Bill Freund, "Theft and Social Protest among the Tin Miners of Northern Nigeria," *Radical History Review* 26 (1982), 68–86; Charles Van Onselen, *Chibaro: African Mine Labour in Southern Rhodesia, 1900–1933* (London: Pluto Press, 1976), 239–42; Van Onselen, *Studies in the Social and Economic History of the Witwatersrand, 1886–1914: New Nineveh* (New York: Longman, 1982), II, 171–95.

7. Linebaugh, *The London Hanged*; E. P. Thompson, "The Moral Economy of the English Crowd in the Eighteenth Century," *Past and Present* 50 (February 1971), 76–135; Douglas Hay, Peter Linebaugh, John G. Rule, E. P. Thompson, and Cal Winslow, *Albion's Fatal Tree: Crime and Society in Eighteenth-Century England* (New York: Pantheon Books, 1975).

8. Hunter, "Household Workers in the Making," 82–83, quotes taken from 137–39; the latter is from Walter L. Fleming, "The Servant Problem in a Black Belt Village," *Sewanee Review* 13 (January 1905), 8. See also, Clifford M. Kuhn, Harlon E. Joye, and E. Bernard West, *Living Atlanta: An Oral History of the City, 1914–1948* (Athens, Ga.: University of Georgia Press, 1990), 113; Jones, *Labor of Love, Labor of Sorrow*, 132.

9. A powerful example from U.S. labor studies is Alvin Ward Gouldner, *Wildcat Strike* (Yellow Springs, Ohio: Antioch Press, 1954); and on British workers, see Steven Box, *Recession, Crime, and Punishment* (Totowa, N.J.: Barnes and

Noble Books, 1987), 34; Jason Ditton, *Part-Time Crime: An Ethnography of Fiddling and Pilferage* (London: Macmillan, 1977); Richard C. Hollinger and J. P. Clark, *Theft by Employees* (Lexington, Mass.: Lexington Books, 1983). For a general discussion of the informal economy and working-class opposition, see Cyril Robinson, "Exploring the Informal Economy," *Crime and Social Justice* 15, nos. 3 and 4 (1988), 3–16.

10. Jones, *Labor of Love, Labor of Sorrow*, 132; Korstad, "'Daybreak of Freedom,'" 102; Janiewski, *Sisterhood Denied*, 124; Robin D.G. Kelley, *Hammer and Hoe: Alabama Communists during the Great Depression* (Chapel Hill: University of North Carolina Press, 1990), 20–21; Julia Kirk Blackwelder, "Quiet Suffering: Atlanta Women in the 1930's," *Georgia Historical Quarterly* 61 (Summer 1977), 119–20.

11. Michel de Certeau, *The Practice of Everyday Life* (Berkeley and Los Angeles: University of California Press, 1984), 25–26.

12. Hunter, "Household Workers in the Making," 85; Jones, *Labor of Love, Labor of Sorrow*, 131; John Dollard, *Caste and Class in a Southern Town*, 3rd ed. (New York: Doubleday, 1957), 108.

13. Korstad, "'Daybreak of Freedom,'" 101.

14. European and African labor historians have been more inclined than Americanists to study industrial sabotage, though much of this work focuses on the nineteenth century. See, for example, Geoff Brown, *Sabotage: A Study in Industrial Conflict* (Nottingham: Bertrand Russell Peace Foundation for Spokesman Books, 1977); Pierre DuBois, *Sabotage in Industry* (New York: Penguin, 1979); Gouldner, *Wildcat Strike*; E. J. Hobsbawm, "The Machine Breakers," in *Labouring Men* (London: Weidenfeld & Nicolson, 1964); Tim Mason's schematic but provocative essay, "The Workers' Opposition in Nazi Germany," *History Workshop* 11 (Spring 1981), 127–30; Donald Quartaert, "Machine Breaking and the Changing Carpet Industry of Western Anatolia, 1860–1908," *Journal of Social History* 19 (Summer 1986), 473–489; Van Onselen, *Chibaro*, 242–44; Crisp, *Story of an African Working Class*, 7. The Industrial Workers of the World offers immense possibilities for studying black working-class sabotage precisely because Wobbly (members of the Industrial Workers of the World) leaders recruited African Americans and openly advocated sabotage as a strategy of resistance. Yet, except for David Roediger's excellent essay, "Gaining a Hearing for Black-White Unity: Covington Hall and the Complexities of Race, Gender and Class," in *Towards the Abolition of Whiteness: Essays on Race, Politics, and Working Class History* (London: Verso, 1994), and brief references in James Green's, *Grass-Roots Socialism: Radical Movements in the Southwest, 1895–1943* (Baton Rouge: Louisiana State University Press, 1978), p. 219, scholars have not attempted to explore whether black Wobblies practiced sabotage. Part of the reason for this has to do with the fact that black workers have been treated by most IWW historians more or less as objects to be debated over rather than subjects engaged in "the class struggle." See especially Paul Brissenden, *The I.W.W.: A Study of American Syndicalism*

(New York: Columbia University Press, 1919), 208; John S. Gambs, *The Decline of the I.W.W.* (New York: Columbia University Press, 1932), 135, 198; Selig Perlman and Philip Taft, *History of Labor in the United States* (New York: Macmillan, 1935), 247; Bernard A. Cook, "Covington Hall and Radical Rural Unionization in Louisiana," *Louisiana History* 18, no. 2 (1977), 230, 235; Melvyn Dubofsky, *We Shall Be All: A History of the Industrial Workers of the World* (Chicago: Quadrangle Books, 1969), 8–9, 210, 213–16; Merl E. Reed, "Lumberjacks and Longshoremen: The I.W.W. in Louisiana," *Labor History* 13 (Winter 1972), 44–58; Philip Foner, "The I.W.W. and the Black Worker," *Journal of Negro History* 55 (January 1970), 45–64; Sterling Spero and Abram L. Harris, *The Black Worker: The Negro and the Labor Movement* (New York: Columbia University Press, 1931), esp. 329–35.

15. My thinking here is partly inspired by Sylvia Wynter's, "Sambos and Minstrels," *Social Text* 1 (Winter 1979), 149–56; David Roediger, *The Wages of Whiteness: Race and the Making of the American Working Class* (London: Verso, 1991), 11–13. For a discussion of the dominant assumptions about black criminality and laziness in the postbellum South, see George Frederickson, *The Black Image in the White Mind: The Debate on Afro-American Character and Destiny, 1817–1914* (Middletown, Conn.: Wesleyan University Press, 1987, orig. 1971), 251–52, 273–75, 287–88; Claude H. Nolen, *The Negro's Image in the South: The Anatomy of White Supremacy* (Lexington, Ky.: University of Kentucky Press, 1967), 13–15, 25–27; Ayers, *Vengeance and Justice*, 176–77.

16. Kelley, *Hammer and Hoe*, 101–103; James C. Scott, *Domination and the Arts of Resistance: Hidden Transcripts* (New Haven: Yale University Press, 1990), 23–36. Of course, the mask of ignorance did not always work as a strategy to mitigate punishment. In some instances, rural African Americans accused of stealing livestock or burning barns were lynched. See clippings in Ralph Ginzburg, ed., *100 Years of Lynchings* (New York: Lancer Books, 1962), 92–93.

17. Kuhn, et al., *Living Atlanta*, 115; Susan Tucker, "A Complex Bond: Southern Black Domestic Workers and Their White Employers," *Frontiers: A Journal of Women's Studies* 11, no. 3 (1987), 6–13.

18. This image is powerfully conveyed in the recent documentary film, "At the River I Stand" (1994), about the Memphis Strike. For one exploration of the masculinist thrust in black politics, see E. Frances White, "Africa on My Mind: Gender, Counter Discourse and African-American Nationalism," *Journal of Women's History* 2, no. 1 (Spring 1990), 73–97. Also, in chapter 5 I examine the common thread of militant politics as a form of male redemption in both black nationalist and Communist discourse.

19. Roediger, *Towards the Abolition of Whiteness*, 168–69.

20. Joe William Trotter, Jr., *Coal, Class, and Color: Blacks in Southern West Virginia, 1915–1932* (Urbana: University of Illinois Press, 1990), 65, 108, 264–65; Evelyn Brooks Higginbotham, *Righteous Discontent: The Women's Movement in the Black Baptist Church, 1880–1920* (Cambridge, Mass.: Harvard University Press, 1993), 177, 211.

21.   This last point was made by Richard Price, "The Labour Process and Labour History," *Social History* 8 (January 1983), 62–63.

22.   See Trotter, *Coal, Class, and Color,* 68–85; 109; William Cohen, *At Freedom's Edge: Black Mobility and the Southern Quest for Racial Control, 1861–1915* (Baton Rouge: Louisiana State University Press, 1991); Earl Lewis, *In Their Own Interests: Race, Class, and Power in Twentieth-Century Norfolk, Virginia* (Berkeley and Los Angeles: University of California Press, 1991), 30–32, 168; James R. Grossman, *Land of Hope: Chicago, Black Southerners, and the Great Migration* (Chicago: University of Chicago Press, 1989); Neil McMillen, *Dark Journey: Black Mississippians in the Age of Jim Crow* (Urbana: University of Illinois Press, 1989), 257–81; Robert G. Athearn, *In Search of Canaan: Black Migration to Kansas, 1879–80* (Lawrence: Regents Press of Kansas, 1978); Nell Irvin Painter, *Exodusters: Black Migration to Kansas after Reconstruction* (New York: Knopf, 1976); Edwin S. Redkey, *Black Exodus: Black Nationalist and Back-to-Africa Movements, 1890–1910* (New Haven: Yale University Press, 1969); Peter Gottlieb, *Making Their Own Way: Southern Blacks' Migration to Pittsburgh, 1916–1930* (Urbana: University of Illinois Press, 1987). For examples of the ways in which black migration is redefined, see Jacqueline Jones, *The Dispossessed: America's Underclasses from the Civil War to the Present* (New York: Basic Books, 1992), 104–26; Dollard, *Caste and Class in a Southern Town,* 115–19; Nolen, *The Negro's Image in the South,* 186–88.

23.   One could go back as far as Charles Wesley, *Negro Labor in the United States, 1850–1925: A Study in American Economic History* (New York: Vanguard Press, 1927); Carter G. Woodson and Lorenzo Greene, *The Negro Wage Earner* (Washington, D.C.: Association for the Study of Negro Life and History, 1930); Spero and Harris, *The Black Worker,* for rich descriptions of racially segregated work. Two of the most sophisticated recent studies that examine the racialized dimension of industrial work and work spaces are Eric Arnesen, *Waterfront Workers of New Orleans: Race, Class, and Politics, 1863–1923* (New York: Oxford University Press, 1991); Trotter, *Coal, Class, and Color,* esp. 65–88, 102–11.

24.   Feminist scholarship on the South, as well as some recent community histories, have begun to examine how the racialized and gendered social spaces in which people work, in addition to the world beyond work, which was also divided by race and—at times—sex, shaped the character of everyday resistance, collective action, and domination. See especially, Hunter, "Household Workers in the Making"; Janiewski, *Sisterhood Denied*; Janiewski, "Sisters under Their Skins," 13–35; Janiewski, "Seeking 'a New Day and a New Way': Black Women and Unions in the Southern Tobacco Industry," in *"To Toil the Livelong Day": American Women at Work, 1780–1980,* eds. Carol Groneman and Mary Beth Norton (Ithaca, N.Y.: Cornell University Press, 1987), 161–78; Korstad, "'Daybreak of Freedom'"; Julia Kirk Blackwelder, "Women in the Workforce: Atlanta, New Orleans, and San Antonio, 1930–1940," *Journal of Urban History* 4 (May 1978), 331–58. My ideas about a "politics of location" are derived from Adrienne Rich, "Notes toward a Politics of Location," in *Women, Feminist Identity, and Society in*

the 1980's: Selected Papers, eds. Myriam Diaz-Diocaretz and Iris M. Zavala (Philadelphia: Benjamins, 1985), 7–22; Linda Alcoff, "Cultural Feminism versus Post-Structuralism: The Identity Crisis in Feminist Theory," *Signs* 13 (1988), 434; Nina Gregg, "Women Telling Stories about Reality: Subjectivity, the Generation of Meaning, and the Organizing of a Union at Yale" (Ph.D. diss., McGill University, 1991).

25. Lewis, *In Their Own Interests*, 47–58, quote from p. 58; see also Brenda McCallum, "Songs of Work, Songs of Worship," *New York Folklore* 14, nos. 1 and 2 (1988), 14.

26. Green, "The Brotherhood of Timber Workers," 185. On the preference of black workers for segregated locals, see Bruce Nelson, "Class and Race in the Crescent City: The ILWU, from San Francisco to New Orleans," in *The CIO's Left-led Unions*, ed. Steven Rosswurm (New Brunswick, N.J.: Rutgers University Press, 1992), 19–45.

27. Janiewski, *Sisterhood Denied*, 97–109 passim.; Janiewski, "Sisters under Their Skins," 27–28; Janiewski, "Seeking a New Day," 166; Beverly W. Jones, "Race, Sex, and Class: Black Female Tobacco Workers in Durham, North Carolina, 1920–1940, and the Development of Female Consciousness," *Feminist Studies* 10 (Fall 1984), 443–50; Jones, *Labor of Love, Labor of Sorrow*, 137–38; and on sexual exploitation of domestic workers, see Hunter, "Household Workers in the Making," 116–17; Kuhn et al., *Living Atlanta*, 115.

28. Three exceptions are Vicki Ruiz, *Cannery Women, Cannery Lives: Mexican Women, Unionization, and the California Food Processing Industry, 1930–1950* (Albuquerque: University of New Mexico Press, 1987); Mary Bularzik, "Sexual Harassment at the Workplace: Historical Notes," in *Workers' Struggles, Past and Present*, ed. James Green (Philadelphia: Temple University Press, 1983), 117–35; Elsa Barkley Brown, "'What Has Happened Here': The Politics of Difference in Women's History and Feminist Politics," *Feminist Studies* 18 (Summer 1992), 302–7.

29. Jones, "Race, Sex, and Class," 449; Korstad, "'Daybreak of Freedom.'"

30. Quote from Eileen Boris, "Black Women and Paid Labor in the Home: Industrial Homework in Chicago in the 1920's," in *Homework: Historical and Contemporary Perspectives on Paid Labor at Home*, eds. Eileen Boris and Cynthia R. Daniels (Urbana: University of Illinois Press, 1989), 47; Hunter, "Household Workers in the Making," 151–86. See also Eileen Boris, *Home to Work: Motherhood and The Politics of Industrial Homework in the United States* (New York: Cambridge University Press, 1994).

31. Kuhn et al., *Living Atlanta*, 115.

32. Elizabeth Clark-Lewis, "'This Work Had a End': African-American Domestic Workers in Washington, D.C., 1910–1940," in *"To Toil the Livelong Day": American Women at Work, 1780–1980*, eds. Carol Groneman and Mary Beth Norton (Ithaca: Cornell University Press, 1987), 207.

33. John Michael Matthews, "The Georgia Race Strike of 1909," *Journal of Southern History* 40 (November 1974), 613–30; Hugh Hammet, "Labor and

Race: The Georgia Railroad Strike of 1909," *Labor History* 16 (Fall 1975), 470–84; Philip S. Foner, *Organized Labor and the Black Worker, 1619–1981*, 2nd ed. (New York: International Publishers, 1981), 105–7; Forth Worth *Telegram*, December 21, 1921, reprinted in Ginzburg, ed., *100 Years of Lynching*, 157–58; William H. Harris, *The Harder We Run: Black Workers since the Civil War* (New York: Oxford University Press, 1982), 45–47; Herbert Shapiro, *White Violence and Black Response: From Reconstruction to Montgomery* (Amherst, Mass.: University of Massachusetts Press, 1988), 338–39.

34. Janiewski, *Sisterhood Denied*, 121; Michael Honey, *Southern Labor and Black Civil Rights: Organizing Memphis Workers* (Urbana: University of Illinois Press, 1993), 208, 276.

35. Roediger, *Wages of Whiteness*, 13–14; Alexander Saxton, *The Rise and Fall of the White Republic: Class Politics and Mass Culture in Nineteenth-Century America* (London: Verso, 1990); Eric Lott, *Love and Theft: Blackface Minstrelsy and the American Working Class* (New York: Oxford University Press, 1993).

36. Arnesen, *Waterfront Workers*, 121–31; Herbert Hill, "Myth-Making as Labor History: Herbert Gutman and the United Mine Workers of America," *International Journal of Politics, Culture, and Society* 2 (Winter 1988), 132–200; Robert J. Norrell, "Caste in Steel: Jim Crow Careers in Birmingham, Alabama," *Journal of American History* 73 (December 1986), 669–94; Horace Huntley, "Iron Ore Miners and Mine Mill in Alabama, 1933–1952" (Ph.D. diss., University of Pittsburgh, 1976), 110–69; David Roediger, "Labor in the White Skin: Race and Working Class History," in *The Year Left 3: Reshaping the U.S. Left: Popular Struggles in the 1980's*, eds. Mike Davis and Michael Sprinker (London: Verso, 1988), 287–308; Roediger, *Wages of Whiteness*, 43–87 passim.

37. Michael Yarrow, "The Gender-Specific Class Consciousness of Appalachian Coal Miners: Structure and Change," in *Bringing Class Back In: Contemporary and Historical Perspectives*, eds. Scott G. McNall, Rhonda F. Levine, and Rick Fantasia (Boulder: Westview Press, 1991), 302–3; Trotter, *Coal, Class, and Color*, 109; Paul Willis, *Learning to Labour: How Working Class Kids Get Working Class Jobs* (New York: Columbia University Press, 1981), 133; and see also his essay, "Shop-Floor Culture, Masculinity, and the Wage Form," in *Working-Class Culture*, eds. John Clarke, Charles Critcher, and Richard Johnson (New York: St. Martin's Press, 1979), 185–98.

38. Scott, *Domination and the Arts of Resistance*, 113.

39. The basis for biracial unions in the South is beyond the scope of my essay, though it is a very important subject that deserves greater examination. For recent critical insights into the racial and class dimensions of interracial unity (and disunity), see Eric Arnesen's, "Following the Color Line: Black Workers and the Labor Movement Before 1930," *Radical History Review* 55 (Winter 1993), 53–87; Arnesen, *Waterfront Workers*; Michael Honey, *Southern Labor and Black Civil Rights*; Roediger, *Towards the Abolition of Whiteness*; Bruce Nelson, "Class and Race in the Crescent City," 19–45; Trotter, *Coal, Class, and Color*.

40. In *Hammer and Hoe*, I document numerous examples of white radicals

and sympathizers in Alabama who were severely beaten (and in one case, lynched) for taking unpopular stands on African American rights. That they crossed the color line was far more important than being Communists; Communists in North Alabama, where the Party was completely white and made up of some ex-Klan members, faced virtually no violence until they began organizing black sharecroppers in the black belt counties. See Kelley, *Hammer and Hoe*, 47, 67–74, 130–31, 159–75 passim. Similar examples can be found in Honey, *Southern Labor and Black Civil Rights*.

41. The literature on the late nineteenth and twentieth centuries alone is extensive. The best overview is Shapiro, *White Violence and Black Response*; see also Dan T. Carter, *Scottsboro: A Tragedy of the American South*, rev. ed. (Baton Rouge: Louisiana State University Press, 1979); James R. McGovern, *Anatomy of a Lynching: The Killing of Claude Neal* (Baton Rouge: Louisiana State University Press, 1982); Anthony J. Blasi, *Segregationist Violence and Civil Rights Movements in Tuscaloosa* (Washington, D.C.: University Press of America, 1980); Arthur Raper, *The Tragedy of Lynching* (Chapel Hill: University of North Carolina Press, 1933); Jacquelyn Dowd Hall, "'The Mind That Burns in Each Body': Women, Rape, and Racial Violence," in *Powers of Desire: The Politics of Sexuality*, eds. Ann Snitow, Christine Stansell, and Sharon Thompson (New York: Monthly Review Press, 1983), 328–49; Charles Crowe, "Racial Violence and Social Reform— Origins of the Atlanta Riot of 1906," *Journal of Negro History* 53 (July 1968), 234–56; Scott Ellsworth, *Death in a Promised Land: The Tulsa Race Riot of 1921* (Baton Rouge: Louisiana State University Press, 1982); and on nonviolent and violent black responses, see Robert L. Zangrando, *The NAACP Crusade against Lynching, 1909–1950* (Philadelphia: Temple University Press, 1980); Kelley, *Hammer and Hoe*, chap. 4; George C. Wright, *Life behind a Veil: Blacks in Louisville, Kentucky, 1865–1930* (Baton Rouge: Louisiana State University Press, 1985), 71–76, 239–41; August Meier and Elliot Rudwick, "Black Violence in the Twentieth Century: A Study in Rhetoric and Retaliation," in *Along the Color Line*, 224–37 passim; William Ivy Hair, *Carnival of Fury: Robert Charles and the New Orleans Race Riot of 1900* (Baton Rouge: Louisiana State University Press, 1976); John D. Weaver, *The Brownsville Raid* (New York: Norton, 1970); Robert V. Haynes, *A Night of Violence: The Houston Riot of 1917* (Baton Rouge: Louisiana State University Press, 1976); J. J. Fyfe, "Blind Justice: Police Shootings in Memphis," *Journal of Criminal Law and Criminology* 73 (1982), 707–22; John Dittmer, *Black Georgia in the Progressive Era, 1900–1920* (Urbana: University of Illinois Press, 1977), 138–39; Howard N. Rabinowitz, "The Conflict between Blacks and the Police in the Urban South, 1865–1900," *Historian* 39 (November 1976), 62–76; Rabinowitz, *Race Relations in the Urban South, 1865–1890* (New York: Oxford University Press, 1978), 41–50.

42. W.E.B. DuBois, and more recently, Michael Schwartz, George Lipsitz, and Rick Fantasia persuasively argue that a radical consciousness often develops as a result of collective struggle. See DuBois, *Black Reconstruction*; Michael Schwartz, *Radical Protest and Social Structure: The Southern Tenant Farmers' Al-*

liance and Cotton Tenancy, 1880–1890 (Chicago and London: University of Chicago Press, 1976); Rick Fantasia, *Cultures of Solidarity: Consciousness, Action, and Contemporary American Workers* (Berkeley and Los Angeles, 1988); George Lipsitz, *"A Rainbow at Midnight": Labor and Culture in the 1940s* (Urbana: University of Illinois Press, 1994).

Chapter 2. "We Are Not What We Seem"

1. Richard Wright, *Twelve Million Black Voices* (New York: Thunder's Mouth Press, 1988, orig. 1941), 10.

2. Zora Neale Hurston, *Mules and Men* (New York: Harper & Row, 1990, orig. 1935), 2.

3. Gloria Wade-Gayles, *Pushed Back to Strength: A Black Woman's Journey Home* (Boston: Beacon Press, 1993), 4.

4. George Lipsitz, *A Life in the Struggle: Ivory Perry and the Culture of Opposition* (Philadelphia: Temple University Press, 1988); Elsa Barkley Brown, "Womanist Consciousness: Maggie Lena Walker and the Independent Order of St. Luke," *Signs: Journal of Women in Culture and Society* 14 (Spring 1989), 610–33; Brown, "Uncle Ned's Children: Richmond, Virginia's Black Community, 1890–1930" (Ph.D. diss., Kent State University, 1994); Michael K. Honey, *Southern Labor and Black Civil Rights: Organizing Memphis Workers* (Urbana: University of Illinois Press, 1993); Tera W. Hunter, "Household Workers in the Making: Afro-American Women in Atlanta and the New South, 1861–1920" (Ph.D. diss., Yale University, 1990); Robin D. G. Kelley, *Hammer and Hoe: Alabama Communists during the Great Depression* (Chapel Hill: University of North Carolina Press, 1990); Robert Korstad, "'Daybreak of Freedom': Tobacco Workers and the CIO, Winston-Salem, North Carolina, 1943–1950" (Ph.D. diss., University of North Carolina, Chapel Hill, 1987); Earl Lewis, *In Their Own Interests: Race, Class, and Power in Twentieth-Century Norfolk, Virginia* (Berkeley and Los Angeles: University of California Press, 1991); Joe William Trotter, *Coal, Class, and Color: Blacks in Southern West Virginia, 1915–1932* (Urbana: University of Illinois Press, 1990). Although Peter J. Rachleff's outstanding book, and his even more prodigious dissertation, is limited to the nineteenth century and therefore beyond the scope of this chapter, he offers one of the most sophisticated discussions of the relationship between community, culture, work, and self-activity. Peter J. Rachleff, *Black Labor in the South: Richmond, Virginia, 1865–1890* (Philadelphia: Temple University Press, 1984), 109–115, and his "Black, White, and Gray: Race and Working-class Activism in Richmond, Virginia, 1865–1890" (Ph.D. diss., University of Pittsburgh, 1981).

5. There has been an enormous amount of work done on the survival and maintenance of black families, and social historians and feminist theorists have made critical contributions to understanding the role of unpaid women's (and, to a lesser degree, children's) work in reproducing the labor power of male industrial workers and maintaining capitalism. For a sampling of historical studies of African American families, see Herbert Gutman, *The Black Family in Slavery*

and Freedom, 1750–1925 (New York: Pantheon Books, 1976); James Borchert, *Alley Life in Washington: Family, Community, Religion, and Folklife in the City, 1850–1970* (Urbana: University of Illinois Press, 1980); Elmer Martin and Joanne Martin, *The Black Extended Family* (Chicago: University of Chicago Press, 1978); Andrew Billingsley, *Black Families in White America* (Englewood Cliffs: Prentice-Hall, 1968); Harriet Pipes McAdoo, ed., *Black Families* (Beverly Hills: Sage Publications, 1981); Sharon Harley, "For the Good of Family and Race: Gender, Work, and Domestic Roles in the Black Community, 1880–1930," *Signs* 15 (1990), 336–49; Jacqueline Jones, *Labor of Love, Labor of Sorrow: Black Women, Work, and the Family, From Slavery to the Present* (New York: Basic Books, 1985); E. H. Pleck, "The Two Parent Household: Black Family Structure in Late Nineteenth-Century Boston," *Journal of Social History* 6 (Fall 1972), 3–31. Important works on the role of unpaid women's labor, the reproduction of male labor power, and the maintenance of capitalism include Emily Blumenfeld and Susan Mann, "Domestic Labour and the Reproduction of Labour Power: Towards an Analysis of Women, the Family, and Class," in *Hidden in the Household: Women's Domestic Labour under Capitalism*, ed. Bonnie Fox (Toronto: Women's Educational Press, 1980), 267–307; Wally Seccombe, "The Housewife and Her Labour under Capitalism," *New Left Review* 83 (January–February 1974), 3–24; Jean Gardiner, "Women's Domestic Labour," *New Left Review* 89 (January–February 1975), 47–58; Margaret Coulsen, Branka Magas, and Hilary Wainwright, "'The Housewife and Her Labour under Capitalism'—A Critique," *New Left Review* 89 (January–February 1975), 59–72; Ira Gerstein, "Domestic Work and Capitalism," *Radical America* 7 (July–October 1973), 101–28; Paul A. Smith, "Domestic Labour and Marx's Theory of Value," in *Feminism and Materialism*, eds. Annette Kuhn and Ann Marie Wolpe (London, 1978), 198–219; Jeanne Boydston, *Home and Work: Housework, Wages, and the Ideology of Labor in the Early Republic* (New York: Oxford University Press, 1990); Martha E. Gimenez, "The Dialectics of Waged and Unwaged Work: Waged Work, Domestic Labor and Household Survival in the United States," in *Work without Wages: Domestic Labor and Self-Employment within Capitalism*, eds. Jane L. Collins and Martha Gimenez (Albany, N.Y.: State University of New York Press, 1990), 25–45; Susan Strasser, *Never Done: A History of American Housework* (New York: Pantheon Books, 1982).

6. Heidi Hartmann, "The Family as the Locus of Gender, Class, and Political Struggle: The Example of Housework," *Signs* 6 (Spring 1981), 366–94; Lois Rita Helmbold, "Beyond the Family Economy: Black and White Working-Class Women during the Great Depression," *Feminist Studies* 13 (Fall 1987), 629–55; Susan Mann, "Slavery, Sharecropping and Sexual Inequality," *Signs* 14, no. 4 (1989), 774–98.

7. Carolyn Steedman, *Landscape for a Good Woman: A Story of Two Lives* (New Brunswick, N.J.: Rutgers University Press, 1987, orig. 1986), 13; Elizabeth Faue, "Reproducing the Class Struggle: Perspectives on the Writing of Working Class History," Paper Presented at Social Science History Association

Meeting, Minneapolis, October 19, 1990 (paper in author's possession), 8; see also Faue, *Community of Suffering and Struggle: Women, Men, and the Labor Movement in Minneapolis, 1915–1945* (Chapel Hill: University of North Carolina Press, 1991), 15; Faue, "Gender, Class, and the Politics of Work in Women's History" (unpublished paper in author's possession).

8. Although these questions have been debated for over two decades, we really do not have adequate answers, since most of the assertions are not based on historical analysis but are drawn from the insights and memories of a handful of black males writing in the shadows of the Moynihan Report. Whereas social scientists such as Calvin Hernton, William Grier, and Price Cobbs suggest that black mothers inflicted irreparable psychological damage on their sons, feminist scholars understood that learning the dominant codes and social conventions of the South was necessary for survival. See, for example, Calvin Hernton, *Sex and Racism in America* (Garden City, N.Y.: Doubleday, 1965); William H. Grier and Price M. Cobbs, *Black Rage* (New York: Basic Books, 1968), 51; Paula Giddings, *When and Where I Enter: The Impact of Black Women on Race and Sex in America* (New York: Morrow, 1984); Patricia Morton, *Disfigured Images: The Historical Assault on Afro-American Women* (Westport, Conn.: Greenwood Press, 1991), 116; Dolores Janiewski, *Sisterhood Denied: Race, Gender, and Class in a New South Community* (Philadelphia: Temple University Press, 1985), 45; Jacquelyn Dowd Hall, *Revolt against Chivalry: Jessie Daniel Ames and the Women's Campaign against Lynching* (New York: Columbia University Press, 1979), 142.

9. The most sophisticated insights into the political ramifications of how Southern black mothers raised their daughters can be found in the work of Elsa Barkley Brown, "Mothers of Mind," *Sage* 6 (Summer 1989), 3–10 and "African-American Women's Quilting: A Framework for Conceptualizing and Teaching African-American Women's History," *Signs* 14 (Summer 1989), 928-29.

10. Elsa Barkley Brown, "To Catch the Vision of Freedom: Reconstructing Southern Black Women's Political History, 1865–1885," in *To Be a Citizen*, ed. Arlene Avakian, John Bracey, and Ann Gordon (Amherst, Mass.: University of Massachusetts Press, forthcoming).

11. Hunter, "Household Workers in the Making," 170–86; Joe William Trotter, Jr., *Coal, Class, and Color: Blacks in Southern West Virginia, 1915–1932* (Urbana: University of Illinois Press, 1990), 199–205; Elsa Barkley Brown, "Womanist Consciousness: Maggie Lena Walker and the Independent Order of St. Luke," *Signs* 14, no. 3 (1989), 175; Bruce Ergood, "The Female Protection and the Sun Light: Two Contemporary Negro Mutual Aid Societies," *Florida Historical Quarterly* 50, no. 1 (July 1971), 25–38; Lewis, *In Their Own Interests*, 72.

12. Elsa Barkley Brown, "Womanist Consciousness," 610–33; Evelyn Brooks Higginbotham, *Righteous Discontent: The Women's Movement in the Black Baptist Church, 1880–1920* (Cambridge, Mass.: Harvard University Press, 1993); Lewis, *In Their Own Interests*; Trotter, *Coal, Class, and Color*; Rachleff, *Black Labor in the South*. Unfortunately, while many of these institutions still exist, they declined in size and importance with the expansion of less expensive commercial

insurance policies, the increasing role of the state in providing unemployment benefits, and the general decline of the economy during the depression. (Trotter, *Coal, Class, and Color*, 198.)

13. Geraldine Moore, *Behind the Ebony Mask* (Birmingham: Southern University Press, 1961), 15.

14. Allison Davis, Burleigh B. Gardner, and Mary R. Gardner, *Deep South: A Social Anthropological Study of Caste and Class* (Chicago: University of Chicago Press, 1941), 230.

15. See William J. Wilson, *The Truly Disadvantaged: The Inner City, the Underclass, and Public Policy* (Chicago: University of Chicago Press, 1987), 56–57; see also Wilson and Loic J. D. Wacquant, "The Cost of Racial and Class Exclusion in the Inner City," *The Annals* 501 (January 1989), 26–47. Recent historical literature and a much older sociological literature challenges Wilson's claim of a "golden age" of black community, especially Lewis, *In Their Own Interests*; Trotter, *Coal, Class, and Color*; Kenneth Marvin Hamilton, *Black Towns and Profit: Promotion and Development in the Trans-Appalachian West, 1877–1915* (Urbana: University of Illinois Press, 1991); Robin D. G. Kelley, "The Black Poor and the Politics of Opposition in a New South City," in *The "Underclass" Debate: Views from History*, ed. Michael Katz (Princeton: Princeton University Press, 1993), 293–333; E. Franklin Frazier, *Black Bourgeoisie* (Glencoe, Ill.: Free Press, 1957); St. Clair Drake and Horace Cayton, *Black Metropolis: A Study of Negro Life in a Northern City* (New York: Harper and Row, 1962, orig. 1945), II, 526–63; Davis, Gardner, and Gardner, *Deep South*, 230–36.

16. Although my general remarks apply to most black denominations, we must remain cognizant of the fact that the "black church" is not a monolithic institution. Not only are there different rituals, modes of worship, and biblical interpretations, but they often differ in terms of class membership. The African Methodist Episcopal Church, for example, has had a much larger middle-class congregation than the Baptist and Pentecostal churches. The Pentecostal churches have had a strong working-class following, especially in the urban North. For more on black churches, see C. Eric Lincoln and Lawrence H. Mamiya, *The Black Church in the African American Experience* (Durham, N.C.: Duke University Press, 1990); Hans Baer, *The Black Spiritual Movement: A Religious Response to Racism* (Knoxville, Tenn.: University of Tennessee Press, 1984); Hans A. Baer and Merrill Singer, eds., *African-American Religion in the Twentieth Century: Varieties of Protest and Accommodation* (Knoxville, Tenn.: University of Tennessee Press, 1992); Arthur Huff Fauset, *Black Gods of the Metropolis: Negro Religious Cults of the Urban North* (Philadelphia: University of Pennsylvania Press, 1944); Higginbotham, *Righteous Discontent*; William E. Montgomery, *Under Their Own Vine and Fig Tree: The African-American Church in the South, 1865–1900* (Baton Rouge: Louisiana State University Press, 1993); Milton C. Sernett, ed., *Afro-American Religious History: A Documentary Witness* (Durham, N.C.: Duke University Press, 1985); Clarence E. Walker, *A Rock in a Weary Land: The African Methodist Episcopal Church during the Civil War and Reconstruction* (Baton Rouge:

Louisiana State University Press, 1982); Edward L. Wheeler, *Uplifting the Race: The Black Minister in the New South, 1865–1902* (Lanham, Md.: University Press of America, 1986); Gayraud Wilmore, *Black Religion and Black Radicalism: An Interpretation of the Religious History of Afro-American People*, 2nd ed. (Maryknoll, N.Y.: Orbis Books, 1983).

17. Higginbotham, *Righteous Discontent*, 195; Wade-Gayles, *Pushed Back to Strength*, 13.

18. Trotter, *Coal, Class, and Color*, 180–81; Higginbotham, *Righteous Discontent*, 192; Elsa Barkley Brown, "Uncle Ned's Children: Richmond, Virginia's Black Community, 1890–1930" (Ph.D. diss., Kent State University, 1994).

19. Robert Korstad and Nelson Lichtenstein, "Opportunities Found and Lost: Labor, Radicals, and the Early Civil Rights Movement," *Journal of American History* 75 (December 1988), 786–811; Korstad, "'Daybreak of Freedom'"; Honey, *Southern Labor and Black Civil Rights*; Kelley, *Hammer and Hoe*.

20. Lucy Randolph Mason, *To Win These Rights: A Personal Story of the CIO in the South* (New York: Harper & Row, 1952), 108; also quoted in Honey, *Southern Labor and Black Civil Rights*, 136.

21. Quoted in Kelley, *Hammer and Hoe*, 149.

22. "Satisfied" quoted in Brenda McCallum, "Songs of Work and Songs of Worship: Sanctifying Black Unionism in the Southern City of Steel," *New York Folklore* 14, nos. 1 and 2 (1988), 27; George Korson, *Coal Dust on the Fiddle: Songs and Stories of the Bituminous Industry* (Hatboro, Pa.: Folklore Associates, 1943).

23. Sterling Spero and Abram L. Harris, *The Black Worker: The Negro and the Labor Movement* (New York: Columbia University Press, 1931), 464–65; Honey, *Southern Labor and Black Civil Rights*, 48, 168; Kelley, *Hammer and Hoe*, 110, 112, 114–16.

24. The narratives I am thinking about are Nell Irvin Painter, *The Narrative of Hosea Hudson, His life as a Negro Communist in the South* (Cambridge, Mass.: Harvard University Press, 1979), 347–51; Jane Maguire, *On Shares: Ed Brown's Story* (New York: Norton, 1975), 125–33; Theodore Rosengarten, *All God's Dangers: The Life of Nate Shaw* (New York: Avon, 1974), 189, 192, 238–40.

25. See Vincent Harding, *There Is a River: The Black Struggle for Freedom in America* (New York: Harcourt Brace Jovanovich, 1981).

26. W.E.B. DuBois, *Black Reconstruction in America: An Essay toward a History of the Part Which Black Folk Played in the Attempt to Reconstruct Democracy in America, 1860–1880* (New York: Harcourt Brace, 1935), 124.

27. LeRoi Jones, *Blues People* (New York: Morrow, 1963); Lawrence Levine, *Black Culture and Black Consciousness: Afro-American Folk Thought from Slavery to Freedom* (New York: Oxford University Press, 1977), xi; Sterling Stuckey, *Slave Culture: Nationalist Theory and the Foundations of Black America* (New York: Oxford University Press, 1987); Sterling Stuckey, "Through the Prism of Folklore: The Black Ethos in Slavery," *Massachusetts Review* 9 (Summer 1968), 417–37; Hazel Carby, "'It Jus Be's Dat Way Sometime': The Sexual Politics of

Women's Blues," *Radical America* 20, no. 4 (1987), 9–22; Charles P. Henry, *Culture and African-American Politics* (Bloomington: Indiana University Press, 1990); John W. Roberts, *From Trickster to Badman: The Black Folk Hero in Slavery and Freedom* (Philadelphia: University of Pennsylvania Press, 1989); McCallum, "Songs of Work and Songs of Worship," 9–33; Gladys-Marie Fry, *Night Riders in Black Folk History* (Knoxville: University of Tennessee Press, 1975).

28. Charles S. Johnson, *The Negro in American Civilization: A Study of Negro Life and Race Relations in the Light of Social Research* (New York: H. Holt, 1930), 299–310; Paul K. Edwards, *The Southern Urban Negro as a Consumer* (College Park, Md.: McGrath, 1969, orig. 1932), 7–8.

29. Lewis, *In Their Own Interests*, 91–92.

30. Higginbotham, *Righteous Discontent*, 199, also 201; Trotter, *Coal, Class, and Color*, 184.

31. W.E.B. DuBois and Augustus Granville Dill, eds., *Morals and Manners among Negro Americans*, Atlanta University Publications, No. 18 (Atlanta: Atlanta University Press, 1914), 82, 85, 87, 93–94.

32. Higginbotham, *Righteous Discontent*, 204.

33. According to Zora Neale Hurston, "jook" was "the word for a Negro pleasure house. It may mean a bawdy house. It may mean the house set apart on public works where men and women dance, drink, and gamble. Often it is a combination of these." Zora Neale Hurston, "Characteristics of Negro Expression," in *Negro Anthology*, ed. Nancy Cunard (New York: Negro Universities Press, 1969), also quoted in Katrina Hazzard-Gordon, *Jookin': The Rise of Social Dance Formations in African-American Culture* (Philadelphia: Temple University Press, 1990), 79.

34. Dunn quoted in Clifford M. Kuhn, Harlon E. Joye, and E. Bernard West, *Living Atlanta: An Oral History of the City, 1914–1948* (Athens, Ga.: University of Georgia Press, 1990), 275. On the social meaning of dance halls and blues clubs in Southern black life, see Hunter, "Household Workers in the Making," 92–93; Lewis, *In Their Own Interests*, 99–100; George Wright, *Life behind a Veil: Blacks in Louisville, Kentucky, 1865–1930* (Baton Rouge: Louisiana State University Press, 1985), 138; Hazzard-Gordon, *Jookin'*.

35. My use of "alternative" cultures is borrowed from Raymond Williams, "Base and Superstructure in Marxist Cultural Theory," in *Problems in Materialism and Culture: Selected Essays* (London: NLB, 1980), 41–42.

36. Hazzard-Gordon, *Jookin'*, 88.

37. Paul Gilroy, "One Nation under a Groove: The Cultural Politics of 'Race' and Racism in Britain," in *Anatomy of Racism*, ed. David Theo Goldberg (Minneapolis: University of Minnesota Press, 1990), 274.

38. Kuhn et al., *Living Atlanta*, 190.

39. Higginbotham, *Righteous Discontent*. My thinking here owes a great deal to Tera Hunter's forthcoming book, *Contesting the New South: The Politics and Culture of Wage Household Labor in Atlanta, 1861–1920* (unpublished manuscript), chapter 5; Kathy Peiss, *Cheap Amusements: Working Women and Leisure in Turn-of-the-Century New York* (Philadelphia: Temple University Press, 1986);

Hazel Carby, "Policing the Black Woman's Body in an Urban Context," *Critical Inquiry* 18 (Summer 1992), 738–755; Judith Walkowitz, *Prostitution and Victorian Society: Women, Class, and the State* (New York, 1980); Victoria Wollcott, "'I'm as Good as Any Woman in Your Town': African-American Woman and the Politics of Identity in Inter-War Detroit" (Ph.D. diss., University of Michigan, in progress); Wollcott, "Mediums, Messages, and Lucky Numbers: African-American Female Leisure Workers in Inter-War Detroit" (unpublished paper in author's possession); and to conversations with Tera Hunter and Victoria Wollcott.

40. Report Involving Race Question, June 1943, p. 1, Box 10, Cooper Green Papers (Birmingham Public Library, Birmingham).

41. Kuhn et al., *Living Atlanta*, 39.

42. Wade-Gayles, *Pushed Back to Strength*, 13; Asa H. Gordon, *The Georgia Negro: A History* (Ann Arbor, Mich.: Edwards Bros., 1937), 91. Of course, Gordon overstates his case. Paul Edwards's 1932 study of black consumers in the urban South reveals that "common and semi-skilled labor families" were less likely to buy brand name clothing, budget constraints being an important factor. Those who did buy brand name products often did so to protect themselves from unscrupulous sales people. Black consumers were more likely to trust national brands than local "bargains" that tended to be overpriced and of poorer quality. (Paul K. Edwards, *The Southern Urban Negro as a Consumer* [New York: McGrath, 1969, orig. 1932], 155–66.)

43. See Donald Bogle, *Toms, Coons, Mulattoes, Mammies and Bucks: An Interpretive History of Blacks in American Films* (New York: Continuum, 1989), 19–94 passim.; Robert C. Toll, *Blacking Up: The Minstrel Show in Nineteenth Century America* (New York: Oxford University Press, 1974); and for a discussion of the "bourgeois promenade" and how it reproduces class hierarchies, see David Scobey, "Anatomy of the Promenade: The Politics of Bourgeois Sociability in Nineteenth-Century New York," *Social History* 17 (May 1992), 203–27.

44. Studies of style politics in the dress of U.S. working people is still underdeveloped. Historical works that deal with this aspect of working-class opposition suggest a range of uses of clothing, from using dress to evade one's oppressors to adorning the body with symbols intended as a militant, resistive statement. For two pathbreaking examples, Jonathan Prude, "To Look upon the 'Lower Orders': Runaway Ads and the Appearance of Unfree Laborers in America, 1750–1800," *Journal of American History* 78 (June 1991), 124–59; Jacquelyn Dowd Hall, "Disorderly Women: Gender and Labor Militancy in the Appalachian South," *Journal of American History*, 73 (September 1986), 372–73.

45. Herbert Shapiro, *White Violence and Black Response: From Reconstruction to Montgomery* (Amherst, Mass.: University of Massachusetts Press, 1988), 147, 305–9.

46. James C. Scott, *Domination and the Arts of Resistance: Hidden Transcripts* (New Haven: Yale University Press, 1990), 120. For similar examples of the importance of monitoring and invading black space for maintaining order,

see Janiewski, *Sisterhood Denied*, 121; Kelley, *Hammer and Hoe*, 161–67; Howard Odum, *Race and Rumors of Race: Challenge to American Crisis* (Chapel Hill: University of North Carolina Press, 1943), 96–104; Shapiro, *White Violence and Black Response*, 224–37; and for the antebellum period, see Herbert Aptheker, *American Negro Slave Revolts* (New York: International Publishers, 1943), 59.

47. Painter, *Narrative of Hosea Hudson*, 162.

48. Lester C. Lamon, *Black Tennesseans, 1900–1930* (Knoxville, Tenn.: University of Tennessee Press, 1977), 18.

Chapter 3. Congested Terrain

1. Henry D. Spalding, comp., *Encyclopedia of Black Folklore and Humor* (Middle Village, N.Y.: Jonathan David Publishing, 1971), 446.

2. Quote from Robert J. Norrell, "Labor at the Ballot Box: Alabama Politics from the New Deal to the Dixiecrat Movement," *Journal of Southern History* 57, no. 2 (May 1991), 227. Wilkinson's own white supremacist organization was formed in part as a response to a black person's insistence on riding with whites on an Anniston train. *Alabama* 7, no. 30 (July 24, 1942), 9.

3. On the political and ideological changes caused by the war, see Pete Daniel, "Going among Strangers: Southern Reactions to World War II," *Journal of American History* 77 (December 1990), 893, 906–8; Robert Korstad and Nelson Lichtenstein, "Opportunities Found and Lost: Labor, Radicals, and the Early Civil Rights Movement," *Journal of American History* 75 (December 1988), 786–811; Bernice Reagon, "World War II Reflected in Black Music: Uncle Sam Called Me," *Southern Exposure* 2 (Winter 1974), 170–84; George Lipsitz, "*A Rainbow at Midnight*": *Labor and Culture in the 1940s* (Urbana: University of Illinois Press, 1994); Harvard Sitkoff, "Racial Militancy and Interracial Violence in the Second World War," *Journal of American History* 58 (December 1971), 661–81.

4. Some of the more sophisticated studies have paid particular attention to American workers and public space, although most of this work focuses on leisure (e.g., sports, public parks, theater, etc.) or public displays of working-class solidarity. Moreover, almost all of this scholarship has been preoccupied with Northeastern white workers. See especially Francis G. Couvares, *The Remaking of Pittsburgh: Class and Culture in an Industrializing City, 1877–1919* (Albany, N.Y.: State University of New York Press, 1984); Susan G. Davis, *Parades and Power: Street Theater in Nineteenth-Century Philadelphia* (Philadelphia: Temple University Press, 1986); Dirk Hoerder, *Crowd Action in Revolutionary Massachusetts, 1765–1780* (New York: Academic Press, 1977); Kathy Peiss, *Cheap Amusements: Working Women and Leisure in Turn-of-the-Century New York* (Philadelphia: Temple University Press, 1986); Steven J. Ross, *Workers on the Edge: Work, Leisure, and Politics in Industrializing Cincinnati, 1788–1890* (New York: Columbia University Press, 1985); Roy Rosenzweig, *Eight Hours for What We Will: Workers and Leisure in an Industrial City, 1870–1920* (New York: Cambridge University Press, 1983); Christine Stansell, *City of Women: Sex and Class in New York,*

1789–1860 (New York: Knopf, 1986); Sean Wilentz, *Chants Democratic: New York City and the Rise of the American Working Class, 1788–1850* (New York: Oxford University Press, 1984). One powerful exception, which is more of an examination of contemporary Los Angeles than a historical monograph, is Mike Davis, *City of Quartz: Excavating the Future in Los Angeles* (London: Verso, 1990).

5. See, for example, August Meier and Elliot Rudwick, "The Boycott Movement against Jim Crow Streetcars in the South, 1900–1906," in *Along the Color Line: Explorations in the Black Experience*, eds. Meier and Rudwick (Urbana: University of Illinois Press, 1976), 267–89; Roger A. Fischer, "A Pioneer Protest: The New Orleans Street-Car Controversy of 1867," *Journal of Negro History* 53 (July 1968), 219–33; Neil McMillen, *Dark Journey: Black Mississippians in the Age of Jim Crow* (Urbana: University of Illinois Press, 1989), 293–95; Lester C. Lamon, *Black Tennesseans, 1900–1930* (Knoxville: University of Tennessee Press, 1977), 20–36; John Dittmer, *Black Georgia in the Progressive Era, 1900–1920* (Urbana: University of Illinois Press, 1977), 16–19; George C. Wright, *Life Behind a Veil: Blacks in Louisville, Kentucky, 1865–1930* (Baton Rouge: Louisiana State University Press, 1985), 52–55, 191–92, 248–49. For specific but brief examples of conflict on Southern public transportation during World War II, see Daniel, "Going among Strangers," 906; Dolores Janiewski, *Sisterhood Denied: Race, Gender, and Class in a New South Community* (Philadelphia: Temple University Press, 1985), 141. Clifford M. Kuhn, Harlon B. Joye, and E. Bernard West, *Living Atlanta: An Oral History of the City, 1914–1948* (Athens, Ga.: University of Georgia Press, 1990), 77–82, is an exception, for they offer several pages of testimony illuminating the day-to-day acts of domination and resistance on Atlanta's busses and streetcars. Likewise, Howard Odum has discovered "stories" of these various acts of opposition on busses, but he leaves the reader with the impression that these incidents were exaggerated, invented, or probable but not documented. See *Race and Rumors of Race: Challenge to American Crisis* (Chapel Hill: University of North Carolina Press, 1943), 113–28.

6. Birmingham *News*, June 25, 1943.

7. Given my use of theater as a metaphor, I end up privileging public conveyances themselves as sites of contestation. However, resistance to conditions on busses and streetcars did not always take place at the point of conflict. Filing complaints with the Birmingham Electric Company was relatively common, but it involved a great deal of time and courage to travel to the BECO office in person or write a letter. Besides, filing complaints often *accompanied* acts of resistance on public transportation. Furthermore, one strategy of dealing with the daily indignities of riding public transportation was to wage individual boycotts. We will never know how many black working people, like Birmingham domestic worker Rosa Jackson, simply refused to ride the bus in protest at the treatment of African Americans. (Rosa Jackson interview, by Peggy Hamrick, July 23 and 24, 1984, p. 7, Working Lives Collection, Oral History Project, University of Alabama, Tuscaloosa (hereafter cited WLC).

8. James Armstrong interview, by Cliff Kuhn, July 16, 1984, p. 9, WLC.

9. Martin P. Knowlton to James Dombrowski, June 27, 1946, Box 3, Southern Conference for Human Welfare Papers, Tuskegee Institute.

10. "Race Complaints for Last Twelve Months," and "Incidents Reported," September 1, 1941 to August 31, 1942, Box 10, Cooper Green Papers, Birmingham Public Library. Unless otherwise indicated, all official reports and documents cited below concerning black resistance on Birmingham busses are located in Box 10, Cooper Green Papers.

11. Report Involving Race Question, August 1943, p. 1.

12. Ibid., October 1943, p. 1.

13. Ibid., June 1943, p. 4; Birmingham *World*, July 27, 1943.

14. "Race Complaints for Last Twelve Months," and "Incidents Reported," September 1, 1941 to August 31, 1942, "Analysis of Complaints and Incidents Concerning Race Problems on Birmingham Electric Company's Transportation System," 12 Months Ending August 31, 1942.

15. Birmingham Electric Co., Transportation Department, "Classification—Complaints & Incidents Involving Race Question"; N. H. Hawkins, Jr., Birmingham Electric Company Transportation Department, n.d.

16. Report Involving Race Question, May 1944, p. 3. See complaints reported in "Race Complaints for Last Twelve Months," September 1, 1941 to August 31, 1942; also Reports Involving Race Question, March 1943, p. 3; September 1943, p. 2; November 1943, p. 2; May 1944, p. 1.

17. N. H. Hawkins, Jr., Birmingham Electric Company Transportation Department, n.d..

18. Report Involving Race Question, February 1943, p. 2. We should presume that he did not win his court case, for it would have forced the company to change its policy.

19. Report Involving Race Question, February 1944, p. 4.

20. Ibid., April 1944, p. 2.

21. Ibid., p. 3, emphasis added.

22. Report Involving Race Question, November 1943, p. 2.

23. Several such cases are documented in Report Involving Race Question, March 1943, pp. 4–5; "Incidents Reported," September 1, 1941 to August 31, 1942, "Analysis of Complaints and Incidents Concerning Race Problems on Birmingham Electric Company's Transportation System," 12 Months Ending August 31, 1942, and also individual incidents in Reports Involving Race Question, February 1943–April 1944.

24. Robert J. Norrell, "Caste in Steel: Jim Crow Careers in Birmingham, Alabama," *Journal of American History* 73, no. 3 (December 1986), 687; Mary Martha Thomas, "Alabama Women on the Home Front, World War II," *Alabama Heritage* 19 (Winter 1991), 9; Geraldine Moore, *Behind the Ebony Mask* (Birmingham: Southern University Press, 1961), 28.

25. "Incidents Reported," September 1, 1941 to August 31, 1942, pp.

5–6; and note incidents on the Travellick line, August 2, 1943, and North Bessemer line, August 1, 1943, in Report Involving Race Question, August 1943, p. 1.

26. "Analysis of Complaints and Incidents Concerning Race Problems on Birmingham Electric Company's Transportation System," 12 Months Ending August 31, 1942; "Incidents Reported," September 1, 1941 to August 31, 1942, p. 4, Report Involving Race Question, October 1943, p. 2.

27. Herbert Shapiro, *White Violence and Black Response: From Reconstruction to Montgomery* (Amherst, Mass.: University of Massachusetts Press, 1988); James A. Burran, "Racial Violence in the South during World War II" (Ph.D. diss., University of Tennessee, 1977); Janiewski, *Sisterhood Denied*, 141; John Hope Franklin, *From Slavery to Freedom: A History of American Negroes*, 5th ed. (New York: Knopf, 1980), 447.

28. Report Involving Race Question, March 1943, p. 3. For other incidents of resistance by servicemen, see Report Involving Race Question, May 1944, pp. 1 and 2; January 1944, p. 1; February 1944, p. 3.

29. Report Involving Race Question, March 1943, p. 5.

30. Ibid., March 1944, p. 1.

31. Ibid., June 1943, p. 5.

32. Ibid., March 1944, p. 2.

33. Ibid., October 1943, p. 1.

34. Odum, *Race and Rumors of Race*, 77–79; and on zoot suit cultural politics during the war, see chapter 7 and Stuart Cosgrove, "The Zoot-Suit and Style Warfare," *History Workshop Journal* 18 (Autumn 1984), 77–91; Mauricio Mazon, *The Zoot-Suit Riots: The Psychology of Symbolic Annihilation* (Austin: University of Texas Press, 1984); Eric Lott, "Double V, Double-Time: Bebop's Politics of Style," *Callalloo* 11, no. 3 (1988), 597–605; Kobena Mercer, "Black Hair/Style Politics," *New Formations* 3 (Winter 1987), 49; Bruce M. Tyler, "Black Jive and White Repression," *Journal of Ethnic Studies* 16, no. 4 (1989), 31–66. In fact, white Southerners not only feared zoot suiters but a false rumor circulated throughout the country that the zoot originated in Gainesville, Georgia, by a young man enamoured with the character Rhett Butler in "Gone with the Wind." "Zoot Suit Originated in Georgia," *New York Times*, June 11, 1943.

35. "Incidents Reported," September 1, 1941 to August 31, 1942, pp. 4, 8; Report Involving Race Question, February 1943, pp. 2 and 3; September 1943, p. 1; see also numerous incidents from Reports (1942–44). For a discussion of "Stagolee" folklore and the political implications of "baaad niggers" in African American working-class consciousness, see John W. Roberts, *From Trickster to Badman: The Black Folk Hero in Slavery and Freedom* (Philadelphia: University of Pennsylvania Press, 1989), 171–215; Lawrence Levine, *Black Culture and Black Consciousness: Afro-American Folk Thought from Slavery to Freedom* (New York: Oxford University Press, 1977), 407–19. Perhaps these men might fall within Eric Hobsbawm's definition of "primitive rebels," but to regard their ac-

tivity as "prepolitical" obscures the fact that most of them are directly challenging racist practices. Hobsbawm, *Primitive Rebels: Studies in Archaic Forms of Social Movements in the 19th and 20th Centuries* (New York: Norton, 1965, orig. 1959).

36. Report Involving Race Question, November 1943, p. 2.

37. Ibid., December 1943, p. 1.

38. Ibid.

39. Report Involving Race Question, March 1943, p. 3.

40. "Race Complaints for Last Twelve Months," September 1, 1941 to August 31, 1942; Willi Coleman, "Black Women and Segregated Public Transportation: Ninety Years of Resistance," in *Black Women in United States History*, ed. Darlene Clark Hine (Brooklyn, N.Y.: Carlson Publishers, 1989), V, 295–301, quote from p. 295.

41. "Race Complaints for Last Twelve Months," September 1, 1941 to August 31, 1942, p. 1; Report Involving Race Question, October 1943, p. 4; Birmingham *World*, October 29, 1943.

42. Report Involving Race Question, March 1943, p. 4.

43. Ibid.

44. Ibid., pp. 5–6.

45. Two such incidents took place on the South Bessemer line, August 2, 1942, and the West End line, June 3, 1942, "Race Complaints for Last Twelve Months," September 1, 1941 to August 31, 1942; Report Involving Race Question, December 1943, p. 2.

46. Report Involving Race Question, September 1943, p. 2; also see May 1944, p. 2.

47. See especially Report Involving Race Question, February 1943, pp. 1, 4; March 1943, p. 4; December 1943, p. 2; May 1944, p. 2.

48. For specific complaints, see Report Involving Race Question, February 1943, p. 3; March 1943, p. 1; September 1943, pp. 1 and 3; November 1943, pp. 1 and 3; December 1943, p. 2; January, 1944, p. 2; February 1944, pp. 2 and 4.

49. See Tera Hunter, "Household Workers in the Making: Afro-American Women in Atlanta and the New South, 1861–1920" (Ph.D. diss., Yale University, 1990).

50. Carol Brooks Gardner, "Analyzing Gender in Public Places: Rethinking Goffman's Vision of Everyday Life," *American Sociologist* 20 (Spring 1989), 42–56.

51. Report Involving Race Question, May 1944, pp. 2–3. "Loud-talking," according to linguistic anthropologist Claudia Mitchell-Kernan, is an age-old discursive strategy among African Americans which "by virtue of its volume permits hearers other than the addressee, and is objectionable because of this. Loud-talking requires an audience and can only occur in a situation where there are potential hearers other than the interlocutors." Moreover, loud-talking assumes "an antagonistic posture toward the addressee." Claudia Mitchell-Ker-

nan, "Signifying, Loud-talking, and Marking," in *Rappin' and Stylin' Out: Communication in Urban Black America*, ed. Thomas Kochman (Urbana: University of Illinois Press, 1972), 329 and 331.

52. Report Involving Race Question, August 1943, p. 1.

53. "Incidents Reported," September 1, 1941 to August 31, 1942, pp. 4–6. On public cursing as an powerful symbolic act of resistance, see James C. Scott, *Domination and the Arts of Resistance: Hidden Transcripts* (New Haven: Yale University Press, 1990), 215.

54. Report Involving Race Question, June 1943, p. 4.

55. Report Involving Race Question, October 1943, p. 3. Report Involving Race Question, August 1942, p. 2.

56. "Race Complaints for Last Twelve Months," and "Incidents Reported," September 1, 1941 to August 31, 1942; Report Involving Race Question, December 1943, p. 2.

57. Reports Involving Race Question, March 1943, p. 1.

58. Ibid., October 1943, p. 2.

59. Birmingham *World*, October 29, 1943; "Southern Negro Youth Congress—Forum," February 6, 1984, presentations by Henry Winston, Esther Cooper Jackson, James Jackson, and Grace Tillman Bassett (untranscribed tape), Oral History of the American Left, Tamiment Library, New York University; FBI Report, "Southern Negro Youth Congress, Birmingham, Alabama," June 14, 1943, File 100-82, p. 5; James Jackson, "For Common Courtesy on Common Carriers," *Worker*, June 4, 1963.

Chapter 4. Birmingham's Untouchables

1. James C. Scott, Domination and the Arts of Resistance: Hidden Transcripts (New Haven: Yale University Press, 1990), 199.

2. Nicholas Lemann, *The Promised Land: The Great Migration and How It Changed Black America* (New York: Knopf, 1991), 291.

3. Robert J. Norrell, "Caste in Steel: Jim Crow Careers in Birmingham, Alabama," *Journal of American History* 73, no. 3 (December 1986), 675, 686–87; George W. Blanks to Cooper Green, September 21, 1945, Louis Pizitz to Cooper Green, August 24, 1945, J. B. Roberts, Jr., to Cooper Green, September 5, 1945, Box 8, Cooper Green Papers. Indeed, the Birmingham Chamber of Commerce was apparently so dominated by TCI that several businessmen supportive of diversification formed the Birmingham District Industrial Development Corporation for the purposes of attracting new industries. Jack Yauger to Cooper Green, May 19, 1945, Box 8, Cooper Green Papers. The most important study of postwar Detroit and the black working class is Thomas Sugrue, "The Origins of the Urban Crisis: Detroit, 1940–1960" (Ph.D. diss., Harvard University, 1992); see also Sugrue, "The Structures of Urban Poverty: The Reorganization of Space and Work in Three Periods of American History," in *The "Underclass" Debate: Views from History*, ed. Michael B. Katz (Princeton, N.J.: Princeton University Press, 1993), 85–117.

4. "Report of the President of the Alabama State Industrial Union Council, Period from March 1, 1949 to March 1, 1950," (typescript, March 1, 1950), 1, 5, Box 2, Philip Taft Papers, Birmingham Public Library; Birmingham *Post-Herald*, May 29, 1949; Birmingham *Post-Herald*, September 4, 1950, Birmingham *World*, May 12, 1949; *Proceedings of the Alabama State Industrial Union Council, Ninth Constitutional Convention, CIO, 1948* (typescript, n.d.), 271–74, Box 2, Philip Taft Papers; *Alabama (CIO) News Digest*, May 4, 1949; Horace Huntley, "The Rise and Fall of Mine Mill in Alabama: The Status Quo against Interracial Unionism, 1933–1949," *Journal of the Birmingham Historical Society* 6, no. 1 (January 1979), 7–13, and "Iron Ore Miners and Mine Mill in Alabama, 1933–1952" (Ph.D. diss., University of Pittsburgh, 1976), 110–69; *Alabama (CIO) News Digest*, April 27, May 18, 25, 1949; Vernon H. Jensen, *Nonferrous Metals Industry Unionism, 1932–1952: The Story of Leadership Controversy* (Ithaca: Cornell University Press, 1954), 233–38; Hosea Hudson, "Struggle against Philip Murray's Racist Policies in Birmingham," *Political Affairs* 53, no. 9 (September 1974), 55–57.

5. Charles L. Joiner, "An Analysis of the Employment Patterns of Minority Groups in the Alabama Economy, 1940–1960" (Ph.D. diss., University of Alabama, 1968), 51–55; John Franklin Pearce, "Human Resources in Transition: Rural Alabama since World War II" (Ph.D. diss., University of Alabama, 1966); Norrell, "Caste in Steel," 675, 686–87.

6. Bobby Wilson, "Black Housing Opportunities in Birmingham, Alabama," *Southeastern Geographer* 17, no. 1 (May 1977), 49–57; George A. Denison, M.D., "Health as an Indication of Housing Needs in Birmingham, Alabama, and Recommendations for Slum Clearance, Redevelopment and Public Housing," Report by Jefferson County Board of Health, April 12, 1950, pp. 1 and 9; Birmingham Housing Authority, *Ninth Annual Report of the Housing Authority of the Birmingham District* (June 30, 1948); "Statement of J. C. De Holl, Manager of the Birmingham Housing Authority, Birmingham, Ala.," U.S. Congress, Joint Committee on Housing, *Study and Investigation of Housing: Hearings before the Joint Committee on Housing*, pt. II (Washington, D.C.: Government Printing Office, 1948), 1280, 1286–92; George Denison, M.D., to Birmingham City Commission, November 10, 1949, Box 8, Cooper Green Papers; Robert A. Thompson, Hylan Lewis, and Davis McEntire, "Atlanta and Birmingham: A Comparative Study in Negro Housing," in *Studies in Housing and Minority Groups*, eds. Nathan Glazer and Davis McEntire, (Berkeley and Los Angeles: University of California Press, 1960), 58, 61, 65.

7. "Statement of Molton H. Gray, Chairman, National Council of Negro Veterans," U.S. Congress, Joint Committee on Housing, *Study and Investigation of Housing: Hearings before the Joint Committee on Housing*, pt. II (Washington, D.C., Government Printing Office, 1948), 1368–71; "Statement of Emory O. Jackson, Representing the Alabama Conference of the NAACP Branches," ibid., p. 1373; Thompson et al., "Atlanta and Birmingham," 59–73.

8. U.S. Department of Commerce, Bureau of the Census, *County and*

City Data Book, 1962 (Washington, D.C.: Government Printing Office, 1962), 433. For a comparison of changes in percentage of black population, see Table III; Robert Gaines Corely, "The Quest for Racial Harmony: Race Relations in Birmingham, Alabama, 1947–1963" (Ph.D. diss., University of Virginia, 1979), 36; Edward S. La Monte, "Politics and Welfare in Birmingham, Alabama: 1900–1975" (Ph.D. diss., University of Chicago, 1976), 245, 251; Thompson et al., "Atlanta and Birmingham," 54.

9. Corely, "The Quest for Racial Harmony," 44–46, 54; Florence S. Adams to Mrs. E. D. Wood, Controller's Office, September 28, 1950, Box 1, Jefferson County Coordinating Committee on Social Forces Papers, Birmingham Public Library.

10. "Organization and Rules of Procedure of the Interracial Committee of Jefferson County Coordinating Council," "Minutes of Interracial Committee Meeting, Friday June 15, 1951," Jefferson County Coordinating Committee on Social Forces Papers, Birmingham Public Library, microfilm.

11. "Minutes, Interracial Committee Meeting," September 18, 1951; January 10, 1952; December 18, 1952; November 4, 1953; May 17, 1955; "Minutes, Interracial Committee, Subcommittee on Housing," July 31, 1951, September 15, 1955, Jefferson County Coordinating Committee on Social Forces Papers, Birmingham Public Library, microfilm.

12. "Minutes, Interracial Committee, Subcommittee on Daycare," September 17, 1951, August 17, 1954, Jefferson County Coordinating Committee on Social Forces Papers, Birmingham Public Library, microfilm.

13. "Minutes, Interracial Committee, Subcommittee on Employment Relations," May 31, 1955, Jefferson County Coordinating Committee on Social Forces Papers, Birmingham Public Library, microfilm.

14. "Minutes of Joint Community Chest–Red Cross Meeting, Executive Committee, April 2, 1956," Box 1, Jefferson County Coordinating Committee on Social Forces Papers, Birmingham Public Library.

15. Jacquelyn M. J. Clarke, "Goals and Techniques in Three Negro Civil Rights Organizations in Alabama" (Ph.D. diss., Ohio State University, 1960), Appendix B, pp. 134–49; Glenn T. Eskew, "The Alabama Christian Movement for Human Rights and the Birmingham Struggle for Civil Rights, 1956–1963," in *Birmingham, Alabama, 1956–1963: The Black Struggle for Civil Rights*, ed. David Garrow (Brooklyn, N.Y.: Carlson Publishers, 1989), 45–46.

16. Petition from Alabama Christian Movement for Human Rights to City Commissioners, July 25, 1965, Box 12, Boutwell Papers; Eskew, "The ACMHR"; Birmingham *News*, September 27, 1960; U.S. Bureau of the Census, *Eighteenth Census of the U.S.: 1960*, Vol. I, Part 2, *Characteristics of the Population: Alabama* (Washington, D.C.: Government Printing Office, 1961), 461.

17. Robin D. G. Kelley, *Hammer and Hoe: Alabama Communists during the Great Depression* (Chapel Hill: University of North Carolina Press, 1990).

18. "Statement by Bessie B. Ammons, Janitress, Smithfield Court Project," January 24, 1951, N. C. Ward, Manager, Smithfield Court to Eugene Con-

nor, Commissioner of Public Safety, January 24, 1951, Box 14, James Morgan Papers, Birmingham Public Library.

19. Report from Earl Heaton—M. S. Davis, City Detectives in Charge Vice Squad to C. F. Eddins, Assistant Chief of Police, May 24, 1943, Box 8, Cooper Green Papers. The literature demonstrating a relationship between poverty and crime is voluminous. See Steven Box, *Recession, Crime and Punishment* (Totowa, N.J.: Barnes and Noble Books, 1987); D. Glaser and K. Rice, "Crime, Age, and Employment," *American Sociological Review* 24 (1959), 679–86; A. J. Reiss and A. L. Rhodes, "The Distribution of Juvenile Delinquency in the Social Class Structure," *American Sociological Review* 26 (1961), 720–43; Elliot Currie, *Confronting Crime* (New York: Pantheon Books, 1985), 146; E. Green, "Race, Social Status, and Criminal Arrest," *American Sociological Review* 35 (1970), 476–90; R. W. Beasley and G. Antunes, "The Etiology of Urban Crime: An Ecological Analysis," *Criminology* 11 (1974), 439–61; J. R. Blau and P. M. Blau, "The Cost of Inequality: Metropolitan Structure and Violent Crime," *American Sociological Review* 47 (1982), 114–29; James W. Messerschmidt, *Capitalism, Patriarchy and Crime* (Totowa, N.J.: Rowman and Littlefield, 1986), 54–58; I. Jankovic, "Labor Market and Imprisonment," *Crime and Social Justice* 8 (1977), 17–31; D. Humphries and D. Wallace, "Capitalist Accumulation and Urban Crime, 1950–1971," *Social Problems* 28 (1980), 179–93; A. D. Calvin, "Unemployment among Black Youths, Demographics, and Crime," *Crime and Delinquency* 27 (1981), 9–41; Richard B. Freeman, "The Relation of Criminal Activity to Black Youth Employment," in *The Economics of Race and Crime*, eds. Margaret C. Simms and Samuel L. Myers, Jr. (New Brunswick, N.J.: Transaction Books, 1988), 99–107; Llad Phillips and Harold Votey, Jr., "Rational Choice Models of Crimes by Youth," in ibid., pp. 129–87; Llad Phillips, H. L. Votey, Jr., and D. Maxwell, "Crime, Youth, and the Labor Market," *Journal of Political Economy* 80 (1972), 491–504.

20. Messerschmidt, *Capitalism, Patriarchy and Crime*, 58–60; Anne Campbell, *The Girls in the Gang: A Report from New York City* (New York: Basil Blackwell, 1984) and *Girl Delinquents* (New York: St. Martin's Press, 1981); Pat Carlen, *Women, Crime and Poverty* (Philadelphia: Open University Press, 1988).

21. Birmingham is not unique in this respect. See Messerschmidt, *Capitalism, Patriarchy and Crime*, 52–53; Jefferey Reiman, *The Rich Get Richer and the Poor Get Prison* (New York: Wiley, 1984); Lee P. Brown, "Bridges over Troubled Waters: A Perspective on Policing in the Black Community," in *Black Perspectives on Crime and the Criminal Justice System; A Symposium* ed. Robert L. Woodson (Boston: G.K. Hall, 1977), 87–88.

22. W. Cooper Green to James E. Chappell, August 9, 1943, Florence Adams to Green, September 7, 1943, Adams to Celia Williams, September 7, 1943, "Minutes of the Executive Committee of the Youth Protective Association," January 31, 1945, W. Cooper Green to J. Edgar Hoover, August 3, 1943, Box 15, Cooper Green Papers; "Youth Protective Association of Jefferson County," *Alabama Social Welfare* 10, no. 5 (May 1945), 12–13.

23. Geraldine Moore, *Behind the Ebony Mask* (Birmingham: Southern University Press, 1961), 15.

24. Birmingham *World*, November 5, 1946.

25. David J. Garrow, *Bearing the Cross: Martin Luther King, Jr., and the Southern Christian Leadership Conference* (New York: Morrow, 1986), 254–55; Eskew, "The ACMHR," 82, 85; Taylor Branch, *Parting the Waters: America in the King Years, 1954–1963* (New York: Simon and Schuster, 1988), 759–60; Lee E. Bains, Jr., "Birmingham, 1963: Confrontation over Civil Rights," in *Birmingham, Alabama, 1956–1963: The Black Struggle for Civil Rights*, ed. David Garrow (Brooklyn, N.Y.: Carlson Publishers, 1989), 181. All of the accounts cited above describing the Birmingham demonstrations refer to those who engage in acts of violence as "onlookers," "spectators," people "along the fringes," or "bystanders.

26. Garrow, *Bearing the Cross*, 261; Branch, *Parting the Waters*, 793–802; Bains, "Birmingham, 1963," 182–83.

27. Eskew, "The ACMHR," 75–77; Bains, "Birmingham, 1963," 228–29; Howell Raines, *My Soul Is Rested* (New York: Putnam, 1977), 190; LaMonte, "Politics and Welfare," 285–91.

28. Glenn T. Eskew is one of the few historians who has commented on this strained relationship between Birmingham's black poor and the civil rights movement. As he points out, "While the demands of the Birmingham movement failed to address the needs of the underclass, the campaign itself led to the involvement of these poor and powerless blacks in the struggle." Eskew, "The ACMHR," 94.

29. Scott, *Domination and the Arts of Resistance*, 277. In some ways this argument resembles Frantz Fanon's interpretation of violence by the oppressed as a transformative process which ultimately alters the personalities of subordinate groups. (See especially, Frantz Fanon, *The Wretched of the Earth* [New York: Grove Press, 1966], 29–74; Luther P. Gerlach and Virginia H. Hine, *People, Power, Change: Movements of Social Transformation* [Indianapolis: Bobbs-Merrill, 1970], 148–49.) However, what I am suggesting is that collective violence served to lay bare the hidden transcript. The feeling of frustration and hatred existed long before the uprising but only occasionally found a public platform. What appeared to be a transformation in personality was really a change in the public posturings of segments of the black poor.

30. Memo from George Seibels to Albert Boutwell, October 15, 1964, Re: "Probable Dope Consumption by Teenagers in the Elyton Housing Project Area"; "Telephone Conversation between Mrs. Virginia Davis and Birmingham Police," May 11, 1964, transcript, Box 30, Boutwell Papers.

31. In 1965, four sociologists and criminologists completed a study which concluded that crimes of violence against other blacks decline when there is a well-organized, direct action campaign, because race-pride replaces self-hatred. The movement allowed "lower-class" blacks to channel their aggression in more positive directions. See Frederick Solomon, Walter Walker, Garrett

J. O'Connor, and Jacob R. Fishman, "Civil Rights Activity and Reduction in Crime among Negroes," *Crime and Social Justice* 14 (Winter 1980), 27–35 (orig. publ. in *Archives of Psychiatry* 12 [1965], 227–36).

32. Juvenile and Domestic Relations Court of Jefferson County, *Annual Report* (1963), 15, 25.

33. Memo from Det. C. L. Pierce to Chief Jamie Moore, September 15, 1963, Re: Shooting of Johnny Robinson, Birmingham Police Department, Statement of Officer J. E. Chadwick, September 16, 1963, Statement of Marvin Kent, September 16, 1963, Statement of Jimmy Sparks, September 16, 1963, Statement of Officer P. C. Cheek, September 16, 1963, Statement of Sidney Howell, September 16, 1963, Box 31, Boutwell Papers. Statements were taken from the whites in the car, though no black people were asked to submit statements or serve as witnesses.

34. Juvenile and Domestic Relations Court of Jefferson County, *Annual Report* (1966), 18; "Negroes Are Calling a 60-Day Period of Mourning for the Dead!" (ACMHR flyer, ca. March 1967), Unsigned, "Racial Notes [Birmingham Police Department]," March 6, 1967, Box 15, Boutwell Papers. A large body of research suggests that black males are more likely to be victims of police homicides than whites. See, for example, G. D. Robin, "Justifiable Homicide by Police Officers," *Journal of Criminal Law, Criminology and Police Science* 54 (1963), 225–31; S. Harring, T. Platt, R. Speiglman, and P. Takagi, "The Management of Police Killings," *Crime and Social Justice* 8 (1977), 34–43; P. Takagi, "A Garrison State in 'Democratic Society,'" *Crime and Social Justice* (Spring–Summer 1978), 2–25; A. L. Kobler, "Figures (and Perhaps Some Facts) on Police Killing of Civilians in the United States, 1965–1969," *Journal of Social Issues* 31 (1975), 163–91; M. W. Meyer, "Police Shootings at Minorities: The Case of Los Angeles," *Annals* 452 (1980), 98–110; J. J. Fyfe, "Blind Justice: Police Shootings in Memphis," *Journal of Criminal Law and Criminology* 73 (1982), 707–22.

35. Statement by Mrs. Catherine McGann (typescript), n.d., Lawrence E. McGinty to Mayor Albert Boutwell, September 15, 1964, Inter-Office Communication from Jamie Moore, Chief of Police to Mayor Boutwell, September 17, 1964, Box 30, Boutwell Papers.

36. "Negroes Are Calling a 60-Day Period of Mourning for the Dead!" (ACMHR flyer, ca. March 1967), Unsigned, "Racial Notes [Birmingham Police Department]," March 6, 1967, Unsigned, "Racial Notes [Birmingham Police Department]," March 8, 1967, Box 15, Boutwell Papers.

37. Jimmie Lewis Franklin, *Back to Birmingham: Richard Arrington, Jr., and His Times* (Tuscaloosa, Ala.: University of Alabama Press, 1989), 92–133, quote from p. 104. In fact, Franklin argues that Arrington's successful bid for mayor can partly be attributed to his stand against police brutality.

38. Norrell, "Caste in Steel," 690–91.

39. Bobby Wilson, "Racial Segregation Trends in Birmingham, Alabama," *Southeastern Geographer* 25, no. 1 (May 1985), 32–33; Marilynn Kindell, "A Descriptive Analysis of the Impact of Urban Renewal on a Relocated Family: A

Case Study of the Medical Center Expansion Project" (M.A. thesis, University of Alabama, Birmingham 1982); U.S. Bureau of the Census, *Seventeenth Census of the U.S.: 1950*, Vol. 3, *Census Tract Statistics* (Washington, D.C.: Government Printing Office, 1952), 7–10; Richard Fussell, *A Demographic Atlas of Birmingham, 1960–1970* (University, Ala.: University of Alabama Press 1975), 65–66; and for a general description of urban renewal policies in the urban South, David R. Goldfield, *Black, White, and Southern: Race Relations and Southern Culture, 1940 to the Present* (Baton Rouge: Louisiana State University Press, 1990), 205.

40. Indeed, if we were to exclude tract 44 from our definition of the inner city, then the percentage of blacks would have increased by 5 percent between 1960 and 1970 rather than decreased by 1 percent, and the percentage of families below the poverty line would rise slightly from 45.5% to 49%.

41. Wilson, "Racial Segregation Trends in Birmingham," 32–33; Fussell, *A Demographic Atlas of Birmingham*, 20–21; U.S. Bureau of the Census, *Twentieth Census of Population and Housing, 1980: Census Tracts* (Washington, D.C.: Government Printing Office 1983), 235–40.

42. Originally called the Birmingham Area Committee for the Development of Economic Opportunity, this precursor to the JCCEO was established in January 1965 to oversee at least forty EOA programs, but its director, Erskine Smith, was forced to resign and the organization had to be restructured following attacks by Governor George Wallace for establishing ties with the Urban League and, later, by the federal government for not complying with its charge of encouraging "maximum feasible participation of the residents." Six months later, however, the organization reemerged as the JCCEO after it was deemed acceptable in both Montgomery and Washington, D.C. LaMonte, "Politics and Welfare," 349–58; Birmingham *Post-Herald*, May 15, 1965.

43. LaMonte, "Politics and Welfare," 281–82, 352–60; Community Service Council, *Family and Children Study of Jefferson County: Priorities and Recommendations* (Birmingham: Community Service Council 1970), pp. 11, 19; Fussell, *A Demographic Atlas of Birmingham*, 20–21. For background on the EOA and its federal administrative arm, the Office of Economic Opportunity, see Michael B. Katz, *The Undeserving Poor: From the War on Poverty to the War on Welfare* (New York: Pantheon, 1989), 79–101, 112–23; James T. Patterson, *America's Struggle against Poverty, 1900–1985* (Cambridge, Mass.: Harvard University Press, 1986), 142–54.

44. LaMonte, "Politics and Welfare," 358, 364–66.

45. Birmingham *News*, July 29, 1969; LaMonte, "Politics and Welfare," 368–70.

46. Carl Braden, "Birmingham Movement Grows," *Southern Patriot* 30, no. 7 (September 1972).

47. Anne Braden, "Law and Order in Birmingham: Two Black Liberation Front Leaders Jailed," *Southern Patriot* 29, no. 3 (March 1971), 5.

48. Ibid., pp. 5–6.

49. Ibid., p. 6.

50. Steven H. Haeberle, *Planting the Grassroots: Structuring Citizen Participation* (New York: Praeger 1989), 123; Philip B. Coulter, *Political Voice: Citizen Demand for Urban Public Services* (Tuscaloosa: University of Alabama Press, 1988), 46–55, 92; and on black politics in Birmingham during the 1970s and 1980s, see Franklin's thorough biography of Arrington, *Back to Birmingham*. Similarly, Jeffrey Berry, Kent Portnoy, and Ken Thomson's study of the political behavior of the poor in four cities, including Birmingham, concludes that the political behavior of the black poor differs little from that of other groups, though African Americans across class lines have a slightly higher participation rate than whites. "The Political Behavior of Poor People," in *The Urban Underclass*, eds. Christopher Jencks and Paul E. Peterson (Washington, D.C., Brookings Institution 1991), esp. 369–70.

Part II. To Be Red and Black

1. Langston Hughes, "A New Song," *Liberator*, October 15, 1932.

Chapter 5. "Afric's Sons With Banner Red"

1. *Harlem Liberator*, June 24, 1933.

2. Harold Cruse, *The Crisis of the Negro Intellectual* (New York: Morrow, 1964), 144, 149, 150–51 passim.; James O. Young, *Black Writers of the Thirties* (Baton Rouge: Louisiana State University Press, 1973), 40, 157–60; Ernest Allen, "The Cultural Methodology of Harold Cruse," *Journal of Ethnic Studies* 5, no. 2 (1977), 26–50; Arthur Paris, "Cruse and the Crisis in Black Culture," *Journal of Ethnic Studies* 5, no. 2 (1977), 63–66; Jabari Simama, "Black Writers Experience Communism: An Interdisciplinary Study of Imaginative Writers, Their Critics, and the CPUSA" (Ph.D. diss., Emory University, 1978), 270.

3. The work of Mark Naison and Paul Buhle, in particular, has explored the politics of black culture during the Popular Front. It was a critical moment, since black culture was elevated to the status as a revolutionary component of American culture, as Communists—especially in Harlem—successfully drew African American artists and performers into their ranks. See Mark Naison, *Communists in Harlem during the Depression* (Urbana: University of Illinois Press, 1983), 193–219; Naison, "Communism and Harlem Intellectuals in the Popular Front: Anti-Fascism and the Politics of Black Culture," *Journal of Ethnic Studies* 9, no. 1 (1981), 1–25; Paul Buhle, *Marxism in the United States: Remapping the History of the American Left* (London: Verso 1987). The more recent important biographies of black radical artists include, Wayne F. Cooper, *Claude McKay: Rebel Sojourner in the Harlem Renaissance, A Biography* (Baton Rouge: Louisiana State University Press, 1986); Arnold Rampersad, *The Life of Langston Hughes, Volume 1: 1902–1941, I, Too, Sing America* (New York: Oxford University Press, 1986); Margaret Walker, *Richard Wright—Daemonic Genius: A Portrait of the Man, A Critical Look at His Work* (New York: Warner Books, 1988); Martin Bauml Du-

berman, *Paul Robeson* (New York: Knopf, 1989); see also Sam G. Kim, "Black Americans' Commitment to Communism: A Case Study Based on Fiction and Autobiographies" (Ph.D. diss., University of Kansas, 1986).

4. On the Socialist Party and African Americans, see Philip Foner, *American Socialism and Black Americans: From the Age of Jackson to World War II* (Westport, Conn.: Greenwood Press, 1977); Jervis Anderson, *A. Phillip Randolph: A Biographical Portrait* (New York: Harcourt Brace Jovanovich, 1973), 85–137; Theodore Kornweibel, *No Crystal Stair: Black Life and the Messenger, 1917–1928* (Westport, Conn.: Greenwood Press, 1975); Henry Williams, *Black Response to the American Left* (Princeton: History Department, Princeton University, 1971); Robert Allen, *Reluctant Reformers: Racism and Social Reform Movements in the United States*, rev. ed. (Washington, D.C.: Howard University Press, 1983), 212–15; Sally Miller, "The Socialist Party and the Negro, 1901–1920," *Journal of Negro History* 56 (July 1971), 220–39; Lawrence Moore, "Flawed Fraternity: American Socialist Response to the Negro, 1901–1912," *The Historian* 33, no. 1 (1969), 1–14; Mark Naison, "Marxism and Black Radicalism in America: Notes on a Long (and Continuing) Journey," *Radical America* 5, no. 3 (1971), 4–10; David A. Shannon, *The Socialist Party of America* (New York: Macmillan, 1955), 49–52; James Weinstein, *The Decline of Socialism in America, 1912–1925* (New York: Monthly Review Press, 1967), 69–70.

5. First quote, *Amsterdam News* September 5, 1917; second quote, *Crusader* 1, no. 8 (April 1919), 8–9; Ibid., 1, no. 12 (August 1919), 4. Anselmo R. Jackson, associate editor of the *Crusader,* wrote that the paper was dedicated "to the doctrine of self-government for the Negro and Africa for the Africans." *Crusader* 1, no. 3 (November 1918), 1. Despite statements in the *Crusader*, Richard B. Moore and W. A. Domingo, two former leaders of the ABB, deny that Briggs, or the ABB, ever advocated such a position. "Richard B. Moore, Interview, January 15, 1958," and "W. A. Domingo, Interview, January 18, 1958," Box 21, Folder 3, Theodore Draper Papers, Emory University. For more on the ABB, see "Cyril Briggs and the African Blood Brotherhood," WPA Writers' Project, No. 1, Reporter: Carl Offord, Schomburg Collection; *Crusader* 2, no. 2 (October 1919), 27; "Program of the African Blood Brotherhood," *Communist Review* (London), April 1922, pp. 449–54; Mark Solomon, "Red and Black: Negroes and Communism, 1929–1932" (Ph.D. diss., Harvard University, 1972), 80–83; For more on the ABB, see Harry Haywood, *Black Bolshevik: Autobiography of an Afro-American Communist* (Chicago: Liberator Press, 1978), 122–30; Naison, *Communists in Harlem*, 3, 5–8, 17–18; Theodore Vincent, *Black Power and the Garvey Movement* (Berkeley, Calif.: Ramparts Press, 1971), 74–85 and passim; Tony Martin, *Race First* (Westport, Conn.: Greenwood Press, 1976); 237–46; Theodore Draper, *American Communism and Soviet Russia* (New York: Viking, 1960), 322–32; Philip S. Foner, *Organized Labor and the Black Worker, 1619–1981*, 2nd ed. (New York: International Publishers, 1981), 148–49; Cedric J. Robinson, *Black Marxism: The Making of the Black Radical Tradition* (London: Zed Press, 1983), 296–301;

David Samuels, "Five Afro-Caribbean Voices in American Culture, 1917–1929: Hubert H. Harrison, Wilfred A. Domingo, Richard B. Moore, Cyril Briggs and Claude McKay" (Ph.D. diss., University of Iowa, 1977); Theman Taylor, "Cyril Briggs and the African Blood Brotherhood: Effects of Communism on Black Nationalism, 1919–1935" (Ph.D. diss., University of California, Santa Barbara, 1981).

    6. Workers (Communist) Party of America, *Program and Constitution: Workers Party of America* (New York: Literature Department, Workers Party of America, 1924), 14; Workers (Communist) Party of America, *The Second Year of the Workers Party of America: Theses, Programs, Resolutions* (Chicago: Literature Department, Workers Party of America, 1924), 125; V. I. Lenin, "The Socialist Revolution and the Right of Nations to Self-Determination (Theses)," in *Lenin on the National and Colonial Questions: Three Articles* (Peking: Foreign Languages Press, 1967), 5; "Theses on the National and Colonial Question Adopted by the Second Congress of the Comintern Congress," in *The Communist International, 1919–1943, Documents*, ed. Jane Degras (London: Oxford University Press, 1956), I, 142. Roy's contribution to the Theses, as well as to the general direction of the Commission was quite substantial. Among other things, he recognized the existence of class distinctions in the colonies and he placed the peasantry in a pivotal position for waging the anticolonial movement. See, Manabendra Nath Roy, *M. N. Roy's Memoirs* (Bombay and New York: Allied Publishers, 1964), 378; see also John Haithcox, *Communism and Nationalism in India: M. N. Roy and Comintern Policy, 1920–1939* (Princeton, N.J.: Princeton University Press, 1971), 14–15; D. C. Grover, *M. N. Roy: A Study of Revolution and Reason in Indian Politics* (Calcutta: Minerva Associates, 1973), 2–13. A copy of Roy's theses are available in V. B. Karnik, *M. N. Roy: A Political Biography* (Bombay: Nav Jagriti Sama, 1978), 107–10. For Lenin's views on Roy's supplementary theses, see "The Report of the Commission on the National and Colonial Questions, July 26, 1920," in *Lenin on the National and Colonial Questions*, 30–37; Draper, *American Communism*, 321. As early as 1913, Lenin wrote a short article entitled "Russians and Negroes," where he compared the plight of blacks to that of emancipated Russian serfs. (*Collected Works* [London: Lawrence & Wishart, 1963], vol. 18, pp. 543–44.) In his "Notebooks on Imperialism," put together in 1916, he was critical of the Socialist Party's position on Afro-Americans, as well as the Mississippi Socialist Party's policy of segregation. (*Collected Works* [London: Lawrence & Wishart, 1965], vol. 39, pp. 590–91.) Lenin's criticism of the American Communists' failure to work among blacks was based on research he had conducted regarding the plight of black sharecroppers and tenant farmers in the United States. And it was in these works, completed in 1915 and 1917, that Lenin suggested that blacks constitute an oppressed nation in the United States. (V. I. Lenin, "New Data on the Laws Governing the Development of Capitalism in Agriculture," in *Collected Works*, [London: Lawrence & Wishart, 1963], vol. 22, pp. 13–102; "On Statistics and Sociology," in *Collected Works* [London: Lawrence & Wishart, 1963] vol. 23, p. 276.)

7. Draper, *American Communism*, 320–21, 327–28; Robinson, *Black Marxism*, 304; Roger E. Kanet, "The Comintern and the 'Negro Question': Communist Policy in the United States and Africa, 1921–1941," *Survey* 19, no. 4 (Autumn 1973), 89–90; Haywood, *Black Bolshevik*, 225; Claude McKay, *A Long Way from Home* (New York: Lee Furman, 1937), 177–80; Billings [Otto Huiswoud], "Report on the Negro Question," *International Press Correspondence* 3, no. 2 (1923), 14–16. The full text of the "Theses on the Negro Question" is available in *Bulletin of the IV Congress of the Communist International* no. 27 (December 7, 1922), 8–10.

8. Workers (Communist) Party of America, *Fourth National Convention of the Workers (Communist) Party of America* (Chicago: Literature Department, Workers Party of America, 1925), 121 and 122.

9. On the CP and Garveyism, see Vincent, *Black Power and the Garvey Movement*, 211; Robert Hill, ed., *The Marcus Garvey and Universal Negro Improvement Association Papers* (Berkeley and Los Angeles: University of California Press, 1984), III, 675–681; (quotation) Workers (Communist) Party of America, *Fourth National Convention of the Workers (Communist) Party of America*, 122; James Jackson [Lovett Fort-Whiteman], "The Negro in America," *Communist International* (February 1925), 52; Robert Minor, "After Garvey—What?" *Workers Monthly* 5 (June 1926), 362–65.

10. Haywood, *Black Bolshevik*, 139, 140–46; "Report of National Negro Committee, CPUSA," (transcript, 1925), Box 12, Folder, "Negro-1924–25," Robert Minor Papers, Butler Memorial Library, Columbia University; James Ford, *The Negro and the Democratic Front* (New York: International Publishers, 1938), Harvey Klehr, *The Heyday of American Communism: The Depression Decade* (New York: Basic Books, 1984), 324; Wilson Record, *The Negro and the Communist Party* (Chapel Hill: University of North Carolina Press, 1951), 29–33.

11. Willy Münzenberg, "Pour une Conférence Coloniale," *Correspondence Internationale* 6, no. 9 (August 1926), 1011; Münzenberg, "La Première Conférence Mondiale contre la Politique Coloniale Impérialiste," *Correspondance Internationale* 7, no. 17 (February 5, 1927), 232; Robin D. G. Kelley, "The Third International and the Struggle for National Liberation in South Africa, 1921–1928," *Ufahamu* 15, nos. 1 and 2 (1986), 110–11; Edward T. Wilson, *Russia and Black Africa before World War II* (New York: Holmes & Meier, 1974), 151; *South African Worker*, April 1, June 24, 1927; "Les Décisions du Congrès: Résolution Commune sur la Question Nègre," *La Voix des Nègres* 1, no. 3 (March 1927), 3.

12. "Resolutions Proposed by Workers Party of America at the Negro Sanhedrin, February 12, 1924," pp. 4, 7, 9, 13, Box 13, and "Report of National Negro Committee, CPUSA," (tsc., 1925), Box 12, Robert Minor Papers; W. A. Domingo Interview, January 18, 1958 (tsc.), p. 4, Box 21, Folder 3, Theodore Draper Papers, Emory University; Ford, *The Negro and the Democratic Front*, 82; Haywood, *Black Bolshevik*, 143–46; Klehr, *The Heyday of American Communism*, 324; Naison, *Communists in Harlem*, 13.

13. Naison, *Communists in Harlem*, 18; (quotation) Gilbert Lewis, "Revolutionary Negro Tradition," *Negro Worker*, March 15, 1930, 8. Cyril Briggs published a whole series of essays on this score, such as "Negro Revolutionary Hero—Toussaint L'Ouverture, *Communist* 8, no. 5 (May 1929), 250–54; "The Negro Press as a Class Weapon," *Communist* 8, no. 8 (August 1929), 453–60; and "May First and the Revolutionary Traditions of Negro Masses," *Daily Worker*, April 28, 1930.

14. William L. Patterson, "Awake Negro Poets," *New Masses* 4 (October 1928), 10.

15. "Draft Program of the League of Struggle for Negro Rights," (tsc., n.d.), pp. 1–3, Box 12, Folder—"Negroes, 1931," Robert Minor Papers; League of Struggle for Negro Rights, *Equality, Land and Freedom: A Program for Liberation* (New York: League of Struggle for Negro Rights, 1933).

16. *Liberator*, February 21, 1931.

17. Resolution of the Central Committee, CPUSA, on Negro Work, March 16, 1931 (tsc.), pp. 2–4, Box 12, Folder—"Negro, 1931," Robert Minor Papers; *Daily Worker*, March 23, 1931; *Liberator*, March 28, 1931.

18. *Daily Worker*, January 19, 1932; Klehr, *The Heyday of American Communism*, 332; [Herman] Mackawain, "The League of Struggle for Negro Rights in Harlem," *Party Organizer* 8 (April 1934), 60; "The Reminiscences of Earl Browder," Interview conducted by Joseph R. Starobin, 1964 (tsc.), vol. III, p. 285, Columbia Oral History Project, Butler Memorial Library, Columbia University; Haywood, *Black Bolshevik*, 439–40.

19. Nell Irvin Painter, *The Narrative of Hosea Hudson, His Life as a Negro Communist in the South* (Cambridge, Mass.: Harvard University Press, 1979), 102.

20. *Liberator*, November 21, 1931.

21. Quoted in Tony Martin, *Literary Garveyism: Garvey, Black Arts and the Harlem Renaissance* (Dover, Mass.: Majority Press, 1983), 43–46, 73.

22. Michael Gold, "Send Us a Critic," in *Mike Gold: A Literary Anthology*, ed. Michael Folsom (New York: International Publishers, 1972), 139; Paula Rabinowitz, "Women and U.S. Literary Radicals," in *Writing Red: An Anthology of American Women Writers, 1930–1940*, ed. Charlotte Nekola and Paula Rabinowitz (New York: The Feminist Press at the City University of New York, 1987), 3; see also, Charlotte Nekola, "Worlds Moving: Women, Poetry, and the Literary Politics of the 1930's," in ibid., 129–31; Stanley Burnshaw, "Notes on Revolutionary Poetry," *New Masses* 10 (February 20, 1934), 22; V. F. Calverton, "Leftward Ho!" *Modern Quarterly* 6 (Summer 1932), 26–32; Paula Rabinowitz, *Labor and Desire: Women's Revolutionary Fiction in Depression America* (Chapel Hill: University of North Carolina Press, 1991).

23. *Liberator*, August 22, 1931.

24. *Daily Worker*, August 10, 1935.

25. *Daily Worker*, December 3, 1932.

26. Elizabeth Faue, *Community of Suffering and Struggle: Women, Men, and*

the Labor Movement in Minneapolis, 1915–1945 (Chapel Hill: University of North Carolina Press, 1991), 71; Sharon Hartman Strom, "Challenging 'Woman's Place': Feminism, the Left, and Industrial Unionism in the 1930's," *Feminist Studies* 9, no. 2 (Summer 1983), 359–86.

27. Richard Frank, "Negro Revolutionary Music," *New Masses* 11, no. 7 (May 15, 1934), 29.

28. Eugene Gordon, "Alabama Massacre," *New Masses* 7 (August 1931), 16; *Daily Worker*, December 3, 1932; Ruby Weems, "The Murder of Ralph Gray," *Liberator*, November 21, 1931; Grace Lumpkin, *A Sign for Cain* (New York, 1935), 223; Robin D. G. Kelley, *Hammer and Hoe: Alabama Communists during the Great Depression* (Chapel Hill: University of North Carolina Press, 1990), 146.

29. William L. Patterson, "The Negro Question," (unpublished ms., April 1933), 1, microfilm, reel 2, International Labor Defense Papers (Schomburg Collection).

30. Harry Haywood, "Against Bourgeois-Liberal Distortions of Leninism on the Negro Question in the United States," *Communist* 8, no. 9 (August 1930), 700.

31. See, for example, David John Ahola, *Finnish-Americans and International Communism: A Study of Finnish-American Communism from Bolshevization to the Demise of the Third International* (Washington, D.C.: University Press of America, 1981); Auvo Kostiainen, *The Forging of Finnish-American Communism, 1917–1924: A Study in Ethnic Radicalism* (Turku: Turun Yliopisto, 1978); Michael Gary Karni, "Yhteishyva—Or For the Common Good: Finnish Radicalism in the Western Great Lakes Region, 1900–1940" (Ph.D. diss., University of Minnesota, 1975); Al Gedicks, "The Social Origins of Radicalism among Finnish Immigrants in Midwest Mining Communities," *Review of Radical Political Economics* 8 (1976), 1–31; Peter Kivisto, *Immigrant Socialists in the United States: The Case of Finns and the Left* (London: Associated University Presses, 1984); George P. Hummasti, "Finnish Radicals in Astoria, Oregon, 1904–1940: A Study in Immigrant Socialism" (Ph.D. diss., University of Oregon, 1975); Paul Buhle, "Jews and American Communism: The Cultural Question," *Radical America* 23 (Spring 1980), 9–33; David P. Shuldiner, "Of Moses and Marx: Folk Ideology within the Jewish Labor Movement in the United States" (Ph.D. diss., UCLA, 1984); Peter Kwong, *Chinatown, New York: Labor and Politics, 1930–1950* (New York: Monthly Review Press, 1979); Karl Yoneda, *Ganbatte: Sixty-Year Struggle of a Kibei Worker*, ed. Yuji Ichioka (Los Angeles: UCLA Asian Studies Center, 1983); Douglass Monroy, "Anarquismo y Comunismo: Mexican Radicalism and the Communist Party in Los Angeles during the 1930's," *Labor History* 24 (Winter 1983): 34–59.

32. Patterson, "Awake Negro Poets," 10.

33. Buhle, *Marxism in the United States*, 157. On the debate over proletarian literature, see ibid., chapter 5; Lawrence Schwartz, *Marxism and Culture: The*

CPUSA and Aesthetics in the 1930's (Port Washington, N.Y.: Kennikat Press, 1980); Alan M. Wald, *The New York Intellectuals: The Rise and Decline of the Anti-Stalinist Left from the 1930's to the 1980's* (Chapel Hill: University of North Carolina Press, 1987), 78 passim.

34. See for instance Walter Carmon's review of Hughes's *Not Without Laughter, New Masses* 6, no. 5 (October 1930). The beginning of a serious black literary critique within Party circles dates back to 1935 with the founding of the American Writers' Congress. See especially Henry Hart, ed., *American Writers' Congress* (New York: International Publishers, 1935), 139–53; Eugene Clay, "The Negro in Recent American Literature," *International Literature* 6 (1935), 79–80; and, of course, Richard Wright, "Blueprint for Negro Writing," *New Challenge* 1 (Fall 1937), 53–61.

35. Michael Gold, "The Negro Reds of Chicago," *Daily Worker*, September 30, 1932.

36. Harold Preece, "Folk Music of the South," *New South* 1, no. 2 (March 1938), 13; also see Harold Preece to Anne Johnson, December 25, 1936, Clyde Johnson Papers, microfilm, reel 13.

37. Philip Schatz, "Songs of the Negro Worker," *New Masses* 5, no. 12 (May 1930), 6–8; Lawrence Gellert, "Negro Songs of Protest," *New Masses* 6, no. 11 (April 1931), 6–8.

38. *Daily Worker*, April 7, 1934; *Southern Worker*, July 1936. As early as 1932, the same song was sung by black Communists in Chicago, but their version was slightly different in that it referred to the "New Communist Spirit." *Daily Worker*, September 30, 1932, quoted in R. Serge Denisoff, *Great Day Coming: Folk Music and the American Left* (Urbana: University of Illinois Press, 1971), 37. For examples of adaptations of "We Shall Not Be Moved," see *Labor Defender* 9, no. 11 (December 1933), 80; Harold Preece to Anne Johnson, December 25, 1936, Clyde Johnson Papers, microfilm, reel 13.

39. *Southern Worker*, July 18, 1931.

40. *Daily Worker*, October 2, 1932.

41. *Liberator*, November 14, 1931.

42. Poet Langston Hughes was unusual among black poets who contributed to the Communist press for his often explicit depiction of ordinary black folk dispensing with or questioning religion altogether. See especially Langston Hughes's works published in *New Masses*, the *Liberator*, and the *Negro Worker*. The more profane works include "Goodbye Christ," "God to Hungry Child," "A Christian Country," "The New Black Blues," and "A New Song." Much of this work has been reproduced in Langston Hughes, *Good Morning Revolution: Uncollected Writings of Social Protest*, ed. Faith Berry (Brooklyn, N.Y.: Lawrence Hill, 1973); see also *Liberator*, October 15 and 31, 1931. The characters in Hughes's poems, however, were not unusual. As I have demonstrated elsewhere, it is likely that some blacks were drawn to the Party as a result of their personal disillusionment with the church. Robin D. G. Kelley, "'Comrades,

Praise Gawd for Lenin and Them!': Ideology and Culture among Black Communists in Alabama, 1930–1935," *Science and Society* 52, no. 1 (Spring 1988), 64–66.

Chapter 6. "This Ain't Ethiopia, But It'll Do"

1. Baltimore *Afro-American*, September 28, 1935; also quoted in Robert Weisbord, *Ebony Kinship: Africa, Africans, and the Afro-American* (Westport, Conn.: Greenwood Press, 1973), 102.

2. *Daily Worker*, February 11, 1939. For an elaboration on the role of Marxist pedagogy among African Americans in the CP, see Robin D. G. Kelley, *Hammer and Hoe: Alabama Communists during the Great Depression* (Chapel Hill: University of North Carolina Press, 1990), 93–99.

3. *Daily Worker*, April 7, 1934; *Southern Worker*, July, 1936.

4. Kelley, *Hammer and Hoe*, 40–42, 95; *Daily Worker*, February 11, 1939; Joe Brandt, ed., *Black Americans in the Spanish People's War against Fascism, 1936–1939* (New York: VALB, 1981), 24; *Southern Worker*, March 21, 1931; Nell Irvin Painter, *The Narrative of Hosea Hudson, His Life as a Negro Communist in the South* (Cambridge, Mass.: Harvard University Press, 1979), 84; Harry Haywood, *Black Bolshevik: Autobiography of an Afro-American Communist* (Chicago: Liberator Press, 1978), 398; "Testimony of Leonard Patterson," State of Louisiana, Joint Legislative Committee, *Subversion in Racial Unrest: An Outline of a Strategic Weapon to Destroy the Governments of Louisiana and the United States*, Public Hearings, Part I (Baton Rouge: State of Louisiana, 1957), 121.

5. Brandt, *Black Americans*, 14, 25; *Daily World*, February 24, 1979.

6. James Yates, *Mississippi to Madrid: Memoir of a Black American in the Abraham Lincoln Brigade* (Seattle: Open Hand Publishers, 1989), 15–28.

7. Ibid., 29–55, 72–73.

8. Arthur Landis, *The Abraham Lincoln Brigade* (New York: Citadel Press, 1967), 73; Steve Nelson, James R. Barrett, and Rob Ruck, *Steve Nelson: American Radical* (Pittsburgh: University of Pittsburgh Press, 1981), 218; Brandt, *Black Americans*, 33–35.

9. Oscar Hunter interview, May 2, 1980, Abraham Lincoln Brigade Archives (Brandeis University), pp. 18–19.

10. Ibid., pp. 6–20, 78; Brandt, *Black Americans*, 23.

11. Admiral Kilpatrick interview, June 8, 1980, Abraham Lincoln Brigade Archives (Brandeis University).

12. William R. Scott, "Black Nationalism and the Italo-Ethiopian Conflict, 1934–1936," *Journal of Negro History* 63, no. 2 (1978), 118–21; Gayraud Wilmore, *Black Religion and Black Radicalism*, 2nd ed. (Maryknoll, N.Y.: Orbis Books, 1983, 120–21, 126–28, 160–61; Edward Ullendorff, *Ethiopia and the Bible* (London: Published for the British Academy by Oxford University Press, 1968); W. A. Shack, "Ethiopia and Afro-Americans: Some Historical Notes,

1920–1970," *Phylon* 35, no. 2 (1974), 142–55; Bernard Makhosezwe Magubane, *The Ties That Bind: African-American Consciousness of Africa* (Trenton, N.J.: Africa World Press, 1987), 160–65; S. K. B. Asante, *Pan-African Protest: West Africa and the Italo-Ethiopian Crisis, 1934–1941* (London: Longman, 1977), 9–38; Weisbord, *Ebony Kinship*, 90–92.

13. Randall K. Burkett, *Garveyism as a Religious Movement: The Institutionalization of a Black Civil Religion* (Metuchen, N.J.: Scarecrow Press, 1978), 34–35, 85–86, 122, 125, 134–35; Arnold Kuzwayo, "A History of Ethiopianism in South Africa with Particular Reference to the American Zulu Mission from 1835–1908" (M.A. thesis, University of South Africa, 1979); George Shepperson, "Ethiopianism and African Nationalism," *Phylon* 14, no. 1 (1953), 9–18.

14. Scott, "Black Nationalism," 121, 128–29; Mark Naison, *Communists in Harlem during the Depression* (Urbana: University of Illinois Press, 1983), 138–140; Magubane, *The Ties That Bind*, 166–67; Cedric J. Robinson, "The African Diaspora and the Italo-Ethiopian Crisis," *Race and Class* 27, no. 2 (Autumn 1985), 51–65; Weisbord, *Ebony Kinship*, 94–100; S.K.B. Asante, "The Afro-American and the Italo-Ethiopian Crisis, 1934–1936," *Race* 15, no. 2 (1973), 167–84.

15. Julian never actually saw combat. For more on Robinson and Julian, see Weisbord, *Ebony Kinship*, pp. 94–95; Hubert Fauntleroy Julian, *Black Eagle: Colonel Hubert Julian, as Told to John Bullock* (London: Jarrolds, 1964); John Peer Nugent, *The Black Eagle* (New York: Stein and Day, 1971). On the war itself, see Angelo Del Boca, *The Ethiopian War, 1935–1941* (Chicago: University of Chicago Press, 1969); George Baer, *The Coming of the Italian-Ethiopian War* (Cambridge, Mass.: Harvard University Press, 1967); Esmonde Robertson, *Mussolini as Empire Builder: Europe and Africa, 1932–1936* (New York: Macmillan, 1977).

16. Quoted in Scott, "Black Nationalism," 129; Naison, *Communists in Harlem*, 138–40.

17. Naison, *Communists in Harlem*, 138–40, 155–58, 174–76.

18. George Padmore, *The Life and Struggles of Negro Toilers* (London: R.I.L.U. Magazine for the International Trade Union Committee of Negro Workers, 1931), 77; James Ford, *The Negro and the Democratic Front* (New York: International Publishers, 1938), 160; on slavery in Ethiopia, see Jon R. Edwards, "Slavery, the Slave Trade and the Economic Reorganization of Ethiopia, 1916–1934," *African Economic History* 11 (1982), 3–14. In addition, Soviet leaders probably realized from the outset that Ethiopia could not have defeated Italy under any circumstances. One of the differences between Haile Selassie's situation in 1935 and the circumstances in which Menelik II was able to rout Italian troops at Adowa was that an arms embargo had been imposed on Ethiopia since 1916 that lasted until 1930. See especially Harold G. Marcus, "The Embargo on Arms Sales to Ethiopia, 1916–1930," *International Journal of African Historical Studies* 16, no. 2 (1983), 263–79.

19. *Daily Worker*, March 2, 6, 22, 27, May 29, 1937, November 12, 17, 24, 1938; Naison, *Communists in Harlem*, 196–97, 212; Scott, "Black National-

ism," 127; Martin Bauml Duberman, *Paul Robeson* (New York: Knopf, 1989), 215–20; Rampersad, *The Life of Langston Hughes* (New York: Oxford University Press, 1986), I, 351; Faith Berry, *Langston Hughes: Before and Beyond Harlem* (Brooklyn, N.Y.: Lawrence Hill, 1983), 261–63; James Baldwin, *Notes of a Native Son* (Boston: Beacon Press, 1955), 3.

20. Chicago *Defender*, March 26, 1938; *Daily Worker*, September 23, 1938, January 7, 1939; Baltimore *Afro-American*, October 1, 1938; Joseph North, *No Men Are Strangers* (New York: International Publishers, 1958), 126; Yates, *Mississippi to Madrid*, 129; Brandt *Black Americans*, 18, 23; Naison, *Communists in Harlem*, 197; Negro Committee to Aid Spain, *A Negro Nurse in Republican Spain* (New York: The Negro Committee to Aid Spain, 1938); *Daily Worker*, March 30, 1937, May 18, 1938.

21. On struggles between the Church and anticlericalists, see especially Gerald Brenan, *The Spanish Labyrinth: An Account of the Social and Political Background of the Civil War* (Cambridge, Eng.: The University Press, 1943); Pierre Broué and Emile Temime, *The Revolution and the Civil War in Spain*, trans. Tony White (Cambridge, Mass.: MIT Press, 1972), 37; Jose M. Sanchez, *Reform and Reaction: The Politico-Religious Background of the Spanish Civil War* (Chapel Hill: University of North Carolina Press, 1964); Frances Lannon, "The Church's Crusade against the Republic," in *Revolution and War in Spain, 1931–1939*, ed. Paul Preston (London: Methuen, 1984), 35–58. For more on Basque and Catalonian nationalism, see Norman Jones, "Regionalism and Revolution in Catalonia," in *Revolution and War in Spain*, 85–111; Martin Blinkhorn, "The Basque Ulster: Navarre and the Basque Autonomy Question under the Spanish Republic," *Historical Journal* 17, no. 3 (1974), 593–613. Catalonia was also the center of Spanish anarchism. See Robert W. Kern, *Red Years/Black Years: A Political History of Spanish Anarchism, 1911–1937* (Philadelphia: Institute for the Study of Human Issues, 1978), 1; Murray Bookchin, *The Spanish Anarchists: The Heroic Years, 1868–1936* (New York: Free Life Editions, 1977); Sam Dolgoff, ed., *The Anarchist Collectives: Workers' Self-Management in the Spanish Revolution, 1936–1939* (New York: Free Life Editions, 1974); George Orwell, *Homage to Catalonia*, 1st American ed. (New York: Harcourt Brace and World, 1952); Gerald W. Meaker, *The Revolutionary Left in Spain, 1914–1923* (Stanford, Calif.: Stanford University Press, 1974); Abel Paz, *Durruti: The People Armed* (Montreal: Black Rose Books, 1977). And for a more extensive discussion of agrarian struggles, see Broué and Temime, *The Revolution and the Civil War in Spain*, 34–35; Paul Preston, "The Agrarian War in the South," in *Revolution and War in Spain*, 159–81; E. E. Malefakis, *Agrarian Reform and Peasant Revolution in Spain* (New Haven: Yale University Press, 1970); Juan Martinez Alier, *Labourers and Landowners in Southern Spain* (London: Allen & Unwin, 1971).

22. Raymond Carr, *Modern Spain, 1875–1980* (New York; Oxford University Press, 1980), 47–116; Gabriel Jackson, *The Spanish Republic and the Civil War, 1931–1939* (Princeton, N.J.: Princeton University Press, 1965), 3–24; Shannon E. Fleming and Ann K. Fleming, "Primo de Rivera and Spain's Moroc-

can Problem, 1923–1927," *Journal of Contemporary History* 12 (January 1977), 85–99; Shlomo Ben-Ami, "The Dictatorship of Primo de Rivera: A Political Reassessment," *Journal of Contemporary History* 12 (January 1977), 65–84; Victor Alba, *Transition in Spain: From Franco to Democracy*, trans. Barbara Lotito, (New Brunswick, N.J.: Transaction Books, 1978), 49–63; Stanley Payne, *A History of Spain and Portugal: Volume II* (Madison: University of Wisconsin Press, 1973), 578–629.

23. On the history of the Second Republic, see Paul Preston, *The Coming of the Spanish Civil War: Reform, Reaction, and Revolution in the Second Republic, 1931–1936* (London: Macmillan, 1978); Jackson, *The Spanish Republic and the Civil War*; Shlomo Ben-Ami, *The Origins of the Second Republic in Spain* (New York: Oxford University Press, 1978); Arthur Landis, *Spain!: The Unfinished Revolution!* (Baldwin Park, Calif.: Camelot, 1972), 9–97; Aviva and Isaac Aviv, "The Madrid Working Class, the Spanish Socialist Party and the Collapse of the Second Republic (1934–1936)," *Journal of Contemporary History* 16 (April 1981), 229–50. On the 1934 uprising, see Paul Preston, "Spain's October Revolution and the Rightist Grasp for Power," *Journal of Contemporary History* 10 (October 1975), 555–78; Manuel Grossi, *L'Insurrection des Austries: Quinze Jours de Revolution Socialiste* (Paris: EDI, 1972); Adrian Shubert, "The Epic Failure: The Asturian Revolution of October 1934," in *Revolution and War in Spain*, 113–36; Kern, *Red Years/Black Years*, 128–30; Jackson, *The Spanish Republic and the Civil War*, 148–68.

24. Paul Preston, "The Creation of the Popular Front in Spain," in *The Popular Front in Europe*, eds. Helen Graham and Paul Preston (New York: St. Martin's Press, 1987), 84–105; Robert G. Colodny, "Notes on the Origin of the Frente Popular of Spain," *Science and Society* 31 (Summer 1967), 257–74.

25. The amount of published work on the Spanish Civil War seems infinite. For just a sampling of the good English-language scholarship on the conflict, see Broué and Temime, *The Revolution and the Civil War in Spain*; Raymond Carr, *The Spanish Tragedy: The Civil War in Perspective* (London: Weidenfeld & Nicolson, 1977); Jackson, *The Spanish Republic and the Civil War*; Hugh Thomas, *The Spanish Civil War*, 4th ed. (New York: Norton, 1986, orig. 1961); Burnett Bolloten, *The Spanish Revolution: The Left and the Struggle for Power during the Civil War* (Chapel Hill: University of North Carolina Press, 1979), and his final comprehensive history published posthumously, *The Spanish Civil War: Revolution and Counterrevolution* (Chapel Hill: University of North Carolina Press, 1990); Brenan, *The Spanish Labyrinth*; Alba, *Transition in Spain*: Franz Borkenau, *The Spanish Cockpit: An Eye-Witness Account of the Political and Social Conflicts of the Spanish Civil War* (Ann Arbor: University of Michigan Press, 1963, orig. 1937); Joan C. Ullman, *The Tragic Week* (Cambridge, Mass.: Harvard University Press, 1968); Cattell, *Communism and the Spanish Civil War*; Robert G. Colodny, *The Struggle for Madrid: The Central Epic of the Spanish Conflict* (New York: Paine-Whitman, 1958); Vernon Richards, *Lessons of the Spanish Revolution: 1936–1939* (London: Freedom Press, 1983, orig. 1953); Stanley Payne, *The Spanish Revolu-*

tion (New York: Norton, 1970); Landis, *Spain!*; Ronald Fraser, *Blood of Spain: An Oral History of the Spanish Civil War* (New York: Pantheon Books, 1979).

26. Broué and Temime, *The Revolution and the Civil War in Spain*, 321–65; Payne, *A History of Spain and Portugal*, II, 669–70; Hugh Kay, *Salazar and Modern Portugal* (New York: Hawthorne Books, 1970); H. Martins, "Portugal," in *European Fascism*, ed. S. J. Woolf (New York: Random House, 1968), 302–36; John Coverdale, *Italian Intervention in the Spanish Civil War* (Princeton: Princeton University Press, 1975); Robert H. Whealey, *Hitler and Spain: The Nazi Role in the Spanish Civil War, 1936–1939* (Lexington: University Press of Kentucky, 1989); Raymond L. Proctor, *Hitler's Luftwaffe in the Spanish Civil War* (Westport, Conn.: Greenwood Press, 1983). The war radicalized a segment of the Portuguese working class; in September 1936 a group of Portuguese seamen mutinied and attempted to join the Spanish Left. Salazar responded by adopting more repressive measures and abandoning what he had called Catholic corporatism for a more blatantly fascist form of government. Ironically, Salazar's downfall was the result of a military coup led by Portugal's version of the "Army of Africa" in 1974. The officers and troops had become war-weary after fighting anticolonial insurgents in Portugal's African colonies. A left-wing military junta helped usher in a democratic regime in Portugal and independence for Mozambique, Angola, Guinea-Bissau, and the Cape Verde Islands. See especially, Barbara Cornwall, *The Bush Rebels* (New York: Holt Rinehart & Winston, 1972), 84–87; R. M. Fields, *The Portuguese Revolution and the Armed Forces* (New York: Praeger, 1976); James H. Mittleman, "Some Reflections on Portugal's Counter Revolution," *Monthly Review* 28 (March 1977), 58–64; Phil Mailer, *Portugal: The Impossible Revolution* (London: Solidarity, 1977); Nicos Poulantzas, *The Crisis of Dictatorship: Portugal, Greece, Spain* (London: NLB, 1976).

27. Their decision to remain "neutral" with respect to Spain has its roots in U.S. and British foreign policy during the 1930s, which consistently viewed the spread of communism as a greater evil than the spread of fascism. Indeed, both countries had shown hostility toward Spain beginning with the Second Republic, and the Popular Front drew even more hostile opposition. See Douglas Little, *Malevolent Neutrality: The United States, Great Britain, and the Origins of the Spanish Civil War* (Ithaca, N.Y.: Cornell University Press, 1985); Richard P. Traina, *American Diplomacy and the Spanish Civil War* (Bloomington: Indiana University Press, 1968).

28. Broué and Temime, *The Revolution and the Civil War in Spain*, 321–365; Dante Puzzo, *Spain and the Great Powers, 1936–1941* (New York: Columbia University Press, 1962); David Carlton, "Eden, Blum, and the Origins of Non-Intervention," *Journal of Contemporary History* 6 (January 1971), 40–55; M. D. Gallagher, "Leon Blum and the Spanish Civil War," ibid., 56–64.

29. In fact, with the exception of Mexico, the USSR was the only country to offer military and other material aid to the Spanish Republic, although Soviet assistance never equaled Italian and German aid to Franco. Broué and Temime, *The Revolution and the Civil War in Spain*, 321–65; Soviet War Veterans' Commit-

tee, *International Solidarity with the Spanish Republic, 1936–1939* (Moscow: Progress Publishers, 1974), 329–30.

30. Even before the Comintern began organizing International Brigades, volunteers from Germany, Italy, France, Austria, and Belgium were slowly trickling across the Spanish border within days of the officers' uprising. Among the first group of volunteers were two Americans, Rosario Negrete of the (Trotskyite) Revolutionary Workers' League and engineer Lee Fleischman, both of whom found their way into the ranks of the Republican army before the Lincoln and Washington battalions had been formed. Robert Rosenstone, *Crusade of the Left: The Lincoln Battalion in the Spanish Civil War* (New York: Pegasus, 1969), 28–31.

31. Rosenstone, *Crusade of the Left*, 95; Subversive Activities Control Board (hereafter SACB), "Herbert Brownell, Jr., Attorney General of the United States v. VALB," September 15, 1954, p. 3265; Landis, *The Abraham Lincoln Brigade*, 17.

32. Landis, *The Abraham Lincoln Brigade*, 15–16; Rosenstone, *Crusade of the Left*, 122–132; quote from Yates, *Mississippi to Madrid*, 112, also see 108–12. For descriptions of the climb over the Pyrenees, see especially Bessie, *Men in Battle*, 18–24; Nelson, Barrett, and Ruck, *Steve Nelson*, 199–202; Nelson, *The Volunteers*, 70–77; Haywood, *Black Bolshevik*, 471–72.

33. Hunter interview, p. 23; SACB, "Herbert Brownell, Jr., Attorney General of the United States v. VALB," September 15, 1954, p. 3203; *Daily Worker*, September 29, 1937.

34. *Daily Worker*, September 29, 1937; Hunter interview; Yates, *Mississippi to Madrid*, 131–52, 155; *Daily Worker*, December 23, 1938; Brandt, *Black Americans*, 20–21, 23, 27–30; Arthur H. Landis, "American Fliers in Spanish Skies," in *Our Fight: Writings by Veterans of the Abraham Lincoln Brigade: Spain, 1936–39*, eds. Alvah Bessie and Albert Prago (New York: Monthly Review Press, with the Veterans of the Abraham Lincoln Brigade, 1987), 27.

35. Brandt, *Black Americans*, 15, 43; Yates, *Mississippi to Madrid*, 176; Eluard Luchell McDaniel interview, March 13, 1978, Radical Elders Oral History Project, 2a–21, pp. 57–58; Letter from Victor Berch in *The Volunteer* 12, no. 1 (May 1990), 23; *Daily Worker*, May 21, 1937; Baltimore *Afro-American*, February 20, 1937; *Chicago Defender*, April 3, 1937. On the Ugandan radical who served in Spain, see Ras Makonnen, *Pan-Africanism From Within*, ed. Kenneth King (New York: Oxford University Press, 1973), 176. I am grateful to Cedric J. Robinson for bringing this to my attention.

36. Rosenstone, *Crusade of the Left*, 46–47, 139–40; Broué and Temime, *The Revolution and the Civil War in Spain*, 370; Landis, *The Abraham Lincoln Brigade*, 34, 65, 72–74, 80, 83, 109, 162, 166, 171, 173, 191; Hunter interview, pp. 27–28, 30–31.

37. Rosenstone, *Crusade of the Left*, 221–22, 266–69, 308–9; Nelson, Barrett, and Ruck, *Steve Nelson*, 187, 203.

38. *Daily Worker*, September 29, 1937; Yates, *Mississippi to Madrid*, 119; Rolfe, *The Lincoln Battalion*, 53; Nelson, Barrett, and Ruck, *Steve Nelson*, 218;

Brandt, *Black Americans*, 8, 33–35; Rosenstone, *Crusade of the Left*, 161–62; Landis, *The Abraham Lincoln Brigade*, 34, 65, 73, 171, 173, 242; Hunter interview, p. 33.

39. Landis, *The Abraham Lincoln Brigade*, 73; Nelson, Barrett, and Ruck, *Steve Nelson*, 218; Brandt, *Black Americans*, 33–35; Rosenstone, *Crusade of the Left*, 184.

40. The most comprehensive account of the battles in which the Lincoln Brigade participated is Landis, *The Abraham Lincoln Brigade*; see also Rosenstone, *Crusade of the Left*, 149–64, 174–212, 230–54, 276–96, 313–33; Bessie, *Men in Battle*; Nelson, *The Volunteers*, 101–88 passim, much of which appears again in Nelson, Ruck, and Barrett, *Steve Nelson*; Rolfe, *The Lincoln Battalion*, 37–293 passim.; Brome, *The International Brigades*, 105–18, 195–225, 236–61; Soviet War Veterans' Committee, *International Solidarity*, 340–345; and Richardson, *Comintern Army*, 81–89.

41. Brandt, *Black Americans*, 32; Joe and Leo Gordon, "Seven Letters from Spain," in Bessie and Prago, eds., *Our Fight*, 196.

42. Thompson quoted in *Daily Worker*, September 29, 1937. While U.S. military policy from the American Revolution through World War II has always remained ambivalent or opposed to placing black troops in combat duty, specific circumstances have always resulted in a suspension of such a policy. For more on the history of blacks in the military through World War I, see Bernard C. Nalty, *Strength for the Fight: A History of Black Americans in the Military* (New York: Free Press, 1986); Jack D. Foner, *Blacks and the Military in American History* (New York: Praeger, 1974); Benjamin Quarles, *The Negro in the American Revolution* (Chapel Hill: University of North Carolina Press, 1961); James McPherson, ed., *The Negro's Civil War: How American Negroes Felt and Acted during the War for the Union* (New York: Pantheon Books, 1965); Arlen Fowler, *The Black Infantry in the West, 1869–1891* (Westport, Conn: Greenwood Press, 1971); William H. Leckie, *The Buffalo Soldiers: A Narrative of the Negro Calvary in the West* (Norman, Okla.: University of Oklahoma Press, 1967); Marvin Fletcher, *The Black Soldier and Officer in the United States Army, 1891–1917* (Columbia, Mo.: University of Missouri Press, 1974); Willard B. Gatewood, *"Smoked Yankees" and the Struggle for Empire: Letters of Negro Soldiers, 1898–1902* (Urbana: University of Illinois Press, 1971); Gerald Wilson Patton, "War and Race: The Black Officer in the American Military" (Ph.D. diss., University of Iowa, 1978); W. Allison Sweeney, *History of the American Negro in the Great World War* (New York: Negro Universities Press, 1969, orig. 1919); Robert W. Mullen, *Blacks in America's Wars: The Shift in Attitudes from the Revolutionary War to Vietnam* (New York: Monad Press, 1973).

43. Duberman, *Paul Robeson*, 217; Dolores Ibarruri, *They Shall Not Pass: The Autobiography of La Pasionaria* (New York: International Publishers, 1966), 265.

44. Haywood, *Black Bolshevik*, 474–87; *Daily Worker*, October 12, 1937; McDaniel interview, 5a–20; Hunter interview, 21 and 25. When he was sta-

tioned at Murcia, one of Hunter's jobs was to pick up deserters. One was a black man whom he had known in Chicago. Hunter interview, 55.

45. Joe and Leo Gordon, "Seven Letters from Spain," 194; Nelson, Barrett, and Ruck, *Steve Nelson*, 219.

46. On the Soviets' role in the Loyalist defense and the tensions between efforts to make a revolution and fight a conventional war, see Bolloten, *The Spanish Revolution*; Broué and Temime, *The Revolution and the Civil War in Spain*, 172–212; Kern, *Red Year/Black Year*, 239–247; Raymond Carr, *Modern Spain*, 137; E. H. Carr, *The Comintern and the Spanish Civil War*, 29–31; Ibarruri, *They Shall Not Pass*, 270–75.

47. Guttman, *The Wound in the Heart*, 100; *Daily Worker*, December 2, 1938.

48. Duberman, *Paul Robeson*, 219; Rampersad, *The Life of Langston Hughes*, I, 345; Rosenstone, *Crusade of the Left*, 196; Tom Page, "Interview with a Black Anti-Fascist," in Bessie and Prago, eds., *Our Fight*, 56; SACB, "Herbert Brownell, Jr., Attorney General of the United States v. VALB," September 15, 1954, p. 3211; McDaniel interview, pp. 5a–23; *Daily Worker*, December 2, 1938. For observations by other black visitors to the front who maintained that Spain was free of prejudice, see William Pickens, "What I Saw in Spain," *Crisis* 45 (October 1938), 321; Edward E. Strong, "I Visited Spain," *Crisis* 43 (December 1936), 358–59; Eslanda Goode Robeson, "Journey to Spain," in *Heart of Spain*, ed. Alvah Bessie (New York: Veterans of the Abraham Lincoln Brigade, 1952), 247.

49. Guttman, *The Wound in the Heart*, 99; Thyra Edwards, "Moors and the Spanish War," *Opportunity* 16 (March 1938), 84–85; Yates, *Mississippi to Madrid*, 127; McDaniel interview, 5a–23.

50. Rampersad, *The Life of Langston Hughes*, I, 349, 351; Baltimore *Afro-American*, October 30, 1937; Hughes, *I Wonder as I Wander*, 327, 351; Berry, *Langston Hughes*, 262; Broué and Temime, *The Revolution and the Civil War in Spain*, 266–67; *Daily Worker*, September 29, 1937.

51. Rolfe, *The Lincoln Battalion*, 266; Yates, *Mississippi to Madrid*, 116, 145–46; Ray Durem, *Take No Prisoners* (London: Paul Bremean, 1971), 3; see also letter from Victor Berch in *The Volunteer* 12, no. 1 (May 1990), 23.

52. McDaniel interview, pp. 5b–27 and 28.

53. Rosenstone, *Crusade of the Left*, 313, 314–21; Bessie, *Men in Battle*, 139–94 passim; Bolloten, *The Spanish Revolution*, 403–77; Broué and Temime, *The Revolution and the Civil War in Spain*, 273–315; Raymond Carr, *The Spanish Tragedy*, 197–201; Cattell, *Communism and the Spanish Civil War*, 169–78; Kern, *Red Years/Black Years*, 225–33; Alba, *Transition in Spain*, 145–57.

54. On the Lincoln battalion's role in the Ebro offensive, see Rosenstone, *Crusade of the Left*, 324–33; Landis, *The Abraham Lincoln Brigade*, 511–588; Bessie, *Men in Battle*, 213–345; Rolfe, *The Lincoln Battalion*, 258–93; James M. Jones, "Hold That Position!" in Bessie and Prago, eds., *Our Fight*, 261–68.

55. Rosenstone, *Crusade of the Left*, 335–338; Rolfe, *The Lincoln Battalion*, 306–10; Ibarruri, *They Shall Not Pass*, 313; Yates, *Mississippi to Madrid*, 158–59.

56. Yates, *Mississippi to Madrid*, 158–59; Tom Page, "Interview with a Black Anti-Fascist," 56; Prowell and McDaniel quoted in Rosenstone, *Crusade of the Left*, 196.

57. Yates, *Mississippi to Madrid*, 160.

58. Hunter interview, pp. 59–60; Yates, *Mississippi to Madrid*, 160; Rosenstone, *Crusade of the Left*, 338–44; SACB, "Herbert Brownell, Jr., Attorney General of the United States v. VALB," September 15, 1954, p. 3213.

59. Kilpatrick interview; Maurice Isserman, *Which Side Were You On?: The American Communist Party during the Second World War* (Middletown, Conn.: Wesleyan University Press, 1982), 28; Rosenstone, *Crusade of the Left*, 341–46; SACB, "Herbert Brownell, Jr., Attorney General of the United States v. VALB," September 15, 1954, pp. 3220–22. On the CP's defense of the Nazi-Soviet Pact, see Harvey Klehr, *The Heyday of American Communism: The Depression Decade* (New York: Basic Books, 1984), 386–409; Isserman, *Which Side Were You On?* 32–54; Naison, *Communists in Harlem*, 287–90.

60. Brome, *The International Brigades*, 290–93; Rosenstone, *Crusade of the Left*, 346–47; Eby, *Between the Bullet and the Lie*, 314–15; Isserman, *Which Side Were You On?* 104–12. On racism and African American participation in the armed forces during World War II, see Richard M. Dalfiume, *Desegregation of the U.S. Armed Forces: Fighting on Two Fronts, 1939–1945* (Columbia: University of Missouri Press, 1969); Herbert Shapiro, *White Violence and Black Response: From Reconstruction to Montgomery* (Amherst: University of Massachusetts Press, 1988), 305–309; Philip McGuire, ed., *Taps for a Jim Crow Army* (Santa Barbara, Calif.: ABC-Clio, 1983); Mary P. Motley, ed., *The Invisible Soldier: The Experience of the Black Soldier, World War II* (Detroit: Wayne State University Press, 1987); Studs Terkel, *The Good War: An Oral History of World War II* (New York: Pantheon Books, 1984), 149–56, 261–67, 274–79, 365–71.

61. Motley, ed., *The Invisible Soldier*, 194–95; SACB, "Herbert Brownell, Jr., Attorney General of the United States v. Veterans of the Abraham Lincoln Brigade." Hearings, September 15, 1954, pp. 3234, 3250, 3282; Yates, *Mississippi to Madrid*, 160–64.

62. Manning Marable, *Race, Reform, and Rebellion: The Second Reconstruction in Black America, 1945–1982* (Jackson, Miss.: University Press of Mississippi, 1984), 13–14; Herbert Garfinkel, *When Negroes March: The March on Washington Movement in the Organizational Politics of the FEPC* (Glencoe, Ill.: Free Press, 1959); SACB, "Herbert Brownell, Jr., Attorney General of the United States v. VALB," September 15, 1954, pp. 3245; Isserman, *Which Side Were You On?* 118–19.

63. Durem, *Take No Prisoners*, 3.

64. Ibid., p. 8.

65. Hunter interview, pp. 68–69; and on the political significance of the bebop counterculture, see chapter 7. Also see Eric Lott, "Double V, Double-Time: Bebop's Politics of Style," *Callaloo* 11, no. 3 (1988), 597–605; Stuart Cosgrove, "The Zoot-Suit and Style Warfare," *History Workshop Journal* 18 (Au-

tumn 1984), 77–91; Bruce M. Tyler, "Black Jive and White Repression," *Journal of Ethnic Studies* 16, no. 4 (Winter 1989), 31–66; Ben Sidran, *Black Talk* (New York: Holt, Rinehart & Winston, 1967), 78–115.

66. Rosenstone, *Crusade of the Left*, 351–55; U.S. Congress, House Un-American Activities, *Communist Activities in the Philadelphia Area* (Washington, D.C.: Government Printing Office, 1952), 4434–41; SACB, "Herbert Brownell, Jr., Attorney General of the United States v. VALB," September 15, 1954, p. 3225; Kilpatrick interview, pp. 64, 68.

67. Brandt, *Black Americans*, 20–21, 25; Durem, *Take No Prisoners*, 3; Yates, *Mississippi to Madrid*, 160–64; Kilpatrick interview, p. 73.

68. John Gerassi, *The Premature Antifascists: North American Volunteers in the Spanish Civil War, 1936–1939: An Oral History* (New York: Praeger, 1986), 155.

Part III. Rebels Without a Cause?

1. Cypress Hill, "How I Could Just Kill a Man," *Cypress Hill* (Columbia, 1991).

Chapter 7. The Riddle of the Zoot

1. Dudley Randall and Margaret G. Burroughs, eds., *For Malcolm: Poems on the Life and Death of Malcolm X* (Detroit: Broadside Press, 1967), 10.

2. *Negro Digest* 1, no. 4 (Winter–Spring 1943), 301.

3. Malcolm X, with Alex Haley, *The Autobiography of Malcolm X* (New York: Grove Press, 1964), 56.

4. A number of scholars, from a variety of different disciplines and standpoints, have illustrated the extent to which the *Autobiography* depended on various rhetorical strategies and literary devices (i.e., conversion narrative). See especially Thomas Benson, "Rhetoric and Autobiography: The Case of Malcolm X," *Quarterly Journal of Speech* 60 (February 1974), 1–13; Werner Berthoff, "Witness and Testament: Two Contemporary Classics," *New Literary History* 2 (Winter 1971), 311–27; Nancy Clasby, "Autobiography of Malcolm X: A Mythic Paradigm," *Journal of Black Studies* 5, no. 1 (September 1974), 18–34; David Demarest, "*The Autobiography of Malcolm X*: Beyond Didacticism," *CLA Journal* 16, no. 2 (December 1972), 179–87; Carol Ohmann, "The Autobiography of Malcolm X: A Revolutionary Use of the Franklin Tradition," *American Quarterly* 22, no. 2 (1970), 131–49; John Hodges, "The Quest for Selfhood in the Autobiographies of W.E.B. DuBois, Richard Wright, and Malcolm X" (Ph.D. diss., University of Chicago, 1980); Stephen Whitfield, "Three Masters of Impression Management: Benjamin Franklin, Booker T. Washington, and Malcolm X as Autobiographers," *South Atlantic Quarterly* 77 (Autumn 1978), 399–417.

5. Part of the reason for this, I believe, has something to do with the unusual proclivity of most Malcolm biographers to adopt a psychobiographical approach in place of an analysis which places the subject within specific historical

and cultural contexts. Examples include Bruce Perry, *Malcolm: The Life of a Man Who Changed Black America* (Barrytown, N.Y.: Station Hill Press, 1991) and Perry's three articles, "Malcolm X in Brief: A Psychological Perspective," *Journal of Psychohistory* 11, no. 4 (Spring 1984), 491–500; "Malcolm X and the Politics of Masculinity," *Psychohistory Review* 13, nos. 2 and 3 (Winter 1985), 18–25; "Escape from Freedom, Criminal Style: The Hidden Advantages of Being in Jail," *Journal of Psychiatry and Law* 12, no. 2 (Summer 1984), 215–30; Lawrence B. Goodheart, "The Odyssey of Malcolm X: An Eriksonian Interpretation," *The Historian* 53 (Autumn 1990), 47–62; Frederick Harper, "Maslow's Concept of Self-Actualization Compared with Personality Characteristics of Selected Black American Protestors: Martin Luther King, Jr., Malcolm X, and Frederick Douglass" (Ph.D. diss., Florida State University, 1970); Cedric J. Robinson, "Malcolm Little as a Charismatic Leader," *Afro-American Studies* 3 (1972), 81–96; Eugene Victor Wolfenstein, *The Victims of Democracy: Malcolm X and the Black Revolution* (Berkeley and Los Angeles: University of California Press, 1981). The worst example thus far is clearly Bruce Perry's massive psychobiography. Ignoring African American urban culture in general, and black politics during World War II in particular, enables Perry to treat Malcolm's decisions and practices as manifestations of a difficult childhood, thus isolating him from the broader social, cultural, and political transformations taking place around him. Throughout the book Perry betrays an incredible ignorance of black culture and cultural politics, and the fact that standard works are omitted from the notes and bibliography further underscores this point. On the other hand, Wolfenstein makes some reference to black politics during the war, but his very thin discussion focuses almost exclusively on organized, relatively mainstream black politics such as A. Philip Randolph's March on Washington Movement. The cultural politics of black zoot suiters, for all its contradictions and apparent detachment from social struggle, is ignored. See also, George Breitman, *The Last Year of Malcolm X: The Evolution of a Revolutionary* (New York: Merit Publishers, 1967); Breitman, *Malcolm X: The Man and His Ideas* (New York: Merit Publishers, 1965); John Henrik Clarke, ed., *Malcolm X: The Man and His Times* (New York: Macmillan, 1969); James Cone, *Martin and Malcolm and America: A Dream or Nightmare* (Maryknoll, N.Y.: Orbis Books, 1991); Peter Goldman, *The Death and Life of Malcolm X* (New York: Harper and Row, 1973); William Moore, "On Identity and Consciousness of El Hajj Malik El Shabazz (Malcolm X)" (Ph.D. diss., University of California, Santa Cruz, 1974).

6. Roi Ottley, *'New World A-Coming': Inside Black America* (Boston: Houghton Mifflin, 1943), 306. On black politics during the war, see Richard Dalfiume, *Fighting on Two Fronts: Desegregation of the Armed Forces, 1939–1953* (Columbia, Mo.: University of Missouri Press, 1969) and "The 'Forgotten Years' of the Negro Revolution," *Journal of American History* 55 (June 1968), 90–106; Herbert Garfinkel, *When Negroes March: The March on Washington Movement in the Organizational Policies for FEPC* (Glencoe, Ill.: Free Press, 1959); Lee Finkle, "The Conservative Aims of Militant Rhetoric: Black Protest during World War

II," *Journal of American History* 60 (December 1973), 692–713; Peter J. Kellogg, "Civil Rights Consciousness in the 1940's," *The Historian* 42 (November 1979), 18–41; Neil A. Wynn, *The Afro-American and the Second World War* (New York: Holmes and Meier Publishers, 1975); John Modell, Marc Goulden, and Magnusson Sigurdur, "World War II in the Lives of Black Americans: Some Findings and an Interpretation," *Journal of American History* 76 (December 1989), 838–48; Harvard Sitkoff, *A New Deal for Blacks: The Emergence of Civil Rights as a National Issue* (New York: Oxford University Press, 1978), 298–325, and Sitkoff, "Racial Militancy and Interracial Violence in the Second World War," *Journal of American History* 58 (December 1971), 661–81; Robert Korstad and Nelson Lichtenstein, "Opportunities Found and Lost: Labor, Radicals, and the Early Civil Rights Movement," *Journal of American History* 75 (December 1988), 786–811; Herbert Shapiro, *White Violence and Black Response: From Reconstruction to Montgomery* (Amherst, Mass.: University of Massachusetts Press, 1988), 301–48.

7. Manning Marable, *Race, Reform, and Rebellion: The Second Reconstruction in Black America, 1945–1990,* 2nd ed. (Jackson, Miss.: University Press of Mississippi 1991), 14–17; Philip S. Foner, *Organized Labor and the Black Worker, 1619–1981* (New York: International Publishers, 1981), 239, 243; Daniel R. Fusfeld and Timothy Bates, *The Political Economy of the Urban Ghetto* (Carbondale, Ill.: Southern Illinois University Press, 1984), 48; William H. Harris, *The Harder We Run: Black Workers since the Civil War* (New York: Oxford University Press, 1982), 113–22; George Lipsitz, *"A Rainbow at Midnight": Labor and Culture in the 1940s* (Urbana: University of Illinois Press, 1994), 14–28; Nelson Lichtenstein, *Labor's War at Home: The CIO in World War II* (New York: Cambridge University Press, 1982), 124–26.

8. Wolfenstein (*Victims of Democracy*, 175–76) makes a similar observation about the intensification of intraracial class divisions, although we disagree significantly as to the meaning of these divisions for the emergence of black working-class opposition. Besides, I am insisting on the simultaneity of heightened intraracial class struggle and racist oppression.

9. Perry, *Malcolm*, 48–49; Malcolm X, *Autobiography*, 38–41; Wolfenstein, *Victims of Democracy*, 154–57.

10. I'm making a distinction here between African American zoot suiters and the Chicano zoot suiters in the Southwest. In predominantly Mexican American urban communities, especially Los Angeles, the zoot suit emerged about the same time, but it also has its roots in the pachuco youth culture, an equally oppositional style politics emerging out of poverty, racism, and alienation. They reappropriated aspects of their parents' and grandparents' Mexican past in order to negotiate a new identity, adopting their own hip version of Spanish laced with English words and derived from a very old creolized dialect known as Calo. For more on Chicano zoot suiters and pachuco culture, see Stuart Cosgrove, "The Zoot-Suit and Style Warfare," *History Workshop Journal* 18 (Autumn 1984), 78–81; Mauricio Mazon, *The Zoot-Suit Riots: The Psychology of*

Symbolic Annihilation (Austin, Tex.: University of Texas Press, 1984); Marcos Sanchez-Tranquilino and John Tagg, "The Pachuco's Flayed Hide: Mobility, Identity, and *Buenas Garras*," in *Cultural Studies*, eds. Lawrence Grossberg, Cary Nelson, and Paula Treichler (London: Routledge, 1992), 566–70; Marcos Sanchez-Tranquilino, "Mano a mano: An Essay on the Representation of the Zoot Suit and its Misrepresentation by Octavio Paz," *Journal of the Los Angeles Institute of Contemporary Art* (Winter 1987), 34–42; Ralph H. Turner and Samuel J. Surace, "Zoot Suiters and Mexicans: Symbols in Crowd Behavior," *American Journal of Sociology* 62 (1956), 14–20; Octavio Paz, *The Labyrinth of Solitude: Life and Thought in Mexico* (New York: Grove Press, 1962), 5–8; Arturo Madrid-Barela, "In Search of the Authentic Pachuco: An Interpretive Essay," *Aztlan* 4, no. 1 (Spring 1973), 31–60. The best general discussions of the zoot in African American culture are Cosgrove, "The Zoot-Suit," 77–91; Bruce M. Tyler, "Black Jive and White Repression," *Journal of Ethnic Studies* 16, no. 4 (1989), 32–38; Steve Chibnall, "Whistle and Zoot: The Changing Meaning of a Suit of Clothes," *History Workshop* 20 (Autumn 1985), 56–81. Malcolm's own description of his zoot suits can be found in *Autobiography*, 52, 58.

11. Cosgrove, "The Zoot-Suit," 78, 80; LeRoi Jones, *Blues People: Negro Music in White America* (New York: William Morrow, 1963), 202; Eric Lott, "Double V, Double-Time: Bebop's Politics of Style," *Callalloo* 11, no. 3 (1988), 598, 600; Ben Sidran, *Black Talk* (New York: Holt, Rinehart and Winston, 1971), 110–11; Tyler, "Black Jive and White Repression," 31–66.

12. Dominic J. Capeci, Jr., *Race Relations in Wartime Detroit* (Philadelphia: Temple University Press, 1984), and *The Harlem Riot of 1943* (Philadelphia: Temple University Press, 1977); Harvard Sitkoff, "The Detroit Race Riot of 1943," *Michigan History* 53 (Fall 1969), 183–206; Shapiro, *White Violence*, 310–337.

13. Kenneth B. Clark and James Barker, "The Zoot Effect in Personality: A Race Riot Participant," *Journal of Abnormal and Social Psychology* 40, no. 2 (April 1945)," 146; and for a broader discussion of police brutality in Harlem during the late 1930s and 1940s, see Cheryl Greenberg, *Or Does it Explode? Black Harlem in the Great Depression* (New York: Oxford University Press, 1991), 193–94, 211.

14. Malcolm X, *Autobiography*, 54.

15. Kobena Mercer, "Black Hair/Style Politics," *New Formations* 3 (Winter 1987), 49; also see Lawrence Levine, *Black Culture and Black Consciousness: Afro-American Folk Thought from Slavery to Freedom* (New York: Oxford University Press, 1977), 291–92. For a general discussion of the ways oppositional meaning can be reinscribed in styles which are essentially a recasting of aspects of the dominant culture, see Dick Hebdige, *Subculture: The Meaning of Style* (London: Methuen, 1979), 17–19. Although Wolfenstein does not completely accept Malcolm's description of the conk as an act of self-degradation, he reduces his transformation to hipster entirely to a negation of waged work, ignoring the creative construction of an ethnic identity that celebrates difference as well as challenges the hegemonic image of the black male body. In Wolfenstein's schema,

oppositional identity becomes merely caricature. Thus he writes, "he was trying to *be* white, but in a black man's way" (Wolfenstein, *Victims of Democracy*, 157).

16. Malcolm X, *Autobiography*, 59–60.

17. Ibid., 72 (first quote), 49.

18. Ibid., 51; and for a description of the Savoy in Harlem, see Jervis Anderson, *This Was Harlem: A Cultural Portrait, 1900–1950* (New York: Farrar, Straus & Giroux, 1981), 307–14.

19. Quoted in Lott, "Double V, Double-Time," 603. Lott's essay is by far the best discussion of the politics of bebop. See also Ira Gitler, *Swing to Bop: An Oral History of the Transition in Jazz in the 1940's* (New York: Oxford University Press, 1985); Jack Chambers, *Milestones 1: The Music and Times of Miles Davis to 1960* (Toronto: University of Toronto Press, 1983); Ira Gitler, *Jazz Masters of the 1940's* (New York: Collier Books, 1966); Jones, *Blues People*, 175–207; Frank Kofsky, *Black Nationalism and the Revolution in Music* (New York: Pathfinder Press, 1970), chapter 1; Robert Reisner, *Bird: The Legend of Charlie Parker* (New York: Citadel Press, 1962); Sidran, *Black Talk*, 78–115; John Wilson, *Jazz: The Transition Years, 1940–1960* (New York: Appleton-Century-Crofts, 1966).

20. See chapter 2, as well as Paul Gilroy, "One Nation under a Groove: The Cultural Politics of 'Race' and Racism in Britain," in David Theo Goldberg, ed., *Anatomy of Racism* (Minneapolis: University of Minnesota Press, 1990), 274; Tera Hunter, "Household Workers in the Making: Afro-American Women in Atlanta and the New South, 1861–1920" (Ph.D. diss., Yale University, 1990), 92–93; and Katrina Hazzard-Gordon, *Jookin': The Rise of Social Dance Formations in African-American Culture* (Philadelphia: Temple University Press, 1990).

21. Malcolm X, *Autobiography*, 71; Gerald R. Gill, "Dissent, Discontent and Disinterest: Afro-American Opposition to the United States Wars of the Twentieth Century" (unpublished book manuscript, 1988), 166–67; Gitler, *Swing to Bop*, 115–16; Tyler, "Black Jive," 34–35. It is interesting to note that in Germany a subculture resembling black hipsters emerged in opposition to "Nazi regimentation." They wore zoot suits, listened to jazz, grew their hair long, and spent as much time as possible in the clubs and bars before they were closed down. The "swing boys," as they were called, faced enormous repression; jailings and beatings were common merely for possessing jazz records. Earl R. Beck, "The Anti-Nazi 'Swing Youth,' 1942–1945," *Journal of Popular Culture* 19 (Winter 1985), 45–53; "Hans Massaquoi," in Studs Terkel, ed., *The Good War: An Oral History of World War Two* (New York: Pantheon Books, 1984), 500–501; Michael H. Kater, "Forbidden Fruit? Jazz in the Third Reich," *American Historical Review* 94 (February 1989), 11–43; Kater, *Different Drummers: Jazz in the Culture of Nazi Germany* (New York: Oxford University Press, 1992).

22. Malcolm X, *Autobiography*, 104–7; Dizzy Gillespie, with Al Fraser, *To Be or Not . . . to Bop: Memoirs* (Garden City, N.Y.: Doubleday, 1979), 119–20. Malcolm's later speeches returned to this very theme. The military was initially reluctant to draft African Americans, Malcolm explained to his audiences, because "they feared that if they put us in the army and trained us in how to use

rifles and other things, we might shoot at some targets that they hadn't picked out. And we would have." Malcolm X, *Malcolm X Speaks: Selected Speeches and Statements*, ed. George Breitman (New York: Merit Publishers, 1965), 140; "Not Just an American Problem, but a World Problem," in Bruce Perry, ed., *Malcolm X: The Last Speeches* (New York: Pathfinder Press, 1989), 176.

23. Malcolm X, *Autobiography*, 71; Clark and Barker, "The Zoot Effect," 145.

24. Gill, "Dissent, Discontent, and Disinterest," 164–68; George Q. Flynn, "Selective Service and American Blacks during World War II," *Journal of Negro History* 69 (Winter 1984), 14–25. Ironically, one of the most widely publicized groups of black conscientious objectors happened to be members of the Nation of Islam. About 100 of its members were arrested for resisting the draft, including its spiritual leader Elijah Muhammad. Yet, despite the fact that a number of jazz musicians had converted to Islam and even adopted Arabic names (e.g., Sahib Shihab, Idris Sulieman, and Sadik Hakim) during the war, Malcolm claims complete ignorance of the Nation prior to his prison stint. On the Nation of Islam during the war, see Gill, "Dissent, Discontent, and Disinterest," 156–57; E. U. Essien-Udom, *Black Nationalism: A Search for Identity* (Chicago: University of Chicago Press, 1962), 80–81; Sidran, *Black Talk*, 82.

25. See especially, Tyler, "Black Jive," 34–39 passim.

26. Tyler, "Black Jive," 38; Mazon, *Zoot-Suit Riots*, 54–77; Cosgrove, "The Zoot-Suit," 80–88; C.L.R. James, George Breitman, Edgar Keemer et al., *Fighting Racism in World War II* (New York: Pathfinder Press, 1980), 254–55; Malcolm X, *Autobiography*, 77.

27. For example, Bruce Perry (who characterizes Malcolm's entire family as a bunch of criminals) not only suggests that theft is merely a manifestation of deviant behavior rooted in unfulfilled personal relationships, but he naturalizes the Protestant work ethic by asserting that Malcolm's resistance to "steady employment" reflected a reluctance to "assume responsibility." (*Malcolm*, 57–61 passim.)

28. Greenberg, *Or Does It Explode?* 198–202; Fusfeld and Bates, *Political Economy*, 45–46.

29. Carol B. Stack, *All Our Kin: Strategies for Survival in a Black Community* (New York: Harper and Row, 1974); Betty Lou Valentine, *Hustling and Other Hard Work: Life Styles in the Ghetto* (New York: The Free Press, 1978); for comparative contemporary and historical examples from Britain, see the brilliant book by Peter Linebaugh, *The London Hanged: Crime and Civil Society in the Eighteenth Century* (London: Allen Lane, The Penguin Press, 1991); Steven Box, *Recession, Crime, and Punishment* (Totowa, N.J.: Barnes and Noble Books, 1987); Jason Ditton, *Part-Time Crime: An Ethnography of Fiddling and Pilferage* (London: Macmillan 1977); Richard C. Hollinger and J. P. Clark, *Theft by Employees* (Lexington, Mass.: Lexington Books, 1983); and for a general discussion of the informal economy and working-class opposition, see Cyril Robinson, "Exploring the Informal Economy," *Crime and Social Justice* 15, nos. 3 and 4 (1988), 3–16.

30. Malcolm X, *Autobiography*, 44, 51; Wolfenstein, *Victims of Democracy*, 157. For a discussion of the "hustler's ethic" as a rejection of the "Protestant work ethic," see Julius Hudson, "The Hustling Ethic," in Thomas Kochman, ed., *Rappin' and Stylin' Out: Communication in Urban Black America* (Urbana, Ill.: University of Illinois Press, 1972), 414–16.

31. Wolfenstein, *Victims of Democracy*, 155; Perry, *Malcolm*, 72. Horace Cayton and St. Clair Drake found numerous examples of poor black residents in Chicago's Southside mutually supporting one another while simultaneously engaged in the illicit economy. *Black Metropolis: A Study of Negro Life in a Northern City*, 2nd ed. (New York: Harper and Row, 1962), II, 570–611 passim.

32. Malcolm X, *Autobiography*, 134; Perry, *Malcolm*, 77–78, 82–83. The evidence Perry provides to make this assertion (which includes simplistic Freudian interpretations of later speeches!) is slim, to say the least. But even if the hearsay Perry's informant passed on is true, it would not contradict my argument. For the manner in which Malcolm allegedly exploited gay men positioned them as Other, and in the cases Perry cites obtaining money was far more important than sexual pleasure. He apparently did not identify with an underground gay community; rather, it was merely another "stunt" in the life of a hustler.

33. Perry, *Malcolm*, 51–52; Wolfenstein, *Victims of Democracy*, 162–63.

34. See, for example, Miles Davis with Quincy Troupe, *Miles: The Autobiography* (New York: Simon and Schuster, 1989), 87–189 passim.; Charles Mingus, *Beneath the Underdog* (Harmondsworth, England: Penguin, 1969); and for some postwar examples beyond the jazz world, see Elliot Liebow, *Tally's Corner: A Study of Negro Streetcorner Men* (Boston: Little, Brown and Co., 1967), 137–44; Christina Milner and Richard Milner, *Black Players: The Secret World of Black Pimps* (New York: Little, Brown, 1972).

35. "Romance without Finance," *Bird/The Savoy Recordings [Master Takes]* (Savoy, 1976).

36. Iceberg Slim [Robert Beck], *Pimp: The Story of My Life* (Los Angeles: Holloway House, 1969), vi.

37. Malcolm X, *Autobiography*, 68.

38. Ibid., 47–48, 75. A number of scholars have suggested that pimps and hustlers, at least in black folklore, were more like modern-day tricksters than "bad men." See, for example, Lawrence Levine, *Black Culture and Black Consciousness*, 381–82; Milner and Milner, *Black Players*, 242.

39. "Not Just an American Problem, but a World Problem," in Perry, ed., *Malcolm X: The Last Speeches*, 161.

40. Malcolm X, *Autobiography*, first quote, 78, second quote, 55.

41. bell hooks, "Sitting at the Feet of the Messenger: Remembering Malcolm X," in *Yearning: Race, Gender and Cultural Politics* (Boston: South End Press, 1990), 84.

42. Malcolm X, *Autobiography*, 43.

Chapter 8. Kickin' Reality, Kickin' Ballistics

1. Quoted in Robert Warshow, *The Immediate Experience: Movies, Comics, Theatre and Other Aspects of Popular Culture* (New York: Atheneum, 1970), 130.

2. Eugene Genovese, *Roll, Jordan, Roll: The World the Slaves Made* (New York: Pantheon Books, 1974), 629.

3. For those who might have forgotten, several thousand people seized the streets on April 29, 1992, in part to protest the acquittal of the four officers who brutally beat a black motorist named Rodney King thirteen months earlier. For more on the L.A. rebellion, see especially Mike Davis, "In L.A., Burning All Illusions," *Nation* 254, no. 21 (June 1, 1992), 743–46; *L.A. Weekly*, 14, no. 23 (May 8–14, 1992); Los Angeles Times, *Understanding the Riots: Los Angeles Before and After the Rodney King Case* (Los Angeles: Los Angeles Times, 1992); Robert Gooding-Williams, ed., *Reading Rodney King, Reading Urban Uprising* (New York: Routledge, 1993).

4. Alan Light, "L.A. Rappers Speak Out," *Rolling Stone* 633 (June 25, 1992), 21; see also Light's "Rappers Sounded Warning," *Rolling Stone* 634/35 (July 9–23, 1992), 15–17, which appeared a month after my own article, "Straight from Underground," *Nation* 254, no. 22 (June 8, 1992), 793–96.

5. MTV News interview, May 3, 1992; Ice Cube, *The Predator* (Priority Records, 1992).

6. Quote from Kofi Buenor Hadjor, *Days of Rage: . . . Behind the Los Angeles Riots* (unpublished manuscript, 1992, in author's possession). I'm grateful to Ula Taylor and Kofi Hadjor for making this manuscript available to me. It is an incredible exploration of the roots and consequences of the L.A. Rebellion. The best sources on recent police brutality cases in Los Angeles are The Independent Commission on the Los Angeles Police Department, *Report of the Independent Commission on the Los Angeles Police Department* (Los Angeles: The Commission, 1991) [hereafter *The Christopher Report*]; Mike Davis, *City of Quartz: Excavating the Future in Los Angeles* (London: Verso, 1990), 267–92; see also Douglas G. Glasgow, *The Black Underclass: Poverty, Unemployment, and Entrapment of Ghetto Youth* (New York: Random House, 1981), 101; M. W. Meyer, "Police Shootings at Minorities: The Case of Los Angeles," *Annals* 452 (1980), 98–110; and for other local and national examples, one might consult, S. Harring, T. Platt, R. Speiglman, and P. Takagi, "The Management of Police Killings," *Crime and Social Justice* 8 (1977), 34–43; P. Takagi, "A Garrison State in 'Democratic Society,'" *Crime and Social Justice* (Spring–Summer 1978), 2–25; Community Relations Service, *The Police Use of Deadly Force: What Police and the Community Can Do About It* (Washington, D.C.: Department of Justice, Community Relations Service, 1977); Jerry G. Watts, "It Just Ain't Righteous: On Witnessing Black Crooks and White Cops," *Dissent* 90 (1983), 347–53; Bruce Pierce, "Blacks and Law Enforcement: Towards Police Brutality Reduction," *Black Scholar* 17 (1986), 49–54; A. L. Kobler, "Figures (and Perhaps Some Facts) on Police Killing of Civilians in the United States, 1965–1969," *Journal of Social Issues* 31 (1975), 163–91; J. J. Fyfe, "Blind Justice: Police Shootings in Memphis," *Journal of Criminal Law and Criminology* 73 (1982), 707–22; Bernard D.

Headley, "'Black on Black' Crime: The Myth and the Reality," *Crime and Social Justice* 20 (1983), 52–53.

7.   For this analysis, which runs throughout much of the chapter, I am indebted to my conversations with Charles Bright and to reading John Irwin, *The Jail: Managing the Underclass in American Society* (Berkeley and Los Angeles: University of California Press, 1985); Diana R. Gordon, *The Justice Juggernaut: Fighting Street Crime, Controlling Citizens* (New Brunswick, N.J.: Rutgers University Press, 1990); Michel Foucault, *Discipline and Punish: The Birth of the Prison*, trans. Alan Sheridan (New York: Pantheon Books, 1977), esp. pp. 195–228.

8.   Tricia Rose, "Black Texts/Black Contexts," in *Black Popular Culture*, ed. Gina Dent (Seattle: Bay Press, 1992).

9.   Charlie Ahearn, *Wild Style* (film) (1982).

10.   David Toop, *Rap Attack 2* (London: Serpent's Tail, 1991), 40; the Morton lyrics are quoted from the "Rockbeat" column in the *Village Voice*, 39, no. 4 (January 25, 1994), 76; on the baaadman narratives, see John W. Roberts, *From Trickster to Badman: The Black Folk Hero in Slavery and Freedom* (Philadelphia: University Pennsylvania Press, 1989), 171–215; and on signifying, see Henry Louis Gates, Jr., *The Signifying Monkey: A Theory of African-American Literary Criticism* (New York: Oxford University Press, 1988), especially 64–88; Claudia Mitchell-Kernan, "Signifying, Loud-talking, and Marking," in *Rappin and Stylin' Out: Communication in Urban Black America*, ed. Thomas Kochman (Urbana: University of Illinois Press, 1972); Bruce Jackson, *"Get Your Ass in the Water and Swim Like Me": Narrative Poetry from Black Oral Tradition* (Cambridge, Mass.: Harvard University Press, 1974); Lawrence W. Levine, *Black Culture and Black Consciousness: Afro-American Folk Thought from Slavery to Freedom* (New York: Oxford University Press, 1977), 407–20.

11.   Darryl James, "Ice-T the Ex-Gangster," *Rappin'* (January 1991), 37; Havelock Nelson and Michael A. Gonzales, *Bring the Noise: A Guide to Rap Music and Hip Hop Culture* (New York: Harmony Books, 1991), 30–31. When this book went to press, Brian Cross's incredible book on the L.A. hip hop scene, *It's Not about a Salary . . . Rap, Race and Resistance in Los Angeles* (London: Verso, 1993), had just come out. Unfortunately, I did not have a chance to incorporate his insights or his interviews with L.A. rappers into this chapter, aside from a few small corrections. It doesn't matter, however, since the material essentially reinforces my interpretation. Nevertheless, I would suggest that all serious readers and hip hop fans check out Cross's book.

12.   James, "Ice-T the Ex-Gangster," 37; "T for Two," *Details* (July 1991), 51–55; Alan Light, "Rapper Ice-T Busts a Movie," *Rolling Stone* (May 16, 1991), 85; Mills, "The Gangsta Rapper," 32; Cross, *It's Not About a Salary*, 24; Ice T, *Rhyme Pays* (Sire Records, 1987).

13.   Mills, "The Gangsta Rapper," 32; Frank Owen, "Hanging Tough," *Spin* 6, no. 1 (April 1990), 34; Nelson and Gonzales, *Bring the Noise*, 80–81, 165–67; NWA, *Straight Outta Compton* (Ruthless Records, 1988).

14.   Sampling refers to the practice of incorporating portions of other

records, or different sounds, into a hip hop recording. Digital samplers are usually used, which enable producers to isolate specific sounds and manipulate
them (change the register, the tempo, etc.).

15. "1993 Summer Jeep Slammers," *Source* (July 1993), 76. There are
some exceptions, the most obvious being Compton's Most Wanted which is
more inclined toward jazz and quiet storm tracks (see especially, CMW, *Straight
Check N' Em* (Orpheus Records, 1991). Nevertheless, funk dominates West
Coast gangsta rap, and the introduction of reggae and jazz, unlike the East
Coast, has been slow coming.

16. The larger hip hop community has maintained an ambivalent, and occasionally critical, stance toward most gangsta rappers. See, for instance, the
criticisms of Kool Moe Dee, YZ, and others in "Droppin' Science," *Spin* 5, no. 5
(August 1989), 49–50; The J, "If you don't know your Culture, You don't Know
Nothin'!: YZ Claims He's 'Thinking of a Master Plan' for Black Awareness," *Rap
Pages* (December 1991), 64; "Views on Gangsta-ism," *Source* (December 1990),
36, 39, 40; as well as critical perspectives in the music itself, e.g., Del the Fun-
kee Homosapien, "Hoodz Come in Dozens," *I Wish My Brother George Was Here*
(Priority Records, 1991); Public Enemy, "No Nigga," *Apocalypse '91* (Def Jam,
1991); Arrested Development, "People Everyday," and "Give a Man A Fish," *3
Years, 5 Months and 2 Days in the Life Of . . .* (Chrysalis Records, 1992); The Dis-
posable Heroes of Hipoprisy, especially "Famous and Dandy (Like Amos N'
Andy)," *Hypocrisy is the Greatest Luxury* (Island Records, 1992); The Coup, *Kill
My Landlord* (Wild Pitch Records, 1993).

17. Ice T, *OG: Original Gangster* (Sire Records, 1991); Ice Cube, *Kill at
Will* (Priority Records, 1992); Ice Cube, *The Predator* (Priority Records, 1992);
Ice T, *Power* (Warner Bros., 1988); CPO, *To Hell and Black* (Capitol Records,
1990); NWA, *100 Miles and Runnin'* (Ruthless, 1990); Dr. Dre, *The Chronic* (Interscope Records, 1992); CMW, *Straight Check N' Em* (Orpheus Records, 1991).
How Ice T's lyrics from "I'm Your Pusher" were misinterpreted was discussed
on the *MacNeil-Lehrer Newshour* on a special segment on rap music.

18. Ice T [and the Rhyme Syndicate], "My Word is Bond," *The
Iceberg/Freedom of Speech . . . Just Watch What You Say* (Sire Records, 1989); Ice
Cube, "J.D.'s Gafflin'," *AmeriKKKa's Most Wanted* (Priority Records, 1990).
West Coast rappers also create humorous countercritiques of gangsterism; the
most penetrating is perhaps Del tha Funkee Homosapien's hilarious, "Hoodz
Come in Dozens," *I Wish My Brother George Was Here* (Priority Records, 1991).

19. Cube quote, David Mills, "The Gangsta Rapper: Violent Hero or Negative Role Model?" *Source* (December 1990), 39; see also Dan Charnas, "A
Gangsta's World View," *Source* (Summer 1990), 21–22; "Niggers With Attitude," *Melody Maker* 65, no. 44 (November 4, 1989), 33; and the Geto Boys'
Bushwick Bill's explanation in J. Sultan, "The Geto Boys," *Source* (December
1990), 33.

20. Digital Underground's, "Good Thing We're Rappin'," *Sons of the P*
(Tommy Boy, 1991) is nothing if not a tribute to the pimp narratives. One hears

elements of classic toasts, including "The Pimp," "Dogass Pimp," "Pimping Sam," "Wicked Nell," "The Lame and the Whore," and perhaps others. Even the meter is very much in the toasting tradition. (For transcriptions of these toasts, see Bruce Jackson, *"Get Your Ass in the Water and Swim Like Me"*, 106–30.) Similar examples which resemble the more comical pimp narratives include Ice Cube, "I'm Only Out for One Thing," *AmeriKKKa's Most Wanted* (Priority, 1990) and Son of Bazerk, "Sex, Sex, and more Sex," *Son of Bazerk* (MCA, 1991).

21. See John Leland, "Rap: Can It Survive Self-Importance?" *Details* (July 1991), 108; Owen, "Hanging Tough," 34; James Bernard, "NWA [Interview]," *Source* (December 1990), 34. In fact, Ice Cube left NWA in part because they were not "political" enough. Though most accounts indicate that financial disputes between Cube and manager Jerry Heller caused the split, in at least one interview he implied that politics had something to do with it as well. As early as *Straight Outta Compton*, Cube wanted to include more like songs "F——the Police," and when the FBI sent a warning to them because of their inflammatory lyrics, Cube planned to put out a twelve-minute remix in response. Of course, neither happened. It finally became clear to Cube that he could not remain in NWA after Jerry Heller kept them from appearing on Jesse Jackson's weekly TV show. Darryl James, "Ice Cube Leaves NWA to Become Amerikkka's Most Wanted," *Rappin'* (January 1991), 20.

22. Davis, *City of Quartz*, 304–7; Edward Soja, *Postmodern Geographies: The Reassertion of Space in Critical Social Theory* (London: Verso, 1989), 197, 201.

23. NWA, *Efil4zaggin* (Priority Records, 1991).

24. The idea that unemployed black youth turn to crime because it is more rewarding than minimum-wage, service-oriented work has been explored by a number of social scientists. See, for example, Richard B. Freeman, "The Relation of Criminal Activity to Black Youth Employment," in Margaret C. Simms and Samuel L. Myers, Jr., eds., *The Economics of Race and Crime* (New Brunswick, N.J.: Transaction Books, 1988), 99–107; Llad Phillips and Harold Votey, Jr., "Rational Choice Models of Crimes by Youth," in ibid., pp. 129–187; Llad Phillips, H. L. Votey, Jr., and D. Maxwell, "Crime, Youth, and the Labor Market," *Journal of Political Economy* 80 (1972), 491–504; Philip Moss and Chris Tilly, *Why Black Men Are Doing Worse in the Labor Market: A Review of Supply-Side and Demand-Side Explanations* (New York: Social Science Research Council Committee for Research on the Underclass, Working Paper, 1991), 90–93. For a discussion of the role of gangs in the illicit economy, see Martin Sanchez Jankowski, *Islands in the Street: Gangs and American Urban Society* (Berkeley and Los Angeles: University of California Press, 1991), 119–31. Despite the general perception that dealers make an enormous amount of money, at least one study suggests that the average crack peddler only makes about $700 per month. See Peter Reuter, Robert MacCoun, and Patrick Murphy, *Money from Crime: A Study of the Economics of Drug Dealing in Washington, D.C.* (Santa Monica, Calif.: Rand, Drug Policy Research Center, 1990); Davis, *City of Quartz*, 322.

25. For discussions of the ways in which the mass media depict black youth gangs, violence, and the crack economy in inner-city neighborhoods, see Jankowski, *Islands in the Street*, 284–302; Jimmie L. Reeves and Richard Campbell, *Cracked Coverage: Television News, The Anti-cocaine Crusade, and The Reagan Legacy* (Durham, N.C.: Duke University Press, 1994); Herman Gray, "Race Relations as News: Content Analysis," *American Behavioral Scientist* 30, no. 4 (March–April 1987), 381–96; Craig Reinarman and Harry G. Levine, "The Crack Attack: Politics and Media in America's Latest Drug Scare," in *Images of Issues: Typifying Contemporary Social Problems*, ed. Joel Best (New York: Aldine de Gruyter, 1989), 115–35; Clarence Lusane, *Pipe Dream Blues: Racism and the War on Drugs* (Boston: South End Press, 1991).

26. "Niggers With Attitude," *Melody Maker* 65, no. 44 (November 4, 1989), 33.

27. James, "Ice T the Ex-Gangster," 38. Of course, the last part of Ice T's pronouncements echoes a range of conspiracy theories that continue to float among communities under siege, and even found a voice in Furious Styles, a lead character in John Singleton's *Boyz N the Hood*. But T's assertion cannot be dismissed so easily, since there are more liquor stores per capita and per square mile in low-income inner-city neighborhoods than anywhere else in the United States. See George A. Hacker, *Marketing Booze to Blacks* (Washington, D.C.: Center for Science in the Public Interest, 1987); Manning Marable, *How Capitalism Underdeveloped Black America: Problems in Race, Political Economy, and Society* (Boston: South End Press, 1983).

28. Ice T, *OG: Original Gangster* (Sire Records, 1991)

29. Bill Moyers interview with Bernice Johnson Reagon, PBS; Abrahams, *Deep Down in the Jungle*, 58–59; Mark Zanger, "The Intelligent Forty-year-old's Guide to Rap," *Boston Review* (December 1991), 34.

30. *AmeriKKKa's Most Wanted*.

31. Bruce Perry, ed., *Malcolm X: The Last Speeches* (New York: Pathfinder Press, 1989), 161.

32. This argument has been made by numerous scholars. For a sampling, see Ken Auletta, *The Underclass* (New York: Random House, 1982), 90–108 passim.; Charles Murray, *Losing Ground: American Social Policy, 1950–1980* (New York: Basic Books, 1984); see also Roger Lane's more historical but equally flawed treatment in *Roots of Violence in Black Philadelphia, 1860–1900* (Cambridge, Mass.: Harvard University Press, 1986). Williams Julius Wilson, *The Truly Disadvantaged: The Inner City, the Underclass, and Public Policy* (Chicago: University of Chicago Press, 1987), 30–32, 37–38, makes a different argument, suggesting that social dislocation is the ultimate cause of criminal behavior, which in turn becomes one out of a set of pathologies brought about by persistent poverty. Nevertheless, there is a large body of research that suggests poverty and joblessness are directly related to crime. In addition to sources cited in note 27, see Steven Box, *Recession, Crime and Punishment* (Totowa, N.J.: Barnes and Noble Books, 1987); D. Glaser and K. Rice, "Crime, Age, and Employment,"

American Sociological Review 24 (1959), 679–86; Jason Ditton, *Part-Time Crime: An Ethnography of Fiddling and Pilferage* (London: Macmillan, 1977); Richard C. Hollinger and J. P. Clark, *Theft by Employees* (Lexington, 1983); A. J. Reiss and A. L. Rhodes, "The Distribution of Juvenile Delinquency in the Social Class Structure," *American Sociological Review* 26 (1961), 720–43; Elliot Currie, *Confronting Crime: An American Challenge* (New York: Pantheon Books, 1985), 146; E. Green, "Race, Social Status, and Criminal Arrest," *American Sociological Review* 35 (1970), 476–90; R. W. Beasley and G. Antunes, "The Etiology of Urban Crime: An Ecological Analysis," *Criminology* 11 (1974), 439–61; J. R. Blau and P. M. Blau, "The Cost of Inequality: Metropolitan Structure and Violent Crime," *American Sociological Review* 47 (1982), 114–29; James W. Messerschmidt, *Capitalism, Patriarchy and Crime* (Totowa, N.J.: Rowman and Littlefield, 1986), 54–58; I. Jankovic, "Labor Market and Imprisonment," *Crime and Social Justice* 8 (1977), 17–31; D. Humphries and D. Wallace, "Capitalist Accumulation and Urban Crime, 1950–1971," *Social Problems* 28 (1980), 179–93; A. D. Calvin, "Unemployment among Black Youths, Demographics, and Crime," *Crime and Delinquency* 27 (1981), 9–41.

33. D. Dub, "We're Not Glamorizin'—But We're Factualizin,'" *Rap Pages* 1, no. 2 (December 1991), 55–56. For Bobby Byrd, however, a job is not something one pulls, but something one has. His lyrics are clearly about wage labor: "You got to have a job/ Put meat on the table/ You got to have a job/ to keep the family stable." (Quoted in Michael Haralambos, *Soul Music: The Birth of a Sound in America* [New York: De Capo, 1974], 115.)

34. W.C. and the MAAD Circle, *Ain't A Damn Thang Changed* (Priority, 1991).

35. Ibid.

36. Ice Cube, *Death Certificate* (Priority, 1991).

37. The phrase "criminal-criminals" is taken from Peter Linebaugh's amazing book, *The London Hanged: Crime and Civil Society in the Eighteenth Century* (London: Allen Lane, The Penguin Press, 1991). Of London's working-class criminals, he writes: "If we categorize them too quickly as social criminals taking from the rich, or criminal-criminals stealing from the poor, in the process of making these judgements we cloud our attentiveness to theirs" (p. xxiii).

38. *Ain't A Damn Thang Changed*.

39. James Bernard, "Ice Cube: Building a Nation," *Source* 27 (December 1991), 34.

40. Da Lench Mob, *Guerrillas in Tha Mist* (Priority, 1992).

41. Quoted in Jankowski, *Islands in the Street*, 103.

42. Davis, *City of Quartz*, 297; *Los Angeles Times*, May 25, 1992; Alexander Cockburn, "Beat the Devil," *Nation* 254, no. 21 (June 1, 1992), 738–39.

43. Ice T, "Pain" and "6 in the Mornin," *Rhyme Pays*, "High Rollers," *Power*, "New Jack Hustler," *OG: Original Gangster*, Ice Cube, "Dead Homiez" *Kill at Will*, "Color Blind," *Death Certificate*, NWA, "Alwayz into Somethin," *Efil4zaggin*; Cypress Hill, *Cypress Hill* (Columbia, 1991).

44. Capitol Punishment Organization, *To Hell and Black* (Capitol Records, 1990). It might be worth noting that even a group as hard as Da Lench Mob suggests that black urban youth should become more religious.

45. D. Dub, "We're Not Glamorizin,'" 57.

46. Messerschmidt, *Capitalism, Patriarchy and Crime*, 58–60, quote p. 59; Tony Platt, "'Street' Crime: A View from the Left," *Crime and Social Justice* 9 (Spring–Summer 1978), 26–34; Walter J. Ong, *Fighting for Life: Contest, Sexuality, and Consciousness* (Ithaca, N.Y.: Cornell University Press, 1981), 68–69; R. W. Connell, *Gender and Power: Society, the Person, and Sexual Politics* (Stanford, Calif.: Stanford University Press, 1987), 57–58, 85–86; R. E. Dobash and R. P. Dobash, *Violence against Wives: A Case against Patriarchy* (New York: The Free Press, 1979); Barbara Ehrenreich, *Hearts of Men: American Dreams and the Flight from Commitment* (Garden City, N.Y.: Anchor Press, 1983), 7–11. One very obvious example of gangsta rappers measuring one's masculinity by his ability and willingness to fight is Ice T's "Bitches 2" from *OG: Original Gangster*. One woman's gangsta group whose music talks about women engaging in drive-by shootings and taking out police in a flurry of buckshot is the New York–based Bytches With Problems. See their "We're Coming Back Strapped" and "Wanted," *The Bytches* (Def Jam, 1991)

47. See "The Drive By," *AmeriKKKa's Most Wanted* and *Kill at Will*.

48. Compton's Most Wanted, *Straight Check N' Em* (Sony, 1991). In a recent article in the *Source*, hip hop critic Reginald C. Dennis, who also shares these gangsta rappers' sensitivity to both the logic of crime and its detrimental effects, has even made a plea for criminals to be socially responsible when engaging in violence: "If you have chosen the lifestyle of the 'gangsta' you can still contribute to the cause by making sure the blood of innocents is not randomly spilled because of your irresponsibility. Do what you gotta do, but keep it limited to your social circle. If you must be criminal minded be professional and responsible—don't drag children and other innocents down with you. . . . In this way we can attempt to find some common ground between the criminal and the activist, and in diverse ways, work towards the same goal." ("After all . . . We are the ones who are Dying: Inner City Crime," *Source* 18 [February 1991], 34.)

49. Ice Cube, *Kill at Will*.

50. NWA, *NWA and the Posse* (Ruthless Records, 1988).

51. From "The Wall," *To Hell and Black*.

52. *Death Certificate* (Priority, 1991).

53. Ice T, "New Jack Hustler," *OG: Original Gangster*.

54. Ice Cube, "Rollin' Wit the Lench Mob," *AmeriKKKa's Most Wanted*.

55. Ice T, *OG: Original Gangster*; Ice Cube, *AmeriKKKa's Most Wanted*.

56. D. Dub, "We're Not Glamorizin,'" 56–57.

57. Quoted in Robert Hilburn, "The Rap Is: Justice," *Los Angeles Times*, May 31, 1992; Ice Cube, "Who's the Mack," MTV video; see also "Niggers With Attitude," *Melody Maker* 65, no. 44 (November 4, 1989), 34. Of course, the complicity of the U.S. government in the distribution of drugs into the black

community is not a new theme, nor is it unique to hip hop. See Sir Mix-a-Lot, "National Anthem," lyrics reprinted in Lawrence A. Stanley, ed., *Rap: The Lyrics* (New York: Penguin Books, 1992), 294; 2 Black, 2 Strong MMG, "War on Drugs," *Doin' Hard Time on Planet Earth* (Relativity Records, 1991); Geto Boys, "City under Siege," *The Geto Boys* (Def American Records, 1989).

58. Davis, *City of Quartz*, 268; Jankowski, *Islands in the Street*, 252, 254; also see Glasgow, *The Black Underclass*, 100–101.

59. NWA, "F——Tha Police," *Straight Outta Compton*; Owen, "Hanging Tough," 34.

60. CMW, *Straight Check N 'Em*; Cypress Hill, *Cypress Hill*; Kid Frost, *East Side Story* (Virgin Records, 1992).

61. George Lipsitz, *Time Passages: Collective Memory and American Popular Culture* (Minneapolis: University of Minnesota Press, 1990), 5; W.C. and the MAAD Circle, *Ain't A Damn Thang Changed*.

62. Although young black women also occupied public space, were victims of police marking, and experienced outright brutality, L.A. gangsta rappers have been silent on the policing of women. Combined with a dominant black political ideology that has framed the issues solely in terms of the problems of black males, the refusal to acknowledge black women's experiences with state-sanctioned violence has effectively rendered them invisible in the whole discourse about police brutality in the aftermath of Rodney King. Even black female rappers have ignored the issue of state-sanctioned violence against women—one exception being "Wanted" by the New York-based rap group, Bytches With Problems. "Wanted" not only reminds listeners that women are victims of police harassment, but briefly adds the dimension of sexual abuse in their descriptions of day-to-day repression. (BWP, *The Bytches* [Def Jam, 1991].) While it is true that the percentage of black male victims of police repression is much, much higher than that of females, we cannot ignore the fact that the most important police homicide and brutality cases over the past decade have had black female victims: Eula Love and Eleanor Bumpurs, to name a few. Unfortunately, scholarship on policing is equally male-focused and thus complicit in rendering black women's experiences invisible. One recent exception is Ruth Chigwada's study of black women in Britain, "The Policing of Black Women," in *Out of Order? Policing Black People*, eds. Ellis Cashmore and Eugene McLaughlin (London: Routledge, 1991), 134–50.

63. *AmeriKKKa's Most Wanted*; also re-mixed on *Kill at Will*.

64. Davis, *City of Quartz*, 274.

65. Ibid., 272. Of course, L.A. is not unique in this respect. See, for example, Box, *Recession, Crime and Punishment*, 46–47; Lee P. Brown, "Bridges over Troubled Waters: A Perspective on Policing in the Black Community," in *Black Perspectives on Crime and the Criminal Justice System*, ed. Robert L. Woodson (Boston: G. K. Hall, 1977), 87–88; Elijah Anderson, *Streetwise: Race, Class, and Change in an Urban Community* (Chicago: University of Chicago Press, 1990), 194–96.

66. "Dress Code," *Ain't A Damn Thang Changed*.

67. Dick Hebdige, *Subculture: The Meaning of Style* (London: Methuen, 1979), 18.

68. This interpretation is derived from a reading of Stuart Hall, "Culture, Media, and the 'Ideological Effect,'" in James Curran, Michael Gurevitch, and Janet Woolacott, eds., *Mass Communication and Society* (Beverly Hills: Sage Publications, 1979), 315–48.

69. From its founding in the mid-1960s, the Five-Percenters believe that every person is God. Less commonly, "G" is used as a shorthand term for "money," which is also used as a form of address. Although my point that this terminology cuts across gender lines is drawn from very unscientific participant observation, one might listen to the music of Yo Yo, M. C. Lyte, or Queen Latifah for their employment of "G" as a form of address.

70. Again, we must be careful not to presume that these styles are merely the authentic expressions of poor black urban youth. Many middle-class suburban black kids and many more white kids—males and females—can be found sporting the "G" style on college and high school campuses, malls, and playgrounds throughout the country. What this means deserves an essay in itself.

71. Ice Cube, *Death Certificate*; Cypress Hill, "Pigs," *Cypress Hill*.

72. Ice Cube, "The Wrong Nigga to F——Wit," *Death Certificate*, and "Endangered Species (Tales from the Darkside)," *AmeriKKKa's Most Wanted*.

73. Marc Mauer, *Young Black Men and the Criminal Justice System: A Growing National Problem* (Washington, D.C.: The Sentencing Project, 1990), 1–11; John Irwin, *The Jail*; Gordon, *The Justice Juggernaut*; Messerschmidt, *Capitalism, Patriarchy and Crime*, 52–53; Jefferey Reiman, *The Rich Get Richer and the Poor Get Prison*, 2nd ed. (New York: Wiley, 1984); R. Sheldon, *Criminal Justice in America: A Sociological Approach* (Boston: Little, Brown, 1982), 39–50; Brown, "Bridges over Troubled Waters," 87–88; Alfred N. Garwood, *Black Americans: A Statistical Sourcebook* 3rd ed. Rev. (Palo Alto, Calif.: Information Publishers, 1993), 210–13. Statistics aside, many rappers take up the subject of incarceration because they know people who are "locked down," and in some instances, a few rap artists have actually served time in the penitentiary. Some examples include MAAD Circle rapper Coolio, East Coast rappers Intelligent Hoodlum (Percy Chapman), K-Solo, and the currently incarcerated Lifer's Group.

74. Michel Foucault, "Intellectuals and Power," *Language, Counter-memory, Practice: Selected Essays and Interviews by Michel Foucault*, trans. Donald F. Bouchard and Sherry Simon (Ithaca, N.Y.: Cornell Univ. Press, 1977), 209.

75. Ice T, "You Shoulda Killed Me Last Year," *OG: Original Gangster*; Ice Cube, "The Nigga Ya Love to Hate," *AmeriKKKa's Most Wanted*; other examples include 2Pac, "Trapped," *2Pacalypse Now*; Public Enemy, "Black Steel in the Hour of Chaos," *It Takes a Nation of Millions to Hold Us Back* (Def Jam, 1988); MMG, 2 Black, 2 Strong, "Up in the Mountains," *Doin' Hard Time on Planet Earth* (Relativity, 1991). Popular texts which suggest that incarceration reflects

part of a conspiracy include Jawanza Kunjufu, *Countering the Conspiracy to Destroy Black Boys* (Chicago: African American Images, 1985–86), 3 vols.; Baba Zak A. Kondo, *For Homeboys Only: Arming and Strengthening Young Brothers for Black Manhood* (Washington, D.C.: Nubia Press, 1991). Although women's voices are absent in these narratives about incarceration, we should keep in mind that 96 percent of the nation's prison population is male. (Franklin E. Zimring and Gordon Hawkins, *The Scale of Imprisonment* [Chicago: University of Chicago Press, 1991], 73.)

76. *Kill at Will* (Priority Records, 1990). A similar point is made in W.C. and the MAAD Circle's "Out on a Furlough," *Ain't A Damn Thang Changed*.

77. Clearly, the roots of homophobia among African American males lay elsewhere, but it is interesting to note how frequently homosexuality is talked about in terms of prison rape. This pervasive image must shape the particular character of homophobia in African American urban communities.

78. *OG: Original Gangster*.

79. Ibid.

80. Claude Brown, "The Language of Soul," *Esquire Magazine* 69 (April 1968), 88.

81. Claudia Mitchell-Kernan, "Signifying, Loud-talking, and Marking," 328; and for numerous examples from folklore, see Levine, *Black Culture*; Roberts, *From Trickster to Badman*, 174–215 passim.; "Niggers With Attitude," *Melody Maker* 65, no. 44 (November 4, 1989), 33. As Ice Cube slowly moves away from gangsta rap, influenced largely by the Nation of Islam, his views on the use of the word seem to have undergone a substantial shift. In a recent interview, he told hip hop journalist James Bernard, "The reason I say 'nigger' is because we are still 'niggers' cuz we got this white man in our heads. Until we get him out our heads, that's when we become Black men [sic] and that's when I'll stop using the word." (James Bernard, "Ice Cube: Building a Nation," *Source* 27 [December, 1991], 32.) Although most cultural nationalist groups critique or avoid the term "Nigga" altogether, X-Clan apparently embraces the phrase as an ironic, often humorous comment on white fears of black militancy. See especially their most recent album, *Xodus: The New Testament* (Polygram Records, 1992).

82. 2Pac, *2pacalypse Now* (Interscope, 1991).

83. NWA, *Efil4zaggin*.

84. Robert H. DeCoy, *The Nigger Bible* (Los Angeles: Holloway House Publishing Co., 1967), 33; William L. Van Deburg, *New Day in Babylon: The Black Power Movement and American Culture, 1965–1975* (Chicago: University of Chicago Press, 1992), 218; *Nigger Uprising* (Los Angeles: Ashanti Art Service, 1968). There are dozens of examples. We might point to the light-skinned character in the film version of "The Spook Who Sat by the Door" who claimed his authenticity by calling himself a "Nigger," or Cecil Brown's reference to James Brown's music as "Nigger feeling" in his brilliant essay, "James Brown, Hoodoo, and Black Culture," *Black Review* (1971), 182. We might also consider the prize-

winning and celebrated narrative compiled by Theodore Rosengarten, *All God's Dangers: The Life of Nate Shaw* (New York: Avon, 1974). When Shaw (whose real name was Ned Cobb) used the word "nigger" as a form of self-designation, it signified more than color. In making distinctions between "niggers" and "better class Negroes," he represented the impoverished, the exploited, the working person.

85. Quoted in Michael Eric Dyson, "The Culture of Hip Hop," *Zeta Magazine* (June 1989), 46; Ice T, *The Iceberg/Freedom of Speech . . . Just Watch What You Say*; see also Ice T, "Radio Suckers," *Power* (Sire Records, 1988), "This One's For Me," *The Iceberg/Freedom of Speech . . . Just Watch What You Say*; Ice Cube, "Turn off the Radio," *AmeriKKKa's Most Wanted*.

86. *Ain't A Damn Thang Changed*.

87. On the complicity of black politicians, see Davis, *City of Quartz*, 290–92.

88. Owen, "Hanging Tough," 34. A comparable line can be found in M. C. Ren's contribution to "Niggaz 4 Life," *Efil4zaggin*.

89. Ice Cube, "Endangered Species (Tales from the Darkside)," *AmeriKKKa's Most Wanted*.

90. W.C. and the MAAD Circle, *Ain't a Damn Thang Changed*; Ice Cube, "The Nigga Ya Love to Hate," *AmeriKKKa's Most Wanted*.

91. Hebdige, *Subculture*, 86.

92. Examples can be found in most gangsta rap, but see especially *Eazy-Duz-It* (Ruthless, 1988); *Straight Outta Compton; 100 Miles and Running*; "Niggaz 4 Life," *Efil4zaggin*.

93. NWA, "Niggaz 4 Life," *Efil4zaggin*; Ice T, "Straight Up Nigga," *OG: Original Gangster*. The black male celebration of stereotypes of black sexuality is common in much black humor. Lawrence Levine writes, "Black humor reflected an awareness that the pervasive stereotype of Negroes as oversexed, hyper-virile, and uninhibitedly promiscuous was not purely a negative image; that it contained envy as well as disdain, that it was a projection of desire as well as fear." *Black Culture*, 338.

94. *Efil4zaggin*.

95. Roger Abrahams, *Deep Down in the Jungle: Negro Narrative Folklore from the Streets of Philadelphia*, rev. ed., (Chicago: Aldine, 1970, orig. 1963), 258.

96. Jackson, *"Get Your Ass in the Water and Swim Like Me,"* 129; see also several other toasts in Jackson's collection as well as Dennis Wepman, Ronald B. Newman, and Murray Binderman, *The Life: The Lore and Folk Poetry of the Black Hustler* (Philadelphia: University of Pennsylvania Press, 1976).

97. Henry Louis Gates, Jr., "Two Live Crew De-Coded," *New York Times*, June 19, 1990; on urban toasts and "baaadman" narratives, see especially Jackson, *"Get Your Ass in the Water and Swim Like Me"*; Levine, *Black Culture*, 407–20; Roberts, *From Trickster to Badman*, 171–215; Abrahams, *Deep Down in the Jungle*; Anthony Reynolds, "Urban Negro Toasts: A Hustler's View from Los Angeles,"

Western Folklore 33 (October 1974), 267–300; Wepman, Newman, and Binderman, *The Life*.

98. "Sexualized Society" is borrowed from John D'Emilio and Estelle Freedman, *Intimate Matters: A History of Sexuality in America* (New York: Harper and Row, 1988), 326–30. The more popular pimp narratives include Iceberg Slim [Robert Beck], *Pimp: The Story of My Life* (Los Angeles: Holloway House, 1969); Christina Milner and Richard Milner, *Black Players: The Secret World of Black Pimps* (New York: Little, Brown, 1972). On the pimp in popular film, see Donald Bogle, *Toms, Coons, Mulattoes, Mammies and Bucks: An Interpretive History of Blacks in American Films*, new ed. (New York: Continuum, 1989), 234–42; Daniel Leab, *From Sambo to Superspade: The Black Experience in Motion Pictures* (Boston: Houghton Mifflin, 1975); David E. James, "Chained to Devilpictures: Cinema and Black Liberation in the Sixties," in *The Year Left 2: Toward a Rainbow Socialism—Essays on Race, Ethnicity, Class and Gender*, ed. Mike Davis et al., (London: Verso 1987), 125–38. Black nationalist narratives that tend to celebrate or romanticize the pimp in African American communities include H. Rap Brown, *Die, Nigger, Die* (New York: Dial Press, 1969); Bobby Seale, *Seize the Time* (New York: Random House, 1970); and *Lonely Rage* (New York: Times Books, 1978) in which Seale himself takes on the characteristics of a pimp; Huey P. Newton, *Revolutionary Suicide* (New York: Harcourt Brace Jovanovich, 1973); Eldridge Cleaver, *Soul on Ice* (New York: McGraw-Hill, 1968).

99. Ice T quoted in Nelson and Gonzales, *Bring the Noise*, 110;

100. Ulf Hannerz, *Soulside: Inquiries into Ghetto Culture and Community* (New York: Columbia University Press, 1969), 105–7; Charnas, "A Gangsta's World View," 22.

101. In the following discussion I limit my critique of sexism to L.A. gangsta rap and thus do not deal with better-know controversies (e.g., the Two Live Crew obscenity trial). For general treatments, see especially, Tricia Rose, "Never Trust a Big Butt and a Smile," *Camera Obscura* 23 (1991), 109–31; Kimberle Crenshaw, "Beyond Racism and Misogyny: Black Feminism and 2 Live Crew," *Boston Review* 16, no. 6 (December 1991), 6, 33; Michelle Wallace, "When Black Feminism Faces the Music and the Music Is Rap," *New York Times*, July 29, 1990; Michael Eric Dyson, "As Complex as They Wanna Be: 2 Live Crew," *Zeta Magazine* (January 1991), 76–78; Paulla Ebron, "Rapping between Men: Performing Gender," *Radical America* 23, no. 4 (June 1991), 23–27.

102. For example, see *Los Angeles Times*, August 22, 1991; Jewell T. Gibbs, *Young, Black and Male in America: An Endangered Species* (Dover, Mass.: Auburn House, 1988); interview with Harry Edwards, *San Francisco Focus* (March, 1984), 100; Murray, *Losing Ground*; Lawrence Mead, *Beyond Entitlement: The Social Obligation of Citizenship* (New York: Free Press, 1985); and for a liberal approach which also suggests that family structure is partly to blame for persistent poverty, see Eleanor Holmes Norton, "Restoring the Traditional Black Family," *New York Times Magazine* (June 2, 1985).

103. "It's a Man's World," *AmeriKKKa's Most Wanted*.

104. D. Dub, "We're Not Glamorizin'" 57; Ice Cube made a similar point in Bernard, "Ice Cube: Building a Nation," 32.

105. Messerschmidt, *Capitalism, Patriarchy and Crime*, 134.

106. Rose, "Never Trust a Big Butt and a Smile," 115. A clear example is Ice T, "I Love Ladies," from his *Rhyme Pays* album.

107. "It's a Man's World (Featuring Yo Yo)," *AmeriKKKa's Most Wanted*. I am grateful to Tricia Rose for her insights into the ways in which Yo Yo's intervention disrupts Cube's masculinist discourse. (Conversation with Tricia Rose, December 26, 1991.) See also Yo Yo's other lyrical challenges to sexism on *Make Way for the Motherlode* (Profile, 1991). It should be noted that some of the most antisexist lyrics on Yo Yo's album were written by Ice Cube.

108. *Kill at Will* (Priority, 1991); a shorter version appeared first on *AmeriKKKa's Most Wanted*.

109. Alan Light, "Beating Up the Charts," *Rolling Stone* (August 8, 1991), 66; Calvin Sims, "Gangster Rappers: The Lives, the Lyrics," *New York Times*, November 28, 1993.

110. *Ain't a Damn Thang Changed*.

111. "The House," *OG: Original Gangster*; "Fuck My Daddy," *Ain't a Damn Thang Changed*. Bay Area gangsta rapper 2PAC has dealt critically with issues such as incest ("Brenda Has a Baby") and the rape of young women by their stepfathers ("Part-Time Mutha"). See *2Pacalypse Now*.

112. Quoted in Sims, "Gangsta Rappers."

113. Light, "L.A. Rappers Speak Out," 21.

114. I credit the music critic Toure with that term; at least that's where I got it from. It's hard to describe, other than a kind of West Coast "twang," a Texas-meets-California accent.

115. Brent Staples, "The Politics of Gangster Rap; A Music Celebrating Murder and Misogyny," *New York Times*, August 27, 1993; Michel Marriot, "Harsh Rap Lyrics Provoke Black Backlash," *New York Times*, August 15, 1993; Sims, "Gangster Rappers: The Lives, the Lyrics"; Donna Britt, "A One-Word Assault on Women," *Washington Post*, November 30, 1993; Scott Armstrong, "Backlash Is Brewing over 'Gangsta Rap' Lyrics as Public Says 'Enough,'" *Christian Science Monitor*, December 13, 1993; Michael Farquhar, "Gangsta Rap Ripped by Protesters: Black Women's Group Arrested at D.C. Store," *Washington Post*, December 22, 1993.

Bibliography

Primary Sources

Collections of Papers

Abraham Lincoln Brigade Archives. Brandeis University, Waltham, Massachusetts.

Boutwell, Albert. Papers. Tutwiler Collection, Birmingham Public Library, Birmingham, Alabama.

Draper, Theodore. Papers. Emory University.

Green, Cooper. Papers. Tutwiler Collection. Birmingham Public Library, Birmingham, Alabama.

International Labor Defense Papers. Schomburg Collection. New York Public Library.

Jefferson County Coordinating Committee on Social Forces. Papers. Birmingham Public Library.

Johnson, Clyde. Papers. Southern Historical Collection. University of North Carolina, Chapel Hill.

Minor, Robert. Papers. Butler Memorial Library, Columbia University.

Morgan, James. Papers. Birmingham Public Library.

Southern Conference for Human Welfare Papers. Tuskegee Institute, Tuskegee, Alabama.

"Southern Negro Youth Congress, Birmingham, Alabama." FBI Report, June 14, 1943. File 100-82. Federal Bureau of Investigation Reading Room, Washington, D.C.

Taft, Philip. Papers. Birmingham Public Library.

Oral Histories

Armstrong, James. Interview conducted by Cliff Kuhn, July 16, 1984. "Working Lives" Oral History Project, University of Alabama, Tuscaloosa.

Browder, Earl. "The Reminiscences of Earl Browder." Interview conducted by Joseph R. Starobin, 1964. Columbia Oral History Project. Butler Memorial Library, Columbia University.

Hunter, Oscar. Interview, May 2, 1980. Abraham Lincoln Brigade Archives. Brandeis University.

Jackson, Rosa. Interview conducted by Peggy Hamrick, July 23 and 24, 1984. "Working Lives" Oral History Project. University of Alabama, Tuscaloosa.

Kilpatrick, Admiral. Interview, June 8, 1980. Abraham Lincoln Brigade Archives, Brandeis University.

McDaniel, Eluard Luchell. Interview, March 13, 1978. Radical Elders Oral History Project. Copy in Brandeis University Spanish Civil War Collection.

Offord, Carl. "Cyril Briggs and the African Blood Brotherhood." WPA Writers' Project, No. 1, 1938. Schomburg Collection, New York.

"Southern Negro Youth Congress—Forum," February 6, 1984. Presentations by Henry Winston, Esther Cooper Jackson, James Jackson, and Grace Tillman Bassett. Untranscribed tape. Oral History of the American Left. Tamiment Library, New York University.

Newspapers and Contemporary Magazines

Alabama (CIO) News Digest
Alabama Magazine
Alabama Social Welfare
Amsterdam News
Baltimore Afro-American
Birmingham News
Birmingham Post-Herald
Birmingham World
Bulletin of the IV Congress of the Communist International
Chicago Defender
Communist
Communist International
Communist Review
Correspondance Internationale
Crisis
Crusader
Daily Worker
Daily World
Detail
International Press Correspondence
La Voix des Nègres
L.A. Weekly
Labor Defender

The Liberator and Harlem Liberator (New York)
Los Angeles Times
Melody Maker
Negro Digest
Negro Worker
New Masses
New South
New York Times
Nigger Uprising
Opportunity
Party Organizer
Rap Pages
Rappin'
Rolling Stone
Source
South African Worker
Southern Patriot
Southern Worker
Spin
Village Voice
Volunteer
Washington Post
Worker's Monthly

Government Publications

Birmingham Housing Authority. *Ninth Annual Report of the Housing Authority of the Birmingham District*, June 30, 1948.

Community Service Council. *Family and Children Study of Jefferson County: Priorities and Recommendations*. Birmingham: Community Service Council, 1970.

George A. Denison, M.D. "Health as an Indication of Housing Needs in Birmingham, Alabama, and Recommendations for Slum Clearance, Redevelopment and Public Housing." Report by Jefferson County Board of Health, April 12, 1950.

Juvenile and Domestic Relations Court of Jefferson County. *Annual Report*. Alabama, 1963–67.

State of Louisiana, Joint Legislative Committee. *Subversion in Racial Unrest: An Outline of a Strategic Weapon to Destroy the Governments of Louisiana and the United States*. Public Hearings, Pt. I. Baton Rouge, 1957.

Subversive Activities Control Board. "Herbert Brownell, Jr., Attorney General of the United States v. Veterans of the Abraham Lincoln Brigade." Hearings, September 15 and 16, 1954. Docket No. 108-53.

U.S. Bureau of the Census. *County and City Data Book, 1962*. Washington, D.C.: Government Printing Office, 1962.

———. *Eighteenth Census of the U.S.: 1960*, vol. I, pt. II, *Characteristics of the Population: Alabama*. Washington, D.C.: Government Printing Office, 1961.

———. *Seventeenth Census of the U.S.: 1950*, Vol. 3, *Census Tract Statistics*. Washington, D.C.: Government Printing Office, 1952.

———. *Twentieth Census of Population and Housing, 1980: Census Tracts*. Washington, D.C.: Government Printing Office, 1983.

U.S. Congress. House. Committee on Un-American Activities. *Communist Activities in the Philadelphia Area*. Washington, D.C.: Government Printing Office, 1952.

U.S. Congress. Joint Committee on Housing. *Study and Investigation of Housing: Hearings before the Joint Committee on Housing*, pt. II. Washington, D.C.: Government Printing Office, 1948.

Secondary Sources

Books and Journal Articles

Abrahams, Roger D. *Deep Down in the Jungle: Negro Narrative Folklore from the Streets of Philadelphia*. Rev. ed. Chicago: Aldine, 1970. Orig. 1963.

Abu-Lughod, Lila. "The Romance of Resistance: Tracing Transformations of Power through Bedouin Women." *American Ethnologist* 17, no. 1 (1990): 41–55.

Ahola, David John. *Finnish-Americans and International Communism: A Study of Finnish-American Communism from Bolshevization to The Demise of The Third International*. Washington, D.C.: University Press of America, 1981.

Alba, Victor. *Transition in Spain: From Franco to Democracy*. Translated by Barbara Lotito. New Brunswick, N.J.: Transaction Books, 1978.

Alcoff, Linda. "Cultural Feminism versus Post-Structuralism: The Identity Crisis in Feminist Theory." *Signs* 13 (1988): 405–36.

Allen, Ernest. "The Cultural Methodology of Harold Cruse." *Journal of Ethnic Studies* 5, no. 2 (1977): 26–50.

Allen, Robert. *Reluctant Reformers: Racism and Social Reform Movements in the United States*. Rev. ed. Washington, D.C.: Howard Univ. Press, 1983.

Anderson, Elijah. *Streetwise: Race, Class, and Change in an Urban Community*. Chicago: Univ. of Chicago Press, 1990.

Anderson, Jervis. *A. Phillip Randolph: A Biographical Portrait*. New York: Harcourt Brace Jovanovich, 1973.

———. *This Was Harlem: A Cultural Portrait, 1900–1950*. New York: Farrar, Straus & Giroux, 1981.

Aptheker, Herbert. *American Negro Slave Revolts*. New York: Columbia Univ. Press, 1943.

———. "Maroons within the Present Limits of the United States." *Journal of Negro History* 24 (April 1939): 167–84.

———. *The Negro in the Civil War*. New York: International Publishers, 1938.

———. *Negro Slave Revolts in the United States, 1526–1860*. New York: International Publishers, 1939.

Arnesen, Eric. "Following The Color Line of Labor: Black Workers and The Labor Movement Before 1930." *Radical History Review* 55 (Winter 1993): 53–87.

———. *Waterfront Workers of New Orleans: Race, Class, and Politics, 1863–1923*. New York: Oxford Univ. Press, 1991.

Asante, S.K.B. "The Afro-American and the Italo-Ethiopian Crisis, 1934–1936." *Race* 15, no. 2 (1973): 167–84.

———. *Pan-African Protest: West Africa and the Italo-Ethiopian Crisis, 1934–1941*. London: Longman, 1977.

Athearn, Robert G. *In Search of Canaan: Black Migration to Kansas, 1879–80*. Lawrence: Regents Press of Kansas, 1978.

Auletta, Ken. *The Underclass*. New York: Random House, 1982.

Aviv, Aviva, and Isaac Aviv. "The Madrid Working Class, the Spanish Socialist Party and the Collapse of the Second Republic (1934–1936)." *Journal of Contemporary History* 16 (April 1981): 229–50.

Ayers, Edward L. *Vengeance and Justice: Crime and Punishment in the 19th Century American South*. New York: Oxford Univ. Press, 1984.

Baer, George. *The Coming of the Italian-Ethiopian War*. Cambridge, Mass.: Harvard Univ. Press, 1967.

Baer, Hans. *The Black Spiritual Movement: A Religious Response to Racism*. Knoxville, Tenn.: University of Tennessee Press, 1984.

Baer, Hans A., and Merrill Singer, eds. *African-American Religion in the Twentieth*

Century: Varieties of Protest and Accommodation. Knoxville, Tenn: Univ. of Tennessee Press, 1992.

Bains, Lee E., Jr. "Birmingham, 1963: Confrontation over Civil Rights." In *Birmingham, Alabama, 1956–1963: The Black Struggle for Civil Rights*, edited by David Garrow, 151–289. Brooklyn, N.Y.: Carlson, 1989.

Baker, Ray Stannard. *Following the Color Line: American Negro Citizenship in the Progressive Era*. 1908. Reprint, New York: Harper and Row, 1964.

Baldwin, James. *Notes of a Native Son*. Boston: Beacon Press, 1955.

Bauer, Raymond A., and Alice H. Bauer. "Day to Day Resistance to Slavery." *Journal of Negro History* 37 (October 1942): 388–419.

Beasley, R. W., and G. Antunes. "The Etiology of Urban Crime: An Ecological Analysis." *Criminology* 11 (1974): 439–61.

Beck, Earl R. "The Anti-Nazi 'Swing Youth,' 1942–1945." *Journal of Popular Culture* 19 (Winter 1985): 45–53.

Bell, Daniel. *Work and Its Discontents: The Cult of Efficiency in America*. Boston: Beacon, 1956.

Ben-Ami, Shlomo. "The Dictatorship of Primo de Rivera: A Political Reassessment." *Journal of Contemporary History* 12 (January 1977): 65–84.

———. *The Origins of the Second Republic in Spain*. New York: Oxford Univ. Press, 1978.

Benson, Thomas. "Rhetoric and Autobiography: The Case of Malcolm X." *Quarterly Journal of Speech* 60 (February 1974): 1–13.

Berry, Faith. *Langston Hughes: Before and Beyond Harlem*. Brooklyn, N.Y.: Lawrence Hill, 1983.

Berry, Jeffrey, Kent Portnoy, and Ken Thomson. "The Political Behavior of Poor People." In *The Urban Underclass*, edited by Christopher Jencks and Paul E. Peterson, 357–72. Washington, D.C.: Brookings Institution, 1991.

Berthoff, Werner. "Witness and Testament: Two Contemporary Classics." *New Literary History* 2 (Winter 1971): 311–27.

Bessie, Alvah. *Men in Battle: The Story of Americans in Spain*. New York: Charles Scribner's Sons, 1939.

———, ed. *The Heart of Spain: Anthology of Fiction, Non-Fiction, and Poetry*. New York: Veterans of the Abraham Lincoln Brigade, 1952.

Bessie, Alvah, and Albert Prago, eds. *Our Fight: Writings by Veterans of the Abraham Lincoln Brigade: Spain, 1936–1939*. New York: Monthly Review Press, with the Veterans of the Abraham Lincoln Brigade, 1987.

Billingsley, Andrew. *Black Families in White America*. Englewood Cliffs, N.J.: Prentice-Hall, 1968.

Blackwelder, Julia Kirk. "Quiet Suffering: Atlanta Women in the 1930's." *Georgia Historical Quarterly* 61, no. 2 (Summer 1977): 112–24.

———. "Women in the Workforce: Atlanta, New Orleans, and San Antonio, 1930–1940." *Journal of Urban History* 4 (May 1978): 331–58.

Blasi, Anthony J. *Segregationist Violence and Civil Rights Movements in Tuscaloosa*.

Washington, D.C.: University Press of America, 1980.

Blau, J. R., and P. M. Blau. "The Cost of Inequality: Metropolitan Structure and Violent Crime." *American Sociological Review* 47 (1982): 114–29.

Blinkhorn, Martin. "The Basque Ulster: Navarre and the Basque Autonomy Question under the Spanish Republic." *Historical Journal* 17, no. 3 (1974): 593–613.

Blumenfeld, Emily, and Susan Mann. "Domestic Labour and the Reproduction of Labour Power: Towards an Analysis of Women, the Family, and Class." In *Hidden in the Household: Women's Domestic Labour under Capitalism*, edited by Bonnie Fox, 267–307. Toronto: Women's Educational Press, 1980.

Bogle, Donald. *Toms, Coons, Mulattoes, Mammies and Bucks: An Interpretive History of Blacks in American Films.* New ed. New York: Continuum, 1989.

Bolloten, Burnett. *The Spanish Civil War: Revolution and Counterrevolution.* Chapel Hill: Univ. of North Carolina Press, 1991.

———. *The Spanish Revolution: The Left and the Struggle for Power during the Civil War.* Chapel Hill: Univ. of North Carolina Press, 1979.

Bookchin, Murray. *The Spanish Anarchists: The Heroic Years, 1868–1936.* New York: Free Life Editions, 1977.

Borchert, James. *Alley Life in Washington: Family, Community, Religion, and Folklife in the City, 1850–1970.* Urbana: Univ. of Illinois Press, 1980.

Boris, Eileen. "Black Women and Paid Labor in the Home: Industrial Homework in Chicago in the 1920's." In *Homework: Historical and Contemporary Perspectives on Paid Labor at Home*, edited by Eileen Boris and Cynthia R. Daniels, 33–52. Urbana: Univ. of Illinois Press, 1989.

———. *Home to Work: Motherhood and the Politics of Industrial Homework in the United States.* New York: Cambridge Univ. Press, 1994.

Borkenau, Franz. *The Spanish Cockpit: An Eye-Witness Account of the Political and Social Conflicts of the Spanish Civil War.* 1937. Reprint, Ann Arbor: Univ. of Michigan Press, 1963.

Box, Steven. *Recession, Crime, and Punishment.* Totowa, N.J.: Barnes and Noble Books, 1987.

Boydston, Jeanne. *Home and Work: Housework, Wages, and the Ideology of Labor in the Early Republic.* New York: Oxford Univ. Press, 1990.

Branch, Taylor. *Parting the Waters: America in the King Years, 1954–1963.* New York: Simon & Schuster, 1988.

Brandt, Joe, ed. *Black Americans in the Spanish People's War Against Fascism, 1936–1939.* New York: VALB, 1981.

Breitman, George. *The Last Year of Malcolm X: The Evolution of a Revolutionary.* New York: Merit Publishers, 1967.

———. *Malcolm X: The Man and His Ideas.* New York: Merit Publishers, 1965.

Brenan, Gerald. *The Spanish Labyrinth: An Account of the Social and Political Background of the Civil War.* Cambridge, England: The University Press, 1943.

Brissenden, Paul. *The I.W.W.: A Study of American Syndicalism*. New York: Columbia Univ. Press, 1919.

Brome, Vincent. *The International Brigades: Spain, 1936–1939*. London: Heinemann, 1965.

Brooks Gardner, Carol. "Analyzing Gender in Public Places: Rethinking Goffman's Vision of Everyday Life." *American Sociologist* 20 (Spring 1989): 42–56.

Broué, Pierre, and Emile Temime. *The Revolution and the Civil War in Spain*. Translated by Tony White. Cambridge, Mass.: MIT Press, 1972.

Brown, Cecil. "James Brown, Hoodoo, and Black Culture." *Black Review*, no. 1 (1971): 180–85.

Brown, Claude. "The Language of Soul." *Esquire Magazine* 69 (April 1968): 88, 160, 162.

Brown, Elsa Barkley. "African-American Women's Quilting: A Framework for Conceptualizing and Teaching African-American Women's History." *Signs* 14 (Summer 1989): 921–29.

———. "Mothers of Mind." *Sage* 6 (Summer 1989): 3–10.

———. "To Catch the Vision of Freedom: Reconstructing Southern Black Women's Political History, 1865–1885." In *To Be a Citizen*, edited by Arlene Avakian, John Bracey, and Ann Gordon. Amherst, Mass.: Univ. of Massachusetts Press. Forthcoming.

———. "'What Has Happened Here': The Politics of Difference in Women's History and Feminist Politics." *Feminist Studies* 18 (Summer 1992): 302–7.

———. "Womanist Consciousness: Maggie Lena Walker and the Independent Order of St. Luke." *Signs* 14 (Spring 1989): 610–33.

Brown, Geoff. *Sabotage: A Study in Industrial Conflict*. Nottingham: Bertrand Russell Peace Foundation for Spokesman Books. 1977.

Brown, H. Rap. *Die, Nigger, Die!*. New York: Dial Press, 1969.

Brown, Lee P. "Bridges over Troubled Waters: A Perspective on Policing in the Black Community." In *Black Perspectives on Crime and the Criminal Justice System: A Symposium*, edited by Robert L. Woodson, 79–100. Boston: G. K. Hall, 1977.

Buhle, Paul. "Jews and American Communism: The Cultural Question." *Radical America* 23 (Spring 1980): 9–33.

———. *Marxism in the United States: Remapping the History of the American Left*. London: Verso, 1987.

Bularzik, Mary. "Sexual Harassment at the Workplace: Historical Notes." In *Workers' Struggles, Past and Present: A Radical America Reader*, edited by James Green, 117–35. Philadelphia: Temple Univ. Press, 1983.

Burkett, Randall K. *Garveyism as a Religious Movement: The Institutionalization of a Black Civil Religion*. Metuchen, N.J.: Scarecrow Press, 1978.

Calverton, V. F. "Leftward Ho!" *Modern Quarterly* 6 (Summer 1932): 26–32.

Calvin, A. D. "Unemployment among Black Youths, Demographics, and Crime." *Crime and Delinquency* 27 (1981): 9–41.

Campbell, Anne. *Girl Delinquents*. New York: St. Martin's Press, 1981.

———. *The Girls in the Gang: A Report from New York City*. New York: Basil Blackwell, 1984.

Capeci, Dominic J., Jr. *The Harlem Riot of 1943*. Philadelphia: Temple Univ. Press, 1977.

———. *Race Relations in Wartime Detroit: The Sojourner Truth Housing Controversy of 1942*. Philadelphia: Temple Univ. Press, 1984.

Carby, Hazel. "'It Jus Be's Dat Way Sometime': The Sexual Politics of Women's Blues." *Radical America* 20, no. 4 (1987): 9–22.

———. "Policing the Black Woman's Body in an Urban Context." *Critical Inquiry* 18 (Summer 1992): 738–55.

Carlen, Pat. *Women, Crime and Poverty*. Philadelphia: Open Univ. Press, 1988.

Carlton, David. "Eden, Blum, and the Origins of Non-Intervention." *Journal of Contemporary History* 6 (January 1971): 40–55.

Carr, E. H. *The Comintern and the Spanish Civil War*, edited by Tamara Deutscher. New York: Pantheon, 1984.

Carr, Raymond. *Modern Spain, 1875–1980*. New York: Oxford Univ. Press, 1980.

———. *The Spanish Tragedy: The Civil War in Perspective*. London: Weidenfeld & Nicolson, 1977.

Carter, Dan T. *Scottsboro: A Tragedy of the American South*. Rev. ed., Baton Rouge: Louisiana State Univ. Press, 1979.

Casdorph, Paul D. *Republicans, Negroes, and Progressives in the South, 1912–1916*. University, Ala.: Univ. of Alabama Press, 1981.

Cattell, David T. *Communism and the Spanish Civil War*. Berkeley and Los Angeles: Univ. of California Press, 1955.

Chambers, Jack. *Milestones 1: The Music and Times of Miles Davis to 1960*. Toronto: Univ. of Toronto Press, 1983.

Chibnall, Steve. "Whistle and Zoot: The Changing Meaning of a Suit of Clothes." *History Workshop* 20 (Autumn 1985): 56–81.

Chigwada, Ruth. "The Policing of Black Women." In *Out of Order? Policing Black People*, edited by Ellis Cashmore and Eugene McLaughlin, 134–50. London: Routledge, 1991.

Clark, Kenneth B., and James Barker. "The Zoot Effect in Personality: A Race Riot Participant." *Journal of Abnormal and Social Psychology* 40, no. 2 (April 1945): 143–48.

Clark-Lewis, Elizabeth. "'This Work Had a End': African-American Domestic Workers in Washington, D.C., 1910–1940." In *"To Toil the Livelong Day": America's Women at Work, 1780–1980*, edited by Carol Groneman and Mary Beth Norton, 196–212. Ithaca, N.Y.: Cornell Univ. Press, 1987.

Clarke, John Henrik, ed. *Malcolm X: The Man and His Times*. New York: Macmillan, 1969.

Clasby, Nancy. "Autobiography of Malcolm X: A Mythic Paradigm." *Journal of Black Studies* 5, no. 1 (September 1974): 18–34.

Cleaver, Eldridge. *Soul on Ice*. New York: McGraw-Hill, 1968.

Cockburn, Alexander. "Beat the Devil." *Nation* 254, no. 21 (June 1, 1992): 738–39.

Cohen, Robin. "Resistance and Hidden Forms of Consciousness among African Workers." *Review of African Political Economy* 19 (1980): 8–22.

Cohen, William. *At Freedom's Edge: Black Mobility and the Southern White Quest for Racial Control, 1861–1915*. Baton Rouge: Louisiana State Univ. Press, 1991.

Coleman, Willi. "Black Women and Segregated Public Transportation: Ninety Years of Resistance." In *Black Women in United States History*, edited by Darlene Clark Hine, vol. 5, 295–302. Brooklyn, N.Y.: Carlson, 1989.

Colodny, Robert G. "Notes on the Origin of the Frente Popular of Spain." *Science and Society* 31 (Summer 1967): 257–74.

———. *The Struggle for Madrid: The Central Epic of the Spanish Conflict, 1936–1937*. New York: Paine-Whitman, 1958.

Community Relations Service. *The Police Use of Deadly Force: What Police and the Community Can Do About It*. Washington, D.C.: Dept. of Justice, Community Relations Service, 1978.

Cone, James. *Martin and Malcolm and America: A Dream or a Nightmare*. Maryknoll, N.Y.: Orbis Books, 1991.

Connell, R.W. *Gender and Power: Society, the Person, and Sexual Politics*. Stanford, Calif.: Stanford Univ. Press, 1987.

Cook, Bernard A. "Covington Hall and Radical Rural Unionization in Louisiana." *Louisiana History* 18, no. 2 (1977): 227–38.

Cooper, Wayne F. *Claude McKay: Rebel Sojourner in the Harlem Renaissance, A Biography*. Baton Rouge: Louisiana State Univ. Press, 1986.

Cornwall, Barbara. *The Bush Rebels: A Personal Account of Black Revolt in Africa*. New York: Holt, Rinehart & Winston, 1972.

Cosgrove, Stuart. "The Zoot-Suit and Style Warfare." *History Workshop Journal* 18 (Autumn 1984): 77–91.

Coulsen, Margaret, Branka Magas, and Hilary Wainwright. "'The Housewife and Her Labour under Capitalism'—A Critique." *New Left Review* 89 (January–February 1975): 59–72.

Coulter, Philip B. *Political Voice: Citizen Demand for Urban Public Services*. Tuscaloosa: Published for the Institute for Social Science Research by the Univ. of Alabama Press, 1988.

Couvares, Francis G. *The Remaking of Pittsburgh: Class and Culture in an Industrializing City, 1877–1919*. Albany, N.Y.: State Univ. of New York Press, 1984.

Coverdale, John. *Italian Intervention in the Spanish Civil War*. Princeton: Princeton Univ. Press, 1975.

Crawford, Marc, and William Loren Katz. *The Lincoln Brigade: A Picture History*. New York: Atheneum, 1989.

Crenshaw, Kimberle. "Beyond Racism and Misogyny: Black Feminism and 2 Live Crew." *Boston Review* 16, no. 6 (December 1991): 6, 33.

Crisp, Jeff. *The Story of an African Working Class: Ghanaian Miners' Struggles, 1870–1980*. London: Zed Books, 1984.

Cross, Brian. *It's Not About a Salary . . . Rap, Race and Resistance in Los Angeles*. London: Verso, 1993.

Crowe, Charles. "Racial Violence and Social Reform—Origins of the Atlanta Riot of 1906." *Journal of Negro History* 53 (July 1968): 234–56.

Cruse, Harold. *The Crisis of the Negro Intellectual*. New York: Morrow, 1964.

Currie, Elliot. *Confronting Crime: An American Challenge*. New York: Pantheon, 1985.

Dalfiume, Richard M. *Desegregation of the U.S. Armed Forces: Fighting on Two Fronts, 1939–1953*. Columbia: Univ. of Missouri Press, 1969.

———. "The 'Forgotten Years' of the Negro Revolution." *Journal of American History* 55 (June 1968): 90–106.

Daniel, Pete. "Going among Strangers: Southern Reactions to World War II." *Journal of American History* 77 (December 1990): 886–911.

Davis, Allison, Burleigh B. Gardner, and Mary R. Gardner. *Deep South: A Social Anthropological Study of Caste and Class*. Chicago: Univ. of Chicago Press, 1941.

Davis, Mike. *City of Quartz: Excavating the Future in Los Angeles*. London: Verso, 1990.

———. "In L.A., Burning All Illusions." *Nation* 254, no. 21 (June 1, 1992): 743–46.

Davis, Miles, with Quincy Troupe. *Miles: The Autobiography*. New York: Simon & Schuster, 1989.

Davis, Susan G. *Parades and Power: Street Theater in Nineteenth-Century Philadelphia*. Philadelphia: Temple Univ. Press, 1986.

de Certeau, Michel. *The Practice of Everyday Life*. Translated by Steven Rendall. Berkeley and Los Angeles: Univ. of California Press, 1984.

DeCoy, Robert H. *The Nigger Bible*. Los Angeles: Holloway House, 1967.

Degras, Jane, ed. *The Communist International, 1919–1943, Documents*, vols. I–III. London: Oxford Univ. Press, 1956–1965.

Del Boca, Angelo. *The Ethiopian War, 1935–1941*. Chicago: University of Chicago Press, 1969.

Demarest, David. "*The Autobiography of Malcolm X*: Beyond Didacticism." *CLA Journal* 16, no. 2 (December 1972): 179–87.

D'Emilio, John, and Estelle Freedman. *Intimate Matters: A History of Sexuality in America*. New York: Harper and Row, 1988.

Denisoff, R. Serge. *Great Day Coming: Folk Music and the American Left*. Urbana: Univ. of Illinois Press, 1971.

Denning, Michael. "The End of Mass Culture." *International Labor and Working-Class History* 37 (Spring 1990): 4–18.

Dittmer, John. *Black Georgia in the Progressive Era, 1900–1920*. Urbana: Univ. of Illinois Press, 1977.

Ditton, Jason. *Part-Time Crime: An Ethnography of Fiddling and Pilferage*. London: Macmillan, 1977.

Dobash, R. E., and R. P. Dobash. *Violence against Wives: A Case against Patriarchy*. New York: Free Press, 1979.

Dolgoff, Sam, ed. *The Anarchist Collectives: Workers' Self-Management in the Spanish Revolution, 1936–1939*. New York: Free Life Editions, 1974.

Dollard, John. *Caste and Class in a Southern Town*. 3rd ed. Garden City, N.Y.: Doubleday, 1957.

Drake, St. Clair, and Horace Cayton. *Black Metropolis: A Study of Negro Life in a Northern City*. 2 vols. 2nd. ed. New York: Harper and Row, 1962.

Draper, Theodore. *American Communism and Soviet Russia: The Formative Period*. New York: Viking Press, 1960.

Duberman, Martin. *Paul Robeson*. New York: Knopf, 1989.

Dubofsky, Melvyn. *We Shall Be All: A History of the Industrial Workers of the World*. Chicago: Quadrangle Books, 1969.

DuBois, Pierre. *Sabotage in Industry*. New York: Penguin, 1979.

DuBois, W.E.B. *Black Reconstruction in America: An Essay Toward a History of the Part Which Black Folk Played in the Attempt to Reconstruct Democracy in America, 1860–1880*. New York: Harcourt, Brace, 1935.

DuBois, W.E.B., and Augustus Granville Dill, eds. *Morals and Manners among Negro Americans*. Atlanta Univ. Publications, No. 18. Atlanta, Ga.: Atlanta Univ. Press, 1914.

Durem, Ray. *Take No Prisoners*. London: P. Bremean, 1971.

Dyson, Michael Eric. "As Complex as They Wanna Be: 2 Live Crew." *Zeta Magazine* (January 1991): 76–78.

———. "The Culture of Hip Hop." *Zeta Magazine* (June 1989): 43–50.

———. *Reflecting Black: African-American Cultural Criticism*. Minneapolis: Univ. of Minnesota Press, 1993.

Ebron, Paulla. "Rapping between Men: Performing Gender." *Radical America* 23, no. 4 (June 1991): 23–27.

Eby, Cecil. *Between the Bullet and the Lie: American Volunteers in the Spanish Civil War*. New York: Holt, Rinehart & Winston, 1969.

Edwards, Jon R. "Slavery, the Slave Trade and the Economic Reorganization of Ethiopia, 1916–1934." *African Economic History* 11 (1982): 3–14.

Edwards, Paul K. *The Southern Urban Negro as a Consumer*. 1932. Reprint, College Park, Md.: McGrath, 1969.

Eley, Geoff. "Labor History, Social History, *Alltagsgeschichte*: Experience, Culture, and the Politics of the Everyday—A New Direction for German Social History?" *Journal of Modern History* 61 (June 1989): 297–343.

Ellsworth, Scott. *Death in a Promised Land: The Tulsa Race Riot of 1921*. Baton Rouge: Louisiana State Univ. Press, 1982.

Ergood, Bruce. "The Female Protection and the Sun Light: Two Contemporary Negro Mutual Aid Societies." *Florida Historical Quarterly* 50, no. 1 (July 1971): 25–38.

Eskew, Glenn T. "The Alabama Christian Movement for Human Rights and the Birmingham Struggle for Civil Rights, 1956–1963." In *Birmingham, Alabama,*

1956–1963: The Black Struggle for Civil Rights, edited by David Garrow, 3–114. Brooklyn, N.Y.: Carlson, 1989.

Essien-Udom, E. U. *Black Nationalism: A Search for an Identity in America*. Chicago: Univ. of Chicago Press, 1962.

Fanon, Frantz. *The Wretched of the Earth*. New York: Grove Press, 1963.

Fantasia, Rick. *Cultures of Solidarity: Consciousness, Action, and Contemporary American Workers*. Berkeley and Los Angeles: Univ. of California Press, 1988.

Faue, Elizabeth. *Community of Suffering and Struggle: Women, Men, and the Labor Movement in Minneapolis, 1915–1945*. Chapel Hill: Univ. of North Carolina Press, 1991.

Fauset, Arthur Huff. *Black Gods of the Metropolis: Negro Religious Cults of the Urban North*. Philadelphia: Univ. of Pennsylvania Press, 1944.

Fields, R. M. *The Portuguese Revolution and the Armed Forces Movement*. New York: Praeger, 1976.

Finkle, Lee. "The Conservative Aims of Militant Rhetoric: Black Protest during World War II." *Journal of American History* 60 (December 1973): 692–713.

Fischer, Roger A. "A Pioneer Protest: The New Orleans Street-Car Controversy of 1867." *Journal of Negro History* 53 (July 1968): 219–33.

Fleming, Shannon E., and Ann K. Fleming. "Primo de Rivera and Spain's Moroccan Problem, 1923–1927." *Journal of Contemporary History* 12 (January 1977): 85–99.

Fleming, Walter L. "The Servant Problem in a Black Belt Village." *Sewanee Review* 13 (January 1905): 1–17.

Fletcher, Marvin. *The Black Soldier and Officer in the United States Army, 1891–1917*. Columbia, Mo.: Univ. of Missouri Press, 1974.

Flynn, George Q. "Selective Service and American Blacks during World War II." *Journal of Negro History* 69 (Winter 1984): 14–25.

Foner, Jack D. *Blacks and the Military in American History: A New Perspective*. New York: Praeger, 1974.

Foner, Philip S. *American Socialism and Black Americans: From the Age of Jackson to World War II*. Westport, Conn.: Greenwood Press, 1977.

———. "The I.W.W. and the Black Worker." *Journal of Negro History* 55 (January 1970): 45–64.

———. *Organized Labor and the Black Worker, 1619–1981*. 2nd ed. New York: International Publishers, 1981.

Ford, James. *The Negro and the Democratic Front*. New York; International Publishers, 1938.

Foucault, Michel. *Discipline and Punish: The Birth of the Prison*. Translated by Alan Sheridan. New York: Pantheon Books, 1977.

———. *Language, Counter-memory, Practice: Selected Essays and Interviews by Michel Foucault*, edited by Donald F. Bouchard, translated by Donald F. Bouchard and Sherry Simon. Ithaca, N.Y.: Cornell Univ. Press, 1977.

Fowler, Arlen. *The Black Infantry in the West, 1869–1891*. Westport, Conn.: Greenwood Press, 1971.

Franklin, Jimmie Lewis. *Back to Birmingham: Richard Arrington, Jr., and His Times.* Tuscaloosa, Ala.: Univ. of Alabama Press, 1989.

Franklin, John Hope. *From Slavery to Freedom: A History of American Negroes.* 5th ed. New York: Knopf, 1980.

Fraser, Ronald. *Blood of Spain: An Oral History of the Spanish Civil War.* New York: Pantheon Books, 1979.

Frazier, E. Franklin. *Black Bourgeoisie.* Glencoe, Ill.: Free Press, 1957.

Frederickson, George. *The Black Image in the White Mind: The Debate on Afro-American Character and Destiny, 1817–1914.* 2nd ed. Middletown, Conn.: Wesleyan Univ. Press, 1987

Freeman, Richard B. "The Relation of Criminal Activity to Black Youth Employment." In *The Economics of Race and Crime*, edited by Margaret C. Simms and Samuel L. Myers, Jr., 99–107. New Brunswick, N.J.: Transaction Books, 1988.

Freund, Bill. "Theft and Social Protest among the Tin Miners of Northern Nigeria." *Radical History Review* 26 (1982): 68–86.

Fry, Gladys-Marie. *Night Riders in Black Folk History.* Knoxville, Tenn.: Univ. of Tennessee Press, 1975.

Fusfeld, Daniel R., and Timothy Bates. *The Political Economy of the Urban Ghetto.* Carbondale, Ill.: Southern Illinois Univ. Press, 1984.

Fussell, Richard. *A Demographic Atlas of Birmingham, 1960–1970.* University, Ala.: Univ. of Alabama Press, 1975.

Fyfe, J. J. "Blind Justice: Police Shootings in Memphis." *Journal of Criminal Law and Criminology* 73 (1982): 707–22.

Gallagher, M. D. "Leon Blum and the Spanish Civil War." *Journal of Contemporary History* 6 (January 1971): 56–64.

Gambs, John S. *The Decline of the I.W.W.* New York: Columbia Univ. Press, 1932.

Gardiner, Jean. "Women's Domestic Labour." *New Left Review* 89 (January–February 1975): 47–58.

Garfinkel, Herbert. *When Negroes March: The March on Washington Movement in the Organizational Politics for FEPC.* Glencoe, Ill.: Free Press, 1959.

Garrow, David J. *Bearing the Cross: Martin Luther King, Jr., and the Southern Christian Leadership Conference.* New York: Morrow, 1986.

Garwood, Alfred N., compiler. *Black Americans: A Statistical Sourcebook 1992.* 3rd ed. Rev. Palo Alto, Calif.: Information Pub., 1993.

Gates, Henry Louis, Jr. *The Signifying Monkey: A Theory of African-American Literary Criticism.* New York: Oxford Univ. Press, 1988.

Gatewood, Willard B. *"Smoked Yankees" and the Struggle for Empire: Letters from Negro Soldiers, 1898–1902.* Urbana: Univ. of Illinois Press, 1971.

Gedicks, Al. "The Social Origins of Radicalism among Finnish Immigrants in Midwest Mining Communities." *Review of Radical Political Economics* 8 (1976): 1–31.

Genovese, Eugene. *Roll, Jordan, Roll: The World the Slaves Made.* New York: Pantheon, 1974.

Gerassi, John. *The Premature Antifascists: North American Volunteers in the Spanish Civil War, 1936–1939: An Oral History*. New York: Praeger, 1986

Gerlach, Luther P., and Virginia H. Hine. *People, Power, Change: Movements of Social Transformation*. Indianapolis: Bobbs-Merrill, 1970.

Gerstein, Ira. "Domestic Work and Capitalism." *Radical America* 7 (July-October 1973): 101–28.

Gibbs, Jewell T., ed. *Young, Black and Male in America: An Endangered Species*. Dover, Mass.: Auburn House, 1988.

Giddings, Paula. *When and Where I Enter: The Impact of Black Women on Race and Sex in America*. New York: Morrow, 1984.

Gillespie, Dizzy, with Al Fraser. *To Be or Not . . . to Bop: Memoirs*. Garden City, N.Y.: Doubleday, 1979.

Gilroy, Paul. "One Nation under a Groove: The Cultural Politics of 'Race' and Racism in Britain." In *Anatomy of Racism*, edited by David Theo Goldberg, 263–82. Minneapolis: Univ. of Minnesota Press, 1990.

Gimenez, Martha E. "The Dialectics of Waged and Unwaged Work: Waged Work, Domestic Labor and Household Survival in the United States." In *Work without Wages: Domestic Labor and Self-Employment within Capitalism*, edited by Jane L. Collins and Martha Gimenez, 25–45. Albany, N.Y.: State Univ. of New York Press, 1990.

Ginzburg, Ralph, ed. *100 Years of Lynchings*. New York: Lancer Books, 1962.

Gitler, Ira. *Jazz Masters of the 1940's*. New York: Collier Books, 1966.

———. *Swing to Bop: An Oral History of the Transition in Jazz in the 1940's*. New York: Oxford Univ. Press, 1985.

Glaser, D., and K. Rice. "Crime, Age, and Employment." *American Sociological Review* 24 (1959): 679–86.

Glasgow, Douglas G. *The Black Underclass: Poverty, Unemployment, and Entrapment of Ghetto Youth*. New York: Random House, 1981.

Gold, Michael. "Send Us a Critic." In *Mike Gold: A Literary Anthology*, edited by Michael Folsom, 138–39. New York: International Publishers, 1972.

Goldfield, David R. *Black, White, and Southern: Race Relations and Southern Culture, 1940 to the Present*. Baton Rouge: Louisiana State Univ. Press, 1990.

Goldman, Peter. *The Death and Life of Malcolm X*. New York: Harper and Row, 1973.

Goodheart, Lawrence B. "The Odyssey of Malcolm X: An Eriksonian Interpretation." *Historian* 53 (Autumn 1990): 47–62.

Gooding-Williams, Robert, ed. *Reading Rodney King, Reading Urban Uprising*. New York: Routledge, 1993.

Gordon, Asa H. *The Georgia Negro: A History*. Ann Arbor, Mich.: Edwards Bros., 1937.

Gordon, Diana R. *The Justice Juggernaut: Fighting Street Crime, Controlling Citizens*. New Brunswick, N.J.: Rutgers Univ. Press, 1990.

Gottlieb, Peter. *Making Their Own Way: Southern Blacks' Migration to Pittsburgh, 1916–1930*. Urbana: Univ. of Illinois Press, 1987.

Gouldner, Alvin Ward. *Wildcat Strike*. Yellow Springs, Ohio: Antioch Press, 1954.

Graham, Helen, and Paul Preston. "The Popular Front and the Struggle against Fascism." In *The Popular Front in Europe*, edited by Helen Graham and Paul Preston, 1–19. New York: St. Martin's Press, 1987.

Gray, Herman. "Race Relations as News: Content Analysis." *American Behavioral Scientist* 30, no. 4 (March-April 1987): 381–96.

Green, E. "Race, Social Status, and Criminal Arrest." *American Sociological Review* 35 (1970): 476–90.

Green, James. "The Brotherhood of Timber Workers, 1910–1913: A Radical Response to Industrial Capitalism in the Southern USA." *Past and Present* 60 (August 1973): 161–200.

———. *Grass-Roots Socialism: Radical Movements in the Southwest, 1895–1943*. Baton Rouge: Louisiana State Univ. Press, 1978.

Greenberg, Cheryl. *Or Does it Explode? Black Harlem in the Great Depression*. New York: Oxford Univ. Press, 1991.

Greene, Lorenzo, and Carter G. Woodson. *The Negro Wage Earner*. Washington, D.C.: The Association for the Study of Negro Life and History, 1930.

Grier, William H., and Price M. Cobbs. *Black Rage*. New York: Basic Books, 1968.

Grossi, Manuel. *L'Insurrection des Austries: Quinze Tours de Revolution Socialiste*. Paris: EDI, 1972.

Grossman, James R. *Land of Hope: Chicago, Black Southerners, and the Great Migration*. Chicago: Univ. of Chicago Press, 1989.

Grover, D. C. *M. N. Roy: A Study of Revolution and Reason in Indian Politics*. Calcutta: Minerva Associates, 1973.

Gutman, Herbert. "Black Coal Miners and the Greenback-Labor Party in Redeemer, Alabama: 1878–1879." *Labor History* 10 (1969): 506–35.

———. *The Black Family in Slavery and Freedom, 1750–1925*. New York, Pantheon Books, 1976.

———. "The Negro and the United Mine Workers of America: The Career and Letters of Richard L. Davis and Something of Their Meaning, 1890–1900." In *The Negro and the American Labor Movement*, edited by Julius Jacobson, 49–127. Garden City, N.Y.: Anchor Books, 1968.

———. *Work, Culture, and Society in Industrializing America: Essays in American Working-Class and Social History*. New York: Knopf, 1976.

Guttman, Alan. *The Wound in the Heart: America and the Spanish Civil War*. New York: Free Press of Glencoe, 1962.

Hacker, George A. *Marketing Booze to Blacks*. Washington, D.C.: Center for Science in the Public Interest, 1987.

Haeberle, Steven H. *Planting the Grassroots: Structuring Citizen Participation*. New York: Praeger, 1989.

Hair, William Ivy. *Carnival of Fury: Robert Charles and the New Orleans Race Riot of 1900*. Baton Rouge: Lousiana State Univ. Press, 1976.

Haithcox, John. *Communism and Nationalism in India: M. N. Roy and Comintern Policy, 1920–1939*. Princeton: Princeton Univ. Press, 1971.

Hall, Jacquelyn Dowd. "Disorderly Women: Gender and Labor Militancy in the Appalachian South." *Journal of American History* 73 (September 1986): 354–82.

———. "'The Mind That Burns in Each Body': Women, Rape, and Racial Violence." In *Powers of Desire: The Politics of Sexuality*, edited by Ann Snitow, Christine Stansell, and Sharon Thompson, 328–49. New York: Monthly Review Press, 1983.

———. *Revolt against Chivalry: Jessie Daniel Ames and the Women's Campaign against Lynching*. New York: Columbia Univ. Press, 1979.

Hall, Stuart. "Culture, Media, and the 'Ideological Effect.'" In *Mass Communication and Society*, edited by James Curran, Michael Gurevitch, and Janet Woolacott, 315–48. Beverly Hills: Sage Publications, 1979.

Hamilton, Kenneth Marvin. *Black Towns and Profit: Promotion and Development in the Trans-Appalachian West, 1877–1915*. Urbana: Univ. of Illinois Press, 1991.

Hammet, Hugh. "Labor and Race: The Georgia Railroad Strike of 1909." *Labor History* 16 (Fall 1975): 470–84.

Hannerz, Ulf. *Soulside: Inquiries into Ghetto Culture and Community*. New York: Columbia Univ. Press, 1969.

Haralambos, Michael. *Soul Music: The Birth of a Sound in America*. New York: De Capo, 1974.

Harding, Vincent. *There Is a River: The Black Struggle for Freedom in America*. New York: Harcourt Brace Jovanovich, 1981.

Harley, Sharon. "For the Good of Family and Race: Gender, Work, and Domestic Roles in the Black Community, 1880–1930." *Signs* 15 (1990): 336–49.

Harring, Sidney, Tony Platt, R. Speiglman, and Paul Takagi. "The Management of Police Killings." *Crime and Social Justice* 8 (1977): 34–43.

Harris, William H. *The Harder We Run: Black Workers since the Civil War*. New York: Oxford Univ. Press, 1982.

Hart, Henry, ed. *American Writers' Congress*. New York: International Publishers, 1935.

Hartmann, Heidi. "The Family as the Locus of Gender, Class, and Political Struggle: The Example of Housework." *Signs* 6 (Spring 1981): 366–94.

Haslam, Jonathan. *The Soviet Union and the Struggle for Collective Security in Europe, 1933–1939*. New York: St. Martin's Press, 1984.

Hay, Douglas, Peter Linebaugh, John G. Rule, E. P. Thompson, and Cal Winslow. *Albion's Fatal Tree: Crime and Society in Eighteenth-Century England*. New York: Pantheon Books, 1975.

Haynes, Robert V. *A Night of Violence: The Houston Riot of 1917*. Baton Rouge: Louisiana State Univ. Press, 1976.

Haywood, Harry. *Black Bolshevik: Autobiography of an Afro-American Communist*. Chicago: Liberator Press, 1978.

Hazzard-Gordon, Katrina. *Jookin': The Rise of Social Dance Formations in African-American Culture*. Philadelphia: Temple Univ. Press, 1990.

Headley, Bernard D. "'Black on Black' Crime: The Myth and the Reality." *Crime and Social Justice* 20 (1983): 50–62.

Hebdige, Dick. *Subculture: The Meaning of Style*. London: Methuen, 1979.

Helmbold, Lois Rita. "Beyond the Family Economy: Black and White Working-Class Women during the Great Depression." *Feminist Studies* 13 (Fall 1987): 629–55.

Henry, Charles P. *Culture and African-American Politics*. Bloomington: Univ. of Indiana Press, 1990.

Hernton, Calvin. *Sex and Racism in America*. Garden City, N.Y.: Doubleday, 1965.

Higginbotham, Evelyn Brooks. *Righteous Discontent: The Women's Movement in the Black Baptist Church, 1880–1920*. Cambridge, Mass.: Harvard Univ. Press, 1993.

Hill, Herbert. "Myth-Making as Labor History: Herbert Gutman and the United Mine Workers of America." *International Journal of Politics, Culture, and Society* 2 (Winter 1988): 132–200.

Hill, Robert, ed., *The Marcus Garvey and Universal Negro Improvement Association Papers*. Vol. 3. Berkeley and Los Angeles: Univ. of California Press, 1984.

Hobsbawm, E. J. "The Machine Breakers." In *Labouring Men: Studies in the History of Labour*. London: Weidenfeld & Nicolson, 1964.

———. *Primitive Rebels: Studies in Archaic Forms of Social Movements in the 19th and 20th Centuries*. 1959. Reprint, New York: Norton, 1965.

Hoerder, Dirk. *Crowd Action in Revolutionary Massachusetts, 1765–1780*. New York: Academic Press, 1977.

Hollinger, Richard C., and J. P. Clark. *Theft by Employees*. Lexington, Mass.: Lexington Books, 1983.

Honey, Michael K. *Southern Labor and Black Civil Rights: Organizing Memphis Workers*. Urbana: Univ. of Illinois Press, 1993.

hooks, bell. *Yearning: Race, Gender and Cultural Politics*. Boston: South End Press, 1990.

Hudson, Hosea. "Struggle against Philip Murray's Racist Policies in Birmingham." *Political Affairs* 53, no. 9 (September 1974): 55–57.

Hudson, Julius. "The Hustling Ethic." In *Rappin' and Stylin' Out: Communication in Urban Black America*, edited by Thomas Kochman, 410–24. Urbana: Univ. of Illinois Press, 1972.

Hughes, Langston. *Good Morning Revolution: Uncollected Social Protest Writings*. Edited by Faith Berry. Brooklyn, N.Y.: Lawrence Hill, 1973.

———. *I Wonder as I Wander: An Autobiographical Journey*. 1956. Reprint, New York: Octagon Books, 1974.

Humphries, D., and D. Wallace. "Capitalist Accumulation and Urban Crime, 1950–1971." *Social Problems* 28 (1980): 179–93.

Hunt, David. "From the Millennial to the Everyday: James Scott's Search for the Essence of Peasant Politics." *Radical History Review* 42 (Fall 1988): 155–72.

Hunter, Tera. *Contesting the New South: The Politics and Culture of Wage Household Labor in Atlanta, 1861–1920*. Forthcoming.

Huntley, Horace. "The Rise and Fall of Mine Mill in Alabama: The Status Quo against Interracial Unionism, 1933–1949." *Journal of the Birmingham Historical Society* 6, no. 1 (January 1979): 7–13.

Hurston, Zora Neale. "Characteristics of Negro Expression." In *Negro: An Anthology,* compiled by Nancy Cunard. New York: Negro Univ. Press, 1969.

———. *Mules and Men*. 1935. Reprint New York: Harper & Row, 1990.

Ibárruri, Dolores. *They Shall Not Pass: The Autobiography of La Pasionaria*. New York: International Publishers, 1966.

Iceberg Slim [Robert Beck]. *Pimp: The Story of My Life*. Los Angeles: Holloway House, 1967.

Ichioka, Yuji. "Early Issei Socialists and the Japanese Community." In *Counterpoint: Perspectives on Asian-America*, edited by Emma Gee. Los Angeles: Asian Studies Center, Univ. of California, 1976.

Independent Commission on the Los Angeles Police Department. *Report of the Independent Commission on the Los Angeles Police Department*. Los Angeles: The Commission, 1991.

Irwin, John. *The Jail: Managing the Underclass in American Society*. Berkeley and Los Angeles: Univ. of California Press, 1985.

Isserman, Maurice. *Which Side Were You On? The American Communist Party during the Second World War*. Middletown, Conn.: Wesleyan Univ. Press, 1982.

Jackson, Bruce. *"Get Your Ass in the Water and Swim Like Me": Narrative Poetry from Black Oral Tradition*. Cambridge, Mass.: Harvard Univ. Press, 1974.

Jackson, Gabriel. *The Spanish Republic and the Civil War, 1931–1939*. Princeton: Princeton Univ. Press, 1965.

James, C.L.R. *Black Jacobins: Toussaint L'Ouverture and the San Domingo Revolution*. 2nd ed., rev. New York: Vintage Books, 1963.

James, C.L.R., George Breitman, and Edgar Keemer et al. *Fighting Racism in World War II*. New York: Monad Press, 1980.

James, David E. "Chained to Devilpictures: Cinema and Black Liberation in the Sixties." In *The Year Left 2: Toward a Rainbow Socialism—Essays on Race, Ethnicity, Class and Gender*, edited by Mike Davis et al., 125–38. London: Verso, 1987.

Janiewski, Dolores. "Seeking 'a New Day and a New Way': Black Women and Unions in the Southern Tobacco Industry." In *"To Toil the Livelong Day": America's Women at Work, 1780–1980*, edited by Carol Groneman and Mary Beth Norton, 161–78. Ithaca, N.Y.: Cornell Univ. Press, 1987.

———. *Sisterhood Denied: Race, Gender, and Class in a New South Community*. Philadelphia: Temple Univ. Press, 1985.

———. "Sisters under Their Skins: Southern Working Women, 1880–1950."

In *Sex, Race, and the Role of Women in the South: Essays*, edited by Joanne V. Hawks and Sheila L. Skemp, 13–35. Jackson, Miss.: University Press of Mississippi, 1983.

Jankovic, I. "Labor Market and Imprisonment." *Crime and Social Justice* 8 (1977): 17–31.

Jankowski, Martin Sanchez. *Islands in the Street: Gangs and American Urban Society*. Berkeley and Los Angeles: Univ. of California Press, 1991.

Jensen, Vernon H. *Nonferrous Metals Industry Unionism, 1932–1954: The Story of Leadership Controversy*. Ithaca, N.Y.: Cornell Univ. Press, 1954.

Johnson, Charles S. *The Negro in American Civilization: A Study of Negro Life and Race Relations in the Light of Social Research*. New York: H. Holt, 1930.

Jones, Beverly W. "Race, Sex, and Class: Black Female Tobacco Workers in Durham, North Carolina, 1920–1940, and the Development of Female Consciousness." *Feminist Studies* 10 (Fall 1984): 443–50.

Jones, Jacqueline *The Dispossessed: America's Underclasses from the Civil War to the Present*. New York: Basic Books, 1992.

———. *Labor of Love, Labor of Sorrow: Black Women, Work and the Family, From Slavery to the Present*. New York: Basic Books, 1985.

Jones, LeRoi. *Blues People: Negro Music in White America*. New York: William Morrow, 1963.

Jones, Norman. "Regionalism and Revolution in Catalonia." In *Revolution and War in Spain, 1931–1939*, edited by Paul Preston, 85–111. London: Methuen, 1984.

Julian, Hubert Fauntleroy. *Black Eagle: Colonel Hubert Julian, as Told to John Bulloch*. London: Jarrolds, 1964.

Kanet, Roger E. "The Comintern and the 'Negro Question': Communist Policy in the United States and Africa, 1921–1941." *Survey* 19, no. 4 (Autumn 1973): 86–122.

Karnik, V. B. *M. N. Roy: A Political Biography*. Bombay: Nav Jagriti Samaj, 1978.

Kater, Michael H. *Different Drummers: Jazz in the Culture of Nazi Germany*. New York: Oxford Univ. Press, 1992.

———. "Forbidden Fruit?: Jazz in the Third Reich." *American Historical Review* 94 (February 1989): 11–43.

Katz, Michael B. *The Undeserving Poor: From the War on Poverty to the War on Welfare*. New York: Pantheon Books, 1989.

Katzman, David. *Seven Days a Week: Women and Domestic Service in Industrializing America*. New York: Oxford Univ. Press, 1978.

Kay, Hugh. *Salazar and Modern Portugal*. New York: Hawthorne Books, 1970.

Kelley, Robin D. G. "An Archeology of Resistance." *American Quarterly* 44 (June 1992): 292–98.

———. "'Comrades, Praise Gawd for Lenin and Them!': Ideology and Culture among Black Communists in Alabama, 1930–1935." *Science and Society* 52, no. 1 (Spring 1988): 59–82.

———. "The Black Poor and the Politics of Opposition in a New South City."

In *The "Underclass" Debate: Views from History*, edited by Michael Katz, 293–333. Princeton: Princeton Univ. Press, 1993.

———. *Hammer and Hoe: Alabama Communists during the Great Depression*. Chapel Hill: Univ. of North Carolina Press, 1990.

———. "Straight from Underground." *Nation* 254, no. 22 (June 8, 1992): 793–96.

———. "The Third International and the Struggle for National Liberation in South Africa, 1921–1928." *Ufahamu* 15, nos. 1 and 2 (1986): 99–120.

Kellogg, Peter J. "Civil Rights Consciousness in the 1940's." *Historian* 42 (November 1979): 18–41.

Kern, Robert W. *Red Years/Black Years: A Political History of Spanish Anarchism, 1911–1937*. Philadelphia: Institute for the Study of Human Issues, 1978.

Kirby, Jack Temple. *Darkness at the Dawning: Race and Reform in the Progressive South*. Philadelphia: Lippincott, 1972.

Kivisto, Peter. *Immigrant Socialists in the United States: The Case of Finns and the Left*. London: Associated Univ. Presses, 1984.

Klehr, Harvey. *The Heyday of American Communism: The Depression Decade*. New York: Basic Books, 1984.

Kobler, A. L. "Figures (and Perhaps Some Facts) on Police Killing of Civilians in the United States, 1965–1969." *Journal of Social Issues* 31 (1975): 163–91.

Kofsky, Frank. *Black Nationalism and the Revolution in Music*. New York: Pathfinder Press, 1970.

Kolchin, Peter. *Unfree Labor: American Slavery and Russian Serfdom*. Cambridge, Mass.: Belknap Press of Harvard Univ. Press, 1987.

Kondo, Baba Zak A. *For Homeboys Only: Arming and Strengthening Young Brothers for Black Manhood* (Washington, D.C.: Nubia Press, 1991).

Kornweibel, Theodore. *No Crystal Stair: Black Life and the Messenger, 1917–1928*. Westport, Conn.: Greenwood Press, 1975.

Korson, George. *Coal Dust on the Fiddle: Songs and Stories of the Bituminous Industry*. Hatboro, Pa.: Folklore Associates, 1943.

Korstad, Robert, and Nelson Lichtenstein. "Opportunities Found and Lost: Labor, Radicals, and the Early Civil Rights Movement." *Journal of American History* 75 (December 1988): 786–811.

Kostiainen, Auvo. *The Forging of Finnish-American Communism, 1917–1924: A Study in Ethnic Radicalism* (Turku: Turun Yliopisto, 1978)

Kuhn, Clifford M., Harlon E. Joye, and E. Bernard West. *Living Atlanta: An Oral History of the City, 1914–1948*. Athens, Ga.: Univ. of Georgia Press, 1990.

Kunjufu, Jawanza. *Countering the Conspiracy to Destroy Black Boys*, 3 vols. Chicago: African American Images, 1985–86.

Kwong, Peter. *Chinatown, New York: Labor and Politics, 1930–1950*. New York: Monthly Review Press, 1979.

Lamon, Lester C. *Black Tennesseans, 1900–1930*. Knoxville, Tenn.: Univ. of Tennessee Press, 1977.

Landis, Arthur. *The Abraham Lincoln Brigade*. New York: Citadel Press, 1967.

————. *Spain! The Unfinished Revolution!* Baldwin Park, Calif.: Camelot 1972.

Lane, Roger. *Roots of Violence in Black Philadelphia,, 1860–1900.* Cambridge, Mass.: Harvard Univ. Press, 1986.

Lannon, Frances. "The Church's Crusade against the Republic." In *Revolution and War in Spain, 1931–1939,* edited by Paul Preston, 35–58. London: Methuen, 1984.

Leab, Daniel. *From Sambo to Superspade: The Black Experience in Motion Pictures.* Boston: Houghton Mifflin, 1975.

League of Struggle for Negro Rights. *Equality, Land and Freedom: A Program for Negro Liberation.* New York: League of Struggle for Negro Rights, 1933.

Leckie, William H. *The Buffalo Soldiers: A Narrative of the Negro Calvary in the West.* Norman, Okla.: Univ. of Oklahoma Press, 1967.

Leidner, Robin. *Fast Food, Fast Talk: Service Work and the Routinization of Everyday Life.* Berkeley and Los Angeles: Univ. of California Press, 1993.

Lenin, V. I. *Collected Works.* Vols. 18–39. London: Lawrence & Wishart, 1960–1965.

————. *Lenin on the National and Colonial Questions: Three Articles.* Peking: Foreign Languages Press, 1967.

Levine, Lawrence. *Black Culture and Black Consciousness: Afro-American Folk Thought from Slavery to Freedom.* New York: Oxford Univ Press, 1977.

Lewis, Earl. *In Their Own Interests: Race, Class, and Power in Twentieth-Century Norfolk, Virginia.* Berkeley and Los Angeles: Univ. of California Press, 1991.

Lichtenstein, Alex. "That Disposition to Theft, with which they have been Branded: Moral Economy, Slave Management, and the Law." *Journal of Social History* 22 (Spring 1988): 413–40.

Lichtenstein, Nelson. *Labor's War at Home: The CIO in World War II.* New York: Cambridge Univ. Press, 1982.

Liebow, Elliot. *Tally's Corner: A Study of Negro Streetcorner Men.* Boston: Little, Brown, 1967.

Lincoln, C. Eric, and Lawrence H. Mamiya. *The Black Church in the African American Experience.* Durham, N.C.: Duke Univ. Press, 1990.

Linebaugh, Peter. *The London Hanged: Crime and Civil Society in the Eighteenth Century.* London: Allen Lane, The Penguin Press, 1991.

Lipsitz, George. *A Life in the Struggle: Ivory Perry and the Culture of Opposition.* Philadelphia: Temple Univ. Press, 1988.

————. *"A Rainbow at Midnight": Labor and Culture in the 1940s.* Urbana: Univ. of Illinois Press, 1994.

————. *Time Passages: Collective Memory and American Popular Culture.* Minneapolis: Univ. of Minnesota Press, 1990.

Little, Douglas. *Malevolent Neutrality: The United States, Great Britain, and the Origins of the Spanish Civil War.* Ithaca, N.Y.: Cornell Univ. Press. 1985.

Los Angeles Times. *Understanding the Riots: Los Angeles Before and After the Rodney King Case.* Los Angeles: Los Angeles Times, 1992.

Lott, Eric. "Double V, Double-Time: Bebop's Politics of Style." *Callaloo* 11, no. 3 (1988): 597–605.

————. *Love and Theft: Blackface Minstrelsy and the American Working Class*. New York: Oxford Univ. Press, 1993.

Lumpkin, Grace. *A Sign for Cain*. New York: Lee Furman, 1935.

Lusane, Clarence. *Pipe Dream Blues: Racism and the War on Drugs*. Boston: South End Press, 1991.

Madhubuti, Haki R., ed. *Why L.A. Happened: Implications of the '92 Los Angeles Rebellion*. Chicago: Third World Press, 1993.

Madrid-Barela, Arturo. "In Search of the Authentic Pachuco: An Interpretive Essay." *Aztlan* 4, no. 1 (Spring 1973): 31–60.

Magubane, Bernard Makhosezwe. *The Ties That Bind: African-American Consciousness of Africa*. Trenton, N.J.: Africa World Press, 1987.

Maguire, Jane. *On Shares: Ed Brown's Story*. New York: Norton, 1975.

Mailer, Phil. *Portugal: The Impossible Revolution?* London: Solidarity, 1977.

Makonnen, Ras. *Pan-Africanism From Within*, edited by Kenneth King. New York: Oxford Univ. Press, 1973.

Malcolm X. *Malcolm X Speaks: Selected Speeches and Statements*, edited by George Breitman. New York: Merit Publishers, 1965.

Malcolm X, with Alex Haley. *The Autobiography of Malcolm X*. New York: Grove Press, 1964.

Malefakis, E. E. *Agrarian Reform and Peasant Revolution in Spain: Origins of the Civil War*. New Haven: Yale Univ. Press, 1970.

Mann, Susan. "Slavery, Sharecropping and Sexual Inequality." *Signs* 14, no. 4 (1989): 774–98.

Marable, Manning. *How Capitalism Underdeveloped Black America: Problems in Race, Political Economy, and Society*. Boston: South End Press, 1983.

————. *Race, Reform, and Rebellion: The Second Reconstruction in Black America, 1945–1990*. 2nd ed. Jackson, Miss.: Univ. Press of Mississippi, 1991.

Marcus, Harold G. "The Embargo on Arms Sales to Ethiopia, 1916–1930." *International Journal of African Historical Studies* 16, no. 2 (1983): 263–79.

Martin, Elmer, and Joanne Martin. *The Black Extended Family*. Chicago: Univ. of Chicago Press, 1978.

Martin, Tony. *Literary Garveyism: Garvey, Black Arts and the Harlem Renaissance*. Dover, Mass.: Majority Press, 1983.

————. *Race First: The Ideological and Organizational Struggles of Marcus Garvey and the Universal Negro Improvement Association*. Westport, Conn.: Greenwood Press, 1976.

Martinez Alier, Juan. *Labourers and Landowners in Southern Spain*. London: Allen & Unwin, 1971.

Martins, H. "Portugal." In *European Fascism*, edited by S.J. Woolf, 302–36. New York: Random House, 1968.

Mason, Lucy Randolph. *To Win These Rights: A Personal Story of the CIO in the South*. New York: Harper, 1952.

Mason, Tim. "The Workers' Opposition in Nazi Germany." *History Workshop* 11 (Spring 1981): 120–37.

Matthews, John Michael. "The Georgia Race Strike of 1909." *Journal of Southern History* 40 (November 1974): 613–30.

Mauer, Marc. *Young Black Men and the Criminal Justice System: A Growing National Problem*. Washington, D.C.: The Sentencing Project, 1990.

Mazon, Mauricio. *The Zoot-Suit Riots: The Psychology of Symbolic Annihilation*. Austin: Univ. of Texas Press, 1984.

McAdoo, Harriet, Pipes, ed. *Black Families*. Beverly Hills: Sage Publications, 1981.

McCallum, Brenda. "Songs of Work and Songs of Worship: Sanctifying Black Unionism in the Southern City of Steel." *New York Folklore* 14, nos. 1 and 2 (1988): 9–33.

McGovern, James R. *Anatomy of a Lynching: The Killing of Claude Neal*. Baton Rouge: Louisiana State Univ. Press, 1982.

McGuire, Philip, ed. *Taps for a Jim Crow Army: Letters from Black Soldiers in World War II*. Santa Barbara, Calif.: ABC-Clio, 1983.

McKay, Claude, *A Long Way from Home*. New York: Lee Furman, 1937.

McMillen, Neil. *Dark Journey: Black Mississippians in the Age of Jim Crow*. Urbana: Univ. of Illinois Press, 1989.

McPherson, James, ed. *The Negro's Civil War: How American Negroes Felt and Acted during the War for the Union*. New York: Pantheon Books, 1965.

Mead, Lawrence. *Beyond Entitlement: The Social Obligations of Citizenship*. New York: Free Press, 1985.

Meaker, Gerald W. *The Revolutionary Left in Spain, 1914–1923*. Stanford: Stanford Univ. Press, 1974.

Meier, August, and Elliot Rudwick. "Black Violence in the Twentieth Century: A Study in Rhetoric and Retaliation." In *Along the Color Line: Explorations in the Black Experience*, edited by August Meier and Elliot Rudwick, 224–37. Urbana: Univ. of Illinois Press, 1976.

———. "The Boycott Movement against Jim Crow Streetcars in the South, 1900–1906." In *Along the Color Line: Explorations in the Black Experience*, edited by August Meier and Elliot Rudwick, 267–89. Urbana: Univ. of Illinois Press, 1976.

Mercer, Kobena. "Black Hair/Style Politics." *New Formations* 3 (Winter 1987): 33–54.

Messerschmidt, James W. *Capitalism, Patriarchy and Crime: Toward a Socialist Feminist Criminology*. Totowa, N.J.: Rowman and Littlefield, 1986.

Meyer, M. W. "Police Shootings at Minorities: The Case of Los Angeles." *Annals* 452 (1980): 98–110.

Miller, Sally. "The Socialist Party and the Negro, 1901–1920." *Journal of Negro History* 56 (July 1971): 220–39.

Milner, Christina, and Richard Milner. *Black Players: The Secret World of Black Pimps*. New York: Little, Brown, 1972.

Mingus, Charles. *Beneath the Underdog*. Harmondsworth, England: Penguin, 1971.

Mitchell, Timothy. "Everyday Metaphors of Power." *Theory and Society* 19 (October 1990): 545–77.

Mitchell-Kernan, Claudia. "Signifying, Loud-talking, and Marking." In *Rappin' and Stylin' Out: Communication in Urban Black America*, edited by Thomas Kochman, 315–35. Urbana: Univ. of Illinois Press, 1972.

Mittleman, James H. "Some Reflections on Portugal's Counter Revolution." *Monthly Review* 28 (March 1977): 58–64.

Modell, John, Marc Goulden, and Magnusson Sigurdur. "World War II in the Lives of Black Americans: Some Findings and an Interpretation." *Journal of American History* 76 (December 1989): 838–48.

Monroy, Douglass. "Anarquismo y Comunismo: Mexican Radicalism and the Communist Party in Los Angeles during the 1930's." *Labor History* 24 (Winter 1983): 34–59.

Montgomery, David. *Workers Control in America: Studies in the History of Work, Technology, and Labor Struggles*. Cambridge and New York: Cambridge Univ. Press, 1979.

Montgomery, William E. *Under Their Own Vine and Fig Tree: The African-American Church in the South, 1865–1900*. Baton Rouge: Lousiana Univ. Press, 1993.

Moore, Geraldine. *Behind the Ebony Mask*. Birmingham, Ala.: Southern University Press, 1961.

Moore, Lawrence. "Flawed Fraternity: American Socialist Response to the Negro, 1901–1912." *Historian* 33, no. 1 (1969): 1–14.

Morton, Patricia. *Disfigured Images: The Historical Assault on Afro-American Women*. Westport, Conn.: Greenwood Press, 1991.

Moss, Philip, and Chris Tilly. *Why Black Men Are Doing Worse in the Labor Market: A Review of Supply-Side and Demand-Side Explanations*. New York: Social Science Research Council Committee for Research on the Underclass, Working Paper, 1991.

Motley, Mary P., ed. *The Invisible Soldier: The Experience of the Black Soldier, World War II*. Detroit: Wayne State Univ. Press, 1975.

Mullen, Robert W. *Blacks in America's Wars: The Shift in Attitudes from the Revolutionary War to Vietnam*. New York: Monad Press, 1973.

Murray, Charles. *Losing Ground: American Social Policy, 1950–1980*. New York: Basic Books, 1984.

Naison, Mark. "Communism and Harlem Intellectuals in the Popular Front: Anti-Fascism and the Politics of Black Culture." *Journal of Ethnic Studies* 9, no. 1 (1981): 1–25.

———. *Communists in Harlem during the Depression*. Urbana: Univ. of Illinois Press, 1983.

———. "Marxism and Black Radicalism in America: Notes on a Long (and Continuing) Journey." *Radical America* 5, no. 3 (1971): 3–25.

Nalty, Bernard C. *Strength for the Fight: A History of Black Americans in the Military*. New York: Free Press, 1986.

Negro Committee to Aid Spain. *A Negro Nurse in Republican Spain*. New York: The Negro Committee to Aid Spain, 1938.

Nekola, Charlotte. "Worlds Moving: Women, Poetry, and the Literary Politics of the 1930's." In *Writing Red: An Anthology of American Women Writers, 1930–1940*, edited by Charlotte Nekola and Paula Rabinowitz, 127–134. New York: The Feminist Press at the City Univ. of New York, 1987.

Nelson, Bruce. "Class and Race in the Crescent City: The ILWU, from San Francisco to New Orleans." In *The CIO's Left-led Unions*, edited by Steven Rosswurm, 19–45. New Brunswick, N.J.: Rutgers Univ. Press, 1992.

———. "Organized Labor and the Struggle for Black Equality in Mobile during World War II." *Journal of American History* 80, no. 3 (December 1993): 952–88.

Nelson, Havelock, and Michael A. Gonzales. *Bring the Noise: A Guide to Rap Music and Hip Hop Culture*. New York: Harmony Books, 1991.

Nelson, Steve. *The Volunteers: A Personal Narrative of the Fight against Facism in Spain*. New York: Masses and Mainstream, 1953.

Nelson, Steve, James R. Barrett, and Rob Ruck, *Steve Nelson: American Radical*. Pittsburgh: Univ. of Pittsburgh Press, 1981.

Newby, I. A. *Black Carolinians: A History of Blacks in South Carolina from 1895–1968*. Columbia, S.C.: Univ. of South Carolina Press for the South Carolina Tricentennial Commission, 1973.

Newton, Huey P. *Revolutionary Suicide*. New York: Harcourt Brace Jovanovich, 1973.

Nolen, Claude H. *The Negro's Image in the South: The Anatomy of White Supremacy*. Lexington, Ky.: Univ. of Kentucky Press, 1967.

Norrell, Robert J. "Caste in Steel: Jim Crow Careers in Birmingham, Alabama." *Journal of American History* 73, no. 3 (December 1986): 669–94.

———. "Labor at the Ballot Box: Alabama Politics from The New Deal to The Dixiecrat Movement." *Journal of Southern History* 57, no. 2 (May 1991): 201–34.

North, Joseph. *No Men Are Strangers*. New York: International Publishers, 1958.

Nugent, John Peer. *The Black Eagle*. New York: Stein and Day, 1971.

Odum, Howard. *Race and Rumors of Race: Challenge to American Crisis*. Chapel Hill: Univ. of North Carolina Press, 1943.

O'Hanlon, Rosalind. "Recovering the Subject: *Subaltern Studies* and Histories of Resistance in Colonial South Asia." *Modern Asian Studies* 22 (February 1988): 189–224.

Ohmann, Carol. "The Autobiography of Malcolm X: A Revolutionary Use of the Franklin Tradition." *American Quarterly* 22, no. 2 (1970): 131–49.

Ong, Walter J. *Fighting for Life: Contest, Sexuality, and Consciousness*. Ithaca, N.Y.: Cornell Univ. Press, 1981.

Orwell, George. *Homage to Catalonia*. First American edition. New York: Harcourt, Brace and World, 1952.

Ottley, Roi. *'New World A-Coming': Inside Black America*. Boston: Houghton Mifflin, 1943.

Padmore, George. *The Life and Struggles of Negro Toilers*. London: R.I.L.U. magazine for the International Trade Union Committee of Negro Workers, 1931.

Painter, Nell Irvin. *Exodusters: Black Migration to Kansas after Reconstruction*. New York: Knopf, 1976.

———. *The Narrative of Hosea Hudson, His Life as a Negro Communist in the South*. Cambridge, Mass.: Harvard Univ. Press, 1979.

Paris, Arthur. "Cruse and the Crisis in Black Culture." *Journal of Ethnic Studies* 5, no. 2 (1977): 63–66.

Patterson, James T. *America's Struggle against Poverty, 1900–1985*. Cambridge, Mass.: Harvard Univ. Press, 1986.

Payne, Stanley. *Basque Nationalism*. Reno: Univ. of Nevada Press, 1975.

———. *A History of Spain and Portugal: Volume II*. Madison: Univ. of Wisconsin Press, 1973.

———. *The Spanish Revolution*. New York: Norton, 1970.

Paz, Abel. *Durruti: The People Armed*. Montreal: Black Rose Books, 1977.

Paz, Octavio. *The Labyrinth of Solitude: Life and Thought in Mexico*. New York: Grove Press, 1962.

Peiss, Kathy. *Cheap Amusements: Working Women and Leisure in Turn-of-the-Century New York*. Philadelphia: Temple Univ. Press, 1986.

Perlman, Selig, and Philip Taft. *History of Labor in the United States*. New York: Macmillan, 1918–35.

Perry, Bruce. "Escape from Freedom, Criminal Style: The Hidden Advantages of Being in Jail." *Journal of Psychiatry and Law* 12, no. 2 (Summer 1984): 215–30.

———. "Malcolm X in Brief: A Psychological Perspective." *Journal of Psychohistory* 11, no. 4 (Spring 1984): 491–500.

———. "Malcolm X and the Politics of Masculinity." *Psychohistory Review* 13, nos. 2 and 3 (Winter 1985): 18–25.

———. *Malcolm: The Life of a Man Who Changed Black America*. Barrytown, N.Y.: Station Hill Press, 1991.

——— ed. *Malcolm X: The Last Speeches*. New York: Pathfinder Press, 1989.

Phillips, Llad, and Harold Votey, Jr. "Rational Choice Models of Crimes by Youth." In *The Economics of Race and Crime*, edited by Margaret C. Simms and Samuel L. Myers, Jr., 129–87. New Brunswick, N.J.: Transaction Books, 1988.

Phillips, Llad, H. L. Votey, Jr., and D. Maxwell. "Crime, Youth, and the Labor Market." *Journal of Political Economy* 80 (1972): 491–504.

Pierce, Bruce. "Blacks and Law Enforcement: Towards Police Brutality Reduction." *Black Scholar* 17 (1986): 49–54.

Platt, Tony. "'Street' Crime': A View from the Left." *Crime and Social Justice* 9 (Spring–Summer 1978): 26–34.

Pleck, E. H. "The Two Parent Household: Black Family Structure in Late Nineteenth-Century Boston." *Journal of Social History* 6 (Fall 1972): 3–31.

Poulantzas, Nicos. *The Crisis of the Dictatorships: Portugal, Greece, Spain.* London: NLB, 1976.

Preston, Paul. "The Agrarian War in the South." In *Revolution and War in Spain, 1931–1939,* edited by Paul Preston, 159–81. London: Methuen, 1984.

————. *The Coming of the Spanish Civil War: Reform, Reaction, and Revolution in the Second Republic, 1931–1936.* London: Macmillan, 1978.

————. "The Creation of the Popular Front in Spain." In *The Popular Front in Europe,* edited by Helen Graham and Paul Preston. New York: St. Martin's, 1987.

————. "Spain's October Revolution and the Rightist Grasp for Power." *Journal of Contemporary History* 10, no. 4 (October 1975): 555–78.

Price, Richard. "The Labour Process and Labour History." *Social History* 8, no. 1 (January 1983): 57–75.

Proctor, Raymond L. *Hitler's Luftwaffe in the Spanish Civil War.* Westport, Conn.: Greenwood Press, 1983.

Prude, Jonathan. "To Look upon the 'Lower Orders': Runaway Ads and the Appearance of Unfree Laborers in America, 1750–1800." *Journal of American History* 78 (June 1991): 124–59.

Puzzo, Dante. *Spain and the Great Powers, 1936–1941.* New York: Columbia Univ. Press, 1962.

Quarles, Benjamin. *The Negro in the American Revolution.* Chapel Hill: Univ. of North Carolina Press, 1961.

Quartaert, Donald. "Machine Breaking and the Changing Carpet Industry of Western Anatolia, 1860–1908." *Journal of Social History* 19 (Summer 1986): 473–89.

Rabinowitz, Howard N. "The Conflict between Blacks and the Police in the Urban South, 1865–1900." *Historian* 39 (November 1976): 62–76.

————. *Race Relations in the Urban South, 1865–1890.* New York: Oxford Univ. Press, 1978.

Rabinowitz, Paula. *Labor and Desire: Women's Revolutionary Fiction in Depression America.* Chapel Hill: Univ. of North Carolina Press, 1991.

————. "Women and U.S. Literary Radicalism." In *Writing Red: An Anthology of American Women Writers, 1930–1940,* edited by Charlotte Nekola and Paula Rabinowitz, 1–16. New York: The Feminist Press at the City Univ. of New York, 1987.

Rachleff, Peter J. *Black Labor in the South: Richmond, Virginia, 1865–1890.* Philadelphia: Temple Univ. Press, 1984.

Raines, Howell. *My Soul Is Rested: Movement Days in the Deep South Remembered.* New York, Putnam, 1977.

Rampersad, Arnold. *The Life of Langston Hughes, Volume 1: 1902–1941: I, Too, Sing America*. New York: Oxford Univ. Press, 1986.

Randall, Dudley, and Margaret G. Burroughs, eds. *For Malcolm: Poems on the Life and Death of Malcolm X*. Detroit: Broadside Press, 1967.

Raper, Arthur. *The Tragedy of Lynching*. Chapel Hill: Univ. of North Carolina Press, 1933.

Rawick, George. "Working-Class Self-Activity." *Radical America* 3 (March–April 1969): 23–31.

Reagon, Bernice. "World War II Reflected in Black Music: 'Uncle Sam Called Me.'" *Southern Exposure* 2 (Winter 1974): 170–84.

Record, Wilson. *The Negro and the Communist Party*. Chapel Hill: Univ. of North Carolina Press, 1951.

Redkey, Edwin S. *Black Exodus: Black Nationalist and Back-to-Africa Movements, 1890–1910*. New Haven: Yale Univ. Press, 1969.

Reed, Merl E. "Lumberjacks and Longshoremen: The I.W.W. in Louisiana." *Labor History* 13 (Winter 1972): 44–58.

Reeves, Jimmie L., and Richard Campbell. *Cracked Coverage: Television News, The Anti-cocaine Crusade, and The Reagan Legacy*. Durham, N.C.: Duke Univ. Press, 1994.

Reiman, Jefferey. *The Rich Get Richer and the Poor Get Prison: Ideology, Class, and Criminal Justice*. 2nd ed. New York: Wiley, 1984.

Reinarman, Craig, and Harry G. Levine. "The Crack Attack: Politics and Media in America's Latest Drug Scare." In *Images of Issues: Typifying Contemporary Social Problems*, edited by Joel Best, 115–35. New York: Aldine de Gruyter, 1989.

Reisner, Robert. *Bird: The Legend of Charlie Parker*. New York: Bonanza Books, 1962; New York: Citadel Press, 1965.

Reiss, A. J., and A. L. Rhodes. "The Distribution of Juvenile Delinquency in the Social Class Structure." *American Sociological Review* 26 (1961): 720–43.

Reuter, Peter, Robert MacCoun, and Patrick Murphy. *Money from Crime: A Study of the Economics of Drug Dealing in Washington, D.C.*. Santa Monica, Calif.: RAND, Drug Policy Research Center, 1990.

Reynolds, Anthony. "Urban Negro Toasts: A Hustler's View from Los Angeles." *Western Folklore* 33 (October, 1974): 267–300.

Rich, Adrienne. "Notes toward a Politics of Location." In *Women, Feminist Identity, and Society in the 1980's: Selected Papers*, edited by Myriam Diaz-Diocaretz and Iris M. Zavala, 7–22. Philadelphia: Benjamins, 1985.

Richards, Vernon. *Lessons of the Spanish Revolution: 1936–1939*. 1953. Rev. ed., London: Freedom Press, 1983.

Richardson, R. Dan. *Comintern Army: The International Brigades and the Spanish Civil War*. Lexington: Univ. Press of Kentucky, 1982.

Roberts, John W. *From Trickster to Badman: The Black Folk Hero in Slavery and Freedom*. Philadelphia: Univ. of Pennsylvania Press, 1989.

Robertson, Esmonde. *Mussolini as Empire Builder: Europe and Africa, 1932–1936*. New York: Macmillan, 1977.

Robin, G. D. "Justifiable Homicide by Police Officers." *Journal of Criminal Law, Criminology and Police Science* 54 (1963): 225–31

Robinson, Cedric J. "The African Diaspora and the Italo-Ethiopian Crisis." *Race and Class* 27, no. 2 (Autumn 1985): 51–65.

———. *Black Marxism: The Making of the Black Radical Tradition*. London: Zed Press, 1983.

———. "Malcolm Little as a Charismatic Leader." *Afro-American Studies* 3 (1972): 81–96.

Robinson, Cyril. "Exploring the Informal Economy." *Crime and Social Justice* 15, nos. 3 and 4 (1988): 3–16.

Roediger, David. "Labor in the White Skin: Race and Working Class History," In *The Year Left 3: Reshaping the U.S. Left: Popular Struggles in the 1980's*, edited by Mike Davis and Michael Sprinker, 287–308. London: Verso, 1988.

———. *Towards the Abolition of Whiteness: Essays on Race, Politics, and Working Class History*. London: Verso, 1994.

———. *The Wages of Whiteness: Race and the Making of the American Working Class*. London: Verso, 1991.

Rolfe, Edwin. *The Lincoln Battalion: The Story of the Americans Who Fought in Spain in the International Brigades*. 1939. Reprint, New York: M.S.G. Haskell House, 1974.

Rose, Tricia. "Black Texts/Black Contexts." In *Black Popular Culture*, edited by Gina Dent, 223–27. Seattle, Wash.: Bay Press, 1992.

———. "Never Trust a Big Butt and a Smile." *Camera Obscura* 23 (1991): 109–31.

Rosengarten, Theodore. *All God's Dangers: The Life of Nate Shaw*. New York: Avon, 1974.

Rosenstone, Robert. *Crusade of the Left: The Lincoln Battalion in the Spanish Civil War*. New York: Pegasus, 1969.

Rosenzweig, Roy. *Eight Hours for What We Will: Workers and Leisure in an Industrial City, 1870–1920*. New York: Cambridge Univ. Press, 1983.

Ross, Steven J. *Workers on the Edge: Work, Leisure, and Politics in Industrializing Cincinnati, 1788–1890*. New York: Columbia Univ. Press, 1985.

Roy, Manabendra Nath. *M. N. Roy's Memoirs*. Bombay and New York: Allied Publishers, 1964.

Rudé, George. *The Crowd in History: A Study of Popular Disturbances in France and England, 1730–1848*. New York: Wiley, 1964.

Ruiz, Vicki. *Cannery Women, Cannery Lives: Mexican Women, Unionization, and the California Food Processing Industry, 1930–1950*. Albuquerque: Univ. of New Mexico Press, 1987.

Sanchez, Jose M. *Reform and Reaction: The Politico-Religious Background of the Spanish Civil War*. Chapel Hill: Univ. of North Carolina Press, 1964.

Sanchez-Tranquilino, Marcos. "Mano a mano: An Essay on the Representation of the Zoot Suit and Its Misrepresentation by Octavio Paz." *Journal of the Los Angeles Institute of Contemporary Art* (Winter 1987): 34–42.

Sanchez-Tranquilino, Marcos, and John Tagg. "The Pachuco's Flayed Hide: Mobility, Identity, and *Buenas Garras*." In *Cultural Studies*, edited by Lawrence Grossberg, Cary Nelson, and Paula Treichler, 566–70. London: Routledge, 1992.

Saxton, Alexander. *The Rise and Fall of the White Republic: Class Politics and Mass Culture in Nineteenth-Century America*. London: Verso, 1990.

Schwartz, Lawrence. *Marxism and Culture: The CPUSA and Aesthetics in the 1930's*. Port Washington, N.Y.: Kennikat Press, 1980.

Schwartz, Michael. *Radical Protest and Social Structure: The Southern Tenant Farmers' Alliance and Cotton Tenancy, 1880–1890*. Chicago and London: Univ. of Chicago Press, 1976.

Scobey, David. "Anatomy of the Promenade: The Politics of Bourgeois Sociability in Nineteenth-Century New York." *Social History* 17 (May 1992): 203–27.

Scott, James C. *Domination and the Arts of Resistance: Hidden Transcripts*. New Haven: Yale Univ. Press, 1990.

———. *The Moral Economy of the Peasant: Rebellion and Subsistence in Southeast Asia*. New Haven: Yale Univ. Press, 1976.

———. *Weapons of the Weak: Everyday Forms of Peasant Resistance*. New Haven: Yale Univ. Press, 1985.

Scott, William R. "Black Nationalism and the Italo-Ethiopian Conflict, 1934–1936." *Journal of Negro History* 63, no. 2 (1978): 118–34.

Seale, Bobby. *Lonely Rage: The Autobiography of Bobby Seale*. New York: Times Books, 1978.

———. *Seize the Time: The Story of the Black Panther Party and Huey P. Newton*. New York: Random House, 1970.

Seccombe, Wally. "The Housewife and Her Labour under Capitalism." *New Left Review* 83 (January–February 1974): 3–24.

Sernett, Milton C., ed. *Afro-American Religious History: A Documentary Witness*. Durham, N.C.: Duke Univ. Press, 1985.

Shack, W. A. "Ethiopia and Afro-Americans: Some Historical Notes, 1920–1970." *Phylon* 35, no. 2 (1974): 142–55.

Shannon, David A. *The Socialist Party of America: A History*. New York: Macmillan, 1955.

Shapiro, Herbert. "The Impact of the Aptheker Thesis: A Retrospective View of American Negro Slave Revolts." *Science and Society* 48 (Spring 1984): 52–73.

———. *White Violence and Black Response: From Reconstruction to Montgomery*. Amherst, Mass.: Univ. of Massachusetts Press, 1988.

Sheldon, R. *Criminal Justice in America: A Sociological Approach*. Boston: Little, Brown, 1982.

Shepperson, George. "Ethiopianism and African Nationalism." *Phylon* 14, no. 1 (1953): 9–18.

Shubert, Adrian. "The Epic Failure: The Asturian Revolution of October 1934." In *Revolution and War in Spain, 1931–1939*, edited by Paul Preston, 113–36. Methuen: London and New York, 1984.

Sidran, Ben. *Black Talk*. New York: Holt, Rinehart & Winston, 1971.

Sitkoff, Harvard. "The Detroit Race Riot of 1943." *Michigan History* 53 (Fall 1969): 183–206.

———. *A New Deal for Blacks: The Emergence of Civil Rights as a National Issue*. New York: Oxford Univ. Press, 1978.

———. "Racial Militancy and Interracial Violence in the Second World War." *Journal of American History* 58 (December 1971): 661–81.

Smith, Albert C. "'Southern Violence' Reconsidered: Arson as Protest in Black Belt Georgia, 1865–1910." *Journal of Southern History* 55 (November 1985): 527–64.

Smith, Paul A. "Domestic Labour and Marx's Theory of Value." In *Feminism and Materialism: Women and Modes of Production*, edited by Annette Kuhn and Ann Marie Wolpe, 198–219. London: Routledge, 1978.

Soja, Edward. *Postmodern Geographies: The Reassertion of Space in Critical Social Theory*. London: Verso, 1989.

Solomon, Frederick, Walter Walker, Garrett J. O'Connor, and Jacob R. Fishman. "Civil Rights Activity and Reduction in Crime among Negroes." *Archives of Psychiatry* 12 (1965): 227–36. Reprinted in *Crime and Social Justice* 14 (Winter 1980): 27–35.

Soviet War Veterans' Committee. *International Solidarity with the Spanish Republic, 1936–1939*. Moscow: Progress Publishers, 1974.

Spalding, Henry D., compiler. *Encyclopedia of Black Folklore and Humor*. Middle Village, N.Y.: Jonathan David, 1972.

Spero, Sterling, and Abram L. Harris, *The Black Worker: The Negro and the Labor Movement*. New York: Columbia Univ. Press, 1931.

Stack, Carol B. *All Our Kin: Strategies for Survival in a Black Community*. New York: Harper and Row, 1974.

Stanley, Lawrence A., ed. *Rap: The Lyrics*. New York: Penguin, 1992.

Stansell, Christine. *City of Women: Sex and Class in New York, 1789–1860*. New York: Knopf, 1986.

Steedman, Carolyn. *Landscape for a Good Woman: A Story of Two Lives*. 1986. Reprint, New Brunswick, N.J.: Rutgers Univ. Press, 1987.

Strasser, Susan. *Never Done: A History of American Housework*. New York: Pantheon, 1982.

Strom, Sharon Hartman. "Challenging 'Woman's Place': Feminism, the Left, and Industrial Unionism in the 1930's." *Feminist Studies* 9, no. 2 (Summer 1983): 359–86.

Stuckey, Sterling. *Slave Culture: Nationalist Theory and the Foundations of Black America*. New York: Oxford Univ. Press, 1987.

———. "Through the Prism of Folklore: The Black Ethos in Slavery." *Massachusetts Review* 9 (Summer 1968): 417–37.

Sugrue, Thomas. "The Structures of Urban Poverty: The Reorganization of Space and Work in Three Periods of American History." In *The "Underclass" Debate: Views from History*, edited by Michael Katz, 85–117. Princeton: Princeton Univ. Press, 1993.

Sweeney, W. Allison. *History of the American Negro in the Great World War*. 1919. Reprint, New York: Negro Universities Press, 1969.

Takagi, Paul. "A Garrison State in 'Democratic Society.'" *Crime and Social Justice* 1 (Spring–Summer 1974): 27–33.

Terkel, Studs, ed. *"The Good War": An Oral History of World War Two*. New York: Pantheon Books, 1984.

Thomas, Hugh. *The Spanish Civil War*. 4th ed. New York: Norton, 1986.

Thomas, Mary Martha. "Alabama Women on the Home Front, World War II." *Alabama Heritage* 19 (Winter 1991): 2–23.

Thompson, E. P. "The Crime of Anonymity," In *Albion's Fatal Tree: Crime and Society in Eighteenth-Century England*, edited by Douglas Hay, Peter Linebaugh, John G. Rule, E. P. Thompson, and Cal Winslow, 255–344. New York: Pantheon Books, 1975.

———. *The Making of the English Working Class*. New York: Vintage Books, 1963.

———. "The Moral Economy of the English Crowd in the Eighteenth Century." *Past and Present* 50 (February 1971): 76–135.

———. *Whigs and Hunters: The Origins of the Black Act*. London: Allen Lane, 1975.

Thompson, Robert A., Hylan Lewis, and Davis McEntire. "Atlanta and Birmingham: A Comparative Study in Negro Housing." In *Studies in Housing and Minority Groups*, edited by Nathan Glazer and Davis McEntire, 13–83. Berkeley and Los Angeles: Univ. of California Press, 1960.

Toll, Robert C. *Blacking Up: The Minstrel Show in Nineteenth Century America*. New York: Oxford Univ. Press, 1974.

Toop, David. *Rap Attack 2: African Rap to Global Hip Hop*. Rev. ed. London: Serpent's Tail, 1991.

Traina, Richard P. *American Diplomacy and the Spanish Civil War*. Bloomington: Indiana Univ. Press, 1968.

Trotter, Joe William, Jr. *Black Milwaukee: The Making of an Industrial Proletariat, 1915–1945*. Urbana: Univ. of Illinois Press, 1985.

———. *Coal, Class, and Color: Blacks in Southern West Virginia, 1915–1932*. Urbana: Univ. of Illinois Press, 1990.

Tucker, Susan. "A Complex Bond: Southern Black Domestic Workers and Their White Employers." *Frontiers: A Journal of Women's Studies* 11, no. 3 (1987): 6–13.

Turner, Ralph H., and Samuel J. Surace. "Zoot Suiters and Mexicans: Symbols in Crowd Behavior." *American Journal of Sociology* 62 (1956): 14–20.

Tyler, Bruce M. "Black Jive and White Repression." *Journal of Ethnic Studies* 16, no. 4 (1989): 31–66.

Ullendorf, Edward. *Ethiopia and the Bible*. London: Published for the British Academy by Oxford Univ. Press, 1968.

Ullman, Joan C. *The Tragic Week: A Study of Anti-clericism in Spain, 1875–1912*. Cambridge, Mass.: Harvard Univ. Press, 1968.

Valentine, Betty Lou. *Hustling and Other Hard Work: Life Styles in the Ghetto*. New York: The Free Press, 1978.

Van Deburg, William L. *New Day in Babylon: The Black Power Movement and American Culture, 1965–1975*. Chicago: Univ. of Chicago Press, 1992.

Van Onselen, Charles. *Chibaro: African Mine Labour in Southern Rhodesia, 1900–1933*. London: Pluto Press, 1976.

———. *Studies in the Social and Economic History of the Witwatersrand, 1886–1914: New Nineveh*. New York: Longman 1982.

Vincent, Theodore. *Black Power and the Garvey Movement*. Berkeley, Calif.: Ramparts Press, 1971.

Wade-Gayles, Gloria. *Pushed Back to Strength: A Black Woman's Journey Home*. Boston: Beacon Press, 1993.

Wald, Alan M. *The New York Intellectuals: The Rise and Decline of the Anti-Stalinist Left from the 1930's to the 1980's*. Chapel Hill: Univ. of North Carolina Press, 1987.

Walker, Clarence E. *A Rock in a Weary Land: The African Methodist Episcopal Church during the Civil War and Reconstruction*. Baton Rouge: Louisiana State Univ. Press, 1982.

Walker, Margaret. *Richard Wright—Daemonic Genius: A Portrait of the Man, A Critical Look at His Work*. New York: Warner Books, 1988.

Walkowitz, Judith. *Prostitution and Victorian Society: Women, Class, and the State*. New York: Cambridge Univ. Press, 1980.

Wall, Brenda. *The Rodney King Rebellion: A Psychopolitical Analysis of Racial Despair and Hope*. Chicago: African American Images, 1992.

Warshow, Robert. *The Immediate Experience: Movies, Comics, Theatre and Other Aspects of Popular Culture*. New York: Atheneum, 1970.

Watts, Jerry G. "It Just Ain't Righteous: On Witnessing Black Crooks and White Cops." *Dissent* 90 (1983): 347–53.

Weaver, John D. *The Brownsville Raid*. New York: Norton, 1970.

Weinstein, James. *The Decline of Socialism in America, 1912–1925*. New York: Monthly Review Press, 1967.

Weisbord, Robert. *Ebony Kinship: Africa, Africans, and the Afro-American*. Westport, Conn.: Greenwood Press, 1973.

Wepman, Dennis, Ronald B. Newman, and Murray Binderman. *The Life: The Lore and Folk Poetry of the Black Hustler*. Philadelphia: Univ. of Pennsylvania Press, 1976.

Wesley, Charles. *Negro Labor in the United States, 1850–1925: A Study in American Economic History*. New York: Vanguard Press, 1927.

Whealey, Robert H. *Hitler and Spain: The Nazi Role in the Spanish Civil War, 1936–1939*. Lexington: Univ. Press of Kentucky, 1989.

Wheeler, Edward L. *Uplifting the Race: The Black Minister in the New South, 1865–1902*. Lanham, Md.: University Press of America, 1986.

White, E. Frances. "Africa on My Mind: Gender, Counter Discourse and African-American Nationalism." *Journal of Women's History* 2, no. 1 (Spring 1990): 73–97.

Whitfield, Stephen. "Three Masters of Impression Management: Benjamin Franklin, Booker T. Washington, and Malcolm X as Autobiographers." *South Atlantic Quarterly* 77 (Autumn 1978): 399–417.

Wilentz, Sean. *Chants Democratic: New York City and the Rise of the American Working Class, 1788–1850*. New York: Oxford Univ. Press, 1984.

Williams, Henry. *Black Response to the American Left: 1917–1929*, Princeton: History Department, Princeton Univ., 1971.

Williams, Raymond. "Base and Superstructure in Marxist Cultural Theory." In *Problems in Materialism and Culture: Selected Essays*. London: NLB, 1980.

Willis, Paul. *Learning to Labour: How Working Class Kids Get Working Class Jobs*. New York: Columbia Univ. Press, 1981.

———. "Shop-Floor Culture, Masculinity, and the Wage Form." In *Working-Class Culture: Studies in Labor and Theory*, edited by John Clarke, Charles Critcher, and Richard Johnson, 185–98. New York: St. Martin's Press, 1979.

Wilmore, Gayraud. *Black Religion and Black Radicalism: An Interpretation of the Religious History of Afro-American People*. 2nd. ed., rev. and enl. Maryknoll, N.Y.: Orbis Books, 1983.

Wilson, Bobby. "Black Housing Opportunities in Birmingham, Alabama." *Southeastern Geographer* 17, no. 1 (May 1977): 49–57.

———. "Racial Segregation Trends in Birmingham, Alabama." *Southeastern Geographer* 25, no. 1 (May 1985): 30–43.

Wilson, Edward T. *Russia and Black Africa before World War II*. New York: Holmes & Meier, 1974.

Wilson, John. *Jazz: The Transition Years, 1940–1960*. New York: Appleton-Century-Crofts, 1966.

Wilson, William J. *The Truly Disadvantaged: The Inner City, the Underclass, and Public Policy*. Chicago: Univ. of Chicago Press, 1987.

Wilson, William Julius, and Loic J. D. Wacquant. "The Cost of Racial and Class Exclusion in the Inner City." *Annals* 501 (January 1989): 26–47.

Wolfenstein, Eugene Victor. *The Victims of Democracy: Malcolm X and the Black Revolution*. Berkeley and Los Angeles: Univ. of California Press, 1981.

Woodson, Carter G., and Lorenzo Greene. *The Negro Wage Earner*. Washington, D.C.: Association for the Study of Negro Life and History, Inc., 1930.

Workers (Communist) Party of America. *Fourth National Convention of the Workers (Communist) Party of America*. Chicago: Literature Department, Workers Party of America, 1925.

———. *The Second Year of the Workers Party of America: Theses, Programs, Resolutions*. Chicago: Literature Department, Workers Party of America, 1924.

Workers (Communist) Party of the United States of America. *Program and Constitution: Workers Party of America*. Chicago: Literature Department, Workers Party of America, 1924.

Worthman, Paul. "Working Class Mobility in Birmingham, Alabama, 1880–1914." In *Anonymous Americans: Explorations in Nineteenth-Century Social History*, edited by Tamara K. Hareven, 172–213. Englewood Cliffs, N.J.: Prentice-Hall, 1971.

Worthman, Paul, and James Green. "Black Workers in the New South, 1865–1915." In *Key Issues in the Afro-American Experience*, edited by Nathan Huggins, Martin Kilson, and Daniel Fox, 47–69. New York: Harcourt Brace Jovanovich, 1971.

Wright, George C. *Life behind a Veil: Blacks in Louisville, Kentucky, 1865–1930*. Baton Rouge: Louisiana State Univ. Press, 1985.

Wright, Richard. "Blueprint for Negro Writing." *New Challenge* 1 (Fall 1937): 53–61.

———. *Twelve Million Black Voices*. 1941. Reprint, New York: Thunder's Mouth Press, 1988.

Wynn, Neil A. *The Afro-American and the Second World War*. New York: Holmes & Meier, 1975.

Wynter, Sylvia. "Sambos and Minstrels." *Social Text* 1 (Winter 1979): 149–56.

Yarrow, Michael. "The Gender-Specific Class Consciousness of Appalachian Coal Miners: Structure and Change." In *Bringing Class Back In: Contemporary and Historical Perspectives*, edited by Scott G. McNall, Rhonda F. Levine, and Rick Fantasia, 285–310. Boulder: Westview Press, 1991.

Yates, James. *Mississippi to Madrid: Memoir of a Black American in the Abraham Lincoln Brigade*. Seattle: Open Hand Publishers, 1989.

Yoneda, Karl. *Ganbatte: Sixty-Year Struggle of a Kibei Worker*. Edited by Yuji Ichioka. Los Angeles: Resource Development and Publications, Asian American Study Center, Univ. of California, 1983.

Young, James O. *Black Writers of the Thirties*. Baton Rouge: Louisiana State Univ. Press, 1973.

Zanger, Mark. "The Intelligent Forty-year-old's Guide to Rap." *Boston Review* 16, no. 6 (December 1991): 7, 34.

Zangrando, Robert L. *The NAACP Crusade against Lynching, 1909–1950*. Philadelphia: Temple Univ. Press, 1980.

Zimring, Franklin E., and Gordon Hawkins. *The Scale of Imprisonment*. Chicago: Univ. of Chicago Press, 1991.

Dissertations and Unpublished Papers

Brown, Elsa Barkley. "Uncle Ned's Children: Richmond, Virginia's Black Community, 1890–1930." Ph.D. diss., Kent State University, 1994.

Burran, James. "Racial Violence in the South during World War II." Ph.D. diss., University of Tennessee, 1977.

Clarke, Jacquelyn M. J. "Goals and Techniques in Three Negro Civil Rights Organizations in Alabama." Ph.D. diss., Ohio State Unversity, 1960.

Corely, Robert Gaines. "The Quest for Racial Harmony: Race Relations in Birmingham, Alabama, 1947–1963." Ph.D. diss., University of Virginia, 1979.

Faue, Elizabeth. "Gender, Class, and the Politics of Work in Women's History." Unpublished paper in author's possession.

———. "Reproducing the Class Struggle: Perspectives on the Writing of Working Class History." Paper presented at the Social Science History Association Meeting, Minneapolis, October 19, 1990. Paper in author's possession.

Gill, Gerald R. "Dissent, Discontent and Disinterest: Afro-American Opposition to the United States Wars of the Twentieth Century." Unpublished book manuscript, 1988.

Gregg, Nina. "Women Telling Stories about Reality: Subjectivity, the Generation of Meaning, and the Organizing of a Union at Yale." Ph.D. diss., McGill University, 1991.

Hadjor, Kofi Buenor. "Days of Rage: . . . Behind the Los Angeles Riots." Unpublished manuscript in author's possession, 1992.

Harper, Frederick. "Maslow's Concept of Self-Actualization Compared with Personality Characteristics of Selected Black American Protestors: Martin Luther King, Jr., Malcolm X, and Frederick Douglass." Ph.D. diss., Florida State University, 1970.

Hodges, John. "The Quest for Selfhood in the Autobiographies of W.E.B. DuBois, Richard Wright, and Malcolm X." Ph.D. diss., University of Chicago, 1980.

Hummasti, George P. "Finnish Radicals in Astoria, Oregon, 1904–1940: A Study in Immigrant Socialism." Ph.D. diss., University of Oregon, 1975.

Hunter, Tera W. "Household Workers in the Making: Afro-American Women in Atlanta and the New South, 1861–1920." Ph.D. diss., Yale University, 1990.

Huntley, Horace. "Iron Ore Miners and Mine Mill in Alabama, 1933–1952." Ph.D. diss., University of Pittsburgh, 1976.

Joiner, Charles L. "An Analysis of the Employment Patterns of Minority Groups in the Alabama Economy, 1940–1960." Ph.D. diss., University of Alabama, 1968.

Karni, Michael Gary. "Yhteishyva—Or For the Common Good: Finnish Radicalism in the Western Great Lakes Region, 1900–1940." Ph.D. diss., University of Minnesota, 1975.

Kim, Sam G. "Black Americans' Commitment to Communism: A Case Study Based on Fiction and Autobiographies." Ph.D. diss., University of Kansas, 1986.

Kindell, Marilynn. "A Descriptive Analysis of the Impact of Urban Renewal on a Relocated Family: A Case Study of the Medical Center Expansion Project." Master's thesis, University of Alabama, Birmingham, 1982.

Korstad, Robert. "'Daybreak of Freedom': Tobacco Workers and the CIO, Winston-Salem, North Carolina, 1943–1950." Ph.D. diss., University of North Carolina, Chapel Hill, 1987.

Kuzwayo, Arnold. "A History of Ethiopianism in South Africa with Particular Reference to the American Zulu Mission from 1835–1908." Master's thesis, University of South Africa, 1979.

LaMonte, Edward S. "Politics and Welfare in Birmingham, Alabama: 1900–1975." Ph.D. diss., University of Chicago, 1976.

Moore, William. "On Identity and Consciousness of El Hajj Malik El Shabazz (Malcolm X)." Ph.D. diss., University of California, Santa Cruz, 1974.

Patton, Gerald Wilson. "War and Race: The Black Officer in the American Military." Ph.D. diss., University of Iowa, 1978.

Pearce, John Franklin. "Human Resources in Transition: Rural Alabama since World War II." Ph.D. diss., University of Alabama, 1966.

Rachleff, Peter J. "Black, White, and Gray: Race and Working-class Activism in Richmond, Virginia, 1865–1890." Ph.D. diss., University of Pittsburgh, 1981.

Samuels, David. "Five Afro-Caribbean Voices in American Culture, 1917–1929: Hubert H. Harrison, Wilfred A. Domingo, Richard B. Moore, Cyril Briggs and Claude McKay." Ph.D. diss., University of Iowa, 1977.

Shuldiner, David P. "Of Moses and Marx: Folk Ideology within the Jewish Labor Movement in the United States." Ph.D. diss., UCLA, 1984.

Simama, Jabari. "Black Writers Experience Communism: An Interdisciplinary Study of Imaginative Writers, Their Critics, and the CPUSA." Ph.D. diss., Emory University, 1978.

Solomon, Mark. "Red and Black: Negroes and Communism, 1929–1932." Ph.D. diss., Harvard University, 1972.

Sugrue, Thomas. "The Origins of the Urban Crisis: Detroit, 1940–1960." Ph.D. diss., Harvard University, 1992.

Taylor, Theman. "Cyril Briggs and the African Blood Brotherhood: Effects of Communism on Black Nationalism, 1919–1935" Ph.D. diss., University of California, Santa Barbara, 1981.

Wollcott, Victoria. "'I'm as Good as Any Woman in Your Town': African-American Women and the Politics of Identity in Inter-war Detroit." Ph.D. diss., in progress, University of Michigan.

———. "Mediums, Messages, and Lucky Numbers: African-American Female Leisure Workers in Inter-War Detroit." Unpublished paper in author's possession.

Discography

Arrested Development. *3 Years, 5 Months and 2 Days in the Life Of* . . . Chrysalis Records, 1992.

Bytches With Problems. *The Bytches*. Def Jam, 1991.

Capital Punishment Organization. *To Hell and Black*. Capitol Records, 1990.

Compton's Most Wanted. *Straight Check N' Em*. Orpheus Records, 1991.

The Coup. *Kill My Landlord*. Wild Pitch Records, 1993.

Cypress Hill. *Cypress Hill*. Columbia, 1991.

Da Lench Mob. *Guerrillas in Tha Mist*. Priority Records, 1992.

Del the Funkee Homosapien. *I Wish My Brother George Was Here*. Priority Records, 1991.

Digital Underground. *Sons of the P*. Tommy Boy, 1991.

The Disposable Heroes of Hipoprisy. *Hypocrisy Is the Greatest Luxury*. Island Records, 1992.

Dr. Dre. *The Chronic*. Deathrow/Interscope, 1992.

Eazy E. *Eazy-Duz-It*. Ruthless, 1988.

Geto Boys. *The Geto Boys*. Def American Records, 1989.

Ice Cube. *AmeriKKKa's Most Wanted*. Priority Records, 1990.

———. *Death Certificate*. Priority Records, 1991.

———. *Kill at Will*. Priority Records, 1992.

———. *The Predator*. Priority Records, 1992.

Ice T. *The Iceberg/Freedom of Speech . . . Just Watch What You Say*. Sire Records, 1989.

———. *OG: Original Gangster*. Sire Records, 1991.

———. *Power*. Warner Bros., 1988.

———. *Rhyme Pays*. Sire Records, 1987.

Kid Frost. *East Side Story*. Virgin Records, 1992.

NWA. *Efil4zaggin*. Priority Records, 1991.

———. *NWA and the Posse*. Ruthless Records, 1988.

———. *100 Miles and Runnin'*. Priority Records, 1990.

———. *Straight Outta Compton*. Ruthless Records, 1988.

Parker, Charlie. *Bird/The Savoy Recordings [Master Takes]*. Savoy, 1976.

Public Enemy. *Apocalypse '91*. Def Jam, 1991.

———. *It Takes a Nation of Millions to Hold Us Back*. Def Jam, 1988.

Snoop Doggy Dogg. *Doggy Style*. Priority Records, 1993.

Son of Bazerk. *Son of Bazerk*. MCA, 1991.

2 Black, 2 Strong MMG. *Doin' Hard Time on Planet Earth*. Relativity Records, 1991.

2Pac. *2Pacalypse Now*. Interscope Records, 1991.

W.C. and the MAAD Circle. *Ain't A Damn Thang Changed*. Priority, 1991.

X-Clan. *Xodus: The New Testament*. Polygram Records, 1992.

Yo Yo. *Make Way for the Motherlode*. Profile, 1991.

Filmography

Ahearn, Charlie. *Wild Style* (1982).

Appleby, David, Margaret Allison Graham, and Steve Ross. *At the River I Stand* (1994).

Dixon, Ivan. *The Spook Who Sat by the Door* (1973).

Singleton, John. *Boyz N the Hood* (1991).

Acknowledgments

This book is a patchwork quilt of sorts. The chapters began as different projects and were shaped by entirely different groups of people some of whose paths never crossed. For that reason, the list of people and institutions to which I'm indebted is enormous. First and foremost, I've got to give big props to Janake Bakhle of the University of Minnesota Press—a brilliant editor and a stellar scholar in her own right. She was the first to envision this book and wanted to publish it, but contractual obligations made it impossible. A phat shout out goes to Deb Chasman of Beacon Press and Mike Sprinker of Verso for their encouragement and insight; to Bruce Nichols, my editor at The Free Press, for believing in *Race Rebels* as well as future projects; and to Denise Stinson, whose hard work and energy make her the James Brown of literary agents.

George Lipsitz has been enormously kind, generous, and supportive from day one—a model of mentorship, intellectual integrity and political commitment. Similarly, Nell Irvin Painter's support and encouragement have been unwavering. She is a master teacher with one of the most brilliant minds in the historical profession. Tricia Rose gets phat, phat, phat props just for being Tricia—pure genius and funny as hell. Her intellectual imprint on this book should be obvious to the dumb, def, and blind. I'm thoroughly indebted to my all-too-brief conversations with Greg Tate and Arthur Jafa, both of whom I think of as modern Renaissance Black Men, towering figures, true intellectuals, sharp critics, or, better yet, contemporary Paul Robesons with a sense of humor and a lot more hair. Tera Hunter's amazing insight into African American culture puts me in the revision mode after every conversation, and her friendship has been life-sustaining. I'm eternally grateful to Elsa Barkley Brown, mentor extraordinaire and font of support even when I'm strong, and to Earl Lewis, a selfless collaborator and a brilliant critic. I also depend on their friendship. The same must be said of Jayne London, Tiffany R. L. Patterson, Michael Eric Dyson, Marcia Dyson, George Sanchez, Gina Morantz-Sanchez, Sid Lemelle, Salima Lemelle, Julius Scott, Denise Greene, Emir Lewis, Michael Awkward, Lauren Rich, Santiago and Emily Colás—all of whom have contributed in one way or another to the manuscript and/or my sanity.

Many, many people read parts of the manuscript, either in draft form or as published articles, and offered useful suggestions, criticisms, and reality checks. Others simply listened to ideas and kept me going. Some of these folks deserve a lengthier, more enthusiastic expression of gratitude since their comradeship proved as important to me as their intellect. To them I must apologize in advance. The list includes Elizabeth Alexander, Susan Armeny, Edward L. Ayers, Houston Baker, Jr., Dana Barron, Eileen Boris, Charles Bright, MariJo Buhle, Paul Buhle, Jane Burbank, Kathleen Canning, George Chauncey, Stuart Clarke, Danny Duncan Collum, Fred Cooper, Fernando Coronil, Marc Crawford, Danny Czitrom, Laura Downs, Alice Echols, Geoff Eley, Glen T. Eskew, Elizabeth Faue, Janet Francendese, Gerald Gill, Herman Gray, Jacquelyn Dowd Hall, Robert L. Harris, Janet Hart, Darlene Clark Hine, Tom Holt, Michael Honey, Tom Jackson, Clyde and Ann Johnson, Michael Katz, Robert Korstad, Cliff Kuhn, Nelson Lichtenstein, Peter Linebaugh, Wahneema Lubiano, Clarence Lusane, Tracye Matthews, Terrence J. McDonald, August Meier, Gary Miles, David Montgomery, Toni Morrison, Bruce Nelson, Eric Perkins, Linda Reed, Jimmie Reeves, Armstead Robinson, David Roediger, Sonya Rose, David Scobey, James Scott, Jonathan Scott, Rebecca Scott, Julie Skurski, James Spady, Thomas Sugrue, David Thelen, Joe W. Trotter, Akinyele Umoja, Maris Vinovskis, Alan Wald, Ken Warren, Cornel West, Victoria Wollcott, Joe Wood, all the members of the Veterans of the Abraham Lincoln Brigade Archives, my new colleagues at New York University, my comrades on the *Radical History Review* editorial collective, and all of my graduate students, too numerous to be named. Props to David Freund, Jamie Hart, Pamela Henry, and Linda Willis for their expert research assistance and critical eye. And juicy phat props to the staff at the Center for Afro-American and African Studies—Gerri Brewer, Tammy Davis, Camille Spencer, and Evans Young—for putting up with me and my incessant requests.

Big up to Ice T, his manager Jorge Hinojosa, and his attorney Eric Greenspan for giving me permission to reprint portions of his lyrics free of charge. Given the rather large fees other music publishing companies require, Ice T's generosity was most welcome. He and his company, Rhyme Syndicate Productions, have consistently demonstrated a strong commitment to those of us serious about examining hip hop and its antecedents. On the music tip, let me also thank all the representatives of publishing companies (gratefully acknowledged on the copyright page) for facilitating my permission requests and the staff at ASCAP and BMI for directing me to the proper sources.

Special thanks to the many archivists and librarians who showed me the way, especially the indefatigable Marvin Y. Whiting, director of the Tutwiler Collection at the Birmingham Public Library, and Victor Berch of the Abraham Lincoln Brigade Archives. Research and writing were supported by generous grants from the Institute for Research on Poverty; the Social Science Research Council Committee for Research on the Urban Underclass; University of Pennsylvania Urban Studies Program (under the direction of Michael Katz); the Stephen A. Stone Research Award, University of Michigan; Rackham Faculty Research Grant, University of Michigan; the Center for Afro-American and African Studies; and the Ford Foundation.

Finally, the folks who count most in my world. Big mackadocious props to my family: my mothers Ananda Sattwa and Annette Rohan; my father Donald Kelley and his wife Mary Kay; my grandmother Carmen Chambers; my sisters and brothers (in-laws and outlaws) Makani Themba, Meilan Carter, Claudine and Stanley Allison, Irie Harris, Don Mitchell, Claudius Harris, Jr., Chris Kelley, Fujiko Kelley, Shannon Patrick Kelley, Benjamin Kelley, Craig Berrysmith, and all their children; and my wife's tribe of supportive cousins (too numerous to name). I'm forever grateful to two of the world's greatest teachers: Jane Andrias and Thelma Reyna. They ought to take credit for whatever I did right and bear no responsibility for my mistakes and stupidity. Their extraordinary commitment to public education and to struggling colored city kids, especially in an era when even progressive political activists are quick to write off the current generation of African American youth, is simply unparalleled. To both I send my deepest love and appreciation.

Last but not least, a crazy psychoalphadiscobeta shout out to all the ladies in the house. Diedra Harris-Kelley, my partner in love and theft, my around-the-way Staten Island girl who stuck it out since our first year at Cal State Long Beach fourteen years ago, deserves serious props for all the work she put into this book. She read it against her will, asked me questions I couldn't answer, corrected typos, and helped me negotiate my way through the complicated maze of commercial publishing. And she found time in her busy schedule to produce yet another beautiful dust jacket. I learned this time around not to ask for a striking illustration after the book is written. Rather, one ought to let the art work inspire the book, which is exactly what I did. The series of small pastel panels on the dust jacket compelled me to think in new ways about the hidden history of African American culture, resistance, and the politics of identity. These haunting faces are the visual equal of Paul Laurence Dunbar's moving poem, "We Wear the Mask." Critics don't know it yet, but Diedra is the future of the New York art scene.

And then there is my newest love and bestest friend, Elleza Carmen Akilah Kelley. She entered this world literally forty-eight hours after I received advance copies of my first book and has come into her own as I wrote virtually all the chapters of this one. Watching her grow has been the most wonderful diversion I've ever had—despite sleepless nights, and her chicken pox and Academy Award–winning tantrums. If the next book takes even longer it will probably be because she and I are spending too much time playing freeze tag, computer games, Aladdin and Jasmine, or our favorite, the Funkadelic chase game. She's Starchild, mommy is the Mothership Connection, and, as always, I'm Sir Nose Devoidoffunk. And if you're familiar with the story, you know that I don't dance until the tiny lady sings—or blasts me with the bop gun.

Index